Primary Health Care in Tanzania through a Health Systems Lens

Primary Health Care in Tanzania through a Health Systems Lens

A History of the Struggle for Universal Health Coverage

Edited by

Ntuli A. Kapologwe

James Tumaini Kengia

Eric van Praag

Japhet Killewo

Albino Kalolo

CABI

CABI is a trading name of CAB International

CABI
Nosworthy Way
Wallingford
Oxfordshire OX10 8DE
UK

Tel: +44 (0)1491 832111
E-mail: info@cabi.org
Website: www.cabi.org

CABI
200 Portland Street
Boston
MA 02114
USA

T: +1 (617)682-9015
E-mail: cabi-nao@cabi.org

A catalogue record for this book is available from the British Library, London, UK.

ISBN-13: 9781800623316 (hardback)
9781800623323 (ePDF)
9781800623330 (ePub)

DOI: 10.1079/ 9781800623330.0000

Commissioning Editor: Alexandra Lainsbury
Editorial Assistant: Lauren Davies
Production Editor: Rosie Hayden

Typeset by Exeter Premedia Services Pvt Ltd, Chennai, India
Printed and bound in the USA by Integrated Books International, Dulles, Virginia

Contents

Contributors

Maryam Amour, Department of Community Health, The Muhimbili University of Health and Allied Sciences, PO Box 65015, Dar es Salaam, Tanzania. Email: maryam.a.amur@gmail.com

Mackfallen Anasel, School of Public Administration and Management, Mzumbe University, PO Box 1, Morogoro, Tanzania. Email: mganasel@mzumbe.ac.tz

Rutasha Dadi, Field Support Services Project (FSSP)–Tanzania, PO Box 45, Dar es Salaam, Tanzania. Email: drrutashadadi@gmail.com

Faisal Issa, Department of Administrative Studies, Mzumbe University, PO Box 20266, Dar es Salaam, Tanzania. Email: kahin2halima@gmail.com

Mwandu Kini Jiyenze, Centre for Educational Development in Health Arusha (CEDHA), PO Box 1162, Arusha, Tanzania. Email: mwandukini@yahoo.com

Godfrey Kacholi, Department of Health Systems Management, School of Public Administration and Management, Mzumbe University, PO Box 2, Morogoro; Centre of Excellence in Health Monitoring and Evaluation, School of Public Administration and Management, Mzumbe University, PO Box 2, Morogoro, Tanzania. Email: gkacholi@gmail.com

Albino Kalolo, Department of Public Health, St Francis University College of Health and Allied Sciences, PO Box 175, Ifakara, Tanzania; Centre for Reforms, Innovation, Health Policies and Implementation Research (CeRIHI), Dodoma, Tanzania. Email: Kaloloa@gmail.com

Antony Kapesa, Department of Community Medicine, School of Public Health, Catholic University of Health and Allied Sciences, PO Box 1464, Mwanza, Tanzania. Email: anthony1kapesa@gmail.com

Ntuli A. Kapologwe, Directorate of Health, Social Welfare and Nutrition Services at the President's Office - Regional Administration and Local Government (PO-RALG), PO Box 1923, Dodoma, Tanzania. Email: nkapologwe2002@gmail.com

Leonard Katalambula, Department of Public Health, University of Dodoma, PO Box 259, Dodoma, Tanzania. Email: katalambula@gmail.com

James Tumaini Kengia, Directorate of Health, Social Welfare and Nutrition Services, President's Office - Regional Administration and Local Government (PO-RALG), PO Box 1923, Dodoma, Tanzania. Email: jtkengia@yahoo.com

Anosisye M. Kesale, Department of Local Government Management, School of Public Administration and Management, Mzumbe University, PO Box 2, Mzumbe-Morogoro, Tanzania. Email: akesale@mzumbe.ac.tz

Stephen M. Kibusi, School of Nursing and Public Health, University of Dodoma, Tanzania. Email: skibusi@gmail.com

Amani Kikula, Muhimbili University of Health and Allied Sciences (MUHAS), Dar es Salaam, Tanzania. Email: amanikikula@gmail.com

Japhet Killewo, Department of Epidemiology and Biostatistics, Muhimbili University of Health and Allied Sciences, Dar es Salaam, Tanzania. Email: jkillewo@yahoo.co.uk

Erick Kitali, Directorate of Information and Communication Technology, President's Office - Regional Administration and Local Government (PO-RALG), PO Box 1923, Dodoma, Tanzania. Email: erick.kitali@tamisemi.go.tz

George Kiwango, Department of Physiology, School of Medicine, Muhimbili University of Health and Allied Sciences, PO Box 65001, Dar es Salaam, Tanzania. Email: georgekiwango@gmail.com

Claud Kumalija, Health Management Information System Unit, Ministry of Health, PO Box 743, Dodoma, Tanzania. Email: claudjohnk@yahoo.com

Hadija Kweka, Enhance Tanzania Foundation, 22 Mtendeni Street 32274, Dar es Salaam, Tanzania. Email: entaf2016@gmail.com

Zarina Shamte Madabida, Expert, Industrial Pharmacy and Marketing. Email: zarinashamte60@gmail.com

Abel Makubi, Ministry of Health, Dodoma, Tanzania. Email: abelmakubi@gmail.com

Maximillian Kassian Kazibure Mapunda, World Health Organization Country Office, Dar es Salaam, Tanzania. Email: mapundam@who.int

Chacha Marwa, Mbeya Medical Research Centre, National Institute for Medical Research, PO Box 2410, Mbeya, Tanzania. Email: mangu.chacha@gmail.com

Innocent Mboya, Department of Translational Medicine, Lund University, 202 13 Malmo, Sweden. Email: ib.mboya@gmail.com

Romuald Mbwasi, Senior Lecturer (Supply Chain), St John University, Dodoma, Tanzania. Email: rmbwasi@gmail.com

William Mfuko, Consultant, Health Supply Chain. Email: wcmfuko@gmail.com

Chipole Mpelembe, President's Office - Regional Administration and Local Government (PO-RALG), PO Box 1923, Dodoma, Tanzania. Email: jo4chipo@gmail.com

Gemini J. Mtei, Abt Associates, Tanzania Public Sector Systems Strengthening Plus (PS3+) Project, Dar es Salaam, Tanzania. Email: gemini.mtei@googlemail.com

Castory Munishi, Muhimbili University of Health and Allied Sciences (MUHAS), Dar es Salaam, Tanzania. Email: castorymunishi@outlook.com

Oresto Michael Munishi, Department of Strategic Information, International Centre for AIDS Programs, Jangid Plaza, Ali Hassan Mwinyi Road, Dar-es-Salaam, Tanzania. Email: munishioresto17@gmail.com

Elihuruma M. Nangawe, PRAXIS in Health and Development – Policy, Systems, Strategies, QI and Capacity Development and Applied Research, 430 Sam Nujoma Road, Mlimani City Tower, Dar es Salaam; Consultant, Public Health, Dar es Salaam, Tanzania. Email: nangawemie@gmail.com

Harrieth P. Ndumwa, Muhimbili University of Health and Allied Sciences (MUHAS), Dar es Salaam, Tanzania. Email: harrieth.peter@gmail.com

Frida N. Ngalesoni, Amref Health Africa, Tanzania, Ali Hassan Mwinyi Road Plot 1019, PO Box 2773, Dar es Salaam, Tanzania. Email: fngalesoni@gmail.com

Jackline E. Ngowi, Muhimbili University of Health and Allied Sciences (MUHAS), Dar es Salaam, Tanzania. Email: jacklinengowi64@gmail.com

Belinda J. Njiro, Muhimbili University of Health and Allied Sciences (MUHAS), Dar es Salaam, Tanzania. Email: belindaj.njiro@gmail.com

William Reuben, President's Office - Regional Administration and Local Government (PO-RALG), Dodoma, Tanzania. Email: willreu66@gmail.com

George M. Ruhago, Department of Development Studies, School of Public Health and Social Sciences, Muhimbili University of Health and Allied Sciences, PO Box 65454, Dar es Salaam, Tanzania. Email: ruhagogm@gmail.com

Bakari Salum, President's Office - Regional Administration and Local Government (PO-RALG), Dodoma, Tanzania. Email: bkrsalum@yahoo.com

Don de Savigny, Swiss Tropical and Public Health Institute, 4002 Basel; University of Basel, 4051 Basel, Switzerland. Email: d.desavigny@swisstph.ch

Aifelo Sichalwe, Ministry of Health, Dodoma, Tanzania. Email: chifurumakb@yahoo.co.uk

Nathanael Sirili, Department of Development Studies, School of Public Health and Social Sciences, Muhimbili University of Health and Allied Sciences, PO Box 65454, Dar es Salaam, Tanzania. Email: drnsirili@gmail.com

Felix Sukums, Directorate of Information and Communication Technology (ICT), The Muhimbili University of Health and Allied Sciences, PO Box 65001, Dar es Salaam, Tanzania. Email: fsukums@muhas.ac.tz

Bruno F. Sunguya, Muhimbili University of Health and Allied Sciences (MUHAS), Dar es Salaam, Tanzania. Email: sunguya@gmail.com

Idda L. Swai, Department of Local Government Management, School of Public Administration and Management, Mzumbe University, PO Box 2, Mzumbe-Morogoro, Tanzania. Email: ilyatonga@mzumbe.ac.tz

Marcel Tanner, Swiss Tropical and Public Health Institute, 4002 Basel; University of Basel, 4051 Basel, Switzerland. Email: marcel.tanner@swisstph.ch

Eric van Praag, Consultant, Health Systems and Community Care, Dar es Salaam; Independent Consultant, PO Box 68260, Dar es Salaam, Tanzania. Email: eric.vanpraag@gmail.com

Desderi Wengaa, Directorate of Digital and Information Systems, USAID/PS3 Plus activity, Abt Associates Inc., Tanzania. Email: Desderi_Wengaa@tanzaniaps3.org

Preface

Tanzania is a country rich in history. Over the years, this history has been well documented from various conventional perspectives and viewpoints. However, missing from the record is a comprehensive history of primary health-care services throughout the many political and cultural transitions experienced by Tanzanians since the 1800s. This book provides, for the first time, a chronicle of the pioneering struggle for universal health coverage in Tanzania. This work intends to inform different generations about the performance, resilience and perseverance of the system and its stakeholders through major political and socio-economic eras. We do this by analysing the history of primary health care (PHC) through a modern health-systems lens. It provides a comprehensive narrative of the context and events that have driven change in the health sector in Tanzania since the 1800s by critically analysing and discussing these events, driving forces, proponents and the outcomes and impacts of such efforts. Policy makers, scholars, global health practitioners, health-system managers, researchers, students, historians and all those interested in primary health care and health-system reforms in Tanzania and beyond will find this as a model reference point. Furthermore, the book can be of use to decision makers and politicians in the context of better understanding how change happens in the health sector.

Chapter 1 provides the historical foundations and timeline of major contextual milestones of PHC in Tanzania. Chapter 2 describes the stewardship of PHC over time. Chapter 3 explores the chronic stresses experienced by the system and the struggles and innovations to resolve workforce challenges. Chapter 4 documents the financing options and shifting landscape from the post-independence era to the present. Chapter 5 highlights supply and demand dynamics, their effects on supply chains, and regulations and practice. Chapter 6 discusses the collaboration between information generated by the system and evidence provided by health research to drive practice and system change. Chapter 7 unpacks the output of Chapters 2 to 6 to produce the services delivered. Chapter 8 underscores how accountability is necessary for people-centred PHC and health systems. Chapter 9 emphasizes the importance of health-system preparedness for unforeseen events and system adaptability to cope with these events. Chapter 10 explores the need to step outside the boundaries of the health system to respond to the influence of external determinants that are having increasingly profound effects on public health. The final chapter attempts to forecast the changes needed and possible solutions.

The information in this book will enable all interested in primary health care to learn where we came from, where we are, and where we want to go.

Dr Ntuli A. Kapologwe
September 2023

Foreword

With great pleasure, we present a Foreword for this exceptional documentation and analysis of Tanzania's struggle to establish a continually improving primary health care system. Tanzania accomplished this over decades through the dedicated efforts of numerous individuals. As seasoned observers of Tanzania's health and social progress over the past forty years, we are privileged to contribute to this comprehensive account.

Tanzania has been a trailblazer in Africa and globally in promoting primary health care, as evidenced by its pioneering efforts since gaining independence in 1961. Tanzania has implemented several national health policies and strategies to realize primary health care, an ideal envisioned in the Arusha Declaration of 1967, which foreshadowed the concept of 'health for all'. These policies articulated the principles and pillars of primary health care as subsequently adopted by the World Health Organization and cemented in their landmark Alma Ata Declaration of Health for All in 1978.

By 1978, Tanzania had already established a robust health services infrastructure, placing a staffed primary care health facility within 5 km of 90% of its predominantly rural population. This achievement was unparalleled in Africa at that time. The fundamental architecture of Tanzania's health system remains essentially unchanged to this day. It is a highly decentralized system organized around a rational hierarchy matching the administrative structure of the country. At the regional level, there is one Public Regional Referral Hospital; at the council (district) level, there is one Council Hospital; at the ward level, there is at least one in-patient Health Centre; and at the village level, there is at least one out-patient Dispensary. These organizational structures have made implementing policies, strategies, and guidelines accessible at all levels.

In the mid-1980s, Tanzania's PHC efforts focused on preventive services to address the shortage of human resources for health, exploring the use of community health workers supporting communities in the catchment areas of their nearest Dispensary. The government-trained community health workers brought much-needed PHC preventive and curative services closer to users while taking some of the load off the dispensaries for the most common, easily treated conditions. However, implementing these innovative community health worker services brought growing concerns among the global health community that felt the emphasis on community participation and intersectoral collaboration, would be too costly, impractical, and slow-paced. Donors shifted their attention away from comprehensive PHC and invested heavily in PHC focused on "selective primary health care" based on vertical technical inputs for selected curative and preventive health services such as immunization, growth monitoring, and oral rehydration. As a result, efforts directed at less qualified community health worker services ended in Tanzania. A disease-driven rather than health-driven prioritization in the health sector emerged and prevailed for many years.

Tanzania's experience managing this complex and evolving primary healthcare scene and donor paradigms accrued since Alma Ata in 1978 is invaluable. The primary health system has undergone several challenges and reforms to reach where it is today. Tanzania has adopted and institutionalized novel health systems definitions and frameworks. However, stakeholders still need to answer questions such as how best to integrate PHC into the overall health system still dominated by a disease-focused approach, given the rising ratio of chronic non-communicable diseases to declining infectious disease rates. How do they deal with health system fragmentation caused by global health actors? How best can PHC be managed and led within rapidly changing adaptive and complex systems such as the health system, which, in turn, is embedded in the ever-changing socio-political-economic systems of which it is a part?

The Tanzanian health sector has documented the attention, investments, and progress across most of the health system framework's building blocks, especially health services, health financing, health informatics, medicines, technologies, and, to some extent, human health resources. However, there has been much less progress in health systems governance and virtually none on the influences beyond the health system building blocks such as the climate change crisis, social and commercial determinants of health, pandemics, and increasingly fractured geopolitics.

This book provides a timely and comprehensive account of Tanzania's struggle to achieve and maintain its primary healthcare system. It will be of great value to those involved in public health policy, research, and practice in the quest for Universal Health Coverage. It is a remarkable joint effort by Tanzanian public health scientists, practitioners, and leaders who have worked tirelessly to document their country's experiences, providing valuable insights and inspiration to current and future generations within Tanzania and far beyond. The book highlights the importance of continual national and global efforts and commitment to maintaining and improving the well-being of citizens, emphasizing that the struggle for health equity is ongoing and requires a sustained commitment to achieving durable results.

Marcel Tanner and Don de Savigny
Basel (Switzerland) and Merrickville (Canada), 24th April 2023

Acknowledgements

This book is based on previous literature and research about the history of primary health care in Tanzania and the struggles it has endured. I am grateful to and I would like to acknowledge a number of colleagues and friends who in one way or another made publication of this historic book possible.

First and foremost, I wish to register and express my sincere gratitude and special thanks to my co-editors Dr James Tumaini Kengia, Dr Eric van Praag, Professor Japhet Killewo and Dr Albino Kalolo for their immense editorial work on the 11 chapters of this book. Second, I wish to acknowledge and express my deep gratitude to the funders of this project, the Fondation Botnar, under leadership of Professor Marcel Tanner and collaborators Professor Don de Savigny and Dr Hassan Mshinda. Furthermore, thanks go to the Center for Reforms, Innovation, Health Policies and Implementation Research (CeRIHI) for the management of this book project.

I am grateful to the minister of state at the President's Office - Regional Administration and Local Government (PO-RALG), the Honourable Angellah J. Kairuki (MP): as a result of her leadership we have been able to publish this book in spite of many challenges. My gratitude also goes to the deputy minister responsible for health at PO-RALG, the Honourable Dr Festo Dugange (MP); permanent secretary at PO-RALG, Professor Riziki S. Shemdoe; and deputy permanent secretary responsible for health at PO-RALG, Dr Grace E. Magembe. Thanks are extended to the minister of health, the Honourable Ummy A. Mwalimu (MP) and permanent secretary minister of health, Professor Abel N. Makubi for their immense support during the process of writing this book.

We are also indebted to the following individuals, who supported this project from its beginning to its submission: the late Dr Leonard Mboera, Dr Paul Chaote, Sarah K. Malima, Nicas Lous, Nick Masanyaji, Michael Macha, Heward Kimambo, Dr Julieth S. Kabengula, Dr Catherine Joachim, Professor Sandi Macoy, Professor Jenny Liu, Dr Prosper Njau, Dr Kasusu Klint, Dr Ahadiel Senkoro, Dr Kijakazi Mashoto, Dr Mary Mwanyika, Professor Michael Mahande, Professor Sia Msuya, Professor Honorath Masanja, Professor Andrew Pembe, Dr Harun Kesale, Michael Mosha, Dr David Sando, Dr John Kahemele, Dr Pius Kagoma and Dr Gwamaka Samson.

To all, I am very grateful for your immense contribution and support for this historic project.

Dr Ntuli A. Kapologwe
Lead Editor

1 Introduction to Primary Health Care

Ntuli A. Kapologwe[1,2]*, Aifelo Sichalwe[3] and Albino Kalolo[4,5]
[1]Directorate of Health, Social Welfare and Nutrition Services at the President's Office – Regional Administration and Local Government, Dodoma, Tanzania; [2]University of Dodoma, Tanzania; [3]Ministry of Health, Dodoma, Tanzania; [4]Department of Public Health, St Francis University College of Health and Allied Sciences, Ifakara, Tanzania; [5]Centre for Reforms, Innovation, Health Policies and Implementation Research (CeRIHI), Dodoma, Tanzania

Abstract

Primary health care (PHC) as a concept and philosophy of health care has evolved over time, globally as well as in Tanzania. This chapter discusses the foundation of the primary health care approach, its evolution over time and how it is currently being implemented. Reflections on how the PHC reforms have been implemented across times and settings are offered. The challenges facing PHC are discussed, as well as the strategies to sustain PHC interventions while also making the PHC system resilient.

1.0 Introduction

The idea to compile this piece of work on primary health care (PHC) reforms and evolution in Tanzania is a result of reflections by the authors on the topic. They feel that documenting the history of PHC, related efforts and the struggles the country has gone through over time is important to inform future reforms and investments in PHC as the country moves towards universal health coverage (UHC). The PHC odyssey in Tanzania, from the pre-independence period, through independence, the Arusha Declaration in 1967, and Alma-Ata in 1978, to the Astana Declaration in 2018, has been challenging. The challenge has been a result of both internal and external influences, which have manifested as a lack of clarity on the conceptual and operational definitions of the PHC package. Other challenges have included debates between vertical and horizontal approaches to PHC, lack of appropriate reforms to influence changes and lack of resources to evaluate and generate evidence for learning within and across settings. In the stride forward to reach UHC (a new direction) in relation to achieving the newly developed sustainable development goals (SDGs), investing in PHC is seen as a quick win among all other options.

The purpose of this book is to compile and document the process of implementation of reforms in the PHC system in Tanzania and related contexts under which such reforms occurred. This exercise is a critical analysis of the reforms, which aims at learning through the reforms to inform future efforts and investments in PHC in order to achieve universal health coverage (UHC) by 2030. The book also intends to inform different generations about resilience and perseverance, and performance of the health system at large.

*Corresponding author: nkapologwe2002@gmail.com

DOI: 10.1079/9781800623330.0001

1.1 Understanding Primary Health Care

1.1.1 Definition and scope of primary health care

Primary health care (PHC) definitions have evolved over time, with some starting before the Alma-Ata Declaration but using different terminologies (WHO, 1978; Greenhalgh, 2013; Giovanella, 2018; Rifkin, 2018b). The most comprehensive definition coined during the Alma-Ata Declaration in 1978 is as follows:

> PHC is an essential health care based on practical, scientifically sound and socially acceptable methods and technology made universally accessible to individuals and families in the community through the full participation and at the cost that the community can afford to maintain at every stage of development in the spirit of self-reliance and self-determination.

What constitutes primary health care is still somehow contested, with a multitude of definitions. The definitions of PHC range from philosophical to aspirational to practical and pragmatic, evolving over time and considering the core values of PHC (holistic, balanced, people centred, rigorous, equitable and reflective) and social changes in terms of demographic transitions, changes in disease patterns, changes in delivery of health care, changes in social roles and changes in technological advancement.

In her book, *Primary Health Care: Theory and Practice*, Greenhalgh (2013) puts forward the defining characteristic of PHC services and alludes to the fact that PHC definitions should include the following dimensions: first-contact care, undifferentiated by age, gender or disease; continuity over time; coordinated within and across sectors; and with a focus on both the individual and the population/community. Simply put, PHC is defined as follows:

> Primary health care is what happens when someone who is ill (or who thinks he or she is ill or who wants to avoid getting ill) consults a health professional in a community setting for advice, tests, treatment or referral to specialist care. Such care should be holistic, balanced, personalised, rigorous and equitable, and delivered by reflexive practitioners who recognize their own limitations and draw appropriately on the strengths of others.

As PHC is the entry point to the health system, where people present their problems, the need for comprehensive and integrated services is critical (Magnussen *et al.*, 2004; Hurley *et al.*, 2010). The primary health service package includes promotive, preventive and curative or rehabilitation care. It looks at comprehensiveness and continuum of care along the referral pathway in order to meet diverse needs and challenges that people face. People take up services more readily if they know a comprehensive spectrum of care is on offer. Rational perspective alludes to the fact that it makes no sense to monitor the growth of children and neglect the health of their mothers (and vice versa), or to treat someone's tuberculosis without considering their HIV status or whether they smoke, and calls for integrated services in primary health care settings. The emphasis is on people's centred care in the context of the prevailing social–economic determinants of health.

Although officially coined at the Alma-Ata conference in 1978, the term PHC has been used previously on several occasions, as reported in the white paper on health care, and in other countries but in different forms, such as primary care, basic health services, family medicine and community services (Newell and WHO, 1975; Giovanella, 2018). PHC serves as a philosophy and a conceptual model to structure essential health care services (WHO, 1978; Greenhalgh, 2013; Rifkin, 2018b). Xu and Wang (2015) report that the concept of PHC has been misinterpreted in many settings to mean entry-level health care, low level or elementary health care, thus, the core meaning of 'primary' as the 'most important, essential or principal' is totally lost in translations. They therefore call for revisiting the way the concept has been conceived as countries move to universal health coverage.

The development of PHC in a given country depends on (i) socio-economic status, (ii) health-care policy orientation (UHC with PHC, free-market health care), (iii) new diseases and other emerging health issues, (iv) stage of PHC development (level of access, health-care workforce, maturity in applying its principles, expansion of service packages and responsiveness of the system) (Vaughan and Walt, 1984; Roemer, 1986; Young, 1986).

1.1.2 PHC implementation experiences and paradigm shifts

Primary health care is a health care approach the discharge of which falls within the realm of district and subdistrict facilities and respective catchment area communities/households (Goergen and Schmidt-Ehry, 2004; Görgen *et al.*, 2004). In the process of searching for pragmatic ways to implement PHC effectively, health-care reforms to support district health and below were conceived within a framework of Sector Wide Approaches (SWAps) (Seco and Martínez, 2001; Hutton and Tanner, 2004; Peters *et al.*, 2013). Its implementation requires that a country understands and implements the deliberations at Alma-Ata which intended PHC to be comprehensive, and to cover the eight elements of PHC. These elements include food supply, proper nutrition, adequate safe water and basic sanitation, health education in prevention and control of prevailing health problems, maternal and child health, immunization, prevention and control of endemic diseases, treatment of common diseases and essential drugs (WHO, 2002). How to apply PHC principles so as to deliver the elements on an effective footing always lagged behind or experienced shortfalls in being attended to (Greenhalgh, 2013; Andrews and Crooks, 2016). Donor dependency emerged as a factor behind strong advocacy for a selective 'less expensive, more easily attainable' approach that attracted funding more than comprehensive PHC. Selected primary health care (SPHC) was suggested in an article in the *New England Journal of Medicine* in 1979, challenging the visionary but idealistic comprehensive primary health care (CPHC) (Walsh and Warren, 1979; Rifkin, 2018b). The SPHC approach focused on tackling the diseases that had high prevalence and greater risk of mortality and which can be controlled cost-effectively. The comprehensive PHC that, in its entirety, required multisectoral action, that is, collaboration between different government sectors such as health, education, and agriculture, was seen to be difficult to translate into practice. Some considered selective PHC as an 'interim' strategy to begin the process of PHC implementation. However, implementing comprehensive PHC has been difficult to date in many low- and middle-income countries, specifically so when donor funding takes a big share of the health-sector budget (Newell, 1988; Magnussen *et al.*, 2004).

The implementation of PHC over time has evolved in relation to how the principles have been taken on board, but also in how the expansion of the essential elements (service package) has been carried out (Young, 1986; Rasanathan *et al.*, 2011; Litsios, 2015; Rifkin, 2018a, Rifkin, 2018b; Appiah-Agyekum, 2020). The epidemiological transitions (Atiim and Elliott, 2016), the health-systems thinking approach (Adam and de Savigny, 2012) and the universal health coverage movement (Latko *et al.*, 2011) are recent paradigm shifts and sector policies that need to be taken on board as PHC is implemented.

Demographic, epidemiological and health transitions: The contemporary PHC system should take into account all forms of transitions, from the epidemiologic and the demographic, to nutritional transitions that are vital in low- and middle-income countries (Martens, 2002; Amuna and Zotor, 2008; Defo, 2014; Atiim and Elliott, 2016). The increasing burden of non-communicable diseases (NCDs), urbanization and the ageing population should be taken onboard when developing PHC policies and related strategies. The PHC system should also be responsive and resilient to shocks, such as that caused by emerging and re-emerging disease threats and other disasters (Jafari *et al.*, 2022).

Health systems thinking: The health systems thinking approach, which takes into account the WHO health system building blocks in the context of implementing PHC services, should be taken as a new direction, given the need to implement comprehensive PHC in any given setting to ensure success. The concept of total quality management (TQM) as an important orientation in the context of systems thinking is cross-cutting within the building blocks with a predominance in the block of Service Delivery (Shortell *et al.*, 1995).

Universal health coverage: Universal health coverage (UHC) is mainly about financing, while PHC is about the right care and at the right time to ensure health for all people.

The situation in the globalized context is characterized by social cohesion within nations being under stress, health systems not performing as expected, impatient people in the context of PHC underperformance, provision of health care that is unsafe, inverse, impoverishing (because of catastrophic expenditure), fragmented and misdirected care. All these drawbacks call for a renewed approach in the stride forwards to accomplish primary health care. This is specifically the case in low- and middle-income countries. Emerging concepts, such as One Health policies or Health-in-All policies, are important in attaining the UHC by showing the path towards attaining the PHC principle of intersectoral collaboration.

PHC and digital technology: The use of digital technology in primary health care comes with a promise of delivery of higher quality, safer and more equitable care. Reforms in this area could focus on (i) patient access to health records, big data analytics and virtual care (remote consulting) (Downie *et al.*, 2022; Neves and Burgers, 2022; WHO, 2022), (ii) the use of digital solutions to conduct robust research in primary health-care settings, and (iii) the use of artificial intelligence (AI) to improve service delivery in PHC settings.

1.1.3 Reforming PHC to meet contemporary demands

The 2008 World Health Organization report, Primary Health Care – Now More Than Ever (WHO, 2008), put forward the following four types of reforms that can revitalize PHC and make it a reliable path towards achieving universal health coverage.

- Universal health coverage reforms (equity, social justice and the end of exclusion, primarily by moving towards universal access and social health protection).
- Service delivery reforms (reorganize health services as primary care, i.e. around people's needs and expectations, so as to make them more socially relevant and more responsive to the changing world while producing better outcomes).
- Public policy reforms (securing healthier communities, by integrating public health actions with primary care and by pursuing healthy public policies across sectors).
- Leadership reforms (inclusive, participatory, negotiation-based leadership required by the complexity of contemporary health systems).

The political economy challenges that need deliberate reforms for a strong PHC include the following:

- Competing demands with limited public budgets that leads to low investment in primary health care.
- Low service productivity in PHC as a result of challenges in health-system inputs (workforce crisis, poor infrastructure, frequent stock outs of health commodities).
- Self-care and private providers are frequently the first resort, but it is not always clear how they are part of the comprehensive PHC system.
- PHC elements are damaged and reliant on donor funding, mainly through vertical programmes that lead to further fragmentation of PHC.
- The role of the private sector in PHC is ill defined, lacks government stewardship and is sometimes unregulated, leading to undue commercialization of PHC services.

1.1.4 Reforming primary health care in Tanzania

Country profile and its policy context

Tanzania Mainland (former Republic of Tanganyika) is part of the United Republic of Tanzania (URT), located in East Africa, and has a population of 61.7 million people, with a population growth rate of 2.98% (URT, 2022). The URT was formed after the union of the Republic of Tanganyika and People's Republic of Zanzibar in 1964. The URT economy is dependent on agriculture, which employs almost 80% of the population. Since July 2021 it has been considered a lower middle-income country by the World Bank. It has a GDP of U$62 million and a GNI per capita of U$1140. Tanzania experienced economic growth of between 5 and 7% per year from 2000 until the global financial crisis in 2009 and the COVID-19 crisis. The poverty rate in Tanzania stands at 33.4% and the country's capacity to collect taxes remains low and hence depends on donor funding of about 29% of the total country budget. Tanzania Mainland gained its independence in 1961; it was ruled by German and British colonialists in the years 1885 to 1918 and 1919 to 1961 respectively. After independence, Tanzania Mainland inherited a classical colonial governance structure (Schneider, 2006). Health services were concentrated in urban areas with a focus on curative services, serving only 4% of the population that resided in urban areas (Mbilinyi, 1985). The colonial government made little effort to expand health services to rural areas. The national development plans post-independence undertook deliberate efforts to expand health services to rural settings and broaden services to include preventive and promotive health services in rural communities.

Health services have been evolving based on the National Health Policy of 1990, which was revised in 2007. The vision of the health policy is to improve the health outcomes of all Tanzanians, with a special focus on the vulnerable and at-risk population. To achieve this, the government of Tanzania aimed at financing the health sector to facilitate the provision of equitable, quality and affordable health services through the national budget by the central government. Other financing models which evolved with time include health insurance, both public and private, grants, credits, development aid from development partners and private financing through user fees from clients. The health sector has undergone several transformations before and after independence geared towards improvement of health services delivery and utilization. After the health-sector reforms in the late 1990s, health sector strategic plans were developed and implemented. The plans immediately after the reforms focused on laying down the foundations of issues addressed by the reform. What was considered critical was to make sure that health sector decentralization was implemented parallel to the primary health care approach, using a district health system approach (Gilson *et al.*, 1994; Bustreo *et al.*, 2019). District-level-based decentralization through local governments helped to increase local autonomy over health budgets and mobilization of resources for core interventions tailored to district needs and demands. To strengthen the district-based PHC approach, the health sector strategic plan III, for example, aimed at improving accessibility of health services through the implementation of the Primary Health Care Strengthening Programme (MMAM in Kiswahili) (Kengia *et al.*, 2013; Jiyenze *et al.*, 2022). The current health sector strategic plan (HPSS V) aims at equipping primary health care facilities to improve equitable provision of PHC.

Overview of the health-care system in Tanzania

Existing evidence attests that health-care systems that can ensure quality, efficiency, access to care, equity and healthy lives are critical for achieving universal health coverage and improving the health status of the population. A health-care system, also known as a health system, is the organization of people, institutions, and resources that deliver health-care services to meet the health needs of target populations. The WHO health-system building-block model, which proposed six blocks of a health-care system, with people at the centre, represents a widely used model to describe the health-care system of a country. The model stipulates that a health-care system is built by six core components or building blocks that consist of: (i) service delivery; (ii) health workforce; (iii) health information systems; (iv) access to essential medicines; (v) financing; and (vi) leadership/governance. At the heart of successful health systems are people and their participatory power as both recipients and producers of health care. In their paper, 'Beyond the building blocks: integrating community roles into health systems frameworks to achieve health for all', Sacks and colleagues have suggested expanding the WHO building blocks, starting with the recognition of the essential determinants of the production of health (Sacks *et al.*, 2019). They suggest an expanded framework that articulates the need for dedicated human resources and quality services at the community level, with strategies for organizing and mobilizing social resources in communities in the context of systems for health. Their proposition comes with an idea that health information is one ingredient of a larger block dedicated to information, learning and accountability; and it recognizes societal partnerships as critical links to the public health sector. To optimize quality, improve equity and maximize population health outcomes, the health-care system in Tanzania has evolved over years and is currently administered by the Ministry of Health (MOH) and the President's Office - Regional Administration and Local Government (PO-RALG).

The MOH provides overall policy guidance and quality control of health system inputs and outputs, but also is responsible for running the regional and national referral hospitals, whereas PO-RALG oversees the regional and district health system and is responsible for the provision of primary health-care services. The Tanzanian health system is guided by national policies, such as the Vision 2025, the National Strategy for Growth and Poverty and the National Health Policy of 2007. Furthermore, international policies, such as sustainable development goals (SDGs), are usually accommodated in the national policies to foster progress in the health-care system. Below, we provide a brief visualization of each of the six health systems building blocks in the Tanzanian context and, later, narrate the PHC reforms in specific time periods.

Service delivery block

Although there have been changing trends over the years, the service delivery block has, since the pre-independence period, predominantly focused on providing curative services. Massive investment in health infrastructure (hospitals, health centres and dispensaries) has been a focus while developing the service delivery block (Scholz *et al.*, 2015; Kapologwe *et al.*, 2020). Services have been predominantly provided by the government and faith-based organizations (FBOs). FBOs and non-governmental organizations (NGOs), for example, have been able to extend health-care availability and accessibility to rural communities. The concept of 'health for all' (HFA), proclaimed in the 1967 Arusha Declaration and later the 1978 Alma-Ata Declaration, led to the development of five-year plans that aimed at deploying the HFA components as stipulated by the declarations, expanding services beyond hospital-based curative services to more comprehensive approaches that recognize preventives, rehabilitative and health promotion services. However, resource constraints undermined implementation of these plans and the government resorted to accepting donor funding in line with the 1987 Bamako Initiative that aimed at revitalizing primary health care in resource-constrained countries. The structural adjustment programmes (SAPs) in the 1990s changed the constellation of service provision from predominantly public service-oriented with free services at the point of care, as it led to major changes, to various inputs that influence service delivery, such as financing modalities, human resource for health and supply of medicines and technologies. Thereafter, especially in the last twenty years (from the early 2000s), an expansion of health-service delivery with a public–private mix has intensified.

To date, Tanzania's health system has been both complex and pluralistic, composed of public, private and donor stakeholders operating at several different levels, including national, regional, district and community levels. Traditional medicine is still widely practised despite the expansion of 'biomedicine' or 'Western medicine' facilities. Faith-based healing is growing stronger, especially in this era of an emerging burden of chronic diseases. The deep-rooted social representations and emerging challenges that biomedicine is not able to address points to the persistence of pluralism. The grandpa's cup, *Kikombe cha Babu*, which induced hundreds of thousands of patients, both Tanzanians and foreigners, to make the tedious journey to the remote village of Samunge to be supposedly healed by Reverend Ambilikile Mwasapila and the growing prevalence of ecstatic preaching or faith healing, mainly by Pentecostal church pastors, are some of the revealing examples of medical pluralism practices (Vähäkangas, 2016). The seeming lack of coordination and robust evaluation and regulatory frameworks relating to this medical pluralism has serious implications for the health outcomes of the population.

Human resources for the health block

The main cadres of health-care workers during the pre-independence period and in the early days after independence were doctors and nurses, trained to provide service in public and missionary hospitals. In the early days after independence, the philosophy was to train doctors and nurses who would stay in rural areas, that is, not training the 'big doctors' who would be difficult to retain. With subsequent policy changes and the increasing complexity of the health-care system there has been a massive expansion of cadres beyond the doctors and nurses to a wide range of professionals who are trained to provide curative, preventive, rehabilitative and health promotion services in a comprehensive manner. The community health-care workers (CHWs) and community drug dispensers have been trained and deployed widely to provide community-based services. The contemporary challenges characterized by epidemiological transitions, emerging and re-emerging diseases and antimicrobial resistance require professionals with an adequate skills mix and who are resilient. Fortunately, there has been a growth in the number of health training institutions over the years with a strong public–private skills mix.

Health information and evidence block

The health information system has evolved from rudimentary paper-based systems based on routine data that aim at capturing information to explain disease trends and their patterns to comprehensive systems that also include learning from the systems. The routine data based on facility records were the only source of information in the colonial and post-independence period. The information system known as 'Kalamazoo' was deployed to collect morbidity and mortality data, which later evolved to a more comprehensive health information management system (HIMS) specifically so in the 1990s, famously known in Kiswahili as MTUHA (Mfumo wa Taarifa za Uendeshaji Huduma za Afya). The MTUHA system later evolved to digitized versions and more customized digital systems, such as the district health information system version 2 (DHIS-2). There are increasing efforts to digitize information systems and make them interoperable in the stride forward to simplify availability and use of data in planning and decision making.

The focus on health information shifted over time from facility-based sources of information to community-based health surveys that use robust research approaches to track demographic and epidemiologic trends over specified time intervals. For example, the Tanzania Demographic Health Surveys (TDHS), the Tanzania HIV and Malaria Indicator Surveys (THMIS) and the National Population Census provide useful periodic health and demographic information. To address emerging and re-emerging diseases, Tanzania adopted the integrated disease surveillance and response (IDSR) strategy during the early 2000s. The IDSR strategy links community, health facility, district, regional and national levels with the overall objective of providing epidemiological evidence for use in making decisions and implementing public health interventions for the control and prevention of diseases. The establishment of demographic sentinel surveillance sites across the country is also a deliberate effort to triangulate the routine data with longitudinal data for better decision making.

Research and learning also evolved over time, with research ranging from those focusing on diseases to those focusing on health systems. The focus of research prior to independence and immediately after independence was disease oriented and mainly focused on tropical diseases such as malaria and bacterial infections. The National Institute for Medical Research (NIMR) act in 1979 saw the establishment of NIMR as an institution with the power and functions to promote medical research in the country. Subsequently, research efforts were intensified, leading to the production of evidence in different thematic areas. Examples of health systems projects that strengthened the PHC system based on the district health systems (reflecting the Harare Declaration and health-sector reforms in Tanzania) are plentiful and include projects such as the Tanzania Essential Health Interventions Package (TEHIP) (de Savigny *et al.*, 2002) and the Health Promotion and Systems Strengthening Project (HPSS) (Kalolo *et al.*, 2017; Wiedenmayer *et al.*, 2019). The use of research evidence was a question that also started to manifest as a problem over time, in that there is plenty of research evidence, but the evidence is not being used to improve policies and practices (Kitua *et al.*, 2000). Deliberate efforts to engage research evidence translation to policy and practice were developed, but the implementation of these efforts remains questionable to date.

Access to essential medicines block

A well-functioning health system requires 'equitable access to essential medical products, vaccines and technologies of assured quality, safety, efficacy and effectiveness, and cost-effective use' (WHO, 2010). To ensure this, the Tanzanian health-care system has strived to reform its supply chain to meet that goal. Despite successful implementation of the reforms, access to essential medical products, vaccines and technologies has not achieved expectations. The development of the medical store department (MSD), after reforms to the central medical stores (a government store responsible for storing and distributing health commodities, but not for procurement) is one of the key milestones in strengthening the supply chain in the country (Githendu *et al.*, 2020). Recent reforms in this domain include the development of the prime vendor system to correct the inefficiencies of the MSD (Wiedenmayer *et al.*, 2019). The current focus in improving the supply chain include improving quantification approaches, alternative financing of the supply chain, strengthening procurement and inbound logistics, strengthening inventory analysis, management and policies, improving storage and transport systems and strengthening the management information system.

Health financing block

Since independence, there have been efforts to ensure equitable access to health care without catastrophic expenditures when seeking health care. To do away with the colonial health financing system that was based on out-of-pocket health expenditure, the Arusha Declaration introduced the free health-care system and a tax-based system. This major reform was hailed by many and was expected to improve access and equity. However, the global financial meltdown in the 1980s and the Uganda–Tanzania War had a tremendous effect on the provision of health services in the country as financial resources were no longer sufficient to provide the basic health-care package as promised in the free health-care policy framework. These events and structural adjustment programmes (SAPs) led to the reform of the financing system by introducing community financing approaches in the form of cost sharing through user fees and prepayment schemes such as the community health funds (Earth, 1996; Mtei and Mulligan, 2007). From 1995 the government embarked on health-sector reforms to address the shortcomings experienced during the SAP, with the aim of improving the equity, efficiency, effectiveness and accessibility of services to the communities. The reforms were organizational, managerial and financial. Prior to 1998, the government financed the provision of services and local development through regional administrations. The enactment of the Regional Administration Act No. 19 of 1997 reduced the role of regional administrations and, as a result, some fiscal powers and service delivery functions were transferred to local government authorities. The amendment of the Local Government Finance Act No. 9 of 1982 in 2000 redefined sources of revenue for local government authorities. Consequently, there was an increase in the percentage of sectoral block grants provided to LGAs over time. These include block grants for education, health, agriculture, water supply and roads. In addition, a recurrent general purpose (administration) grant has been provided since 2003 (initially as compensation for abolished local revenue sources).

The health financing reforms introduced social insurance schemes, such as the National Health Insurance Fund (NHIF) which was meant for formal public sector employees, and the Community Health Fund (CHF) which was to cater for the informal sector. One of the key reforms was the devolution of health-service management to local government (otherwise known as councils). The devolution of decision making space to the councils provided authority to develop plans and budgets, including the participation of the community, and paved the way for direct health facility financing (DHFF) as part of public financial management reforms (Kapologwe *et al.*, 2019).

Leadership and governance block

Across different periods, the Tanzanian health-care system has implemented various reforms to improve governance and leadership. The leadership and management practices during colonial rule focused on developing and enforcing a regulatory framework that mainly ensured provision of health-care services (Beck, 1977). After independence, the focus shifted to five-year development plans that strategically streamlined actions based on the targeted goals. The policy directions emanating from the Arusha

Declaration led to the development of decentralization reforms that in turn led to changes across the different blocks of the health-care system in terms of leadership and management. The first health policy was developed in 1990 and thereafter health sector strategic plans began to be developed to guide the development in the health-care system. The ideological and managerial reforms that were proposed by the health-sector reforms in 1994 have shaped the modern management and leadership practices (Mujinja and Kida, 2014).

1.1.5 Evolution of PHC reforms

Evolution of PHC reforms before 1880

In the pre-colonial period (before 1880) the health system was predominantly a traditional health-care system. As in other African countries, African traditional medicine is said to be one of the oldest and most diverse of all medicine systems, though poorly documented. Although it is acknowledged that traditional health-care systems existed and evolved over time commensurate to the level of human development, there is a limited written account of the pre-colonial health-care systems. However, it is undisputed that the traditional health-care system existed and evolved over time as people gained knowledge and skills. Traditional medicine – defined as the sum total of knowledge, skills and practices based on the theories, beliefs and experiences indigenous to different cultures that are used to maintain health, as well as to prevent, diagnose, improve or treat physical and mental illnesses – was practised in pre-colonial Tanzania. The traditional health-care system was organized around three core functions, namely: (i) local healing using herbs and traditional remedies, (ii) religious healing in which traditional religious practitioners (local priests) played a key role and (iii) the witch doctor or sorcerer, who could either prevent people from getting ill (as illness was conceived as invasion by evil spirits) or could inflict diseases or misfortunes to others, especially when they misbehaved or there was a need to do so for societal or personal gains. Traditional birth attendants also were part of the traditional health system.

The traditional healing system was not structured in levels of referral (primary, secondary, tertiary) like the modern health-care system, rather referrals were made to providers based on experience and the nature of the illness to be attended. The practice of Western medicine was introduced in 1887 and began to be used in the period 1889–1916 by German missionaries, while vaccination against polio began in 1891. In 1928 the first legislation was made to allow traditional medicine in the country.

Evolution during the German and British administrations

The colonial period in Tanzania (1880–1960) can be viewed as a time when, for the first time, the biomedicine (Western medicine) was introduced in Tanzania. German colonial rule commenced in the 1880s, and in 1891 the Germans declared the region a protectorate as part of German East Africa. To consolidate their rule and benefit from their undertakings, the Germans developed a health-care system that saw the construction of physical health infrastructure throughout the country, with a focus on their areas of production. The very basic rudimentary health system that was developed at this time focused on containing epidemic diseases. Also, there was a great focus of research activities on the (exotic) diseases with the aim of hastening the discovery of innovative ways to control the diseases. For example, in 1895, German doctors were officially advised to collect specimens and send them to Germany for scientific investigation (Görgen *et al.*, 2001).

After Germany were defeated in World War I and were forced to leave the Tanganyika Territory, British colonial rule began. British colonial rule, which lasted up to 1959, further expanded the existing health infrastructure and added an extensive component of training health personnel.

The colonial health-care system had a strong emphasis on curative services, prevention and control measures assigned to health inspectors and their assistants. Most of the health facilities were constructed in urban or semi-urban areas where there was intense colonial government activity. The missionary health facilities established during colonial rule were most often constructed in rural areas.

Both the colonial government and missionary facilities charged user fees and were therefore more accessible to affluent segments of the population. The health-care system worked in favour of foreigners working for the colonial government. It focused on the conservation and restoration of the health of Europeans residing in tropical areas. The health of the natives was usually only considered when their diseases also threatened Europeans, as in the case of malaria or the plague.

Health-care services during the colonial era were either run by the colonial government or by missionaries (Jennings, 2008, Jennings, 2019). By 1926, in Shinyanga district, a government-run hospital and two government dispensaries were operational and provided services to the community. In the same year, the Africa Inland Mission Hospital at Kola Ndoto provided services to the community (Jennings, 2008, Jennings, 2019). By 1936, the Universities Mission to Central Africa (UMCA) attended patients in its hospitals and outpatient health facilities in Masasi and Zanzibar Diocese. Modern medicine which began to be offered included treatment against malaria, leprosy, the plague and trypanosomiasis, and was mainly for German civil servants, business people and police officers. The first hospital was built in Mamboya, Mpwapwa. In 1886, Sewahaji provided money for the construction of a hospital in Bagamoyo, with the foundation stone laid in 1891 (Brennan and Burton, 2007). Also in the 1890s, two hospitals were built in Dar es Salaam – Sewahaji Hospital and Ocean Road Hospital. The mission-owned health facilities conceived and set up the Tanganyika Christian Medical Association around the 1930s to share experiences and discuss challenges. This motivated and precipitated the formation of the Christian Medical Board of Tanganyika (CMBT), which served as a link, representing various mission health departments and facilities at formal meetings with the government (MOH).

With regards to traditional medicine practice, the British government introduced a witchcraft ordinance and a medical and dentist ordinance in 1929. The ordinances were meant to regulate medical practice (including the practice of traditional medicine) and ban witchcraft (Görgen *et al.*, 2001).

Evolution immediately after independence, 1961–1963

By the time of independence (1961), Tanzania (by then Tanganyika) had a total of 737 dispensaries and health centres and a total of 3172 health-care workers of different types (mainly medical assistants, dispensers, African laboratory assistants, medical auxiliaries, tribal dressers and urban sanitary inspectors), and there were a total of 400 medical doctors, 20 of them Tanzanians. There was no district hospital, however, there were 98 provincial hospitals (central government hospitals and voluntary agency hospitals) (Kilama *et al.*, 1974). Those hospitals were located in Dar es Salaam, Tanga (Bombo), Moshi, Peramiho, Mwanza (Bugando), Tabora (Kitete), Morogoro (Turiani), Bumbuli in Lushoto, Ifakara, Mvumi in Dodoma, Ndanda in Lindi and Sumve in the Mwanza area. The patient-to-bed ratio was one bed per 1000 patients and the facility per population ratio was one facility per 40,000 or 50,000 people.

However, much progress in the health sector was made after independence, especially during 61 years of independence as compared to 71 years of colonialism (Germany 1889–1916 and Britain 1916–1960).

Immediately after independence, there was lots of 'trial and error' in trying to establish a basic health-care system, extending coverage of care to the local population. Disease was pronounced as one among the three enemies to be fought against by the new government; the others were ignorance and poverty. The government received advice from different sources and tried to implement this to see whether it worked or not. After independence, the government had expanded the health services with a vision to improve the health and well-being of all Tanzanians, with a focus on those most at risk, and to encourage the health system to be more responsive to the needs of the people. The policy mission was to facilitate the provision of equitable, quality and affordable basic health services, which were gender-sensitive and sustainable, delivered for the achievement of improved health status. The training of health personnel who could run the health system was one of the measures that was meant to be expanded, and as time passed auxiliary clinical staff were replaced by qualified medical doctors at the district hospital level. This trial faced challenges as, with time, it was realized that the paramedical staff were the ones who were readily available to run rural health facilities and they could not be phased out abruptly, but needed to be trained and upgraded in status to assistant medical officers. The concept of rural health centres, which was proposed as early as 1956, was successfully trialled and brought a full range of well-equipped, well-staffed health services to the rural population, which were also assigned to provide support to satellite dispensaries in their catchment areas.

Evolution during the period between 1964 and 1977

During this period, Tanzania set ambitious social and human development plans that aimed at the eradication of the aforementioned 'three enemies of the nation' (*umasikini, ujinga na maradhi*) in a matter of two decades. This was followed by the development of numerous top-down policies and plans, such as the first five-year development plan (1964–1969), the Arusha Declaration (1967), the second five-year development plan (1969–1974) and the decentralization policy (1972). Much of the widespread health-care services infrastructure that is evident now in rural areas of mainland Tanzania is a result of the re-emphasis of the Arusha Declaration in 1971. With conscious efforts to restructure society in the context of eradicating poverty, ignorance and diseases, the government embarked on a comprehensive basic health services (BHS) approach that put high emphasis on community participation. The implementation of the BHS approach, promoted with development plans and the decentralization policy, faced several implementation challenges, including severe resource constraints that resulted after the war with the regime of Idi Amin's Uganda.

Evolution during the post–Alma-Ata Declaration period, 1978–1994

The third five-year development plan (1975–1980) saw the coming of the Alma-Ata Declaration on primary health care in 1978, where the BHS experience of Tanzania shaped some of the declaration's content. This meant that the plan had to be restructured to accommodate the rapid inflow of development partners who came to support PHC projects outlined in the eight elements of primary health care. Given the ambitious objective of 'health for all' by the year 2000, the local funds set aside in the annual plans could not suffice and therefore excessive dependence on donor funding was inevitable, particularly precipitated by the economic crisis that followed the war with Uganda under Idi Amin. The twenty-year plan (1980–2000) that was developed to achieve 'health for all' by 2000 ended up being highly donor funded, therefore lacking country ownership.

Evolution since the Astana declaration, 1995 to date

Following the observation that the country's health-care plans were lagging behind in terms of achieving the 'health for all' goals and other equally important goals in the health sector, proposals for major reforms were laid down. In October 1995, a meeting between the government and development partners was held and proposed major reforms in the health sector. At a key WHO-organized consultation of countries in Africa held at Zimbabwe (1997), the district focus of PHC was articulated and recommended. A proposal for health-sector reform was developed by December 1995 and included reforms at various levels of the health-care system, including primary health-care services. A health-sector reform plan (1996–1999) was developed and its implementation endorsed by all stakeholders. Some issues proposed for reforms had been raised earlier and received little attention in implementation. Such areas included the Decentralization Act (1974), the un-banning of private medical practice in 1991/92 and the introduction of cost sharing in 1993. Reforms relevant to PHC services included decentralized decision making and planning (the CCHP), the Council Health Service Board (CHSB) and health facility governing committees (HFGC). Generally, the reform actions were grouped into eight strategies, namely: (i) district health services, (ii) secondary and tertiary hospitals, (iii) a central Ministry of Health, (iv) human resource development, (v) central support systems, (vi) health-care financing, (vii) the public–private mix and (viii) Ministry of Health and donor relationships.

Primary health care 40 years after the Alma-Ata Declaration focused on achieving sustainable development goals. This comes with a comprehensive approach that takes PHC as one of the means (quick wins) to reach to UHC. The Astana Declaration comes with, first, a commitment of making bold political choices for health across sectors, thus promoting multisectoral actions through Health in All policies. Second, it aims at building a sustainable PHC that takes research and continuous learning on board in relation also to ensuring sustainability and resilience. Third, it aims at empowering individuals and communities. In this regard, Tanzania has implemented a number of demand- and supply-side reforms in the PHC system. These include health financing reforms such as the *CHF iliyoboreshwa* (improved CHF) and direct health facility financing (DHFF), and availability of medicine, the Jazia Prime Vendor System (Kalolo *et al.*, 2017; Kapologwe *et al.*, 2019; Wiedenmayer *et al.*, 2019).

1.2 The Model Guiding the Current Book

The narratives in this book have been informed by a framework that provides a comprehensive picture of the context under which the PHC processes and struggles overtime have happened. The contexts that inform the reforms are described as economic situation, political climate, social environment and legal and policy environment. Table 1.1 provides details of the context and the reforms (events) in different time periods from before 1880 to the present day.

1.3 Conclusion

The PHC concept and its implementation in real-life settings over time and across settings has constantly evolved to reflect the changing health needs of the population and their desires in terms of maximizing population health gains. The changing context, manifested as changes in economic situation, politics, social systems, legal frameworks and technological advancement, has in particular influenced the implementation approaches of PHC and reforms to improve it. In addition, the paradigm shifts over time have influenced the implementation of PHC. The paradigm shifts considered over time include: the selective vs comprehensive PHC approaches in implementation, health systems thinking, universal health coverage movement, accommodating transitions and changing technology (PHC digitalization).

In its own way Tanzania, over time, has implemented a series of reforms on PHC to meet time-related demands. Although it is acknowledged that traditional health-care systems existed and evolved over time, commensurate to the level of human development, there is a limited written account of pre-colonial health-care systems. During the colonial period, Western medicine, which forms the basis of contemporary thinking regarding PHC, was introduced in Tanzania. PHC services were organized (and reformed) to safeguard the needs of the colonial government and mainly focused on curative services. PHC reforms after independence could be visualized through the Arusha Declaration (1967), the Alma-Ata Declaration, the 1990s health-sector reforms, and beyond. In this period, several reforms (sometimes radical reforms) have been implemented to cope with the country's development goals and also as a result of global actors and actions.

To meet equity goals and maximize gains in health outcomes, during this time several notable reforms have been implemented. The major reforms that have had a wider impact on population health and health system outcome include the decentralization of PHC to district-based health systems, the formulation of a national health policy and subsequent health-sector strategic plans and reforms in each of the health system building blocks.

The lessons from each period of PHC reforms have led to continuous improvement over time and have guided future investments. Documenting the evolution of struggles to reform PHC in Tanzania has importance beyond what it tells us about the reforms, however. To start with, looking ahead, the narratives on the evolution of the concepts related to PHC and their implementation over time may reflect the changing health needs of the population

Table 1.1. Country contexts and processes for PHC reforms through history in Tanzania.

Country contexts	Before 1880	1880–1960	1961–1963	1964–1977	1978–1994	1995 to present day
Economic situation	Day-earners (subsistence farming and livestock keeping) Small-scale trade Feudalism	Colonial-driven economy not benefiting the citizens	Stagnation of economy	Nationalization Government as employer Economic stagnation Central planning Price control	Structural adjustment programmes Limited privatization Liberalization of economy	Debt relief privatization Lower middle-income economy (a mixture of command and market economy)
Political climate	Chiefdoms and councils of elders	External rulers: sultanates, Germans, British Limited urban authorities Protectorate Country preparing for independence	Indigenous political activism Reform the system to reach rural areas Training of health personnel to meet growing needs	Formation of United Republic of Tanzania Arusha Declaration Declaration to fight poverty/diseases/ ignorance Villagization Second five-year development plan (1969–1975) Formation of the Chama cha Mapinduzi (CCM)	Slow growth of the middle class National Health policy (1990) Introduction of multiparty system (1992) Health-sector reform proposal (1994)	National Health Policy (2007) Public–private partnership (PPP) policy (2009) One Plan II (2008) Primary health-care development programme (MMAM) (2007) Roll out of iCHF (2018) Establishment of division of health at PO-RALG (2014) Introduction of DHFF (2017) Health-sector strategic plans
Social environment	Herbal/traditional care and sporadic missionary care	Colonial health care mainly in urban settings, outbreak control mainly in plantations Poor nutrition Tribal conflicts High illiteracy rate	Trial and error to try to reform the health-care system	Strong role of mission health facilities Focus on peripheral facilities and human resources Community-oriented curricula Centralized decision making	PHC strategies Poor social protection Limited absorption of trained workforce	Reforming vertical programmes, TEHIP SWAp Introduction of health basket fund

Continued

Table 1.1. Continued

Country contexts	Before 1880	1880–1960	1961–1963	1964–1977	1978–1994	1995 to present day
Legal and policy environment	Traditions and customs/local laws	Local Government Act of 1953		Decentralization in 1972 (by deconcentration)	Comprehensive local government legislation passed (1982) Comprehensive system of local government re-established (D by D policy) (1984)	NHIF Act (1999) CHF Act (2001) Proposal for universal health insurance
International health policies/goals				Alma-Ata Declaration	Harare Declaration (Primary health care through a district health system) (1987)	Abuja Declaration (2001) Ouagadougou Declaration (2008) The 2008 World Health Organization report: Primary Health Care – Now More Than Ever Astana Declaration (2018)
Paradigm shifts on conceptualizing PHC		Health for urban elites/plantation workers	Focus on most at risk Responsive to the needs of the people	Health for all	Health for all	Transitions (demographic, epidemiological, health and nutritional) Health-system thinking Universal health coverage

and the constant struggle to improve systems that can deliver services that meet their needs. In addition, future investment in PHC should be context-driven in order to be relevant and impactful. Finally, the gains and failures in the course of struggling to reform PHC in Tanzania could provide a lesson to be learned for future reforms in Tanzania and beyond.

Bibliography

Adam, T. and de Savigny, D. (2012) Systems thinking for strengthening health systems in LMICs: need for a paradigm shift. *Health Policy and Planning* 27(suppl 4), iv1–iv3. DOI: 10.1093/heapol/czs084.

Amuna, P. and Zotor, F.B. (2008) Epidemiological and nutrition transition in developing countries: impact on human health and development. *The Proceedings of the Nutrition Society* 67(1), 82–90. DOI: 10.1017/S0029665108006058.

Andrews, G.J. and Crooks, V.A. (2016) *Primary Health Care: People, Practice, Place*. Routledge, Abingdon, UK. DOI: 10.4324/9781315602127.

Appiah-Agyekum, N.N. (2020) Primary healthcare implementation in practice: evidence from primary healthcare managers in Ghana. *African Journal of Primary Health Care & Family Medicine* 12(1), 1–7. DOI: 10.4102/phcfm.v12i1.2183.

Atiim, G.A. and Elliott, S.J. (2016) The global epidemiologic transition: noncommunicable diseases and emerging health risk of allergic disease in Sub-Saharan Africa. *Health Education & Behavior: The Official Publication of the Society for Public Health Education* 43(1 Suppl), 37S–55S. DOI: 10.1177/1090198115606918.

Beck, A. (1977) Medicine and society in Tanganyika, 18901930: a historical inquiry. *Transactions of the American Philosophical Society* 67(3), 1–59. DOI: 10.2307/1006330.

Brennan, J. and Burton, A. (2007) The emerging metropolis: a short history of Dar es Salaam circa 1862–2005. In: Brennan, J.R., Burton, A. and Lawi, Y. (eds) *Dar es Salaam: Histories from an Emerging African Metropolis*. African Books Collective, Oxford, UK, pp. 13–75.

Bustreo, F., Mshinda, H., Hinton, R., Hausmann-Muela, S. and Tanner, M. (2019) Commentary: primary health care in Tanzania – Leading the way through innovation. *eClinicalMedicine* 13, 12–13. DOI: 10.1016/j.eclinm.2019.07.010.

de Savigny, D., Kasale, H., Mbuya, C., Munna, G., Mgalula, L, *et al.* (2002) *Tanzania Essential Health Interventions Project: TEHIP 'Interventions', An Overview*. Discussion paper/Ministry of Health's Tanzania Essential Health Interventions Project (TEHIP), No. 2. Available at: https://idl-bnc-idrc.dspacedirect.org/bitstream/handle/10625/40912/129019.pdf?sequence=1 (accessed 18 May 2023).

Defo, B.K. (2014) Demographic, epidemiological, and health transitions: are they relevant to population health patterns in Africa? *Global Health Action* 7, 22443. DOI: 10.3402/gha.v7.22443.

Downie, A., Mashanya, T., Chipwaza, B., Griffiths, F., Harris, B. *et al.* (2022) Remote consulting in primary health care in low- and middle-income countries: feasibility study of an online training program to support care delivery during the COVID-19 pandemic. *JMIR Formative Research* 6(6), e32964. DOI: 10.2196/32964.

Earth, B. (1996) Structural adjustment and its effects on health and education in Tanzania. *Canadian Woman Studies* 16(3), 122–128.

Gilson, L., Kilima, P. and Tanner, M. (1994) Local government decentralization and the health sector in Tanzania. *Public Administration and Development* 14(5), 451–477. DOI: 10.1002/pad.4230140503.

Giovanella, L. (2018) Basic health care or primary health care? Cadernos de Saúde Pública (accessed 15 May 2023). 34(8). DOI: 10.1590/0102-311X00029818.

Githendu, P., Morrison, L., Silaa, R., Pothapregada, S., Asiimwe, S. *et al.* (2020) Transformation of the Tanzania medical store department through global fund support: an impact assessment study. *BMJ Open* 10(11), e040276. DOI: 10.1136/bmjopen-2020-040276.

Goergen, H. and Schmidt-Ehry, B. (2004) The concept of the district health system (DHS). In: *The District Health System*. p. 27. Available at: https://www.uio.no/studier/emner/matnat/ifi/IN5330/v20/pensumliste/district_health_system.pdf (accessed 21 April 2023).

Görgen, H., Bruchhausen, W., Kuelker, K. and Eckart, W.U. (2001) *The History of Health Care in Tanzania*. GTZ, Dar es Salaam, Tanzania.

Görgen, H., Kirsch-Wolk, T. and Schmidt-Ehry, B. (2004) *The District Health System: Experiences and Prospects in Africa, Manual for Public Health Practitioners*. Deutsche Gesellschaft für Technische Zusammenarbeit (GTZ) GmbH, Eschborn, Germany.

Greenhalgh, T. (2013) *Primary Health Care: Theory and Practice*. Wiley, Oxford, UK.

Hurley, C., Baum, F., Johns, J. and Labonte, R. (2010) Comprehensive primary health care in Australia: findings from a narrative review of the literature. *Australasian Medical Journal* 1(2), 147–152. DOI: 10.4066/AMJ.2010.201.

Hutton, G. and Tanner, M. (2004) The sector-wide approach: a blessing for public health? *Bulletin of the World Health Organization* 82(12), 893.

Jafari, H., Mousavi, S.M., Ghoshouni, H., Nemati, M. and Kelishadrokhi, S.F. (2022) Strengthening the primary health care system in the face of emerging and re-emerging epidemics; providing a native and applicable model based on best practices of countries. *Disaster and Emergency Medicine Journal* 8(1), 41–54. DOI: 10.5603/DEMJ.a2022.0024.

Jennings, M. (2008) 'Healing of bodies, salvation of souls': missionary medicine in colonial Tanganyika, 1870s–1939. *Journal of Religion in Africa* 38(1), 27–56. DOI: 10.1163/157006608X262700.

Jennings, M. (2019) *Cooperation and Competition: Missions, the Colonial State and Constructing a Health System in Colonial Tanganyika*. Manchester University Press, Manchester, UK, pp. 153–173. Available at: https://www.manchesteropenhive.com/view/9781526137074/9781526137074.00012.xml (accessed 15 May 2023).

Jiyenze, M.K., Tundui, C., Sirili, N. and Mollel, H. (2022) Effects of implementing a health sector strategic plan: evidence from Tanzania. *East African Medical Journal* 99(9), 5147–5155.

Kalolo, A., Gautier, L., Radermacher, R., Stoermer, M., Jahn, A. *et al.* (2017) Implementation of the redesigned community health fund in the Dodoma region of Tanzania: a qualitative study of views from rural communities. *The International Journal of Health Planning and Management* 33(1), 121–135. DOI: 10.1002/hpm.2403.

Kapologwe, N.A., Kalolo, A., Kibusi, S.M., Chaula, Z., Nswilla, A. *et al.* (2019) Understanding the implementation of direct health facility financing and its effect on health system performance in Tanzania: a non-controlled before and after mixed method study protocol. *Health Research Policy and Systems* 17(1), 11. DOI: 10.1186/s12961-018-0400-3.

Kapologwe, N.A., Meara, J.G., Kengia, J.T., Sonda, Y., Gwajima, D. *et al.* (2020) Development and upgrading of public primary healthcare facilities with essential surgical services infrastructure: a strategy towards achieving universal health coverage in Tanzania. *BMC Health Services Research* 20(1), 218. DOI: 10.1186/s12913-020-5057-2.

Kengia, J.T., Igarashi, I. and Kawabuchi, K. (2013) Effectiveness of health sector reforms in reducing disparities in utilization of skilled birth attendants in Tanzania. *The Tohoku Journal of Experimental Medicine* 230(4), 241–253. DOI: 10.1620/tjem.230.241.

Kilama, W., Nhonoli, A.M. and Makene, W.J. (1974) Health care delivery in Tanzania. In: Ruhumbika, G. (ed.) *Towards Ujamaa. 20 Years of TANU Leadership. A Contribution of the University of Dar Es Salaam to the 20th Anniversary of TANU*. Kampala, pp. 191–217.

Kitua, A.Y., Mashalla, Y.J. and Shija, J.K. (2000) Coordinating health research to promote action: the Tanzanian experience. *BMJ* 321(7264), 821–823. DOI: 10.1136/bmj.321.7264.821.

Latko, B., Temporão, J.G., Frenk, J., Evans, T.G., Chen, L.C. *et al.* (2011) The growing movement for universal health coverage. *The Lancet* 377(9784), 2161–2163. DOI: 10.1016/S0140-6736(10)62006-5.

Litsios, D.S. (2015) On the origin of primary health care. In: Medcalf, A., Bhattacharya, S., Momen, H., Saavedra, M. and Jones, M. (eds) *Health for All: The Journey to Universal Health Coverage*. Orient Blackswan, Hyderabad, India. Available at: https://www.ncbi.nlm.nih.gov/books/NBK316278 (accessed 15 May 2023).

Magnussen, L., Ehiri, J. and Jolly, P. (2004) Comprehensive versus selective primary health care: lessons for global health policy. *Health Affairs* 23(3), 167–176. DOI: 10.1377/hlthaff.23.3.167.

Martens, P. (2002) Health transitions in a globalising world: towards more disease or sustained health? *Futures* 34(7), 635–648. DOI: 10.1016/S0016-3287(02)00005-8.

Mbilinyi, M. (1985) 'City' and 'Countryside' in colonial Tanganyika. *Economic and Political Weekly* 20(43), WS88–WS96.

Mtei, G. and Mulligan, J. (2007) *Community Health Funds in Tanzania: A Literature Review*. Ifakara Health Research and Development Centre, Ifakara, Tanzania.

Mujinja, P.G.M. and Kida, T.M. (2014) *Implications of Health Sector Reforms in Tanzania: Policies, Indicators and Accessibility to Health Services*. Economic and Social Research Foundation, Dodoma. Available at: https://books.google.co.uk/books/about/Implications_of_Health_Sector_Reforms_in.html?id=EwHUjwEACAAJ&redir_esc=y (accessed 15 May 2023).

Neves, A.L. and Burgers, J. (2022) Digital technologies in primary care: Implications for patient care and future research. *The European Journal of General Practice* 28(1), 203–208. DOI: 10.1080/13814788.2022.2052041.

Newell, K.W. (1988) Selective primary health care: the counter revolution. *Social Science & Medicine* 26(9), 903–906. DOI: 10.1016/0277-9536(88)90409-1.

Newell, K.W. and WHO (1975) *Health by the People*. World Health Organization, Geneva, Switzerland. Available at: https://apps.who.int/iris/handle/10665/40514 (accessed 15 May 2023).

Peters, D.H., Paina, L. and Schleimann, F. (2013) Sector-wide approaches (SWAps) in health: what have we learned? *Health Policy and Planning* 28(8), 884–890. DOI: 10.1093/heapol/czs128.

Rasanathan, K., Montesinos, E.V., Matheson, D., Etienne, C. and Evans, T. (2011) Primary health care and the social determinants of health: essential and complementary approaches for reducing inequities in health. *Journal of Epidemiology & Community Health* 65(8), 656–660. DOI: 10.1136/jech.2009.093914.

Rifkin, S.B. (2018a) Health for all and primary health care, 1978–2018: a historical perspective on policies and programs over 40 years. In: *Oxford Research Encyclopedias: Global Public Health*. Oxford University Press, Oxford, UK. Available at: https://oxfordre.com/publichealth/view/10.1093/acrefore/9780190632366.001.0001/acrefore-9780190632366-e-55 (accessed 15 May 2023).

Rifkin, S.B. (2018b) Alma Ata after 40 years: primary health care and health for all – from consensus to complexity. *BMJ Global Health* 3(Suppl 3), e001188. DOI: 10.1136/bmjgh-2018-001188.

Roemer, M.I. (1986) Priority for primary health care: its development and problems. *Health Policy and Planning* 1(1), 58–66. DOI: 10.1093/heapol/1.1.58.

Sacks, E., Morrow, M., Story, W.T., Shelley, K.D., Shanklin, D, *et al*. (2019) Beyond the building blocks: integrating community roles into health systems frameworks to achieve health for all. *BMJ Global Health* 3(Suppl 3), e001384. DOI: 10.1136/bmjgh-2018-001384.

Schneider, L. (2006) Colonial legacies and postcolonial authoritarianism in Tanzania: connects and disconnects. *African Studies Review* 49(1), 93–118. DOI: 10.1353/arw.2006.0091.

Scholz, S., Ngoli, B. and Flessa, S. (2015) Rapid assessment of infrastructure of primary health care facilities – a relevant instrument for health care systems management. *BMC Health Services Research* 15(1), 1–10. DOI: 10.1186/s12913-015-0838-8.

Seco, S. and Martínez, J. (2001) *An Overview of Sector Wide Approaches (SWAps) in Health: Are They Appropriate for Aid-Dependant Latin American Countries?* DFID Health Systems Resource Centre, London. Available at: https://www.heart-resources.org/wp-content/uploads/2012/10/An-overview-of-Sector-Wide-Approaches-in-Health.pdf (accessed 21 April 2023).

Shortell, S.M., O'Brien, J.L., Carman, J.M., Foster, R.W., Hughes, E.F. *et al*. (1995) Assessing the impact of continuous quality improvement/total quality management: concept versus implementation. *Health Services Research* 30(2), 377–401.

URT (2022) *National Bureau of Statistics: 2022 Population and Housing Census, Preliminary Report in Swahili Language*. United Republic of Tanzania, Dodoma. Available at: https://www.nbs.go.tz/index.php/en/census-surveys/population-and-housing-census/802-matokeo-ya-mwanzo-ya-sensa-ya-watu-na-makazi-ya-mwaka-2022 (accessed 15 May 2023).

Vähäkangas, M. (2016) The Grandpa's cup: a Tanzanian healing ritual as a temporary Interreligious platform. *Suomen Antropologi: Journal of the Finnish Anthropological Society* 41(4), 14–28.

Vaughan, J.P. and Walt, G. (1984) Implementing primary health care: some problems of creating national programmes. *Tropical Doctor* 14(3), 108–113. DOI: 10.1177/004947558401400304.

Walsh, J.A. and Warren, K.S. (1979) Selective primary health care. *New England Journal of Medicine* 301(18), 967–974.

WHO (1978) *Declaration of Alma-Ata*. World Health Organization, Regional Office for Europe, Geneva, Switzerland.

WHO (2002) *Declaration of Alma-Ata 1978*. World Health Organization, Regional Office for Europe, Geneva, Switzerland.

WHO (2008) *The World Health Report 2008: Primary Health Care Now More than Ever*. World Health Organization, Geneva, Switzerland. Available at: https://apps.who.int/iris/handle/10665/43949 (accessed 15 May 2023).

WHO (2010) *Monitoring the Building Blocks of Health Systems: A Handbook of Indicators and Their Measurement Strategies*. World Health Organization, Geneva, Switzerland. Available at: https://apps.who.int/iris/bitstream/handle/10665/258734/9789241564052-eng.pdf (accessed 18 May 2023).

WHO (2022) *Digital Technologies: Shaping the Future of Primary Health Care*. World Health Organization, Geneva, Switzerland. Available at: https://apps.who.int/iris/handle/10665/326573 (accessed 15 May 2023).

Wiedenmayer, K., Mbwasi, R., Mfuko, W., Mpuya, E., Charles, J. *et al*. (2019) Jazia prime vendor system- a public-private partnership to improve medicine availability in Tanzania: from pilot to scale. *Journal of Pharmaceutical Policy and Practice* 12, 4. DOI: 10.1186/s40545-019-0163-4.

Xu, G. and Wang, J. (2015) Primary health care, a concept to be fully understood and implemented in current China's health care reform. *Family Medicine and Community Health* 3(3), 41–51. DOI: 10.15212/FMCH.2015.0127.

Young, T.K. (1986) Socialist development and primary health care: the case of Tanzania. *Human Organization* 45(2), 128–134. DOI: 10.17730/humo.45.2.17p75666m4347g14.

2 Leadership and Governance for Primary Health Care in Tanzania

Mwandu Kini Jiyenze[1]*, Elihuruma M. Nangawe[2], Idda L. Swai[3], Anosisye M. Kesale[3], Godfrey Kacholi[4,5] and James Tumaini Kengia[6,7]
[1]Centre for Educational Development in Health Arusha (CEDHA), Tanzania; [2]PRAXIS in Health and Development – Policy, Systems, Strategies, QI and Capacity Development and Applied Research, Dar es Salaam, Tanzania; [3]Department of Local Government Management, School of Public Administration and Management, Mzumbe-Morogoro, Tanzania; [4]Department of Health Systems Management, School of Public Administration and Management, Mzumbe University, Tanzania; [5]Centre of Excellence in Health Monitoring and Evaluation, School of Public Administration and Management, Mzumbe University, Tanzania; [6]President's Office – Regional Administration and Local Government, Dodoma, Tanzania; [7]University of Dodoma, Tanzania

Abstract
Leadership and governance, also called stewardship, play a pivotal role in ensuring success in the implementation of strategies for improving primary health care (PHC). Tanzania, through a series of reforms, has organized herself into a robust health system that has leadership and governance structures and tools to ensure efficiency and effectiveness in the provision of PHC services. The main focus of this chapter is to describe how leadership and governance in the context of PHC evolved over time in Tanzania. After presenting concepts and instruments for PHC leadership and governance, the historical development of primary health care is presented in five phases: 1880–1960; 1961–1963; 1964–1977; 1978–1994; and 1995–2022. Also, the chapter outlines the current practices in PHC leadership and governance, existing structures, systems in place and efforts to strengthen PHC leadership and governance in Tanzania. Lastly, the chapter presents lessons learnt and recommendations for improving future PHC leadership and governance in Tanzania.

2.0 Introduction

Effective leadership and governance (also called stewardship) are important for the functionality of any health system and play critical roles in the planning, implementation, monitoring and evaluation of health interventions at all levels (West *et al.*, 2015). Leadership and governance practices, systems and structures impact the overall direction of the health system, priority setting and implementation of strategies to ensure better access to health services (WHO, 2007; Brinkerhoff and Bossert, 2008). According to WHO (2007), the key functions of leadership and governance include: policy guidance, intelligence and oversight, collaborations and

*Corresponding author: mwandukini@yahoo.com

DOI: 10.1079/9781800623330.0002

coalition building, regulation, system design and accountability. Leadership and governance ensure that policies, standards and norms that determine the practices are developed and used at all levels of the health system within the political and socio-economic contexts (Pourbohloul and Kieny, 2011).

Leadership and governance play a crucial role in ensuring the provision of quality primary health care (PHC) services within the context of a well-established efficient system that operates under carefully crafted, long-term policy frameworks (WHO and UNICEF, 2018). Policies and strategic decisions taken by government officials at the national and subnational levels have always been crucial for determining how well the health system is governed and managed (WHO and UNICEF, 2018).

Despite recognizing the universality of leadership and governance within the context of PHC these concepts have numerous definitions. Box 2.1 provides key concepts used in this chapter.

In Tanzania, the leadership and governance of PHC has evolved over time, and significant milestones have been reached to date. In this chapter, the important milestones, events and

Box 2.1. Definition of key concepts

Health (system) leadership and governance: According to the WHO, leadership and governance of the health system 'involve ensuring strategic policy frameworks exist and are combined with effective oversight, coalition building, the provision of appropriate regulations and incentives, attention to system-design, and accountability' (WHO, 2007). Leadership and governance also refer to processes and practices that ensure the health sector has a vision, strategic direction, policy instruments and organizational structures to facilitate health service delivery and improve individual and population health. As part of the health system, PHC leadership and governance is exercised at various levels of a country's health system: community, health facility, council, regional, health system and national levels (WHO and UNICEF, 2018). To exercise successful leadership and governance, it is necessary to ensure that strategic policy frameworks are in place and complemented by effective regulation, coalition-building, oversight, and system design.

PHC leadership and governance: PHC leadership and governance 'involves ensuring strategic policy frameworks exist and are combined with effective oversight, coalition building, the provision of appropriate regulations and incentives, attention to system design, and accountability' to guide provision and governance of primary health care. These are the processes and practices that promote, facilitate and support effective and efficient delivery of primary health care and improved health of individuals, households and communities through a council (district) health system. PHC leadership and governance are exercised at various levels of a country: community, health facility, council, regional, health system and national levels (WHO and UNICEF, 2018). PHC leadership and governance involves three processes: setting priorities for the maintenance and improvement of the population's health; assessing progress towards attainment of those priorities; and ensuring that all relevant actors are held properly to account for their actions (Smith *et al.*, 2012).

Health system leadership: This is the process of providing vision, effective coordination and integration of work and taking responsibility to ensure the organization or national reach the desired health goal. Leadership is about people, and it involves using the manager's power, personality, influence, persuasion, and communication skills to coordinate people, the team and their activities and efforts to achieve organizational objectives and targets (Jones *et al.*, 2019).

Health system governance: This refers to the process of setting strategic health direction through establishing legal frameworks, institutions and mechanisms and making decisions carried out by the government and other stakeholders to achieve national health development objectives (WHO, 2020). It includes identifying and correcting unfavourable trends and distortions, making a case for health in national development, and regulating the behaviour of various actors, such as health-care providers, financiers and beneficiaries.

Therefore this chapter adopts the WHO definition that leadership and governance refer to all practices that involve ensuring strategic policy frameworks exist and are combined with effective oversight, coalition building, regulation, attention to system design and accountability (WHO, 2007).

turning points are outlined and discussed with the view of understanding the struggles in strengthening leadership and governance of PHC. Throughout this chapter, the documentation of significant decisions, established policy frameworks and authoritative circulars that have transformed or facilitated the evolution of PHC are highlighted.

After this introductory section, the chapter has the following sections. Sections 2.1 and 2.2 of the chapter provide a general introduction and outline the key concepts related to leadership and governance, respectively. Instruments and the history of PHC leadership and governance in Tanzania are described in Sections 2.3 and 2.4 respectively. Section 2.5. of the chapter outlines the current PHC leadership and governance structures in Tanzania, and the current efforts to strengthen PHC leadership and governance in Tanzania are explained in Section 2.6, while Section 2.7 outlines the lessons learned and recommendations for future PHC leadership and governance in Tanzania.

2.1 Key Leadership and Governance Concepts

Primary health care leadership and governance refer to processes and practices that promote, facilitate and support the effective and efficient delivery of primary health care to individuals, households and communities through a council (district) health system. PHC leadership and governance are exercised at various levels of a country: community, health facility, council, regional, health system and national levels (WHO and UNICEF, 2018). A more detailed summary of leadership and governance concepts is given in Box 2.1.

2.2 Leadership and Governance Instruments for PHC in Tanzania

In Tanzania, PHC is guided and governed by various instruments (Barbazza and Tello, 2014; Brinkerhoff *et al.*, 2019; MOHCDGEC, 2020). These instruments provide practical guiding statements for the leadership and provision of primary health-care services. The instruments are categorized into international, national and sector-specific health instruments.

2.2.1 International instruments

These are international policies and declarations adopted by countries to achieve specific purposes. The contribution of the international policies and declarations in shaping primary health care at the global level as well as in Tanzania cannot be underestimated. For instance, in 1978, the Alma-Ata Declaration reshaped the governance of health systems and primary health care in particular by integrating community/users/people in governance and management of their own health in primary health care. The declaration placed stress on the importance of people as individuals and collectively to participate in the planning, implementation and monitoring of health-service delivery in primary health care. Despite the fact that during the first years after independence Tanzania had already started engaging the community in designing and governing basic health care, the Alma-Ata Declaration significantly accelerated Tanzania's government efforts to strengthen the participation of communities in planning, implementing and monitoring health-service delivery in their areas, and this played a major role in improving the quality of service provision that responds to community needs, preference and taste.

The Declaration of Astana of 2018, which came at a time of an increasing global movement for stronger investment in primary health care to achieve universal health coverage, acknowledged the commitment laid down by the Alma-Ata Declaration and underscored the critical role of primary health care. In governance perspective for instance, among other things the Astana Declaration committed itself by making a bold political choice for health in all sectors and stressing that the primary role of the government at all levels is to ensure that the rights of everyone are promoted and protected by participating local communities, engaging all stakeholders and promoting multisectoral action in strengthening

PHC, including the expansion and provision of primary health care to the population.

Furthermore, the Ouagadougou Declaration on Primary Health Care and Health Systems in Africa calls for the member states to review and update their national health strategies, policies, guidelines and plans according to the PHC approach as a strategy to strengthening overall health systems. This declaration basically focuses on nine major priority areas, namely: (i) leadership and governance for health, (ii) health service delivery, (iii) human resources for health, (iv) health financing, (v) health information systems, (vi) health technologies and supplies, (vii) community ownership and participation, (viii) partnerships for health development, and (ix) research for health. Likewise, the Agenda 2063 and the Common African Position (CAP) of the African Union underscore that a prosperous Africa should base on inclusive growth and sustainable development and that the development should be people-driven, relying on the potential of African people, especially its women and youth and caring for the children – which falls with the principles of PCH. Notwithstanding, the Abuja Declaration of 2001 contributed to the improved PCH as it aimed at increasing government funding for health by allocating at least 15% of the annual budget to improve the health sector. This forced countries to increase spending priorities for primary health care and overall health systems in order to ensure accessible and affordable quality health care. Similarly, the East Africa Community (EAC) and Southern Africa Development Community (SADC) blocks have stipulated various priorities in the health sector to be implemented by the member states, which includes strengthening the PHC.

2.2.2 National instruments

These are cross-cutting instruments affecting both the public and private sectors in Tanzania. Such instruments include the Constitution of the United Republic of Tanzania of 1977, acts of Parliament, regulations, standing orders, policies and guidelines and circulars. The most common guiding instruments are the Tanzania Development Vision 2025, five-year national development plans, public finance acts and regulations, local government authorities acts, Public Procurement Act and Regulations and Public Service Act and Regulations. These instruments provide overall guidance on leadership and governance and provision of public services, including primary health services. The instruments generally set national priorities, objectives, principles and responsibilities, including priorities, objectives and responsibilities for improving the health of the population through the primary health-care approach. The relevance of some of the key instruments to primary health care is summarized in Table 2.1.

2.2.3 Health-sector instruments

The health sector in Tanzania is guided by various instruments that provide guidance on how the primary health services are led and governed in Tanzania. The instruments that govern the health sector, including leadership and governance of primary health care comprise, but are not limited to, health policy which provides the direction of leadership and governance of PHC in institutional arrangements to some extent. For instance, the health policy (2003) provides for the organization of the health system in Tanzania including PHC. The policy mentions that the health system in Tanzania is pyramidal in shape, but specifies that for PHC the lowest level is the village level where there are dispensaries, at the ward level there are health centres and at the district level there are district hospitals. On the other side the health policy has tried to integrate government structures and health system within PHC; acts and regulations; standing orders; guidelines and circulars; health-sector strategic and operational plans; essential health service packages; health programmes; national targets, goals and performance measures; codes of conduct for health service provision ethics and research. Other instruments include signed contracts and memoranda; manuals related to the health sector (financial, procurement, training manuals); financial audit reports in the health sector; health services reports; progress reports; mission/vision statements of health organizations; organizational charts; resource allocation formulae; and computerized support systems, such as health information systems. The health-sector instruments are useful in a number of ways, as shown in Box 2.2 for general health services and for primary health care in Tanzania.

Table 2.1. Some of the national instruments and their relevance to PHC.

National instrument	Specific role/relevance to PHC in Tanzania
Constitution of the United Republic of Tanzania	Has provisions that require the government to improve 'welfare of the people' and require the government to use national wealth for 'development of people and in particular is geared toward the eradication of poverty, ignorance and diseases'.
The Tanzania Development Vision 2025	Envisages Tanzania, among others, with high quality livelihood and good governance. The vision calls for achieving the following goals related to primary health: access to quality primary health care for all; access to quality reproductive health services for all; reduction of infant and maternal mortality rate; universal access to safe water. The vision calls for decentralization of responsibilities to local government.
Five-Year National Development Plan	A tool for implementing the Tanzania Development Vision and it sets a national development agenda within 5 years. Example, the plan for 2021 and 2026 set seven health-sector targets to be achieved using various strategies, including expanding and improving the quality of primary health care in Tanzania.
Public Finance Act and Local Government Finance Act (and their regulations)	Provides overall guidance on mobilization and use of financial resources to improve social services, including primary health services.
Public Procurement Act and Regulations	Provides principles and procedures on procurement of goods and services for provision of social services, including primary health services.
Public Service Act and Regulations	Has provisions and guidance on management of public servants, including public servants and the provision of primary health services.

Box 2.2. The usefulness of health instruments for primary health care

Generally, the development and use of health instruments helps to:

- set directions in terms of health priorities and objectives;
- identify means (interventions) and resources required to achieve health objectives;
- identify principles (values), actions and actors required to achieve health objectives;
- rationalize and facilitate decision making;
- define the frame of reference and criteria for evaluation and reporting;
- rally professionals and other stakeholders around health issues;
- build consensus;
- facilitate the introduction of viable and effective actions; and
- guide provision and leadership and governance of health services and organization.

(From Dussault and Dubois, 2003; Wizara ya Afya na Usitawi wa Jamii, 2007; MOHCDGEC, 2021a, b; MOHSW, 2015)

The government, in collaboration with stakeholders, has implemented various steps to strengthen leadership and governance of the health sector at regional and council levels, where PHC services are provided to individuals, families and communities (Wizara ya Afya na Usitawi wa Jamii, 2007; MOHCDGEC, 2021a, b).

2.3 Historical Development of Leadership and Governance for PHC in Tanzania

The history of leadership and governance for PHC in Tanzania is linked to three historical periods: before the German and British

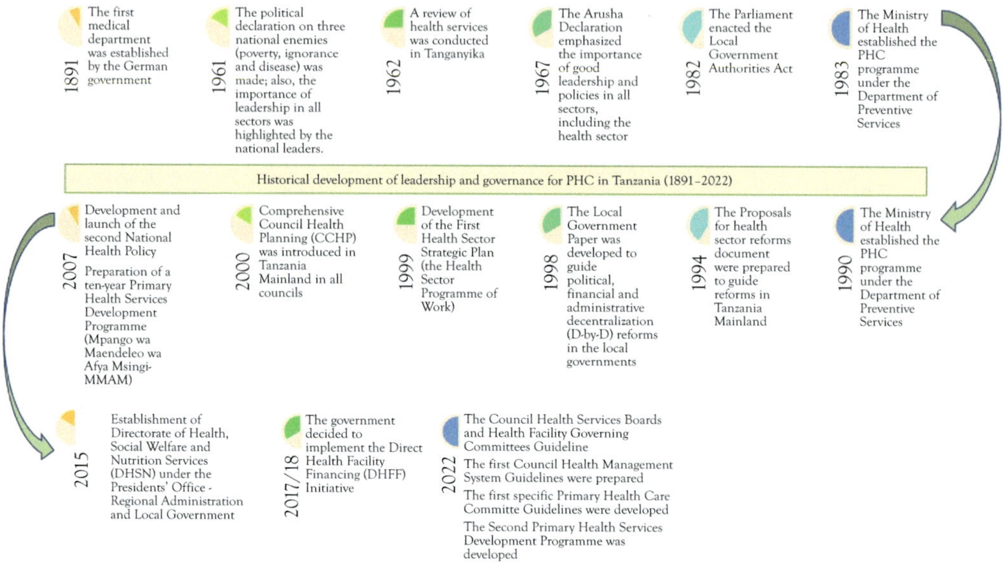

Fig. 2.1. Historical development of leadership and governance for PHC in Tanzania.

administrations (before 1880); during German and British administration (1880–1960); and after the German and British administrations (1961–2022). Some of the key historical events for developing, enhancing and strengthening PHC leadership and governance are outlined in Fig. 2.1, and details on the implication of the major events are detailed in Table 2.2.

2.3.1 Leadership and governance for PHC before the German and British administrations, pre-1880

During this period, only traditional medicines were provided to people. Mostly, traditional healers and birth attendants dominated traditional medicines in their respective communities (MOH, 1983; Organizing Committee, 2000). The practices of traditional medicines had different governance arrangements based on how the communities were organized. Often, the traditional rulers (chiefs) and the councils of elders were responsible for managing the delivery of traditional medicine on behalf of the people, while simultaneously the elders were responsible for health promotion and community wellbeing (Beck, 1977; MOH, 1983; Organizing Committee, 2000).

2.3.2 Leadership and governance for health services during the German and British administrations, 1880–1960

The period covers the German and British administrations, which started early in the 17th century and lasted until the period when Tanzania gained its independence from colonial rule in 1961. The German and British governments laid the foundation for current health services in Tanzania (Organizing Committee, 2000). The German and British administration period established the primary (basic) but, to some extent, organized medical care that was managed mainly by missionary agencies around the coast and expanded further into the interior with the establishment of hospitals that were meant to serve the German and British government's interests. The German policy preferred hospitals in urban areas over small health units in rural areas and primary health care focused on diseases that mainly affected the Germans (Msambichaka *et al.*, 1997). The Germans first introduced modern and to some extent structured medical health services in 1891 and the first medical department was established in 1891 (Chagula and Tarimo, 1975; Beck, 1977). The medical department was responsible for coordinating and managing

Table 2.2. Major leadership and governance events and their implications for PHC.

S/N	Major event	Implication of the event to the PHC
1	Germans first introduced modern medical health services in 1891 and the first medical department was established in 1891.	The purpose of the medical department was to coordinate and manage the provision of modern medical services offered in economical strategic areas and administrative centres/urban areas.
2	Townships Ordinance and the Food and Drugs Ordinance were enacted in the 1930s.	The purpose was to regulate urban health services at all levels.
3	The first medical policy review was conducted in 1949.	The purpose of the reviews was to generate evidence to inform decisions on how to improve urban curative and environmental services in Tanganyika.
4	Tanganyika became Independent in 1961.	The political leaders identified the need for leaders to guide and react in all sectors, including the health sector. Teaching institutions were established to produce skilled and qualified personnel, especially management and leadership.
5	Declaration of war against poverty, ignorance and diseases in 1961.	The purpose of this declaration was to provide overall guidance to the leaders in all sectors to address poverty, ignorance and diseases.
6	Review medical service survey in Tanganyika in 1962.	The survey was conducted in 1961 and 1962, and the purpose was to collect evidence to inform the development of the health sector. The survey emphasized shifting from curative urban and medical services to promotive services and rural areas.
7	The first health-sector plan was developed in 1964.	The first health-sector plan was developed as part of the first five-year national development plan for the 1964–1969 period to guide development in the health sector.
8	The Arusha Declaration in 1967.	The declaration was made in 1967, and the implementation started immediately after the declaration. The purpose was to guide the socio-economic development of the country and emphasized the importance of good leadership and policies in all sectors, health included.
9	The second five-year development plan was developed in 1969.	The second five-year development plan was developed to emphasize equality in social services for the period 1969 to 1974.
10	The second health plan for 1972 to 1980 was developed in 1972 as part of the second five-year development plan.	The plan's purpose was to implement the directive by the party (TANU) that requires the government to provide free and comprehensive basic health services to all of Tanzania.
11	Decentralization of power and authority to regions and districts in 1972.	Regions and districts were given some administrative power and authority, but the regions and districts lacked skilled and qualified leaders. This led to increased dependence on central government and declining quality of services.
12	The act to abolish the provision of health services for profit was introduced in 1977.	The provision of free health services was restricted, and the engagement of voluntary agencies and parastatal organizations to provide health services started.
13	Formulation of the long-term objectives for the health sector in 1980.	The purpose of the long-term objectives was to strengthen health management and supervision of health services at different levels.

Continued

Table 2.2. Continued

S/N	Major event	Implication of the event to the PHC
14	The economic crisis in the 1980s.	Tanzania experienced a severe economic crisis in the 1980s, which affected the management of PHC and health-care delivery in general.
15	Introduction of Local Government Authorities Act in 1982.	The local government authorities were introduced and given the mandate to supervise and provide basic social services, including primary health services
16	The first guidelines for the implementation of the primary health-care programme was developed in 1983.	The Ministry of Health developed the first guidelines for implementing the primary health care programme in Tanzania. The programme, among others, clarified the composition, roles and functions of primary health care (PHC) committees at all levels.
17	Primary health-care review conducted in 1984.	The Ministry of Health conducted a preliminary health-care review in 1984 and documented the successes and challenges in implementing the primary health-care strategy.
18	The first written health policy was developed in 1990.	The policy was developed to guide the planning, implementation and evaluation of health services, PHC included. The health sector was guided by the ruling party directives, general government policies, and directives in the five-year development plans before this policy. The policy was informed by the PHC Declaration, and it guides the successful implementation of PHC. The policy specifically stipulated the roles of the community structures, including primary health-care committees and community members.
19	The preparation of the health planning and management training manual in 1991.	The purpose of the manual was to strengthen management and leadership competencies for health managers, health facility health management teams and other health workers at the district and regional levels.
20	Private sector was allowed to practice in 1991.	The act allowed providers of health services to provide health services for profit.
21	Proposal to reform the health sector was prepared in 1994.	The Ministry of Health proposed various reforms to address key problems of the health sector, including weak management and leadership and weak health governance structures.
22	An act to reform the regional administration passed in 1997.	The act reformed the regional administration by forming a regional secretariat to support local governments in a region. In line with this act and the 1990 health policy, the regional health management team (RHMT) was established as a technical resource to support health development in local government authorities.
23	Private Laboratories Act was passed in 1997.	The act allowed private organizations to establish laboratory services that expand medical laboratory facilities in the health sector.
24	The development of the local government policy paper in 1998.	The paper was developed to guide the reforms of local governments in Tanzania. The paper, together with the Local Government Act of 1982 and the health policy of 1990, establishes CHMT, membership and their responsibilities. The reform also changed the naming from district health management team (DHMT) to council health management team (CHMT).

Continued

Table 2.2. Continued

S/N	Major event	Implication of the event to the PHC
25	The first health-sector strategic plan was prepared in 1999.	The SP was developed to continue reforming the health sector, strengthening health management and leadership at council and regional levels.
26	The first CCHP guideline was developed in 2000.	The guideline was developed to guide the preparation of CCHPs. It was further reviewed in 2004, 2007, 2011 and 2021 to accommodate the requirements for planning and the management and governance issues in PHC.
27	The first national package of essential health interventions was approved in 2000 and rolled out in 2005.	The package was for primary health services and it was rolled out in the councils in two phases: from two districts (Rufiji and Morogoro Rural) to two regions, namely Coast and Morogoro, under the UNF support, 2003–2006; from 2006 onwards, to the whole country through zonal training centres, now known as zonal health resource centres.
28	Health management training programmes and manuals were developed in 2000.	The programmes and manuals were developed to strengthen the health management capacities of CHMT between 2000 and 2003.
29	In 2002, Tanzania's development vision 2025 was developed.	Tanzania development vision 2025 was developed in 2002 to guide socio-economic development in Tanzania; the vision emphasizes the need for improving the health and welfare of people through the provision of primary health care.
30	The second health-sector strategic plan was developed in 2003.	The plan was named as strengthening health management and leadership at council and regional levels and aimed to set priorities and direction for the health sector for 5 years from 2003 to 2008.
31	The third health-sector strategic plan was developed in 2009.	The plan was developed to get a firmer grip on PHC management and leadership and provided general direction and priorities for the health sector for 5 years, from 2009 to 2015. The document emphasized the need for strengthening health management and leadership at the council and regional levels.
32	A fourth health-sector strategic plan was developed in 2015.	The SP set out priorities and direction for the health sector and emphasized strengthening health management and leadership at council and regional levels, as well as developing community-based health care (reaching households with quality health care).
33	Performance contract for nutrition was introduced in mainland Tanzania in 2017.	For the first time, the performance contract was introduced in 2017 as a governance tool for promoting accountability for nutritional services at regional and council levels. The contract is between the president and regional and district commissioners.
34	A fifth health-sector strategic plan was developed in 2021.	The plan was set to provide direction for the health sector over 5 years, from 2021 to 2025. Strengthening health management and leadership at all levels is also emphasized in the document.

modern medical services in Tanzania Mainland (formerly known as Tanganyika). The first chief medical officer of the medical department was Dr Alexander Becker, a senior surgeon appointed in 1890 (Beck, 1977). Before World War I, the Germans had established 12 small hospitals, including a sanatorium in Usambara and a mental hospital in Lutindi (Organizing Committee, 2000).

After World War I, Tanganyika became under British rule, which continued to develop medical health services in Tanganyika (Chagula and Tarimo, 1975). The health services operated during this time served public sector employees and the military, mostly in urban settings. Rural areas benefited from the attention accorded by early missionaries, who formed the Tanzania Christian Medical Association in 1930. The health sector in general was not given a high priority compared with other sectors and the services favoured people who lived in urban areas, with minimal community involvement (MOH, 1983). In 1949, the first review of medical policy was conducted by Dr E.D. Pride, the chief medical advisor to the British administration, to assess the implementation of the first medical development plan (Chagula and Tarimo, 1975; Organizing Committee, 2000). The second medical policy review was carried out by the medical department in 1956. These reviews were used by the British medical department to develop the second and third five-year medical development plans for health services in Tanganyika. The first review provided recommendations that were used by the British to strengthen curative services and environmental services in urban areas. The first and second reviews also recommended the development of health centres in rural areas (Chagula and Tarimo, 1975). Also developed during the British administration was the formulation and enforcement of regulations and by-laws to regulate urban environmental health services. The major achievement during the British administration was the establishment of hospitals (which formed government regional hospitals and council hospitals after independence) in major urban areas. Another development during the British administration was the introduction of the first training of African medical staff: urban sanitary supervisors (1919); African dispensers (1924); tribal dressers and district sanitary inspectors (1925); laboratory technicians (1930); and medical assistants (1940). Moreover, during British rule, the native authorities were given responsibility for managing rural health services provided by 22 health centres and 715 dispensaries (MOH, 1983). Other health facilities available in 1961 were 52 central governmental hospitals, 48 voluntary agencies (religious) hospitals and 19 special hospitals.

2.3.3 Leadership and governance of health services after independence, 1961–2022

The provision of health services in Tanzania took a different shape immediately after independence in 1961 (Msambichaka *et al.*, 1997). The efforts to develop and strengthen leadership and governance of health services (including primary health care) during the post-independence period can be divided into four major periods: 1961–1963; 1964–1977; 1978–1994; and 1995 to the 2020s.

Leadership and governance of health services between 1961 and 1963

PHC leadership and governance began to take shape immediately after Tanganyika's independence. At independence in 1961, the elected government of Tanganyika pronounced three national enemies: poverty, ignorance and disease (Nyerere, 1966; Chagula and Tarimo, 1975). Also, the new government of Tanganyika started to restructure the health system to meet the political expectations of increased health-care coverage, focusing on rural underprivileged people and communities. Also, the importance of leadership in all sectors was highlighted by the national leader, who stated that it was the government's responsibility to make 'relentless professionals, for the responsibilities they must shoulder to manage and lead health services (Nyerere, 1966). Also, a review of Tanganyika health services was conducted in 1961 and 1962; the purpose was to collect evidence and make recommendations to inform the development of the health sector. The health services review report gave various recommendations. Some recommendations included shifting from curative and urban medical services to promotive and rural-oriented services, constructing health-care facilities to provide basic health services and strengthening information for decision making (Titmuss, 1964; Chagula and Tarimo, 1975). It was at this time that the chief medical officer, Dr Akim, suggested restructuring the Ministry of Health and a decentralization to zones instead of directorates at the central level: this idea was not taken forward then but would be modified later into zonal coordination and resource centres.

Leadership and governance of health services, 1964–1977

PHC Leadership and governance of health services in this period were influenced by the directives of the political party and the Arusha Declaration (Chagula and Tarimo, 1975):

> The Arusha Declaration directed that rural areas should receive priority in development programmes. Poverty, ignorance, and disease were declared priority areas. At the 1971 TANU [Tanganyika African National Union] Biennial Conference, the need for increased rural development was re-emphasized. TANU directed, in particular, that health services, adequate and wholesome water, and education for the people, particularly in the rural areas, should receive priority in all the country's future annual development plans. Since these declarations, many leaders, including the President himself, have frequently spent long periods in rural areas helping implement various development projects. On the whole, considerable development has taken place in the rural areas. The Ministry of Health has had to translate this and other Party directives into action. The present approach towards meeting the basic health needs of the country can therefore be traced to the Party, which has directed the Government.

The role of good leadership and good policies are also summarized by the same (Chagula and Tarimo, 1975):

> The conviction is held in Tanzania that better coverage of the population with basic health services can be achieved through good policies and good leadership.... With a policy and a social system that places value on the health of all citizens, an advance can be made – despite limited resources – towards the better distribution of health services.

Also, during this period, the second five-year development plan (1969–1974) proposed and initiated a further radical expansion of health services and the plan focused primarily on preventive services in rural areas – with a strong emphasis on decentralization (deconcentration) to regional and district development directorates (MOH, 1990; Organizing Committee, 2000). During this deconcentration era (Madaraka Mikoani) local governments took guidance and direction from regional development directors (RDDs) and district development directors (DDDs) and the role of cooperatives was less clear. Again, in 1967, the Arusha Declaration was introduced, emphasizing self-reliance, rural development, equity, and community participation as a means to socio-economic development (Chagula and Tarimo, 1975). The declaration emphasized central planning and government provision of free health services (Chagula and Tarimo, 1975). The declaration also highlighted the importance of 'good leadership' and 'good policies' as one of the means and prerequisites for socio-economic development in all sectors, including the health sector (Nyerere, 1968). Resettling citizens in Ujamaa villages was a major undertaking with a view to making social services readily accessible to the majority.

At the material time, creating and tasking RDDs and DDDs enabled the expansion of health-care services. Expansion of basic health services (both preventive and curative services) was done through the construction of new health centres and dispensaries, training various types of primary health-care providers (e.g. MCH Aids, RMAs, increasing medical assistants later called Cos, increasing health assistants) and tackling major diseases (Chagula and Tarimo, 1975). To address major diseases, three significant campaigns were conducted: smallpox eradication, Mtu ni Afya tackling cholera and Chakula ni Uhai tackling nutrition issues as emphasized by the second five-year development plan between 1969 and 1974 (Chagula and Tarimo, 1975; MOH, 1990). In 1972, the Ministry of Health prepared a second health plan for 1972 to 1980 as part of the second five-year development plan, emphasizing providing free and comprehensive basic health services to all Tanzanians (MOH, 1990).

Leadership and governance during and after the Alma-Ata declaration, 1978 to 1994

The period between 1978 and 1994 witnessed tremendous changes in the health sector's leadership and governance, particularly of PHC. Although the country experienced challenges from the structural adjustment programmes (a set of economic reforms that a country must adhere to in order to secure a loan from the International Monetary Fund and/or the World Bank), the government worked hard to increase the number of personnel and facilities throughout the country. The key development milestones recorded during this period include: (i) formulation of long-term objectives for strengthening the health sector; (ii) establishment of the grants aid scheme for faith-based health facilities; (iii) re-establishment of local governments; (iv) development of specific PHC programme; (v) review of primary health-care services; (vi) formulation of national health policy; (vii) development of a short course to strengthen health management; and (viii) introduction of health-sector reforms.

In 1980, the Ministry of Health formulated long-term objectives for strengthening the health sector to realize the social goal of health for all in Tanzania (Magari *et al.*, 1991). Three objectives related to leadership and governance were formulated: (i) 'to strengthen leadership and supervision'; (ii) 'to involve people in the implementation and management of health programmes and projects'; and (iii) 'to cooperate with other ministries, parastatals, non-governmental organisations and the party' (Magari *et al.*, 1991). At the same time, the Ministry of Health established the grants aid scheme for faith-based health facilities. Leader Stirling, the minister of health in 1978, developed the scheme as an early example of public–private partnership in health-service provision in Tanzania.

Another key event was the re-establishment of local government authorities through the Local Government (Urban and District) Authorities Act of 1982 (Organizing Committee, 2000). The act paved the way for decentralizing decision making to the lower local councils. Specifically, the act established a standing committee responsible for health at the council level and village council social committee level (which includes health, education and water). Therefore, the act establishes these governance organs, which allow communities to participate in providing their leadership to health-service provision. The health-service providers of primary health care account themselves to these committees. Informed by the Alma-Ata Declaration of 1978, the Ministry of Health established the PHC programme in 1983 under the Department of Preventive Services. In 1983 the first guideline for the Primary Health Care Programme in Tanzania was completed and distributed for implementation (MOH, 1983). The guideline was a tool to guide implementation of the Alma-Ata Declaration in Tanzania Mainland and it provided specific guidelines for the provision and management of primary health care. Among other things, the guideline directed the establishment of PHC Committees from the village to the national level and stipulated their roles and functions. In addition, the guideline emphasized the strengthening of leadership skills in PHC structures to accelerate the delivery of health services and community participation in resource mobilization, planning, implementation and monitoring of health-service delivery in PHC.

A PHC review to establish the baseline for basic health services was conducted by the Ministry of Health in 1984, in which improved coverage of health services and infrastructure distribution were noted (Magari *et al.*, 1991). In addition, the review identified several challenges, such as inadequate leadership skills, high turnover of district medical officers, and donor dependence, that were to be addressed by PHC.

Another key development in 1990 was the formulation of the first National Health Policy to guide the planning, implementation and evaluation of health services in Tanzania. Before the policy, the health sector was guided by ruling party directives, general government policies and directives stated in the five-year national development plans. The Alma-Ata Declaration informed the health policy and set directions and priorities for the health sector in Tanzania (MOH, 1990). It stipulated requirements for the successful implementation of PHC, including decentralization of health services to district medical officers, district health management teams and district primary health-care committees. The policy also stipulated the duties and responsibilities of the district medical officer and district health management teams, including planning, coordinating and supervising health services in the district. Moreover, the National Health Policy stipulated the roles of the community members and community structures (for example, primary health-care committees) in problem identification, planning, implementation and monitoring and evaluation of health services and programmes from village to community levels.

Close follow up on faith-based institutions and NGOs (Maasai Health Services Project, Mvumi Community Health Promoters Project, Hanang Village Health Workers, Oxfam, AMREF and others supported within the CMBT umbrella) resulted in progressive interaction with the MOH PHC programme. Those that were in active pursuit of PHC implementation in the field were assigned to submit performance reports to the MOH PHC Secretariat, which was organized under DANIDA support covering 13 primary health-care project components from the central level. A report on community participation in health, outlining field experiences and lessons, was submitted to the CMO and the PHC Secretariat (MOH Secretariat, 1989). From this report the submitting agency was assigned to show an example related to organizing intersectoral collaboration. This assignment produced two documents titled 'Health Action by All – A development challenge into the 1990s', with an example of working with Ministry of Labour Youth and Sports and 'National Health Culture Initiative', that appealed to working with other sectors starting with strengthening school health by introducing a school nurse (MOH Secretariat, 1991). Subsequently a team of consultants was recruited to work on 'Strengthening Decentralization of Health Education to Districts', led by Franz Staugard. This is elaborated here to note that leadership in the Ministry of Health changed hands at least three times in a short period (Hence three PSs, three CMOs and three DPSs/DPPs); the effort that was invested in clarifying pragmatic intersectoral collaboration for PHC lost some direction. Subsequently there was a renaming of the PHC Secretariat to a 'Health Sector Resource Secretariat'. This was a significant change in assignment and responsibilities.

In 1991, a specific health planning and management manual was prepared to strengthen leadership competencies for health managers and other health workers at the district and regional levels (Magari *et al.*, 1991). The manual indicated various health challenges, including weak health leadership and governance capacities at district and regional levels. The manual focused on strengthening the capacities of the district (council), regional and health facility health-management teams on health planning and management to support the implementation of primary health-care strategy in Tanzania. In 1991, the Private Sector Practice Act was passed to allow and regulate private-for-profit providers to provide health services, including primary health services, to supplement government efforts. The act removed restrictions on private health providers for profit imposed by the 1977 Act.

Following the World Bank (WB) report of 1993, the movements for reforms started to take shape in several countries, including Tanzania. The Proposals for Health Sector Reforms Document in Tanzania was developed in 1994 to guide how the health sector could be reformed. The proposed reforms included: empowering regional administrations and local governments to offer and manage comprehensive health services in the councils through district hospitals and primary health facilities; establishing and strengthening health leadership and governance teams and committees; developing competency-based training for health managers and leaders; developing operational guidelines for health management and governance teams and committees; and empowering two zonal health resources centres (Centre for Educational Development in Health Arusha (CEDHA) and Primary Health Care Iringa (PHC-I)) to develop and offer courses on health planning and management for CHMT members, facilitated through biennial plans between the MOH and WHO. In addition, the health-sector reforms document stipulated the duties of the district and regional medical officers. The proposed health-sector reforms were governmental decisions geared to address critical problems of the health sector, which included: weak leadership and governance capacities among health managers; weak training programmes that emphasized knowledge transfer rather than skill development; and weak community health governance structures (lack of or weak health boards, health facility committees, PHC committees).

Leadership and governance of primary health services during the health-sector reforms, 1995 to date

Tanzanian PHC experienced leadership and governance changes during the 1990s, health-sector reforms famously referred to as the second phase of decentralization. The second phase of decentralization involved was mainly in the form of decentralization by devolution, which involved transferring operational decision making power and resources to regional administration and local governments. The changes included the establishment of various structures and organs. For instance, the Regional Administration Act No. 19 of 1997 established a regional secretariat which consists of the regional health management teams (RHMT). The RHMT members are assigned the role of coordinating the provision of health services and providing technical support to local government authorities with regard to primary health-service delivery. RHMTs are led by the regional medical officer (RMO); the RHMT is expected to provide vision and leadership and make decisions in their roles. The RHMT is expected to guide PHC committees at all levels and ensure that they work responsibly and effectively to accomplish the delegated mandates.

Again in 1998, a local government paper was developed to guide reforms of local governments in Tanzania (Ministry of Regional Administration and Local Governments, 1998). The paper set a new vision and guided the reforms in political, financial, administrative and central–local relations to allow local governments to exercise their powers in these four key areas of reform. The local government reform paper, the 1982 Local Government Act, and the 1990 health policy guided the establishment of the district health management team (DHMT) for each council and its membership. Compared to the core RHMT members, the core DHMT membership has evolved from six members in 1991 to nine core members in 2022. The overall DHMT responsibility is to oversee PHC in the district, in addition to planning, coordinating, managing, monitoring and evaluating resources and provision of primary health-care services in the area of jurisdiction, meaning that the DHMT was responsible for all councils in the districts. This was seen as a challenge to the DHMT and the local government and health-sector reforms instigated a change of name of the district health management team (DHMT) to council health management team (CHMT) to establish a clear accountability mechanism for the team and ultimately reduce the potential confusion of being accountable to more than one council. The CHMTs work hand in hand with the district PHC committees responsible for extending health services to the peri-urban areas and health promotion, particularly preventive services.

The sector-wide approaches (SWAps) programme was established in 1998 as a result of an agreement between the Ministry of Health and development partners as a response to dissatisfaction with the fragmented donor-sponsored projects and poor coordination of development partners (COWI, 2007). The SWAps were intended to provide a more coherent way to coordinate and build effective relationships between government and donor agencies supporting the health sector and enhance transparent mechanisms through basket funding. In 1999 the first health-sector strategic plan (HSSP) was prepared to continue reforming the health sector to strengthen primary health care (MOH, 1990). The plan stipulated the health-sector reform process and set activities and timeframe to implement the reforms from 1999 to 2002. In addition, the plan identified weaknesses related to health-sector leadership and governance and emphasized the need for strengthening the same at regional and council levels. Specifically, the HSSP goals were to: devolve responsibility to council health committees; strengthen health governance structures; improve planning and budgeting, strengthen community participation; strengthen inter-sector collaboration; provide cost-effective essential clinical and public health packages; and strengthen the referral system.

In addition, comprehensive council health planning (CCHP) was introduced in Tanzania Mainland in 2000. The CHMT and other planning team members were and are still vested with the responsibility of preparing the CCHP. The implementation of CCHP began with 37 districts in 2000 and 45 districts in 2001/2; the remaining districts were covered in 2003 (COWI, 2007). The CCHP is the principal prerequisite for a well-functioning district health system. Furthermore, the first CCHP guideline was developed in 2000 to guide the preparation of the CCHPs. It was reviewed in 2004, 2007, 2011 and 2021 to accommodate the increasing needs of planning and reporting for primary health care at the council level, specifically thus maximizing participation of stakeholders in the planning processes (Kiologwe *et al.*, 2022)

The 1990 health policy was reviewed to accommodate the changes and transformations that were taking place in the country. The second National Health Policy was developed and launched in 2007. The new policy emphasized strengthening primary health care in the context of health-sector reforms. In the same year, and as a response to the 2007 health policy, a ten-year primary health services development programme (PHSDP), famously known as Mpango wa Maendeleo wa Afya Msingi (MMAM), was prepared (MOHSW, 2007). The programme emphasized the expansion of primary health-care infrastructures to ensure that each village or urban street in Tanzania has a health facility. The programme rarely addressed and emphasized leadership and governance capacity, as highlighted in the programme evaluation report. As a result of this neglect, primary health-care governance structures had limited capacities to implement and govern the PHC programme in the councils.

In 2008, a specific health leadership and management training programme and manuals for regional health-management teams were developed by the MOH through JICA support (MOHSW, 2011). The manuals were used to strengthen the leadership and management capacities of all regional health-management teams to perform their duties and responsibilities (RHMTs). In 2019, the MOH and PO-RALG redefined the duties and responsibilities of the regional health-management teams into 11 functions, which are shown in Table 2.3. These functions are similar to the functions of CHMTs. The functions cover four general duties and responsibilities of RHMTs: curative services, preventive services, community engagements and coordination of health services in the region.

In 2009, a third health-sector strategic plan was developed. The plan set out priorities and directions for the health sector for 5 years, from 2009 to 2015. A mid-term review of HSSP III was conducted in 2013 and informed adjustments and planning for a successor HSSP IV and the revitalization of the community health programme. The HSSP IV was developed in 2015 and emphasized strengthening leadership and governance at council and regional levels (MOHSW, 2015). The plan emphasized the need to reach all households with quality health care. This went hand to hand with the initiation of the National Big Results Now (BRN) initiative in 2015 that contributed to setting immediate focus priorities in the health sector as part and parcel of HSSP IV (MOHSW, 2015). The assessment of the health-sector strategic plan indicated that health managers used practices recommended by experts to implement and monitor progress of the strategic plan (Jiyenze *et al.*, 2022a) and implementation of the plan led to the achievement of three planned results at the council: improved actors' alignment with health-sector priorities; improved health services coverage; and increased availability of some resources, specifically medicines (Jiyenze *et al.*, 2022b).

Table 2.3. RHMT functions by 2019. FromMOHCDGEC and PO-RALG (2019).

SN	Functions of the RHMTs
1	Function 1: Develop and operationalize RHMTs plans and strategies annually from the five-year strategic plan
2	Function 2: Disseminate and support the translation of the policies, strategies and guidelines
3	Function 3: Support an appropriate environment for private-sector development
4	Function 4: Coordinate services in the region
5	Function 5: Support human resource management
6	Function 6: Ensure the quality of services at all health and social welfare facilities
7	Function 7: Facilitate emergency and disaster preparedness and response
8	Function 8: Support and backstop regional referral hospitals
9	Function 9: Institute network system
10	Function 10: Conduct innovative supervision
11	Function 11: Enhance data management and operational research

Also, one of the major governance decisions in Tanzania in February 2015 was establishing the Directorate of Health, Social Welfare and Nutrition Services (DHSN) under the Presidents' Office-Regional Administration and Local Government (PO-RALG). The purpose of establishing the DHSN was to improve the coordination of primary health-care services. The directorate was mandated to coordinate and monitor the implementation of health policies and guidelines and the provision of primary health nutrition and social welfare services by the local government authorities. The directorate also conducts operational research, interprets health policies and guidelines for the regions and council, and coordinates the implementation of health programmes. The formation of this directorate has aided in delineating the tasks of the Ministry of Health, which are policy formulation, resource mobilization and evaluation of primary health-care programme implementation. Primary health facilities in Tanzania operate under the local government authorities.

Before the establishment of the DHSN at PO-RALG in the 2000s, the health service was coordinated by two appointed officers who were attached to or working under the department of local government under PO-RALG. The two officers were responsible for coordinating health services; one was coordinating or overseeing the health-basket fund, and the second was coordinating health issues. Other health-related issues, including appointments, and implementation of primary health-care activities, were under the Ministry of Health.

Due to the establishment of DHSN in 2015, the Tanzanian government, through President's Office - Public Service Management and Good Governance, decided to strengthen primary health-care governance by delegating the appointment powers of the RMOs and DMOs to the Prime Ministry Office Regional Administration and Local Government. This greatly improved RMO/DMO coordination and responsibility to PO-RALG, addressing the issue of the appointment of RMOs and DMOs. Before the establishment of DHSN, the Ministry of Health would appoint an RMO/DMO.

The government of Tanzania has continued to make enormous efforts to strengthen primary health care. Current efforts have been to deepen fiscal decentralization from the council to the facility level (Kapologwe *et al.*, 2019). This is because the first decentralization mainly transferred powers and responsibilities from the centre to the council (Kesale *et al.*, 2022c). Even when the government decided to transfer powers and responsibilities from the council to primary health-care facilities, only political and administrative powers and responsibilities were devolved. Retaining fiscal powers and responsibilities at the council level generated many challenges for the primary health facilities. This is because all the facility funds were deposited into the council and controlled by the district medical officers (Boex *et al.*, 2015). Then the DMO and council officials were responsible for governing the disbursement and utilizing facility funds. One of the major challenges was that the funds were not sent in time, leading to delays in implementing health interventions. Another challenge with this practice is that councils would sometimes relocate facility funds to other council activities; governance and management actors at the facility level lacked fiscal autonomy, which constrained the actors from participating in other facility operations, such as planning and budgeting and implementing health intervention at the facility level.

In 2017/18, the government decided to implement fiscal decentralization through direct health facility financing (DHFF). DHFF has strengthened the implementation of other types of decentralizations, such as administrative and decision making powers at the facility. Now, all facility funds are deposited in facility accounts and managed and governed by the facility managers and governance actors (health facility governing committees). The implementation of DHFF has empowered health facility leaders and has increased their autonomy in making major decisions about their facility (Kesale *et al.*, 2022a). Community ownership of the primary health facility has improved since they participate in overseeing service delivery at their facility (Kesale *et al.*, 2022b). Through the current practices, facility decision makers can find solutions for facility and community health challenges by using available resources. The regional health management teams (RHMTs) and council health management teams (CHMTs) currently support and provide mentorship on financial management and implementation of annual plan budgets to the health facilities, as per the guidelines.

Another milestone reached in primary health care in 2017 was the development of the community score card guideline based on practical experience from SIKIKA, an NGO that has been active in service accountability monitoring (SAM). The guideline was developed to facilitate the generation of views from users and managers regarding performance and other leadership issues related to primary health care. The community score card is a participatory assessment tool expected to contribute to health systems improvement and better leadership within governance structures. The tool is significant in accelerating community feedback on the service delivery of primary health care, particularly in reaching the vision of the Alma-Ata Declaration of 1978 and Astana Declaration, which stresses community participation in planning, implementation and monitoring health services. Even though the Tanzania Health Policy 2007 stipulates community participation in delivering health care, the community scorecard operationalizes policy by providing frameworks for involving the community in monitoring and evaluating health-service delivery.

In 2021, a fifth health sector strategic plan was developed after conducting a mid-term review of HSSP IV (MOHCDGEC, 2021a). The plan set out priorities and direction for the health sector for 5 years, from 2021 to 2025. At the same time, the National Health Policy for 2007 was reviewed to cater to the requisites to respond to the sustainable development goals (successor to MDGs), and rededicate to universal health coverage by tracking the primary health-care principles on a more effective footing. Moreover, the HSSP V document re-emphasizes the need for strengthening health management and leadership at all levels, including the community. To support the process of strengthening leadership and governance, comprehensive health leadership and governance training manuals for regional, council and health facility health-management teams were developed. The training programme, and related manuals, accommodated new developments and reforms in the health sector.

In 2022, the review of council health-services boards and health-facility governing-committee guidelines was initiated and the process is under way. The first council health-management-system guideline was prepared to provide guidelines on managing primary health care in the councils. In 2022, the first specific primary health-care committee guideline was developed to provide guidelines on the establishment and operation of primary health care at all levels in Tanzania Mainland. Also, in 2022, the second primary health-services development programme has been developed to strengthen PHC leadership and governance at the council, health facility and community.

To summarize, the historical development of PHC leadership and governance in Tanzania evolved over the years and its critical assessment of leadership and governance functions is presented in Table 2.4.

2.4 The Current PHC Leadership and Governance Structures in Tanzania

By 2022, the government of Tanzania had established various governance structures (organs) for primary health care (COWI, 2007; MOHCDGEC, 2020; Wizara ya Afya na Usitawi wa Jamii, 2007). These structures carry out the functions required for effective leadership and governance. Tables 2.5 and 2.6 identify the key responsibilities of the various structures at the national, regional, council ward and village levels.

2.5 The Current Efforts to Strengthen PHC Leadership and Governance in Tanzania

Leadership and governance are critical for effective primary health-care delivery to individuals, families and communities (WHO, 2008). Towards universal health coverage in Tanzania, the government, through the MOH, PO-RALG and other actors, are currently implementing various initiatives to strengthen leadership and governance (MOHCDGEC, 2021a, b). The major initiatives and efforts include the following:

1. Reviewing, updating and development of new guidelines to facilitate leaders to execute their leadership and governance roles effectively. Key guidelines under review and or development include primary

health-services development programme, guidelines for council health-management teams and health-facility management teams, guidelines for council health-service boards and health-facility governing committee. Health in All policies (HiAP) and guidelines for primary health committees.

2. Designing competency-based continuing professional development training for strengthening capacities of regional, council and health-facility management teams on leadership and governance to support PHC through a problem-solving approach.
3. Strengthening capacities in research to generate and use data and evidence to inform decision making processes, including policy making and planning, especially at the regional, council and facility levels.
4. Development of a guideline that provides objective criteria for the appointment and dismissal of individuals who can take a leadership position in regions' and councils' health-management teams. The guideline also outlines key indicators for monitoring their performance.
5. Revitalization and improvement of the functionality of governance structures in PHC and strengthening community engagement.

Table 2.4. Critical assessment of leadership and governance functions for PHC.

Leadership and governance	Critical assessment of the function in relation to PHC
Formulating and enforcing policies, laws, regulations, and guidelines	Generally, this function has evolved over the years and Tanzania has successfully formulated policies, regulation and guidelines to inform PHC implementation. However, enforcement and accountability still need to be improved in future.
Setting vision and direction	Overall, Tanzania has successfully set the relevant vision and directions for PHC as reflected in instruments such as the constitution, Tanzania's development vision, health policy, health-sector strategic plans, primary health development programme regulation and guidelines to inform PHC implementation including community-based health care.
Setting priorities and conducting consensus building	The function of setting priorities and conducting consensus building has also improved over the years. Key actors are involved in setting priorities and reaching consensus through various opportunities such as health-policy making, health-sector strategic plan development and review and annual health planning and reviews at technical and sector leadership levels.
Coordinating and promoting health in other health-related sectors and policies to advance health goals	Coordinating and promoting health in other health-related sectors and policies to advance health goals has improved to some extent through strategies such as 'Health in All' policies. But this function needs to be improved further in future to realize benefits provided by other sectors improving the health of the population, particularly through enhancing visibility of lower-level integrated approaches.
Improving and protecting population health	The function of improving and protecting population health has evolved over the years through reviews of the Public Health Act, collection of data and establishing structures for responding to disasters and emergencies in the population. However, this function needs to be strengthened in terms of strengthening capacities of various structures for effective protection of population health.
Monitoring and evaluating performance of health organizations in health-sector institutions	This function is related to collecting intelligence (data to inform decision making). Some development has been recorded, ensuring Tanzania has relevant data and evidence to inform policy and practice through conducting specific surveys (e.g. Tanzania Demographic and Heath Survey and development of health-related information systems. However, efforts are still needed to use collected data and evidence to inform PHC decisions at various level of the health system.

Table 2.5. Summary of roles and responsibilities of PHC leadership and governance structures at national and zonal levels in Tanzania. Prepared in 2022 from Wizara ya Afya na Usitawi wa Jamii (2007) and MOHCDGEC (2020, 2021a, b).

No.	Structure (organ)	Key roles/responsibilities of structures (organs)
1	Parliament and the Parliamentary Social Service Committee	Oversees health services provision, including primary health care, in Tanzania.
2	Controller and auditor general	Conducts auditing related to primary health-care services and resources.
3	MOH	Formulates and reviews primary health-care guidelines and programmes; mobilizes and allocates resources for primary health care; monitors and evaluates the implementation of primary health guidelines and programmes; supports building management, leadership and governance capacities for primary health care in line with health policy, regulations and ethics of practice.
4	PO-RALG	Mobilizes and allocates resources for primary health care; monitors and evaluates the implementation of primary health guidelines and programmes; supports building management, leadership and governance capacities for primary health care, including advocating for and monitoring private sector partners and stakeholders from other sectors.
5	Development and implementing partners	Mobilize and provide resources for primary health care; provide technical assistance for primary health care; support provision and management of primary care; support building management, leadership and governance capacities for primary health care.
6	Zonal health resource centres and other training institutions	Conduct training needs assessment; design long and short training programmes; conduct training on health management, leadership and governance; monitor and evaluate training programmes and undertake implementation research.

2.6 Leadership and Governance Lessons and Recommendations for PHC in Tanzania

Tanzania recorded major achievements in delivering primary health services to the population (Chagula and Tarimo, 1975; MOH, 1983, 1999; COWI, 2007; MOHCDGEC, 2021a) despite the challenges experienced. Reflecting on the evolution of PHC leadership and governance outlined in this chapter, Tanzania has learnt five important lessons related to PHC. Such lessons are summarized in Box 2.3 and the recommendations for future leadership and governance are summarized in Box 2.4.

Table 2.6. Summary of roles and responsibilities of PHC leadership and governance structures at regional, council, ward and village/street levels in Tanzania. Prepared in 2022 from Wizara ya Afya na Usitawi wa Jamii (2007) and MOHCDGEC (2020, 2021a, b).

No.	Structure (organ)	Key roles/responsibilities of structures (organs)
1	Regional health management teams (RHMTs)	Supervise and provide technical primary health-care support to the council; mobilize and monitor resources for primary health care; and evaluate the implementation of primary health guidelines and programmes.
2	The full councils and council social services committee	Oversee implementation of primary health-care programme and guidelines; oversee resources mobilization for primary health care services; approve plans and budget for primary health care; monitor primary-care services provision and implementation of approved plans and budgets.
3	CHMT	Coordinate, plan, supervise and evaluate the implementation of primary health guidelines and programmes; mobilize and monitor resources for primary health care.
4	Council health services boards	Oversee provision and management of primary health care in their councils; oversee resources mobilization for primary health-care services, including oversight of accountability.
5	Health-facility governing committees	Oversee provision and management of primary health care in the health facility; oversee resources mobilization for primary health-care services, including oversight of accountability.
6	Primary health-care committees	Oversee implementation of primary health-care guidelines and programmes in their area; oversee mobilize resources for primary health care; promote intersectoral collaboration in their jurisdiction or area.
7	Health-facility management teams	Manage health resources and provision of primary health care in the health facility and link to CHVs for their technical supervision and managing referrals and continuum of care.
8	Ward-development committees	Oversee primary health-care planning and incorporate this into ward development plans; mobilize and allocate resources for primary health care; monitor implementation of primary health plan at ward level.
9	Village/street governments through social services committees for education, health and water	Oversee primary health-care planning and incorporate this into village development plans; mobilize and allocate resources for primary health care; monitor and supervise the provision and implementation of primary health plan at the village level.

Box 2.3. Key PHC leadership and governance lessons

1. *Leadership and governance matter for PHC*: Effective leadership and governance and structures at various levels contribute to improved coordination, management and governance of primary health services.
2. *Policy frameworks and programmes are critical tools for success*: The development of policy frameworks and programmes is a key leadership and governance practice that facilitated partnerships and the coordination of various actors. Specifically, the policy frameworks and programmes set the directions, priorities and structures (organs) for expanding and improving the delivery of primary health services in Tanzania Mainland.
3. *Decentralization empowers the delivery and management of primary health services*: Decentralization of power, authority and resources to local government organs accelerated progress of PHC delivery.
4. *Operational research, reviews and evaluations empower decision making*: Operational research, reviews and evaluations are key to providing evidence and informing various policies and strategic decisions related to primary health care.
5. *Partnerships and the engagement of key stakeholders are important for PHC's success*: Partnerships and the engagement of key stakeholders, such as the government, donors, training and research institutions, the private sector, faith-based organizations and communities in PHC, enhance coordination and support the smooth delivery of primary health services.

Box 2.4. The recommendations for building the future vibrant PHC

1. Strengthen capability in leadership at all levels through tailor-made capacity-building programmes and the appointment of qualified high-performing individuals to leadership roles.
2. Periodic monitoring of the functionality of PHC governance structures to ensure members fulfil their duties and responsibilities.
3. Strengthening fiscal decentralization (procurement of medicine and medical commodities) is required to empower primary health-care facilities and primary health-care governance structures to accomplish their mandates.
4. Capacity of health providers and incentives to conduct operational research should be provided to enhance data use in decision making.
5. Enhance collaboration and partnership of all actors.
6. Completion of key guidelines for PHC under development and or review and dissemination.
7. Strengthen working links with professional councils to monitor and ensure adherence to ethics of practice at every level.

Bibliography

Barbazza, E. and Tello, J.E. (2014) A review of health governance: definitions, dimensions and tools to govern. *Health Policy (Amsterdam, Netherlands)* 116(1), 1–11. DOI: 10.1016/j.healthpol.2014.01.007.

Beck, A. (1977) Medicine and society in Tanganyika, 1890–1930: a historical inquiry. *Transactions of the American Philosophical Society* 67(3), 1–59. DOI: 10.2307/1006330.

Boex, J., Fuller, L. and Malik, A. (2015) *Decentralized Local Health Services in Tanzania*. Urban Institute, Washington, DC.

Brinkerhoff, D.W. and Bossert, T.J. (2008) Health governance: concepts, experience, and programming options. *Bethesda: Health Systems* 20, 20.

Brinkerhoff, D.W., Cross, H.E., Sharma, S. and Williamson, T. (2019) Stewardship and health systems strengthening: an overview. *Public Administration and Development* 39(1), 4–10. DOI: 10.1002/pad.1846.

Chagula, W.K. and Tarimo, E. (1975) Meeting basic health needs in Tanzania. In: Newell, K.W. (ed.) *Health by the People*. World Health Organization, Geneva, Switzerland, pp. 145–168.
COWI (2007) *Joint External Evaluation of the Health Sector in Tanzania, 1999–2006*. COWI, Copenhagen.
Dussault, G. and Dubois, C.A. (2003) Human resources for health policies: a critical component in health policies. *Human Resources for Health* 1(1), 1–16. DOI: 10.1186/1478-4491-1-1.
Jiyenze, M.K., Tundui, C. and Mollel, H. (2022a) Practices of implementing and monitoring the progress of health sector strategic plan: the perspectives of the Council health managers in Tanzania. *East African Medical Journal* 99, 5280–5288.
Jiyenze, M.K., Tundui, C., Sirili, N. and Mollel, H. (2022b) Effects of implementing a health sector strategic plan: evidence from Tanzania. *East African Medical Journal* 99, 5147–5155.
Jones, G.R., George, J.M., Haddad, J. and Rock, M. (2019) *Essentials of Contemporary Management*. McGraw-Hill Irwin, Boston, Massachusetts.
Kapologwe, N.A., Kalolo, A., Kibusi, S.M., Chaula, Z., Nswilla, A. *et al.* (2019) Understanding the implementation of Direct Health Facility Financing and its effect on health system performance in Tanzania: a non-controlled before and after mixed method study protocol. *Health Research Policy and Systems* 17(1), 1–13. DOI: 10.1186/s12961-018-0400-3.
Kesale, A.M., Mahonge, C. and Muhanga, M. (2022a) The quest for accountability of Health Facility Governing Committees implementing Direct Health Facility Financing in Tanzania: a supply-side experience. *PloS ONE* 17(4), e0267708. DOI: 10.1371/journal.pone.0267708.
Kesale, A.M., Mahonge, C. and Muhanga, M. (2022b) The functionality variation among health facility governing committees under direct health facility financing in Tanzania. *PLOS Global Public Health* 2(5), e0000366. DOI: 10.1371/journal.pgph.0000366.
Kesale, A.M., Mahonge, C.P. and Muhanga, M. (2022c) The functionality of health facility governing committees and their associated factors in selected primary health facilities implementing direct health facility financing in Tanzania: a mixed-method study. *Health Science Reports* 5(3), e611. DOI: 10.1002/hsr2.611.
Kiologwe, J.C., Kusirye, U., Hoffman, A. and Kalolo, A. (2022) Operational challenges of engaging development partners in district health planning in Tanzania. *BMC Public Health* 22(1), 200. DOI: 10.1186/s12889-022-12520-6.
Magari, F., Malangalila, E.G., Mukoyo, S.M., Ndeki, S.S. and Nyoni, C.J. (1991) *Planning and Management of Primary Health Care in Tanzania: A Manual for District Health Teams*. Ministry of Health, Dar es Salaam, Tanzania.
Ministry of Regional Administration and Local Governments (1998) *Policy Paper on Local Government Reform*. Ministry of Regional Administration and Local Governments, Dar es Salaam, Tanzania.
MOH (1983) *Guidelines for the Implementation of the Primary Health Care Programme in Tanzania*. Ministry of Health, Dar es Salaam, Tanzania.
MOH (1990) *Health policy*. Ministry of Health, Dar es Salaam, Tanzania.
MOH (1999) *The Health Sector Programme of Work*. Ministry of Health, Dar es Salaam, Tanzania.
MOHCDGEC (2020) *Tanzania Health Enterprise Architecture*. MOHCDGEC, Dodoma.
MOHCDGEC (2021a) *The Health Sector Strategic Plan V 2021–2026*. MOHCDGEC, Dodoma.
MOHCDGEC (2021b) *National Human Resources for Health Strategy for 2021–2026*. MOHCDGEC, Dodoma.
MOHCDGEC and PO-RALG (2019) *Functions of Regional Health Management System*, Third edition. Dar es Salaam, Tanzania.
MOH Secretariat (1989) *Community Involvement in Health: A Desk Study and Field Experiences*. A report to the Chief Medical Officer, Ministry of Health, Dar es Salaam, Tanzania.
MOH Secretariat (1991) *Health Action by All, a Development Challenge in the 90s*. Workbook. Ministry of Health, Dar es Salaam, Tanzania.
MOHSW (2007) *Primary Health Services Development Programme 2007–2017*. MOHSW, Dar es Salaam, Tanzania.
MOHSW (2011) *RHMT Training on Leadership and Management*. MOHSW, Dar es Salaam, Tanzania.
MOHSW (2015) *The Health Sector Strategic Plan IV 2015–2020*. MOHSW, Dar es Salaam, Tanzania.
Msambichaka, L., Kilindo, A., Kiwara, A. and Mkusa, E. (1997) *Economic Adjustment Policies & Health Care in Tanzania*. University of Dar es Salaam, Dar es Salaam, Tanzania.
Nyerere, J.K. (1966) *Freedom and Socialism*. Oxford University Press, Dar es Salaam, Tanzania.
Nyerere, J.K. (1968) *Freedom and Socialism*. Oxford University Press, Dar es Salaam, Tanzania.

Organizing Committee (2000) *Essentials of Muhimbili Medical Centre Reforms: A Prototype for Hospital Reforms*. Muhimbili Medical Centre, Dar es Salaam, Tanzania.

Pourbohloul, B. and Kieny, M.-P. (2011) Complex systems analysis: towards holistic approaches to health systems planning and policy. *Bulletin of the World Health Organization* 89(4), 242. DOI: 10.2471/BLT.11.087544.

Smith, P.C., Anell, A., Busse, R., Crivelli, L., Healy, J. *et al.* (2012) Leadership and governance in seven developed health systems. *Health Policy* 106(1), 37–49. DOI: 10.1016/j.healthpol.2011.12.009.

Titmuss, R.M. (1964) *The Health Services of Tanganyika: A Report to the Government*. Pitman Medical Publishing Company, London.

West, M., Armit, K., Loewenthal, L., Eckert, R., West, T. *et al.* (2015) *Leadership and Leadership Development in Health Care: The Evidence Base*. The King's Fund, London.

WHO (2007) *Everybody's Business – Strengthening Health Systems to Improve Health Outcomes: WHO's Framework for Action*. World Health Organization, Geneva, Switzerland.

WHO (2008) *The World Health Report 2008 Primary Health Care: Now More than Ever*. World Health Organization, Geneva, Switzerland.

WHO (2020) *Operational Framework for Primary Health Care: Transforming Vision into Action*. World Health Organization, Geneva, Switzerland.

WHO and UNICEF (2018) *A Vision for Primary Health Care in the 21st Century: Towards Universal Health Coverage and the Sustainable Development Goals*. World Health Organization and UNICEF, Geneva, Switzerland.

Wizara ya Afya na Usitawi wa Jamii (2007) *Sera ya afya*. Wizara ya Afya na Usitawi wa Jamii, Dar es Salaam, Tanzania.

3 Human Resources for Health

Nathanael Sirili[1]*, George Kiwango[2], Chipole Mpelembe[3], Faisal Issa[4] and Hadija Kweka[5]

[1]Department of Development Studies, School of Public Health and Social Sciences, Muhimbili University of Health and Allied Sciences, Dar es Salaam, Tanzania; [2]Department of Physiology, School of Medicine, Muhimbili University of Health and Allied Sciences, Dar es Salaam, Tanzania; [3]President's Office - Regional Administration and Local Government, Dodoma, Tanzania; [4]Department of Administrative Studies, Mzumbe University, Dar es Salaam, Tanzania; [5]Enhance Tanzania Foundation, Dar es Salaam, Tanzania

Abstract

This chapter presents an account of primary health-care cadres' evolution in Tanzania from before independence to 2022. It highlights which cadre existed, the developments in bringing in new cadres and upgrading existing ones, and the reasons behind those shifts. Additionally, the chapter presents the human resource for health (HRH) availability and distribution status, including policy, planning and practice responses devised, adapted and implemented. Finally, it considers innovations in the area, their contribution to addressing the shortage, and how local decisions regarding staff and staffing levels were guided. The chapter focuses mainly on HRH delivering services in facility settings or mobile clinics, not community health workers. However, a section on community health workers is comprehensively covered in Chapter 8. The chapter identifies lessons in each area and outlines their implications for the future. This chapter gathers information from reports, academic publications, policies and guidelines. Stories from health-sector veterans who worked in the health sector in the 1970s were also used. The evolution of HRH for primary health care is an example of strategic efforts adopted by a developing country to reach its population with services using personnel with skills. The history indicates an incremental development in cadres' skills and portfolios of services provided at the primary care level. It also shows guidelines about which type of staff are placed progressed in alignment with the development of health systems and ensuring equity. This is evident by decentralizing cadres such as medical doctors below district hospitals and ongoing efforts to expand specialized care to district hospitals.

3.0 Introduction

This chapter presents an account of primary health-care cadres' evolution in Tanzani from before independence to 2022. We highlight existing staff categories, the decline of some cadres, the introduction of new ones and the upgrading of other health cadres, including the reasons behind those shifts. We also discuss the availability and distribution of human resources for health (HRH), including policy, planning and practice responses set to guide HRH supply, recruitment, retention and productivity. Lastly, we consider innovations around HRH and responses in addressing health and staff shortages. The chapter focuses mainly on HRH delivering services in

*Corresponding author: drnsirili@gmail.com

 Primary Health Care in Tanzania through a Health Systems Lens (eds N.A. Kapologwe *et al.*)
DOI: 10.1079/9781800623330.0003

facility settings or mobile clinics, not on community health workers. Community health workers are covered in detail in Chapter 8.

We have gathered information from reports, academic publications, policies and guidelines. Stories from health-sector veterans who worked in the 1970s have also been used.

3.1 Human Resources for Health: Fundamental Concepts

The struggle to balance health workforce supply to health workforce demand remains a constant struggle for many countries. Human resources for health (HRH), which is also known as health workforce or human health resources (HHR), can be defined as every person engaged in an activity whose primary intent is to enhance health (Guilbert, 2006). Equitable distribution of skilled and motivated health workforce is central to primary health care (PHC) and universal health coverage's (UHC) achievement. HRH has gained much attention due to challenges associated with training, recruiting, deploying, placement and the performance of health workers. As such, HRH planning is of paramount importance. Human resource planning constitutes all processes in forecasting the supply and demand of the health workforce for adequate health services provision, promotion and prevention. It has since been expanded to include policy settings, which are key instruments in delivering health-care services (Guilbert, 2006).

Different frameworks exist in explaining HRH development and its management. In this chapter, two main frameworks are used to guide the discussions:

1. Health workforce development stages (Guilbert, 2006).
2. Health labour market dynamics (Sousa *et al.*, 2013).

3.1.1 Health workforce development stages

The World Health Organization (WHO) conceptualizes the development of HRH into three critical stages (Fig. 3.1) of:

1. Entry.
2. Available workforce.
3. Exit.

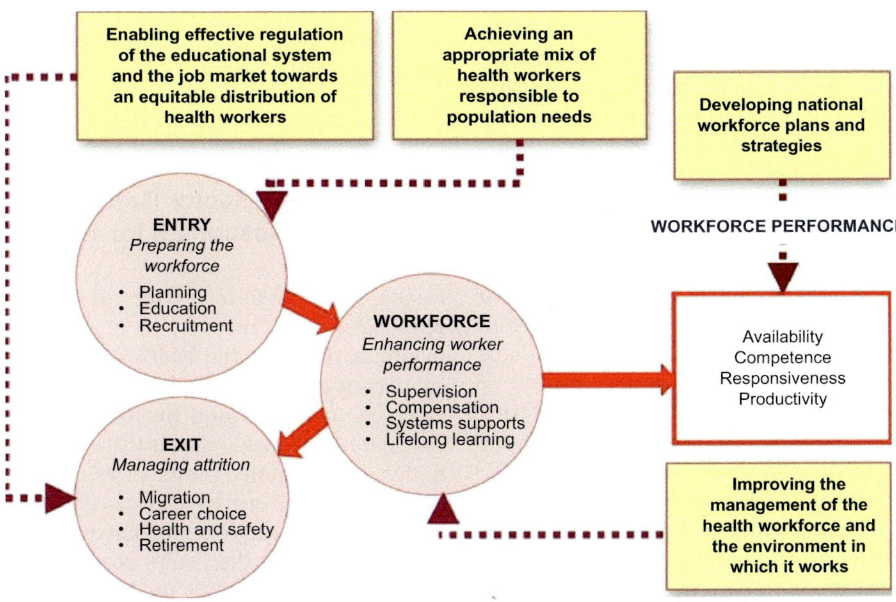

Fig. 3.1. Human resource for health development stages. (From WHO, 2006.)

First stage: Entry stage

This stage usually considers the pre-service training and the deployment of trained human resources for health. The organization or country needs to forecast the number of health workforce required to adequately deliver quality health care services to all and therefore plan the number appropriately to be trained. This stage advocates forecasting the increasing demands of health services and the attrition of the health workforce (HW) due to different reasons, such as ageing, death, change of job and migration. To prepare these HW, this stage advocates for the availability of adequate trainers and trainees, equipped training institutions and quality outputs per the demand for trained health-care personnel.

Second stage: Available workforce and motivation

In this stage, the health managers at the working sites and the multisectoral managers need to ensure that the available HRH is well-motivated, updated and readily equipped to provide the needed services effectively. HRH's challenges in services provision must be identified and addressed engagingly with the available HW. Planners need to forecast the expansion of the service recipients, dynamics of diseases and the market imperfections that might affect the provision of the services at large.

Third stage: Retention and exit

As for the previous stages, this stage is not a solitary stage. In this stage, the managers and planners need to ensure that the available HRH in a particular organization, facility or jurisdiction are kept and not drained or wasted elsewhere. This is contingent upon many factors, from individuals and society to the health system. For this to happen, managers need to invest in the pull and push factors while trying to address the push factors. This stage also needs to consider succession planning on the exits due to ageing, death, change of jobs and other reasons.

3.1.2 Health labour-market dynamics

Sousa *et al.* (2013) developed a framework that considered the life cycle of HRH and the macroeconomic policies (Fig. 3.2). This cycle included policies related to HRH production, development and management. The labour-market policy framework prioritizes the use of the market lens to allow a comprehensive understanding of the forces that drive shortages and surpluses, geographical imbalances and suboptimal HRH contributions in the services delivery setting. The framework highlights how policies on pre-service education affect HRH production and quality; for example, how many students are enrolling in health education programmes and the available capacity of the instructors. In addition, the framework notes how labour markets, including migration flow (abroad and into other sectors), and supply and demand for jobs in the health sector, affect the availability of health workers and, as a result, feature in HRH management.

Although the following sections do not vividly indicate the components of the framework discussed, the frameworks were used to provide basis to take account of the evolution of HRH management in Tanzania in line with the three concepts of entry, management of the workforce and exit. It helped in identifying major conceptual components in which the historical perspectives were drawn.

3.2 Health-Sector Reforms and Human Resources for Health

Health-sector reforms refer to sustained, purposeful and fundamental changes in the health sector. From the 1940s until now, three significant health-regime-sector reforms have emerged, and the World Health Assembly has championed all three regimes through the international community (Sirili, 2018). The three generations of reform have involved an ideological, organizational, managerial and financial transformation in the health sector. Although not specific and explicit for the health workforce, global health-sector reforms have affected and been affected by health workforce development.

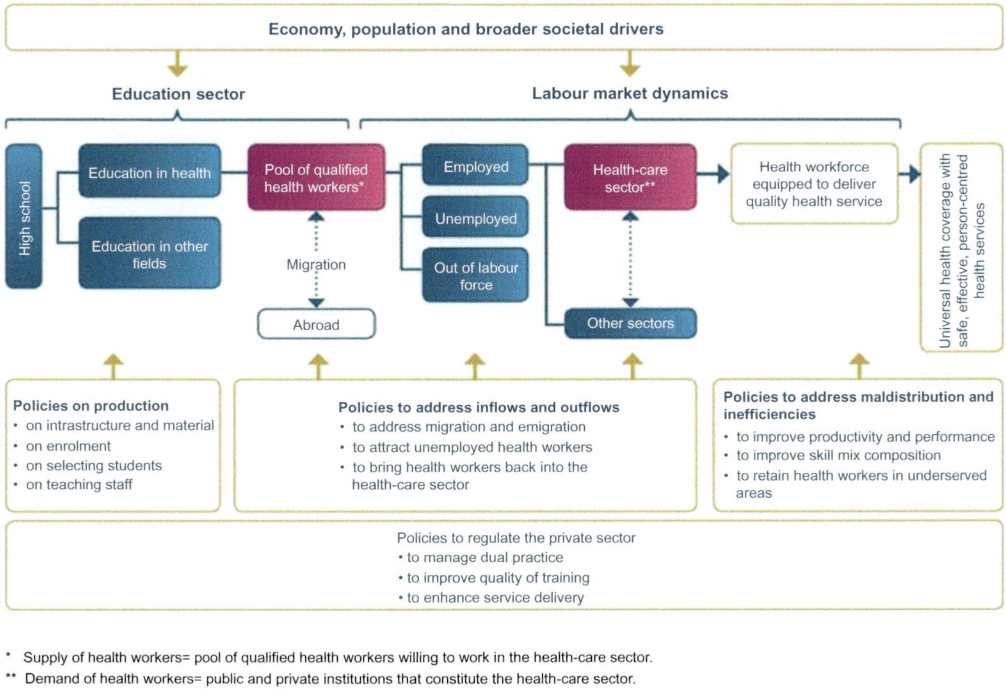

Fig. 3.2. Health labour market framework. (Modified from Sousa *et al.*, 2013 under CC-BY.)

3.2.1 The three generations of health-sector reforms

From the 1940s to the 1960s, the world implemented the first generation of health-sector reforms. The first generation emphasized hospital care; thus, countries invested in the foundation of health-care systems by building health facilities to ensure their populations have access to health-care services. However, by the 1960s, many health-care systems were under great stress due to the rising costs of care resulting from the increased volume and intensity of hospital-based care. In places where systems were nominally universal, coverage for the poor was still limited. Most of the health facilities were built in urban areas, and only better-off people could afford the cost, thus leaving the majority of the poor and disadvantaged rural population without access to affordable health-care services. Furthermore, around 50% of all inpatient spending went towards treating conditions that could be managed by ambulatory care (Sirili, 2018).

After policy makers realized that hospital care had failed to address most of the health challenges, beginning in the 1970s, the second generation of reforms was designed to address the health challenges through PHC. PHC is guided by the fundamental principles of universal access to care, need-driven coverage, health equity, community participation in defining and implementing health agendas and intersectoral approaches to health. However, the implementation of the PHC strategy faced many challenges. The main difficulties were low state funding, increased population needs and a shortage of adequately trained health workers. Therefore, the second generation of health-sector reforms did not endure for long, lasting only to the early 1980s.

By the early 1980s, many low and middle-income countries (LMICs) were in critical economic situations. They had failed to fund their health-sector budgets adequately. Conditionally, the International Monetary Fund (IMF) and World Bank (WB) initiated the implementation of the third generation of health-sector reforms in LMICs to support these countries in dealing with economic downfalls (Gilson and Mills, 1995; Mubyazi *et al.*, 2007; Sirili *et al.*, 2017).

Implementation of the third-generation health-sector reforms required a sector-wide approach. This involved structural adjustment programmes (SAPs) in the LMICs. SAPs involved monetary and fiscal policies as well as institutional reforms. SAPs aimed to make LMICs reduce their spending on the social sector, get rid of excessive government control and encourage market competition.

Despite the need for health-sector reforms in LMICs in the 1980s, following the failure of the previous reform regimes due to different reasons, including economic downfalls, the 1990s health-sector reforms in many LMICs were not demanded or driven locally. Instead, the reforms followed those from high-income countries. The literature shows that the initial reform efforts were carried out in Europe. Ideologically, in the welfare states of Western Europe, the reforms were driven by changes in demographic profiles—mainly the increasingly aged population and thus changes in health-care needs and demands. In other countries, the transformation in economies was the main driver for the health-sector reforms. For instance, in Eastern Europe, especially in the republics of the former Soviet Union, restructuring the economies from centrally planned to market economies drove the health-sector reforms. Due to their economic downfalls, the WB and the IMF pushed many LMICs into reforms unwillingly. Therefore, unlike in many high-income countries, where the design of the reforms involved many local stakeholders and was accepted by their governments, many governments in LMICs were reluctant to buy these reforms (Mubyazi *et al.*, 2007; Sirili *et al.*, 2017).

The third generation of reforms emphasized a sector-wide approach to addressing health challenges. Although, as for the previous generations of reforms, the third-generation reforms' main objective was to improve health systems' performance and respond to population needs, perhaps the primary driver for these 1980s reforms was the global economic depression from the late 1970s to the early 1980s.

Although many governments resisted implementing SAPs, conditions established by the IMF and WB that led to a massive reduction of donor support to these countries rendered many LMICs unable to achieve even 50% of their health-sector budgets. Therefore, many governments reluctantly involved the private sector to fill the gap. As a result, by the early 1990s, many developing countries had launched the third generation of health-sector reforms (Mujinja and Kida, 2014).

3.3 Evolution of Human Resources for Health in Primary Health Care in Tanzania

In this section, we document the evolution of Tanzania's health workforce in PHC and consider how policies and global events shaped and affected them. We have organized this section following the three health-workforce development stages as advocated by the World Health Organization. We summarize the events related to the macro-economic policy change that took place from time to time. Moreover, we discuss the challenge facing the health workforce and how some landmark policy changes (e.g. structural adjustment programmes) had long-lasting and unintended consequences on Tanzania's health workforce. Historically, Tanzania has been suffering from a chronic shortage of skilled health workers. The severity of the shortage has varied with time and location. In this subsection, we provide a brief account of health workers' availability and distribution in Tanzania from before independence to the early 2020s.

3.3.1 Health workforce demand and supply: Before independence

In his budget speech of July 1972, the then minister for health, Ali H. Mwinyi, declared the importance of adequate, well-distributed and motivated health workers in expanding health services, especially in rural areas. He said that the country's health success would depend on the adequacy and morale of health service workers (Bech *et al.*, 2013).

Pre-independence before 1884

Little is known about health workers' availability and distribution before the German colonial administration in Tanzania. The existing literature indicates that medical matters mainly were the responsibilities of individuals taken care of within their households, often by a traditional healer, except for medical matters that required the intervention of ruling elites, often those believed to be caused by spirits and sorcery (Beck, 1977; Waite, 1987).

Family elders often supervised and directed health-care provision within the family, including the propitiation of spirits as need directed. On the other hand, chiefs, kings and priests were in charge of matters considered of public health interest. This included the spirit of founders and sorcery control in their area of administration (ruling) and management of public taboos. Chiefs and kings controlled public taboos such as epidemics and catastrophic societal events. In such a case, rulers (chiefs, kings or priests), depending on the area, instituted several measures, including prohibiting people from engaging in certain everyday activities, such as conjugal/marital relationships and house-to-house visitations. These prohibitions were practical and symbolic since nuclear and extended family contacts were important in pre-capitalist societies. The suspension of normal activities reminded the community that it was in a dangerous state (Waite, 1987). Even before the German protectorate, missionaries, traders and explorers in Tanganyika were engaged in providing health-care services (Beck, 1977).

German protectorate, 1884–1919

Modern biomedicine can be considered to have begun around 1888 when the appointed imperial commissioner for German East Africa (GEA), Herrmann von Wissmann, added two doctors to his staff to start his rule in the newly acquired East African colony. They were tasked with establishing a functioning health-care system to protect the administration and increase investment in the protectorate (Beck, 1977).

Two doctors to service a population of well over 5,000,000 people was a challenging task. Further, the initial colonization of the GEA necessitated dispatching officers to the outposts to pacify and secure the colony. These outposts also had to offer various services, including medical services, which was considered one way to win over the Africans. They would later be the frontrunners of dispensaries.

With the limited human resources at his disposal, the dispatching of officers meant medical services were severely stretched, and many posts had to improvise and administer health services without having a medical professional. Things began to improve in 1890, with the formation of a civilian government and the establishment of the Department of Health. For the first time, the country appointed a chief medical officer, Dr Alexander Becker, who ran medical services in the protectorate. With Dr Becker's appointment, more medical officers were sent in from the German government and were now stationed along the coast in Lindi, Pangani, Kilwa and Tanga. By 1891, there were about 16 doctors in the country, catering for a population of 5,406,000. Still, apart from a small government hospital at Bagamoyo, the original base of government operations, there were no facilities for treating Asians and Africans in hospitals (Beck, 1977).

The German administration dictated that colonies take care of themselves, including administratively. Being a newly established colony, German East Africa had limited revenue and was very dependent on subsidies from the German government. This affected their decisions concerning health-care staffing and expanding access through the construction of facilities. Moreover, the price of hiring doctors was also high.

Aware of fund shortages, Dr Becker approached a wealthy Indian merchant, Sewa Haji, to carry out his plan to construct a much-needed hospital. In return, Sewa Haji was granted commercial privileges for his commercial enterprises. He gave the imperial government the sum of 12,400 rupees for establishing a hospital and a school that were to bear his name. He stipulated that 'the school and the hospital were to serve the natives whatever their origin, be they Indians, Arabs, Swahili and the like'. The hospital provided free treatment for the poor. It opened on a limited basis in 1893 with a dispensary, a laboratory, an operating room, and a waiting room. In 1895 the Germans built a government hospital in Dar es Salaam on a healthy spot overlooking the ocean. Up until this time, medical services provision was to a large degree provided by the non-Africans. By 1918, the German government started training medical auxiliaries, a move that would later be scaled up by the British. However, information on the actual number of medical auxiliaries trained (mostly Africans) is limited (Beck, 1977).

British protectorate, 1918–1961

British wanted to improve its Africans' public health and increased the number of workers by staffing all districts with European medical officers and Indians at small stations. The scheme was set in motion by 1926. By 1929 the British formally introduced training of district inspectors and the principle of rural dispensaries and were now treating many patients. However, their number was small, and dispensers were often underqualified for the paramedical services which they performed in their isolated outposts without supervision. Expanding rural health centres would have required coordinated action by the Education and Medical and Sanitary Services departments and support from the governor's office and the Treasury in London. Moreover, regulation of the services further necessitated a body strengthening the role of the Medical Council of Tanganyika (Beck, 1977).

FORCES OF GERMAN AND BRITISH ADMINISTRATION AND THEIR EFFECT ON ADEQUACY AND DISTRIBUTION OF THE HEALTH WORKFORCE. Various forces brought by the German and British protectorates affected Tanzania's health workforce's availability and distribution. They include regional specialization, direct taxation, centralization of authority, colonial medical institutions and profession (Gottlich, 2018). We briefly expand on each force below.

Direct taxation was a vital policy implemented by the British government to minimize the need to provide financial assistance to communities not engaged in growing cash crops. Consequently, it justified restricting services to groups based on what local tax revenue afforded. However, an issue with this stance is that the formal tax base was almost exclusively confined to Tanganyikans employed in growing cash crops, reinforcing the geographical fragmentation of health services in the country. In addition, the *centralization of authority* started by Germany and continued by the British emphasized the role of central government administrators throughout Tanganyika. Their primary goal was to establish order in the colony and maximize the production of cash crops. The system only supported the development of health services that catered to an exclusive minority of affluent rulers and did not substantially engage in preventive health measures. Such a system promoted unequal development of health services, with more care allocated to urban and areas of commercial viability. The remnants of the policy can be seen in the location of major hospitals in Tanzania, as shown in Fig. 3.3.

Medical institutions: To improve health-care services, the British government commissioned a team to propose an arrangement to guide the development of health care in Tanganyika. The first such report was the Pridie Report, released in 1949. It brought a balance between curative and preventive services. However, it still advocated for health provision through European-style hospitals. Hospitals, though, were ill-equipped to serve average Tanganyikans due to the increased cost of technologies and physician salaries. While a more decentralized system consisting of health-extension workers or primarily preventive health approaches with smaller health centres would be better suited for the colony, care confined to a hospital-based setting was favoured. Hospital care was ill-suited for the rural Tanganyikan population, as hospitals primarily care for patients within a few square miles. The colonialist health model aimed not to provide equitable health care but to treat the colonist minority.

Medical professional model: The medical professional model under the British administration is as crucial to understanding the colonial health-care system as hospital-based care. European doctors almost exclusively managed the care of European patients, who were Tanganyika's sole demographic with reliable access to health care. The only medical role for Tanganyikans was as hospital assistants to these European physicians. After independence, these Tanganyikan hospital assistants transitioned to full physicians, but their lack of autonomous training presented issues in their clinical care. Despite their limited clinical knowledge base, these physicians expected to receive similar status and salaries as European physicians.

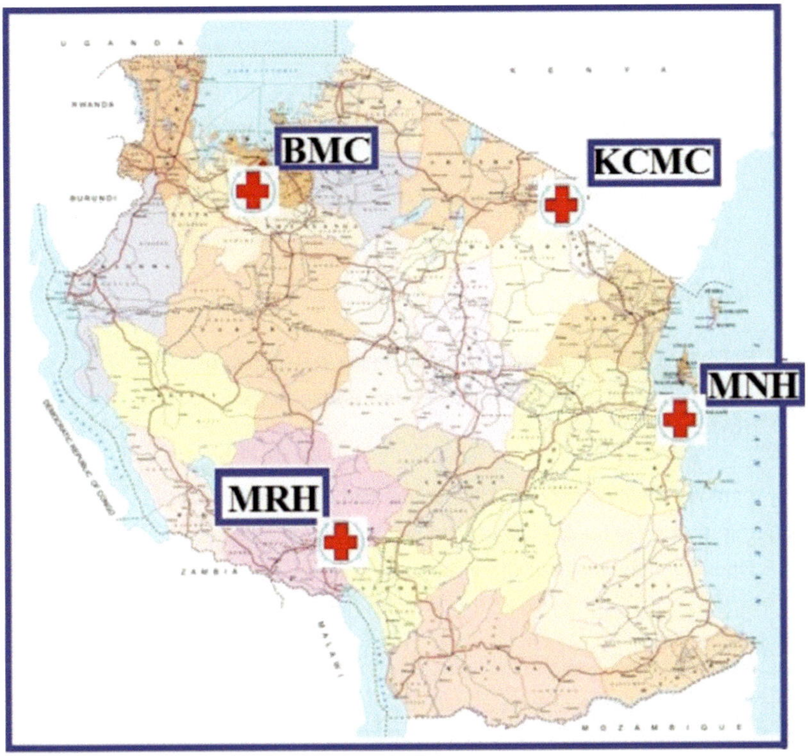

Fig. 3.3. Map of Tanzania showing the location of the four referral hospitals. (From http://www.tanzania.go.tz; last accessed 26 May 2014.)

Instead of adapting to the need for flexible professionals, the colonial medical profession model entrenched itself in the first generation of Tanzanian doctors, presenting issues for developing a preventive-focused care system. These changes would shape the health-care system and health workforce for years (see Table 3.1 for a summary of major developments affecting HRH in Tanzania).

3.3.2 Management of available workforce

The first 50 years: From 1961 to 2010

AFTER INDEPENDENCE, 1961–1977. The first 5 years the Africans' health training was limited to lower-level cadres during the German and British administrations. As a result, by the time Tanzania got its independence in 1961, only 12 out of the 400 registered doctors in Tanganyika were Africans. Moreover, many non-African doctors were to leave soon afterwards, leaving the country in shortage (Bech *et al.*, 2013).

In addition to the inadequate number of health workers, there was unequal distribution influenced by German and British policies, with doctors concentrated in urban areas. The next 5 years post-independence would not see much change as the health plan in the country between 1964 and 1965 would be primarily influenced by the Pridie Report (Bruchhausen, 2016; Gottlich, 2018). The report emphasized British medical institutions and roles, which meant that hospital-led services were favoured. In addition, the government closed the medical assistant programme in favour of professional medical programmes, which further reduced the supply. Moreover, British medical roles meant training and keeping professional doctors who cost more and often refrained from going to rural areas, accentuating geographical imbalances.

Table 3.1. Major developments of HRH in Tanzania.

Period	Development
Before the German administration	< 1884
Before 1884	The health workforce comprised of traditional healers, chiefs, kings and priests
Before independence	
German protectorate	1884–1920
	Sewa Haji, the first modern hospital, opens in Bagamoyo
	Health services provided by the German administration
British protectorate	1918–1965
	Establishment of training of inspectors and rural medical aides
	Introduction of Medical Council of Tanganyika
	Opening of the first midwifery school
After independence	
First 5 years	1961–1967
	Pridie and Titmuss reports
	Centralization of the recruitment system
	Establishment of the first medical school
Arusha Declaration	1967–
	Villagization with emphasis on rural health care
	Opening of primary health training centres
	Training of lower health cadres
	Economy stagnation
	Ban on private practice
Structural adjustment programmes	1986–1994
	Freeze on hiring and downsizing of employment apparatus
	Ban on private practice lifted
Crisis and reforms	1993–2006
	Introduction of public–private partnership
	Establishment of the first private medical training university
	Establishment of centre for distance learning
	Increasing student enrolment for all health-training institutions
	Partial decentralization of recruitment
	Establishment of BMAF to increase staff retention

Continued

Table 3.1. Continued

Period	Development
	Human Resource for Health Strategic Plan 2008–2013
Post-2010	2014–present
	Roll-out of HRHIS and TIIS
	Addition of POA to WISN
	Establishment of a national e-learning platform and CPD guidelines
	Centralization of recruitment
	Human Resource for Health and Social Welfare Strategic Plan 2014–2019
	Endorsement of National Health Workforce Volunteering guidelines
	Task-sharing policy guidelines for health-sector services
	National Human Resources for Health Strategy 2021–2026

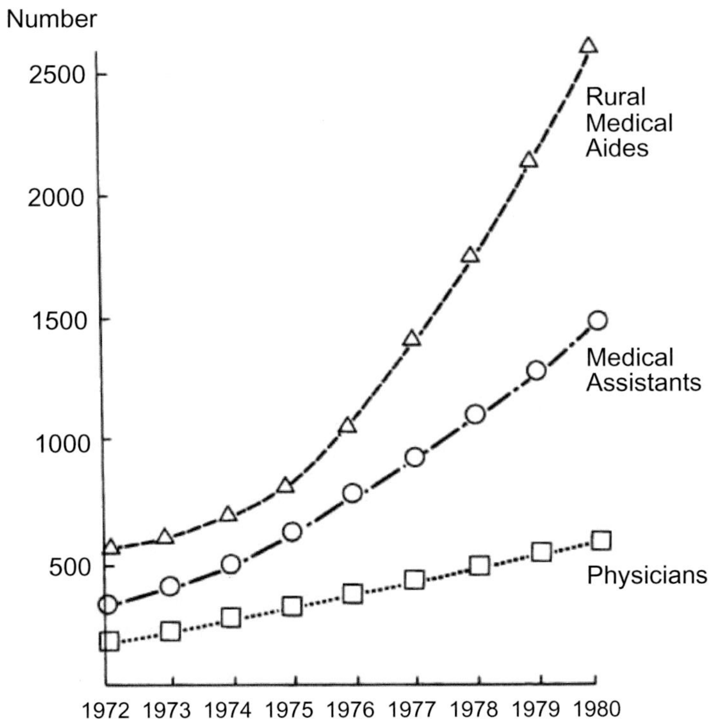

Fig. 3.4. Growth in the supply of physicians, medical assistants and rural medical aides in Tanzania from 1972 to 1980. (From Young, 1986.)

This was to change upon the release of a report by British medical planners led by Richard M. Titmuss, who advocated for the health plan for Tanganyika, which was firmly based on the realities of economics and population. This report pursued training more rural health professionals and integrating them within the existing system (Titmuss, 1964). That way, Tanzania would achieve a more equitable distribution of its health workforce, one that met the needs of its people. Titmuss's report would lead to a health-system restructuring and affected the training, availability and distribution of health workers in Tanzania.

ARUSHA DECLARATION, 1967–1985. Under the Arusha Declaration, emphasis was placed on increasing access to health-care services in rural areas where the Tanzanian population lived. Under the plan, the direction of training changed to basic health training centres and not large institutions such as the medical school in Dar es Salaam. This increased the number of human resources for health in the subsequent years (Fig. 3.4).

This initiative was reaffirmed in 1971 in the Bi-annual National Conference of TANU, which further pressed for investments in rural health care and renewed attention to strengthening the administrative focus of development (Bech *et al.*, 2013). However, while more resources were being devoted to rural health care, in 1972, curative services still amounted to over 91.3% of Tanzanian health expenditures. For example, Muhimbili hospital received 41% of all the health government's drug and equipment budget (Bech *et al.*, 2013; Gottlich, 2018). Recognizing the unsustainability of providing curative services, Tanzania issued a 1972 policy forbidding large hospitals and channelling money to construct smaller health centres. Nevertheless, the 1972 policy led to a 30% increase in the total number of health facilities, with approximately 6–8 employees working in each dispensary, 77 of which better adhered to the Arusha Declaration's goal by ensuring that more than 90% of the Tanzanian population lived within 10 kilometres of one of these health facilities (Bech *et al.*, 2013).

ECONOMIC STAGNATION, 1970s. Tanzania's economy began to stagnate from the mid-1970s due to several factors: the international oil crisis of 1973 and 1979, the breakup of EAC in 1977, the war in Uganda in 1978 and the decline in agricultural production and export because of drought and floods. The economic crisis translated into poor funding for social services, including health care (Bech *et al.*, 2013; Mujinja and Kida, 2014; Sirili *et al.*, 2017).

The medical sector was among the most affected and decreasing funding for the industry led to the deterioration of working conditions. Around the same time, the local currency was devalued, which decreased purchasing power (Mujinja and Kida, 2014). This severely affected health workers' morale and impacted performance.

Health workers started to engage in other activities to supplement their income, and some abandoned their practice altogether. The situation peaked in 1977 when the government officially banned private practice. This further pushed the migration of health professionals out of practice. A Tanzanian national health-sector evaluation in 1979 identified the significant constraints experienced in the shortage of trained health personnel. Statistics by the social scientist Angwara D. Kiwara claimed that close to 26% of government doctors, or 170 physicians, left Tanzania between the mid- and late 1980s (Kwesigabo *et al.*, 2012; Bech *et al.*, 2013).

STRUCTURAL ADJUSTMENT PROGRAMMES, 1986. Following the crisis in 1986, the World Bank and IMF intervened, and Tanzania implemented structural adjustment programmes (SAP) with monetary and austerity measures (Sirili, 2018). As part of the SAP the civil sector was to undergo significant reformations. It was argued that the public sector lay at the core of the stagnation and decline in growth in Africa and 'fundamental reform of the public sector was needed to reverse the economic decline'. Policy implementation led to freezing hiring and downsizing the employment apparatus, with unskilled and semi-skilled cadres affected the most. Freezing and retrenchment policy coupled with the limited investments in infrastructure, training and retention in the public health and medical sectors would have long-term consequences on the health-care workforce.

Reducing staff in the civil service during the 1990s did not lead to the intended efficiency among government health workers. On the contrary, the significantly reduced health workers were under enormous strain, leading to low motivation and performance. As a result, more health workers would eventually leave the public sector. Moreover, downsizing the apparatus led to the loss of many experienced and skilled health workers (Bech *et al.*, 2013).

The drain to other sectors, primarily to the private health sector and out of the country,

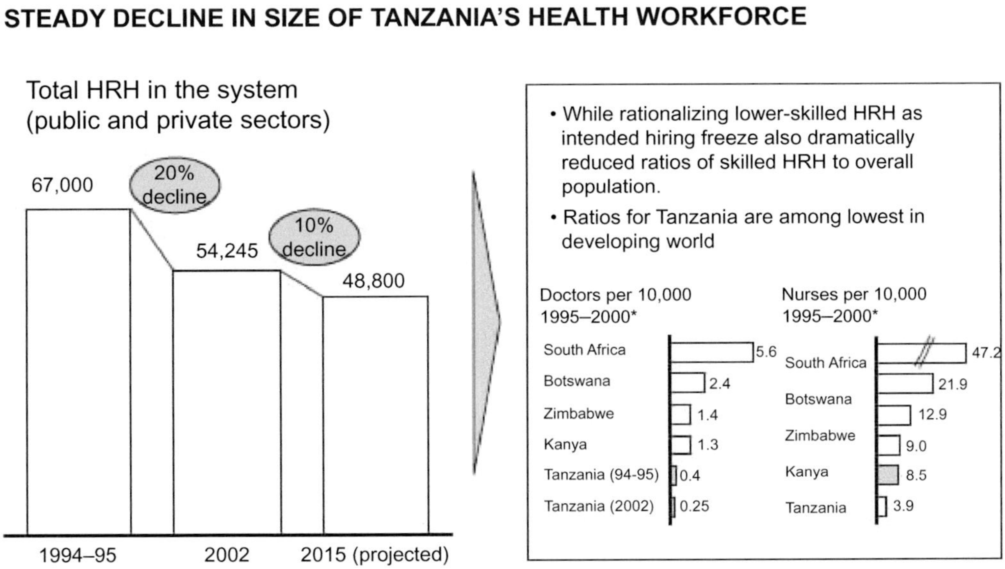

Fig. 3.5. Reduction in the size of the health-care workforce in Tanzania between 1994/95 and 2002. (From McKinsey & Company, 2004.)

continued in the 1990s. According to the Organization for Economic Co-operation and Development (OECD), Tanzania was among the top ten countries with the highest doctor expatriation rates since 55.3% of Tanzanian medical doctors (1018 doctors) were working abroad around the year 2000. The expatriation rate for Tanzanian nurses was 6.8% (970 nurses) (Bech *et al.*, 2013).

HEALTH WORKER CRISIS, 1996. HRH was first declared a crisis in 1996. The retrenchment policy, coupled with the freeze on hiring implemented in 1993, had led to a sharp decline in the health workforce. Statistics indicate that Tanzania's total active health workforce declined from 67,600 workers in 1994/95 to 48,500 workers in 2001/02 (Fig. 3.5) (McKinsey & Company, 2004). Over the same period, the population grew by 20%, representing a decline per capita of 40%, with most of the decline occurring in lower-skilled cadres. In addition, the employment freeze was having an effect, with data showing that only 16% (3,836) of 23,474 health-care professionals trained over the last decade were employed by the government in 2005 (McKinsey & Company, 2004).

The downsizing of the workforce had negative consequences due to the loss of experienced and skilled health workers (Fig. 3.5). By 2004, Tanzania had the world's lowest physician coverage, with only 0.02 medical officers or specialists per 1000 persons (McKinsey & Company, 2004). Moreover, even after the freeze was lifted in the mid-2000s, the budget ceiling implied that the government could not recruit doctors fast enough to mitigate the shortage (MOHSW, 2008).

The health sector faced other challenges, such as weak planning and forecasting of human resource requirements. An even more significant deficit was expected as HIV/AIDS would potentially increase demand for health workers, and the existing health workers retired due to old age. There were also problems of inadequate involvement of the private sector in human resource planning (MOHSW, 2008).

The country was also facing challenges with geographical distribution, with most shortages seen in rural areas. Rural staffing challenges included a lack of attractive retention schemes, poor remuneration, and defective equipment and medicines to do the work. As a result, physicians preferred practising in urban settings where they could 'moonlight' or work at multiple hospitals and clinics to supplement low salaries.

A tracking analysis report for the posted health workers in financial years 2007/2008/2009/2010 showed that only 63% of doctors assigned to rural areas showed up. Of those who went to their post, 13% left within 1 year due to quality of life, delays in clearing hardship claims, moving costs, bad roads and lack of social services. In addition, Tanzania has a diffuse system of monitoring health-care workers and limited information on where trainees went (MOHSW, 2008; Kwesigabo *et al.*, 2012; Bech *et al.*, 2013).

The social welfare sector also faced shortages. Proposed factors were: the retrenchment policy of the 1993 decentralization policy, which required social welfare services to be rolled out to the lower levels, and the government policy of 2002, which prohibited standard seven leavers from being employed in the government facilities.

To address the health workforce shortage, the government rolled out several changes, including allowing the establishment of private medical training institutions, increasing student enrolment of students in health-care universities and increasing salaries for physicians and other public health workers. For example, IMTU, a private institution, first opened to increase the production of medical doctors in 1997 (Mkony, 2012; Sue *et al.*, 2016). Although a positive move, there were a few drawbacks, in particular with increasing government salaries, which drew many private-sector physicians back to the public sector and exacerbated private-sector human resource shortages, raising concerns about the quality of care at private facilities (MOHSW, 2008). In 2008 the government published a second five-year HRH strategic plan, having renewed efforts in planning, policy development, education, training, workforce management and utilization, partnership creation, research and development and adequate financing and leadership promotion. In addition, the plan also recognized mid-level cadres (MOHSW, 2008).

SUMMARY. 1967 – Arusha Declaration, and renewed efforts in training of mid-level cadres and free services for all. Growth in the supply of physicians, medical assistants and rural medical aides in Tanzania from 1971 to 1980.

1970 – Economic stagnation: international oil crisis of 1973 and 1979, the breakup of the EAC in 1977, the war in Uganda in 1978 and the decline in agricultural production led to the stagnation of the economy and decreasing funding for health and social services. Ban on private practice.

1986 – Structural adjustment programmes: freezing hiring and downsizing the employment apparatus, with unskilled and semi-skilled cadres affected the most. Resumption of private practice and introduction of cost sharing.

1996 – Health workforce crisis: loss of experienced cadres, reduced health-care workforce further strained remaining staff and led to emigration of skilled workforce.

2000s reforms – Establishment of private medical universities, increased enrolment of students and increasing health workers salaries.

Table 3.2. HRH requirements by facilities in Tanzania, 2019.

Level of care	HRH required	HRH available	Deficit (%)
Dispensary	99,060	30,625	68,435 (69.08)
Health centre	32,487	17,954	14,533 (44.73)
District hospital	21,600	17,443	4157 (19.25)
Other hospital	26,400	11,243	15,157 (57.41)
Regional hospital	14,226	11,373	2853 (20.05)
National, zonal, spec. referral hospital	14,509	10,349	4160 (28.67)
Total health facilities	208,282	98,987	109,295 (52.47)
Health training institution	2632	726	1906 (72)

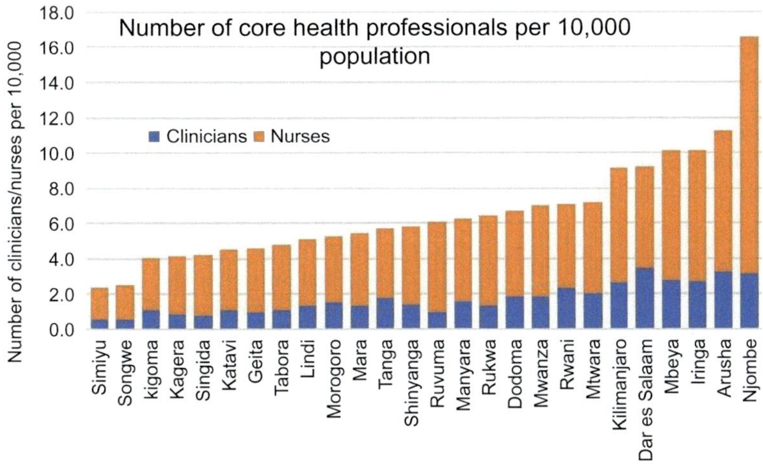

Fig. 3.6. Distribution of nurses and midwives, and clinicians per 10,000 population per region. (From MOHCDGEC, 2020.)

The demand and supply situation of health-care personnel after 2010

Tanzania continues to experience a shortage of health-care workers. According to the staffing levels guideline (2014–2019) (MOHCDGEC, 2019), the minimum number of health workers required to provide quality health services in health-care facilities in 2019 was 208,282. However, the actual number of health workers available was 98,987, indicating a shortage of 109,295, which is about 52.47%. Moreover, this shortage is severe at lower levels of health-care provision, with dispensaries reporting a deficit of more than two-thirds (69%) (MOHSW, 2013; URT, 2020) (Table 3.2).

Similarly, the number of workers required in the health training institutions is insufficient. For example, in 2019, only 28% (726) of the human resources necessary for health training was available (MOHCDGEC, 2019). In addition, the rapidly ageing workforce poses a severe threat, as their retirement will further deplete the health workforce.

HEALTH WORKFORCE DISTRIBUTION BY REGION IN 2020. As of 2020, geographical disparities regarding HRH availability continue, with some regions having better staffing and showing urban–rural maldistribution. For instance, health workers' density ranged from 4/10,000 population in good, staffed parts like Kilimanjaro to 10/10,000 population in understaffed areas (Fig. 3.6). Also, there was a maldistribution of health workers among rural and urban areas, whereby one doctor served 78,880 people in rural areas while one served 9095 people in urban areas (MOHCDGEC, 2019; URT, 2020).

PHARMACEUTICAL STAFF IN PHC. Like many countries in sub-Saharan Africa, Tanzania is experiencing a severe shortage of pharmaceutical personnel. According to Tanzania's pharmaceutical human resources report, by 2009, the country had only 640 pharmacists, 479 pharmacy technicians, and 376 pharmacy assistants, with a mean density of pharmacists of only 0.18 per 10,000 population (MOHSW, 2009). In addition to a shortage, there is a challenge of maldistribution with most pharmacists working in urban areas and at higher levels of the health systems. As a result, there are often vacancies at lower levels and in rural areas, which are often forced to be filled by other cadres without pharmaceutical competencies.

Under Tanzania's decentralized health-care system, local governments are responsible for providing health services in their areas. Concerning pharmaceutical staffing, each district is required to have a minimum of one pharmacist overseeing all matters related to pharmacy practices. The revised national staffing guidelines of 2014–2019 also mandate that a minimum of one pharmacist (degree holder) and two pharmacy technologists (a diploma holder) serve at the district hospital (MOHCDGEC, 2019). The health centre and dispensary requirements are pharmaceutical technologists and assistant pharmaceutical and pharmaceutical assistant (a certificate holder), respectively.

3.3.3 Training of health-care personnel

Training local people for health-care service delivery is key to the availability of adequate and quality health-care services. Therefore, the Tanzanian government has strived to increase health-care personnel by continuously expanding training resources and adopting appropriate policies to promote professional health-care services in the country. The developments and efforts are summarized below.

Immediately after independence, the government started a move toward equality in the provision of social services to all people, which led to a strategic increase in the numbers of health professionals in the country. The objective was to increase the number of Tanzanian health-care providers. By then, the government only had its first 12 Tanzanian medical doctors who had graduated from Makerere College Uganda (University of London).

In Tanzania, up until the time of independence from the British administration in 1961, there were no universities available locally. Africanizing the workforce became the main challenge of nationalistic leadership, establishing the University College Dar es Salaam as a college of the University of London with fourteen students. It became a constituent college of the University of East Africa in 1963 (UDSM, 2011). The University of East Africa was initially instituted as an independent external college of the University of London and offered programmes and degrees from the University of London until 1966. The dissolution of the University of East Africa in 1970 led to the creation of the three first autonomous public universities of Dar es Salaam (UDSM), Makerere and Nairobi in Tanzania, Uganda and Kenya, respectively (Mkony, 2012).

Some of the renowned events in the country's HRH development include the opening of the Muhimbili College of Medicine in 1963, which started by training assistant medical officers (AMOs) and later medical doctors. The first students of the Muhimbili College were enrolled in 1964 and graduated with a medical diploma in 1968. By 1968 Muhimbili College had graduated from the faculty of medicine, College of Dar es Salaam under the University of East Africa. It started offering a Bachelor of Medicine and Surgery (MBChB).

In 1970 the dissolution of the East Africa Community led to Tanzania establishing the University of Dar es Salaam, and Muhimbili faculty becoming a college of the university. In 1973 Muhimbili College started offering postgraduate training, ten years after its establishment. At the time, there were 28 medical specialists, with the other 23 being abroad for medical specialist training, mainly in Russia and Cuba. In 1974 the Faculty of Medicine at Muhimbili started offering a bachelor's degree in pharmacy. However, due to lack of qualified professionals in the Faculty of Medicine, training was collaboratively offered by the Faculty of Science at UDSM. As a result, the existing MUHAS school of pharmacy (SOP) is the first and only public-owned academic institution that trains pharmacists from baccalaureate to doctorate degrees. To date, the SOP has graduated approximately 1000 pharmacists in the country and averages 70 graduates per year (Mbilinyi *et al.*, 2021). By 1974 the country had 280 assistant medical officers and 500 rural assistant medical aids. By 1976 there were already about 30 established health cadres, 106 colleges of health for nurses training and other health cadres. In 1989 the Ministry of Health established eight health cadres training zones for continuing education, i.e. HRH development for the existing health-care workers.

Following the continued health-sector reforms since 1994, the first HRH Strategic Plan (1996–2001) was endorsed. In Tanzania, the first HRH Strategic Plan was developed in 1996 and implemented between 1996 and 2001. The plan's focus was mainly to elevate HRH issues to be recognized in the health-sector reforms and decentralization. One of the significant results of the programme has been the devolution of primary health services, including management of HRH, to the local government authorities.

The increase in the number of medical colleges/universities from only Muhimbili since 1963, producing about 50 doctors from four colleges (IMTU – 1997; Hubert Kairuki Memorial University – 1997; KCM College – 1997), yielded about 600 per year. By 1998 a centre for distance learning education for health-care workers' continued education and development was established. The establishment of other medical colleges/universities in Bugando (2004), and Dodoma (2007) increased the number of MD admissions to 950 per year. From 2005 to 2021 there was a curriculum review for middle cadres training to comply with NACTE requirements to strengthen training for such cadres.

Between 2007 and 2020 there was an increase in the number of student admissions into colleges from 1018 in 2007 to 25,077 in 2020, about 167.2 of the target of 15,000 students who were to be admitted by 2020 (NEC CCM, 2015), increasing the number of graduating students from 6890 in 2015 to 13,450 in 2019 for middle cadres, and for bachelor level from 1141 in 2015 to 1810 in 2019. Also, the number of medical specialists' enrolments increased from 420 in 2015/16 to 784 in 2019/20.

Between 2009 and 2014, the national rollout of HRHIS and TIIS was carried out in four phases. Together with other activities, the rollout process included conducting system operation and data utilization training for evidence-based planning, development and management of HRH, social welfare workers and health-training institutions.

In the period 2014 to 2019 this strategic plan was developed to call for a more collaborative effort to address the HRH crisis in the country. It provided guidance on key issues to be discussed in relation to HRH production,

Table 3.3. Evolution of health professional training universities in Tanzania.

	Year of admission				
University/university college	Dentist DDS	Doctors MD or MBBS	Environmental health officers (BSc EHS)	Nurses and midwives (BSc N)	Pharmacist BPharm
Muimbili University of Health and Allied Science	1979	1963	2001	1990	1974
International Medical and Technological University (IMTU)	–	1997	–	2006	–
Kilimanjaro Christian Medical Center (KCMC)	–	1997	–	1997	–
Hubert Kairuki Memorial University (HKMU)	–	1998	–	1998	–
Aga Khan University	–	–	–	2001	–
Catholic University of Health and Allied Science (CUHAS)	–	2003	–	–	2010
St John's University of Tanzania (SJUT)	–	–	–	2007	2007
College of Health Science University of Dodoma (UDOM)	–	2007	–	2009	–
St Francis University College of Health and Allied Science (SFUCHAS)	–	2010	–	–	–

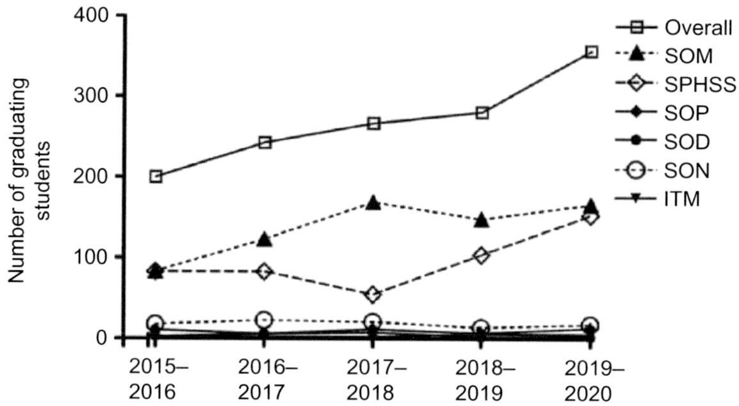

Fig. 3.7. Number of graduating students at Muhimbili University of Health and Allied Sciences (MUHAS) from 2015 to 2019. (From Balandya *et al.*, 2022.)

planning, development, management, utilization and monitoring of HR within the health sector and social welfare.

In 2020/21 the National e-Learning platform was established, a CPD guideline for continuous development of health-care workers in Tanzania.

3.3.4 Training institutions

More than 170 registered training institutions offer health and social welfare workers various training programmes. The non-degree-level programmes for health professionals fall under the Ministry of Health and Social Welfare and are accredited by the National Council for Technical Education (NACTE). The degree programmes are under the Ministry of Education and Vocational Training and are regulated by the Tanzania Commission for Universities (TCU). Involvement of the private sector has grown as of late, as shown in the programme offered and the ownership table (Table 3.3).

In 2010, the MOHSW asked all 116 national health-training institutions to increase their enrolment by 100%, specifically focusing on the mid-level cadres. Despite new attention to increasing human resources for health, the percentage of skilled health workers did not dramatically increase between 2008 and 2012 for health workers per head of population 2008 and 2012. The MOHSW encouraged new schools to open, and a sixth private medical school opened in 2015.

Enrolment and output of health-training institutions

The number of enrolled students has been increasing progressively. For example, at MUHAS, the number of students who registered/enrolled at the university grew from 358 in 2015–2016 to 536 in 2019–2020. Moreover, within the same period, the students graduating at MUHAS steadily increased, from 200 to 357 (79% increase), as shown in Fig. 3.7.

Continued professional development for health workforce

In terms of practical exposure to students, due to a critical shortage of staff in health facilities, trainees often get limited exposure time with clinical instructors. In addition, the increased number of students with limited training space limits adequate exposure to patients and practical sessions. Moreover, there is a weak quality management framework for ensuring quality training in schools and adaptation of new technology to increase efficiency in training is limited.

Midwifery education and training

The development of midwifery as a healthcare profession has been evolving alongside

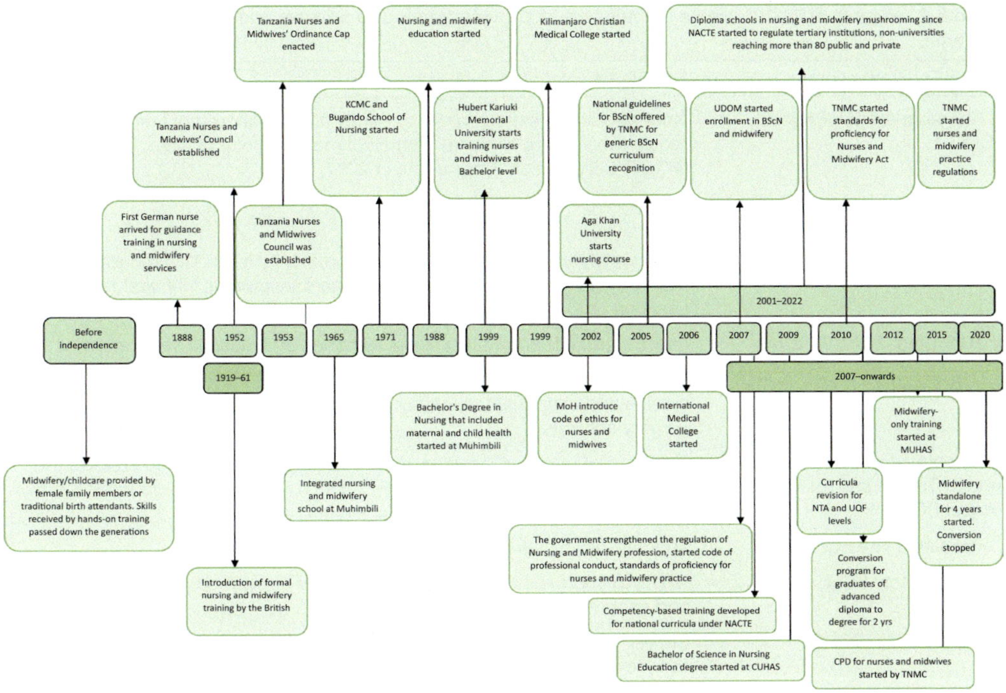

Fig. 3.8. Evolution of midwifery training in Tanzania.

developments in scientific medicine. Midwifery schools in Tanzania extend back to the pre-independence period, as summarized in Fig. 3.8. Tanzania records the first nurse from Germany who arrived in 1888, and after that, between 1919 and 1961, British nurses came to introduce formal nursing and midwifery services. In 1952 the Nursing Council was established, followed by the Tanzania Nurses and Midwives Ordinance, enacted in 1963. The first nursing and midwifery school was opened in the same year, producing certificate-level graduates.

After independence, nursing training development continued as an integrated programme. The nursing and midwifery schools were established in 1965 in Muhimbili, followed by Bugando and Kilimanjaro Christian Medical Centre schools in 1971. Nursing and midwifery practice and training continued to improve to produce bachelor's degree level graduates from 2005 at Muhimbili and other universities, such as Aga Khan University, University of Dodoma, Kilimanjaro Christian Medical University College (KCMUCo) and the Catholic University of Health and Allied Sciences (CUHAS). As of 2021, ten institutions were providing university degree programmes, 57 clinical officers, and six training centres for assistant medical officer (AMO) programmes. With respect to nursing training institutions, 59 HTI were offering nursing certificates, 49 nursing diplomas and 8 university degree programmes. In Tanzania, midwifery education is delivered together as a comprehensive nursing-midwifery programme for a Certificate and Diploma in Nursing and Midwifery. There are no stand-alone midwifery programmes in Tanzania except for bachelor's and master's degrees in midwifery offered by the Muhimbili University of Health and Allied Sciences (MUHAS) and the University of Dodoma as of 2021.

e-learning systems and CPD

Since the 1990s, several initiatives have been implemented to enhance e-learning. Some of the earliest initiatives were the establishment of the Centre for Distance Education (CDE) by

Table 3.4. Project ECHO™ clinics established to provide training to primary health-care workers in Tanzania.

Project ECHO™ clinic	Specific focus
1. HIV rapid-testing Project ECHO™	Non-laboratory testers: target to certify all non-laboratory testers as a requirement of the National Framework for the Point of Care Testing (POCT) Certification Programme in 2017.
2. HIV care and treatment Project ECHO™	Improve services to people living with HIV/AIDS.
3. HIV viral load Project ECHO™	Improve HIV viral-load testing at the community level. This focuses on reaching stakeholders, experts and testers to improve HIV viral-load services.
4. TB Project ECHO™ clinic	Implemented through discussing TB cases and didactic sessions.
5. Safe surgery Project ECHO™	Improve service and safety in surgery units. This focuses on equipment service and maintenance, safety practices and technical guidance on surgery services.
6. Differentiated service delivery model (DSDM) and task-sharing Project ECHO™	Provision of technical assistance (TA) to high-volume sites to support the adoption of quality differentiated HIV care for paediatrics and adolescents.
7. Paediatric HIV ECHO™	Improve clinical services to children living with HIV.
8. Blood safety ECHO™	NBTS to improve blood and safety services through sharing knowledge and experience among HCWs.
9. Supply chain ECHO™	Supply chain and management ECHO strengthening of supply-chain services.
10. COVID-19 ECHO™ clinics – emerging and re-emerging diseases	Emerging and re-emerging diseases ECHO to strengthen disease prevention and management of emerging and re-emerging diseases through sharing knowledge and experience.

the Ministry of Health in 1997. The CDE was tasked with coordinating continuous professional development (CPD) studies through distance learning. In addition, the CDE aimed to enable the development of health workers while still at their workplace. This arrangement ensures health workers are present at their working sites while learning and developing. Other actions included the construction of the e-learning facility at Morogoro in 2017 and creating of telemedicine hubs in 2021–2022. Up to September 2022, a total of 31,487 users from the medical council of Tanganyika, 7743 from the pharmacy council and 9789 from Tanzania nursing and midwifery have been linked with the National e-Learning Platform. The majority of these providers are those working at primary health-care facilities.

Extension for community outcome (ECHO™)

Project ECHO™ (Extension for Community Healthcare Outcomes) is a known model for improving patient outcomes through health-provider education. It has proliferated since its initial success in treating diseases, particularly hepatitis C, in the 1990s. This viewpoint of Project ECHO™ is that the right knowledge in the right place and at the right time can save millions of lives.

Since the provision of high-quality, accessible and affordable health-care services has been a priority of the government of Tanzania, the Ministry of Health adopted the Project ECHO™ model to conduct mentorship, training and share knowledge with health-care providers while at their working stations. The model was officially launched in November 2016 as a training and mentorship model for non-laboratory testers who perform HIV rapid tests (non-laboratory testers certifications framework, 2016). It aimed to facilitate the certification programme of non-laboratory testers who perform HIV rapid tests in primary health care due to the shortage of laboratory practitioners in Tanzania (Table 3.4).

3.3.5 Recruitment and deployment

Recruitment of HRH is part of the first stage of health workforce development, the entry stage. It is defined as a process of searching for and obtaining a pool of potential candidates with the desired knowledge, skills and experience to allow an organization to select the most appropriate people to fill job vacancies against defined position descriptions and specifications.

Process and procedures

During the German occupation, there were no formal medical systems. Traditional medicine was the only existing option. Systems of medicine based on cultural beliefs and practices were handed down from generation to generation. The concept includes traditional herbal medicine, mystical and magical healing. The community's sickness was attended by traditional doctors, herbalists, traditional birth assistants (TBAs) and sorcerers who had inherited the expertise from their ancestors. Society would afford to cater to these services in exchange with the service providers for items like farm products, chicken and livestock.

Until the end of the German administration the Tanzanian health system had been dictated by foreigners who advocated for the development of an exclusive curative-based health-care system catering to the minority, that is, administrators and Tanzanians engaged in the growing of cash crops (Gottlich, 2018). The curative-based system had racialized the workforce and ignored the vast need for preventive-focused initiatives to combat the then-endemic tropical diseases in Tanzania.

The racialist settler government did recruitment, and the private sector/missionaries owned health facilities. The first president, Julius Nyerere, pursued a preventive health-care system after Tanzanian independence to achieve his health goal for all Tanzanians. Deployment was done by the independent government of Tanganyika and the private sector (mostly missionary-owned)

Between 1964 and 1967, Tanzania began to formally address this health-services inequity by developing a governmental preventive-focused health-care delivery system. Using a centralized recruitment system, the government was the then sole employer in the public service. As a result, the government recruited qualified and unqualified personnel with specific potential in the health sector who were trained locally and abroad to fill the gap in medical staff needs. Although deployment was done solely by the independent government of Tanzania, nationalization moves provided no room for the private (for-profit) sector.

Domestic and international pressures in the 1990s led to the dismantling of a socialist system in favour of a privatized health model and public–private partnership model. However, the deployment of health-care providers, as for all other public servants in the public sector, was still centralized. The Ministry of Health directly posted all workers who graduated from training and working stations in regions and LGAs with a letter of employment from the MOH.

Under the public–private partnership umbrella, FBOs, which had many health facilities in the country, started obtaining health-care workers who were government employees under service agreements between the government and FBOs.

After the reforms in 1994, districts were fully responsible for the retention of the health workforce. Later, districts and central government combined efforts and policies were made and implemented, for example, the HR bonding policy.

Due to a critical shortage of staff in regions and LGAs in the aftermath of the employment freeze for about ten years, between 2005 and 2010, the President's Office Public Service Management (POPSM) gave a directive for a decentralized recruitment process where districts would identify their needs and hire new employees following the prescribed process (advertisement, interviews, providing offer letters and submitting names to the sector ministry which would then request POPSM approval and entry into the payroll).

In 2006, the deployment system changed to a partially centralized system. In this system, the districts identified vacancies and the Ministry of Health and Social Welfare (MOHSW) filled vacancies in collaboration with the Ministry of Finance and Economic Affairs (MOFEA), the Prime Minister's Office Regional Administration and Local Government (PO-RALG) and POPSM.

The aim of this new system, as for the previous one, was to ensure an equal distribution of health-care workers and address ongoing challenges of the recruitment system in the LGAs. Many LGAs were not doing very well in terms of revenue collection and therefore could not afford to carry out the processes and hire as many staff as they needed to, so there were uneven numbers of recruited staff in LGAs.

In 2011, due to unequal health workforce distribution, MOHSW fully started conducting the recruitment process through its Department of Administration and Human Resource Management. The MOH received the approved permits from POPSM and advertised all the job positions. It would later obtain and scrutinize graduates' applications. To maximize the quantity of recruited candidates, there were no interviews. All requested graduates were posted to fill these positions based on their qualifications and the needs of the regions and LGAs. In these previous years, offers to new recruits were made via letters which would be submitted to employers upon reporting for work.

The service scheme for health cadres was reviewed to include other health-related cadres such as social welfare officers and health secretaries and has evolved over the years to include medical recorders (2018), CHWs and biomedical engineers (2019). These cadres are now requested in HRH permits, recruited and posted to their working stations in primary health facilities.

In 2016 and in later years, placement lists could be accessed on the MOHSW website, but there were no offer letters. This new system has helped reduce forgery because districts can quickly confirm the credentials of all arriving staff through the website.

New employee details are uploaded to the online system (LAWSON) and entered into the payroll. Typically, staff begin receiving their salaries one to two months after reporting; before the online system was introduced, it took a minimum of four to six months to receive their first salaries.

Based on the permit for each institution, the MOH advertises for staff of its institutions and PO-RALG for primary health facilities; the recruitment process is done jointly, and each ministry uses its own Ajira management systems. The systems receive shortlists and places, receive reporting feedback and are used for applicants' replacements in the unfilled posts. Starting in 2019, health-care workers are posted directly to the working stations as they have requested in the application system. Responsible officers verify those who have qualified and place them into different employer votes/districts.

After the 1990s health-sector reforms, there has been centralized recruitment by five key players – by the MOH, PO-RALG, POPSM, MOF and PSRS. Responsible officers verify those who have qualified and place them into different employer votes/districts. Ministries do not directly post non-medical/health-related cadres but this is done by PSRS. It takes a month to receive the first salary if certificates are verified and submitted before the fifteenth day of the month.

Of importance is that HRH recruitment has taken into account social considerations by prioritizing candidates with special needs, that is, people with disabilities, in the recruitment process.

The Big Results Now initiative in 2014, a multisector national initiative, had significant importance to the health sector, and it provided an opportunity for a massive HRH analysis. There were key results in these areas: redistribution of HCW to reduce the unequal and inequitable distribution; prioritization of application of employment permits to regions with a critical shortage of HRH; ring-fencing subsistence allowances for new recruits; and providing HRH through PPP (BMAF).

After the Big Results Initiative, the HRH team obtained 9735 employment permits for 2014/15; several cadres in the permit that were not in the labour market were converted into skilled primary health care cadres. In addition, subsistence allowance, orientation and other innovative retention mechanisms for new recruits were a condition for employers and a directive was provided on the same from PO-RALG.

Summary of the recruitment process for new health workers since 2005

According to key respondent interviews, recruitment of HWs involves a complex interplay of five government entities: LGAs, PO-RALG, POPSM, the MOF and the MOH. Each body has a different role in facilitating the recruitment process.

The district human resource officer (DHRO) develops the personnel emolument (PE) budget

Table 3.5. Table showing recruitment trends from PO-RALG for health-care personnel, 2017–2022.

No.	May 2017	November 2017	2018	2019	2020	2021	Total
GOVT	206	2058	6180	477	2726		12,257
BMAF			281	198	559		1038
GRAND TOTAL							13,295

(using the staffing norms) and PE budget ceiling from the previous year. The PE budget includes salaries for existing staff, promotions and new staff. Hiring priority is given to key sectors that include social services: health, education and agricultural and livestock.

The district health secretary and CHMT members use the existing staffing levels and the previous year's PE budget to prepare a list of new staff requests by cadre. The DHRO reviews the new staff requests for all departments, consulting them for clarification when needed. The DHRO then prepares the PE budget projection to be sent to POPSM.

In previous years, districts would send a team to POPSM to defend the PE budget requests before approval. In 2013/14, POPSM introduced the LAWSON system, a web-based human-resource database. Therefore, councils are now submitting requests for new staff online. POPSM verifies that all information from each district is accurate and in line with staffing norms, that there are facilities to accommodate the new staff, and that their roles and responsibilities have been clearly stipulated. If these conditions are met, POPSM approves the PE budget for salaries for existing staff and new employees, subject to the availability of funds and ceiling from MOF. Table 3.5 shows the recruitment trends of health-care personnel under PO-RALG.

3.4 Human Resource for Health and Decentralization in Tanzania

Like other countries in sub-Saharan Africa, Tanzania implemented health-sector reforms in the 1990s. One of the features of the health-sector reform was the decentralization of health services planning and delivery to district councils. Health-sector reforms were implemented alongside reforms in the local governments. Decentralization of issues regarding HRH was stipulated in the local government reform paper of 1998, where it was quoted that:

> Administrative decentralisation: ... involves de-linking local authority staff from their respective ministries and procedures for the establishment of a local payroll. Local governments will thus have and recruit their own personnel, organised in a way decided by the respective councils in order to improve service delivery. Administrative decentralisation makes local government staff accountable to local councils.
>
> (Local Government Reform Paper, p. 57)

In addition, this involved a change in central–local relations, where line ministries also changed their role and functions and remained to be (i) policy-making bodies, (ii) supportive and capacity-building bodies, (iii) monitoring and quality assurance bodies within the local government legislation framework, and (iv) regulating bodies (legal control and audit). The structural arrangements of HRH recruitment and management under the decentralized settings included the engagement of an array of actors. Externally, the MOHSW undertakes human-resource function in partnership with POPSM, PO-RALG, the Ministry of Finance, local government authorities and Ministry of Education, Science and Technology (MOEVT) (Table 3.6).

Basically, the prevailing practice indicates a deconcentrated mode of recruitment and management of health workers. LGAs in decentralized settings are not well positioned in assuming HRH management roles as per the decentralization proposal. Consequently, multiple actors are engaged in HRH management; recruitment, training, transfer, recategorization of cadres and promotions. Experience indicates delays in transfers and promotion of staff including delayed recategorization for staff who have upskilled. The major challenge is limited financial capacity leading to dependency on central grants. Fig. 3.9 presents interaction

Table 3.6. Roles of ministries in HRH.

Ministry stakeholders	Roles
Ministry of Health	Oversight function for the collection and analysis of human resource information, including the provision of statistical estimates of present and future human resource requirements at all health system levels. Provides technical support to the local authorities and regions to achieve their human resources requirements. Formulates policies, regulations and standards. The employer for referral hospitals and training institutions, and also handles health technical issues at all levels of health care.
Presidents' Office Public Service Management and Good Governance	Sets policies for human resource management, provides a national framework for human resource planning; approves manning levels for health facilities.
Ministry of Finance	Provides and approves finance allocations.
PO-RALG	The employer for regional hospitals through the regional administrative secretary, and district hospitals, health centres and dispensaries through district executive director.
Ministry of Education, Science and Technology	Sets national educational policies and national qualification frameworks, provides oversight to health-related education up to university level.

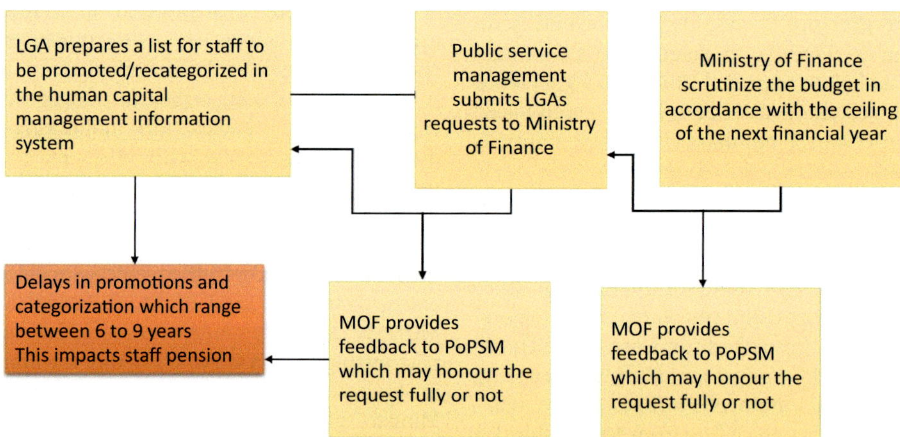

Fig. 3.9. Initiation and approval process of staff promotion/recategorization.

between actors in the process of recruitment/recategorization of staff.

3.4.1 Challenges in staff deployment in subnational government

The recruitment of health workers happens when there is permission from the public-service management ministry. After the cessation of the employment freeze and the implementation of the decentralization policy, recruitment responsibilities were also decentralized to councils. However, the councils' performance were below expectations. According to the tracking report of 2011, councils were able to utilize only 57% of the employment permits since the financial year 2007/8. The MOHSW was called to rescue the situation. In response to this challenge, zonal health resource centres (ZHRCs) were called to assist in posting health workers. As a result, the utilization of permits increased to 75%. This indicated a potential substantial gain in the posted/permit ratio through the involvement of ZHRCs in the recruitment process. To date this role is assumed centrally, except for operational cadres such as drivers and security guards.

Lessons from the decentralization of hiring roles to the council are that central–local relations features of decentralization by default determine the local government authorities' chances to utilize the decentralized discretion. Limited financial space of local authorities and accountability concerns of line ministries are among the inherent challenges of decentralization contributing to poor performance of councils in hiring staff. Structurally the line ministries are accountable to quality-of-service delivery; the MOH and PO-RALG continue to take the lead in the hiring process of skilled health workers to safeguard quality, professionalism and staff security in the overall process of HRH management. Council-specific factors also played a role. For instance, in some councils, there were few candidates who presented for interviews; this was the case for remote and hard-to-reach areas. Due to limited knowledge of the roles of health cadres, when councils were given authority to hire, some focused on less qualified personnel like medical attendants, hence shifting recruitment priorities from recruiting skilled staff to favouring the recruitment of non-skilled staff.

3.5 Strategies to Respond to HR Shortages in Tanzania

3.5.1 Task sharing

Evidence-based interventions exist, and more evidence is always generated to address health problems and disease burdens. However, practical coverage of these interventions has always been a challenge. The availability of qualified cadres to deliver these interventions to reach those who need them most is among the important factors. HRH shortage is a global challenge, and Tanzania is not an exception. For example, contraception is an inexpensive and cost-effective intervention. Still, health workforce shortages and restrictive policies on the roles of mid- and lower-level cadres limit access to effective contraceptive methods in many settings. The same challenge is felt in other interventions as well. Since addressing the shortage is not a one-time endeavour, at least in the health sector, it is labour intensive, and the service delivery financial requirement is too demanding. The WHO started promoting task sharing in the mid-2000s as a coping mechanism for living with the HRH crisis. This section of the chapter introduces the concepts of task sharing and provides its history and application in Tanzania.

Basic concepts

Although various terms exist to define task shifting, in this monograph we define task shifting as the process of delegation of functions, often from skilled to low or unskilled health workers. Moreover, we use the terms 'task shifting' and 'task sharing' interchangeably.

Manongi *et al.* coined vertical and horizontal task shifting to describe the different task-shifting practices commonly practised in Tanzania. Manongi further divided the vertical task-shifting into upward and downward acting to reflect how it is practised. Upward acting is where, for whatever reasons, lowly trained health personnel (or untrained ones) take the duties of adequately trained health personnel or higher-cadre health workers. Downward acting, on the other hand, involves a highly trained health workers taking the duties of a lower-level cadre or unskilled health worker. 'Horizontal' task shifting is also practised and is more widespread than 'vertical' task shifting. It involves a situation whereby in the context of a shortage of appropriate personnel, physicians' clinical tasks are delegated to non-physicians, for example, from clinical officers to nurses or laboratory personnel (Manongi *et al.*, 2006).

Task sharing involves the rational redistribution of tasks among health-care workers within the health-care system (WHO, 2008). It involves sharing functions related to health-care delivery from highly qualified cadres to health workers with fewer qualifications in that field. Task sharing is a prominent strategy in addressing the shortage of health workforce in many parts of the world (Hermann *et al.*, 2009). The objectives of task sharing are to make efficient use of available resources, expand access to interventions in remote facilities where skilled staff are not available to cope with a shortage

Table 3.7. Non-physician clinicians in selected countries in Africa.

Country	Name	Duration of training	Scope of practice
Angola	Clinical officer	Secondary education +3 years	Medicine, minor surgery, obstetrics (but no caesarean section)
Ethiopia	Health officer	Secondary education + Bachelor of Science or Registered Nurse + 3 years + 1 year internship	Medicine, minor surgery, obstetrics, including caesarean section
Ghana	Medical assistant	Secondary education + 3 years + 1 year internship	Medicine, minor surgery, obstetrics, including caesarean section
Kenya	Clinical officer	Secondary education + 3 years + 1–1.5 years of internship	Medicine, minor surgery, orthopaedics, dermatology, anaesthesia, otolaryngology
Mozambique	Clinical officer	Secondary education + 2.5 years + 1–1.5 years of internship	Medicine, minor surgery, obstetrics including caesarean section, dermatology, public health
Malawi	Clinical officer	Secondary education + 3 years + 1 year internship	Medicine, minor surgery, obstetrics including caesarean section, orthopaedics, dermatology, ophthalmology
Tanzania	Assistant medical officer[a]	Secondary education + 3 years of clinical officer's training + 2 years training + 0 years of internship	Medicine, minor surgery, obstetrics, including caesarean section
Zambia	Medical licentiate[a]	Secondary education + 4 years of associate clinicians' training + 3 years training + 0 years of internship	Medicine, paediatrics, obstetrics and gynaecology, surgery

[a]Senior associate clinicians based on WHO classification.

of HRH and reduce missed opportunities by enhancing the communities to receive service in constrained settings. Literature on task sharing provides several examples of where task sharing is used. For example, more than 300,000 non-physician clinicians practise alongside physicians in the USA. In sub-Saharan Africa, many countries opted for non-physician clinician cadres in places with critical shortages of physician clinicians (Table 3.1). Likewise, lower cadres of nurses and midwives exist in high- and low-income countries to address the shortage of qualified nurses and midwives. In different parts of the world, non-physician clinicians have other names, for example, in Canada they are termed medical licentiate; in the USA they are known as assistant practice clinicians, and as physician assistants in South Africa. In Africa, 25 out of 47 countries have active non-physician clinicians named differently as of 2015. The scope of practice and duration of training varies from one country to another (Table 3.7).

Although task sharing began as an interim solution to the critical shortage of health workers, it is now seen as an important strategy in addressing the ever-growing shortage of health workers. The redistribution of roles in some countries were extended to community cadres. These are given different names in different places, for instance, health extension workers in Ethiopia, lay health workers in Pakistan, lay health workers in India and community health workers in many other parts of the world. Due to the growing skilled health workforce shortage, these groups of health workers have now been trained and assigned more roles in nutrition, health promotion, vaccination and reproductive health.

Task sharing has two important elements that must be considered before venturing into it at all points. The first and foremost element is the quality of services provided by the cadre that was initially solely providing those tasked services. The delegation of the tasks must ensure that the quality of the service will be maintained to ensure equity in the service provided by the newly task-shared cadre and the original provider. The second element is ensuring that the task distribution is done rationally. That is, the capacity of the new cadre for task-sharing must be weighed by the services to be provided. Furthermore, both elements of task sharing must ensure that the benefits exceed the consequences.

Historical background of task sharing in Tanzania

Tanzania's human resource crisis in the health sector primarily affects the rural population. It dramatically impacts the quality of health-service delivery, universal health coverage and achieving desirable health outcomes. Many other countries in the world have for many years suffered a critical shortage of skilled health workforce. The struggle to address this shortage dates back to before independence. In the 1930s, Tanganyika introduced non-physician clinicians to serve at the lower-level facilities to cater to the critical shortage of physicians. These included rural dispensary assistants, assistant clinical officers (formerly known as rural medical aid) and clinical officers (formerly medical assistants). Rural medical aids, pharmacy and health auxiliaries, medical assistants and assistant medical officers formed the real army against misery, disease and death from the 1960s to 2000.

The British government during this time realized that its officials in rural areas lacked quality health-care services due to a lack of an adequate skilled workforce. Among the major struggles was battling the malaria infection that was killing administration officials in many rural areas (Beck, 1977). Below this cadre was a junior cadre of rural medical aids, which evolved with time to be named assistant clinical officers (ACOs) in the 1960s.

In the early 1960s, the independent Tanganyika made a health policy decision to train a middle-level cadre of clinical practitioners as a response to the acute shortage of medical doctors. Therefore, in 1963 the training of assistant medical officers started in Tanganyika. To cater for the critical shortage of oral health personnel, Tanganyika started training dental assistants in 1955. The latter was interrupted for ten years, from 1961 to 1971. Furthermore, in 1981 another mid-level cadre for oral health, the training of assistant dental officers, started.

The experience of utilizing task sharing in Tanzania

Albeit informally, task shifting in Tanzania was a common practice at all health facility levels and practised both within cadres (medical officers, assistant medical offices and clinical officers) and between cadres (for example, between clinical officers and nurses) (Munga *et al.*, 2012). However, although considered a common practice, there was still no formalization of the service in the country and the African continent. The absence of formalization brought with it many challenges. It included a lack of regulatory mechanism, certification and remuneration for health workers. Furthermore, task shifting was associated with challenges in the quality of care, especially when done without proper supervision.

Recognizing the utility of task shifting and the problems brought about by the lack of formalization, in 2010 the World Health Organization issued global recommendations on the steps to be considered by all countries which consider scaling up task shifting as one of the interventions to deal with their health personnel crises (WHO, 2008). These recommendations stated that:

- Task shifting must be implemented in such a manner that it will improve the overall quality of care. It should not, and must not, be associated with second-rate health-care services.
- Task shifting must be implemented with systems containing checks and balances sufficient to protect both health workers and patients. This will involve both the presence of effective regulatory mechanisms, certification and remuneration of health workers who assume new/delegated tasks.

- Regulation and certification must neither decelerate the speed at which action is already taking place nor usher in restrictions that may have a constraining effect on others or future public health-service delivery effort.

As a stakeholder of the WHO and among countries already practising task shifting, albeit informally, Tanzania embarked on formalizing task shifting in the country. The process faced several challenges from various stakeholders having different vested interests. A qualitative assessment of task shifting for HIV services in Tanzania reported barriers to adoption, such as strong opposition from professional associations, legal hurdles, territorialism among cadres and pre-service training not matching the required competencies (Lunsford *et al.*, 2019). Other barriers included: inappropriate job descriptions; complex government functions and processes; political resistance; lack of legal protections; limited financial resources to roll out; lack of operational guidelines; and state autonomy. However, despite the challenges, Tanzania's government completed the formalization process and officially launched the task-sharing policy guideline for health sector services in Tanzania in 2016 (MOHCDGEC, 2016).

Among the successes of task shifting in Tanzania was the recruiting and training of non-professional members of the community, known as community health workers (CHWs), to provide health care by professionals conducting patient outreach, education and basic treatment (Arshad *et al.*, 2014). In addition, CHWs were used and were instrumental in supporting HIV treatment in Tanzania through a national programme called Community-Based HIV Services (Munga *et al.*, 2012). Under the arrangement, a cohort of volunteer CHWs is assigned to each care and treatment clinic (CTC) site. A designated nurse oversees the CHWs and maintains a schedule so that at least one CHW is on-site during all clinic hours. All persons initiating HIV care are informed of the CBHS programme, given the option to enrol and introduced to a CHW if they decide to opt in. The CHW maintains regular contact with the patient to provide ongoing education and support. CHWs in the CBHS programme are considered volunteers and receive a monthly stipend of 45,000 Tanzanian shillings (approximately USD 19.50) to assist with transportation and logistical costs associated with their role. With their use, the government managed to increase reach and access to HIV services and reduce the cost of maintaining patient contact, thus allowing for cost-efficient outreach to people living with HIV (PLWH) (Forsythe *et al.*, 2019).

Task shifting has also been instrumental in helping Tanzania address its inability to meet millennium development goals (MDGs) related to infant and maternal mortality. In the early 2010s, the Tanzanian Training Centre for International Health (TTCIH), in collaboration with St Francis Referral Hospital, developed a comprehensive emergency obstetrics care (CEmOC) course for AMOs (Sue *et al.*, 2016). Over three months, the course addressed how to differentiate between uncomplicated and complicated labour, determine the need for a Caesarean section and take care of select infant pathology. Participants also participated in newborn resuscitation, management of postpartum haemorrhage, normal caesarean sections and laparotomies for ectopic pregnancies. The centre also developed a complementary course for nurses/midwives, and COs on the most widely available and easy-to-use forms of anaesthesia, which was necessary for caesareans. During the first year of CEmOC, June 2009–2010, 45 participants performed 278 major obstetric surgeries and 1161 anaesthetic procedures. Their results align with other data showing that the performance of obstetric surgeries by non-physician clinicians, or AMOs, was comparable to the results of medical doctors. With funding from the World Lung Foundation, staff from many health centres in the Kigoma, Morogoro and Pwani districts had trained in CEmOC at TTCIH by 2014. As a result, maternal mortality rates decreased by 22% in Morogoro and 25% in Pwani.

3.5.2 Benjamin Mkapa Foundation and the Mkapa fellows programme

In addition to task sharing, several innovations have been attempted in order to address the human resource shortage in Tanzania. Another success story is the Mkapa Fellows Programme, run by the Benjamin Mkapa Foundation (BMF) (BMF, 2022). Under the arrangement, BMF, in

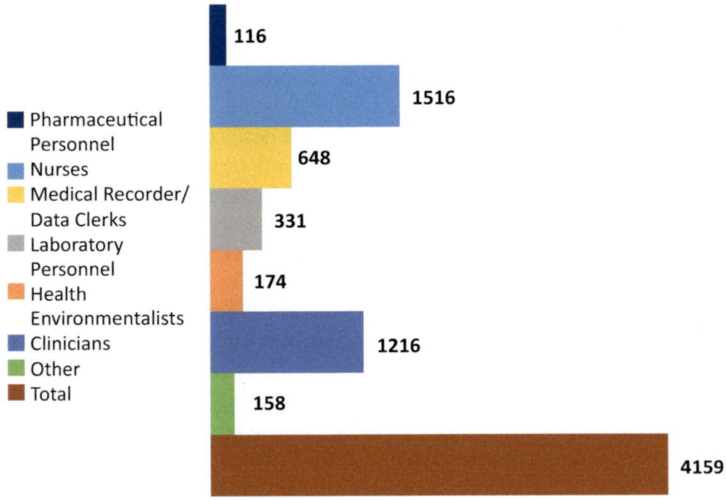

Fig. 3.10. Distribution of BMF-supported health-care workers by cadre (*N*=4159). (Copyright © Mkapa Foundation.)

collaboration with PO-RALG, is responsible for recruiting health-care workers and covering the employment cost for the first 3 years. The government then absorbs these workers. To facilitate the placement of workers, particularly in hard-to-reach areas, the BMF provides extra incentives, including staff housing and additional allowances.

Available data support the utility of the Mkapa Fellows Programme. For instance, from the programme's initiation in 2006 to 2021, the programme has recruited 10,041 health workers, including a total of 4159 facility-based health-care workers of different cadres placed at the facility level and 5882 community health workers placed in villages and at ward level (see Fig. 3.10).

One of the presumed important motivators for retention of these workers was the health infrastructure improvement, such as staff houses and good health-care facilities. Over the 16 years of its existence, BMF has been involved in constructing 482 in 268 health facilities in 17 regions. In addition, it has renovated four health-care facilities, built and equipped 13 operating theatres and created five maternity wards.

BMF has not only succeeded in health-care workers' recruitment and retention but has also been active in their continued education development. In collaboration with the Ministry of Health, BMF developed and enrolled an e-learning platform to assist with providing continuous learning education. As a result, 34,357 health-care workers have been trained through the system over the years, and 11,507 health-care workers are undertaking various training using the e-learning platform.

The BMF has also facilitated the development and reviews of various national documents for effective human resources for health management. They include the National Pay Incentive Policy (2012), the National Guideline for Developing Council Health Plans, the National Health Workforce for Volunteering Guideline and National Orientation Manual for newly recruited public servants (July 2017).

The BMF has also assisted in training, coaching and mentoring LGA health managers on effective planning, supervision and management of health workers. By 2021, the BMF had trained at least 4500 LGA health managers in more than 23 districts (BMF, 2022).

3.5.3 Volunteering scheme

The National Health Workforce for Volunteering Guideline has formalized a relatively new strategy, formalized after 2015, the Volunteering Scheme (MOHCDGEC, 2020). Several health workers had been working as volunteers, for example, the CHWs. Still, due to government policies of increased production of the skilled workforce, the country has produced more skilled health workers than its ability to recruit them. Also, the private sector in health care is not well established, with a limited capacity to absorb many graduates. To address this issue of supply–demand mismatch, in 2019 the government, in partnership with CSO, convened a meeting that spearheaded a new dialogue on HRH strategies and the planning of HRH. Among the key resolutions from that meeting was to establish a mechanism/framework for health graduates to volunteer in facilities with critical HRH shortages. The initiative aimed to address the HRH challenges partly while providing an opportunity for short-term on-the-job training in lifelong skills for a career as a health professional.

The National Health Sector Volunteering strategy is implemented at all levels of service delivery, including health training institutions. The levels include:

1. Hamlet level (community level).
2. Village level (dispensary level).
3. Ward level (health centre level).
4. District level (district hospital level).
5. Regional level (regional referral hospital level).
6. Zonal referral hospital and national level.
7. Health training institutions.

Public–private partnership in HRH

The history of engagement with private for-profit and private not-for-profit providers in Tanzania's health sector gained its due recognition following the implementation of health-sector reforms which were introduced in the 1990s. The organization and management relationship between the public and private sectors is gaining momentum in Tanzania. Several public–private partnership (PPP) arrangements exist concerning HRH's public–private partnership. This includes HRH in service delivery and training of human resources. Regarding service delivery, the secondment of government-employed staff to faith-based hospitals is one of the HRH interventions to improve access to skilled personnel in communities where government facilities do not exist. This arrangement is prominent in district designated hospitals at the primary care level and tertiary services. PPP arrangements also exist in the area of training. Faith-based organizations (FBOs) were more active in training middle-level cadres and nurses from the 1960s to the 1990s, and progression to higher learning is now prominent. In such instances, contracts have been managed within short-term parameters, with the government continuing the payment of salaries. Critical issues, such as welfare benefits and related entitlement and tenure, are often not clearly defined.

Furthermore, the government provides grants in aid to FBOs on a contractual basis to support the running of the health facilities and training institutions depending on the priority needs. The existing partnership between government and non-governmental institutions is inadequate to harness the potential of existing non-governmental institutions in the country. The primary health-care cadre training was regulated through government mechanisms.

3.5.4 Accredited drug-dispensing outlets and human resource challenge

Shops selling medicines have always been principal players in promoting access to medicines in low- and middle-income countries, including Tanzania. For example, statistics show that caretakers' use of retail drug outlets for child health ranged from 15 to 82%, with a median of around 50%. In addition to increasing access to medicines, these shops have generally acted as the first entrance into primary health care, particularly for the poorest in these regions. In Tanzania, before 2003, shops selling medicines, commonly referred to as *duka la dawa baridi*, constituted the largest network of licensed outlets for basic essential medicines in Tanzania and catered for the largest segment of the population, especially in rural areas (Rutta *et al.*, 2012).

Despite their popularity and potential, medicine shops are not considered part of the more extensive health system and are mostly missing from countries' health strategies, policies and monitoring. Also, these drug outlets are associated with problems that include:

- questionable medicine quality;
- inadequate storage of medicines;
- untrained staff;
- inadequate regulatory enforcement and supervision;
- authorization to sell only a limited list of over-the-counter medicines; and
- illegal dispensing of prescription medicines.

Recognizing the need for access to good quality medicines and the already key role played by these outlets, the Tanzania Food and Drugs Authority (TFDA) and Management Sciences for Health designed the accredited drug-dispensing outlet (ADDO) programme to address these problems. The programme aimed to improve access to affordable, quality medicines and pharmaceutical services in retail drug outlets in rural or peri-urban areas with few or no registered pharmacies. Also, the programme offered an opportunity to train a new cadre of health workers. Dispensers, as they became known, would provide relief by increasing access to medicine and serving as a platform for community-based public health interventions. For example, a child-health training module for dispensers is based on the integrated management of childhood illness initiative. It includes danger signs of pneumonia in children and the appropriate action – co-trimoxazole treatment or referral – depending on the situation. Other programmes that have been integrated include tuberculosis case identification and referrals, distribution of subsidised artemisinin-based combination therapies and knowledge and control of antimicrobial resistance.

Although many interventions targeting retail medicine sellers have been carried out in Africa and Asia, they have usually focused on training or other capacity-building activities. They have often been limited to a particular concern, such as malaria or child health. ADDO was different in that it took a comprehensive approach to address public- and private-sector issues as well as consumer demand by:

- developing accreditation based on government instituted standards and regulations;
- creating a public-sector-based regulatory and inspection system and strengthening local regulatory processes and capacity; and
- developing drug shop owners' business skills.

Providing ADDO owners with business incentives, such as access to microfinancing and legal authorization to sell a limited list of essential prescription medicines, including some antimicrobials.

ADDO dispenser curriculum topics

- Laws, regulations and ethics
- Good dispensing practices and rational medicines use
- Common medical conditions in the community
- Reproductive health and HIV/AIDS
- Communication skills and counselling
- Child health
- Record-keeping
- Some antimicrobials
- Facilitating access to convenient and reliable sources of quality medicines
- Changing the behaviour of dispensing staff through training and supervision
- Improving awareness of customers regarding quality and the importance of treatment compliance through marketing and public education

As a result, the ADDO programme not only fills a human resource niche in the health system but can also be a career pathway for dispensers. Indeed, in a survey of owners' views of the ADDO programme, dispenser training was ranked as the most highly valued programme benefit. Due to ADDO implementation, Tanzania has over 20,000 dispensers trained with government-approved curricula. This equates to approximately 43 trained personnel per 100,000 population.

Also, ADDO had a significant impact on women, mainly rural women who have few employment options. By the time the last region was rolled out in mid-2013, approximately 90% of ADDO dispensers and 39% of ADDO owners were women. This programme, therefore, provides a unique opportunity for many women to supplement their family's income, while at the same time taking on a leadership role within their community.

3.5.5 Workload indicator of staffing needs and prioritization and optimization analysis (POA)

An important HR management innovation is the use of digital tools for improved health-workforce management. The tools include the workload indicator of staffing needs (WISN) and the prioritization and optimization analysis (POA) (Sukums, 2017). The WISN is a human-resource-management and planning tool that assesses the workload by analysing the service delivery data (e.g. outpatient department attendance) vs available health-care workers. In addition, the system is configured to consider other parameters, for example, the proposed number of clients to be seen by a specific provider in each department. Combining this information, WISN then computes the demand and provides recommendations for the optimal number of the health workforce in the facility.

Although WISN provided information on the need, there remained a challenge with placement prioritization since many facilities may report needs. Therefore, to mitigate this, the Tanzanian government, in association with developmental partners, developed POA, leveraging WISN output to support data-driven HRH planning in Tanzania. POA integrates demand information from WISN with the available slots provided by the Public Office Private Service Management to suggest allocation with the optimal mix of cadres.

Community health workers

A community health worker (CHW) is a health worker who is selected by, belongs to, is trained in and is answerable to the community s/he works in under the support of the health system, and receives less training than formally trained health workers. Thus, they are embedded in the formal health systems and the communities they serve and can be considered boundary spanners between community and formal health systems. CHWs are enormously diverse in roles and activities, which often exist between and across programmes. Regardless of the typology, CHWs usually carry out one or more functions related to health-care delivery and are often trained in some way for the intervention they are expected to perform. The importance of CHWs was reiterated in the Alma-Ata Declaration of 1978, which advised that health systems consider community participation as a core principle in managing primary health care and established CHWs as essential elements of a comprehensive primary health-care approach. Numerous works of the literature suggest that CHWs can make a valuable contribution to community development, specifically through improving access to and coverage of communities with essential health services. There is robust evidence that actions undertaken by CHWs can lead to improving health outcomes in many areas, such as improving child nutrition, reducing maternal and neonatal mortality, increasing child immunization uptake, expanding family planning access, and contributing to the control of HIV, tuberculosis and malaria. However, for CHWs to be able to make an effective contribution, they must be carefully selected, trained and, more importantly, governed.

HISTORY. In Tanzania, the concept of community health workers started as far back as the 1960s with the introduction of village health workers (VHWs). The introduction of the VHWs aimed to extend services to remote rural areas. This followed the decision made by the government to strengthen primary health care and to know that it would not be realistic for all villages to have dispensaries. The VHWs worked voluntarily for many years, and the available local government system partly remunerated some places. However, with the growth of the health-facility networks, the majority of the VHWs found themselves working as assistants to the facility-based providers and being remunerated by vertical programmes.

In the late 1990s and early 2000s, research evidence from other places showed that community health-based programmes were more appropriate for reducing maternal and under-fives mortality, hence there was a need to reinvent community-based health workers. With the Primary Health Services Development Programme in 2007–2017 that aimed at establishing a dispensary in every village and a health centre at every ward, Tanzania embarked on the establishment of a new cadre, community health workers (CHWs),

Case study: Task sharing – the utilization of medical students in cholera outbreak control in Bagamoyo (personal experience recalled by Dr Elihuruma Nangawe)

In the 1970s the Faculty of Medicine of the University of Dar es Salaam established a community medicine field-training exposure facility at the Bagamoyo Teaching Unit (BTU) adjacent to the district hospital in Bagamoyo. During the fourth-year rotation for Community Medicine staying at the BTU in 1978, I recall we were mobilized to visit a site from where cases of cholera had occurred and undertake specific tasks aimed at bringing the outbreak under control, guided by expert supervision of Dr Eric van Praag (The Community Medicine faculty member heading the BTU based at Bagamoyo). We went to Kidogozero village, which was a remote place along the banks of the Ruvu River where many households were only reachable by boat (canoes made out of trees), and took samples from a number of household contacts of cases that had been detected as infected with cholera. Simultaneous with taking samples, we carried out health education of groups of households on recognition of the disease, administering plenty of oral fluids as cases awaited IV drips to be administered by health staff to avert severe dehydration eventuality and carrying out disinfection of all discharge from the patients (vomitus, diarrhoea), and spreading the message of boiling all drinking water, washing eating utensils with boiled water, washing hands with soap and water after using latrines and eating food that is served hot (avoiding cold and left-over foods). We made sure all households had received the control measures and every household had a latrine available and been used so as to avoid indiscriminate defecation. The impact of applying these measures at the village was the curtailment of the long distances that new cases would be undertaking to reach the nearest health facility: in other words we set up a makeshift cholera treatment post in the field (at a suitable shed in the village) and administered the case management on site, while others went house to house to deliver education on prevention measures.

Later, when I graduated and started medical practice at Selian Hospital in Arusha, it was relatively easy for me to establish field-treatment sites for cholera control and house-to-house education on strict personal hygiene, food and water safety measures, as well as sanitation (safe disposal of excreta) in all affected neighbourhoods when I encountered an outbreak in catchment-area villages. I simply recalled what I learnt at Kidogozero village in Bagamoyo and applied it, resulting in effectively controlling the outbreak through local leaders' involvement and participation at Selian in 1982. I did not have the privilege of students at Selian, but maximized cooperation of village leaders, faith leaders and some support from the district medical officer for Arumeru. The experience reinforced the relevance and ease with which we introduced selection and training of CHWs at Selian and other Maasai health project sites.

The key observation here is the rapid coverage and reach of all households within a very short time-span (at Kidogozero done within the span of two days, at Selian villages were covered within four days) helped to cut transmission more rapidly and attain control within a week of starting field operationalization. Measures were low-cost and effective due to optimizing resources (human, materials/medicines, time) efficiently, underscoring a lesson that students involved at Kidogozero and local community-resource persons involved at Selian demonstrated the yield of an inclusive participatory approach.

who will act as a link between the community and health facilities.

Apart from doing other roles in primary health care, the introduction of CHWs was expected to contribute to the efforts of reducing maternal and under-fives mortality. Community health workers in Tanzania are trained in family planning services and home-based life-saving skills to educate communities on the danger signs, birth preparedness and complication readiness regarding childbirth. By doing this role properly, it is expected that they will help in reducing the delay of care-seeking, timely referral to health facilities and good postpartum care. (For more on community health workers, please see Chapter 8 on community health systems.)

Acknowledgements

The authors also thank Professor Marcel Tanner and Don de Savigny, who took time out of their busy schedules to read our work and provide valuable input. In addition, we acknowledge the personal stories as told by Dr Harun Kasale, which have greatly enriched our chapter and PHC team members who critiqued our work. Finally, we are most grateful to the following institutions: Muhimbili University of Health and Allied Sciences, National Institute of Medical Research, Ministry of Health, President's Office - Regional Administration and Local Governments and Mzumbe University for providing their experts for working with us in writing of the book.

Conflict of interest: The authors declare that they have no competing interests.

Bibliography

Arshad, A., Salam, R.A., Lassi, Z.S., Das, J.K., Naqvi, I. *et al.* (2014) Community based interventions for the prevention and control of tuberculosis. *Infectious Diseases of Poverty* 3(1), 1–10. DOI: 10.1186/2049-9957-3-27.

Balandya, E., Hyuha, G., Mtaya, M., Otieno, J., Sunguya, B. *et al.* (2022) Advances in training of the specialized human resources for health in Tanzania: the case of Muhimbili University of Health and Allied Sciences. *BMC Medical Education* 22(1), 1–10. DOI: 10.1186/s12909-022-03102-6.

Bech, M.M., Lawi, Y.Q., Massay, D.A. and Rekdal, O.B. (2013) Changing policies and their influence on government health workers in Tanzania, 1967–2009: perspectives from rural Mbulu district. *The International Journal of African Historical Studies* 46(1), 61–103.

Beck, A. (1977) Medicine and society in Tanganyika, 1890–1930; a historical inquiry. *Transactions of the American Philosophical Society* 67(3), 1. DOI: 10.2307/1006330.

BMF (2022) *MKAPA Foundation Profile 2022: For a Healthier, More Prosperous, Inclusive and Resilient Society*. Benjamin Mkapa Foundation, Dar es Salaam, Tanzania. Available at: https://mkapafoundation.or.tz/mkapa-foundation-about-us/ (accessed 15 May 2023).

Bruchhausen, W. (2016) From precondition to goal of development: health and medicine in the planning and politics of British Tanganyika. In: Hodge, J.M., Hödl, G. and Kopf, M. (eds) *Developing Africa*. Manchester, Manchester University Press, UK, pp. 207–221. DOI: 10.7228/manchester/9780719091803.001.0001.

Forsythe, S., Lee, B., Tarimo, K., Silvan, B., Balampama, M. *et al.* (2019) HIV treatment support services in Tanzania: a cost and efficiency analysis at facility and community levels. *African Journal of AIDS Research* 18(4), 306–314. DOI: 10.2989/16085906.2019.1676805.

Gilson, L. and Mills, A. (1995) Health sector reforms in sub-Saharan Africa: lessons of the last 10 years. *Health Policy* 32(1–3), 215–243. DOI: 10.1016/0168-8510(95)00737-d.

Gottlich, H.C. (2018) *Colonialism and the development of the Tanzanian health system*. Thesis, Baylor University, USA.

Guilbert, J.-J. (2006) The World Health Report 2006: working together for health. *Education for Health (Abingdon, England)* 19(3), 385–387. DOI: 10.1080/13576280600937911.

Hermann, K., Van Damme, W., Pariyo, G.W., Schouten, E., Assefa, Y. *et al.* (2009) Community health workers for ART in sub-Saharan Africa: learning from experience--capitalizing on new opportunities. *Human Resources for Health* 7(1), 1–11. DOI: 10.1186/1478-4491-7-31.

Kwesigabo, G., Mwangu, M.A., Kakoko, D.C., Warriner, I., Mkony, C.A. *et al.* (2012) Tanzania's health system and workforce crisis. *Journal of Public Health Policy* 33(1), S35–S44. DOI: 10.1057/jphp.2012.55.

Lunsford, S., Broughton, L.E. and Fatta, K. (2019) *Task Shifting/Sharing for HIV Services in 26 PEPFAR-Supported Countries: A Qualitative Assessment*. USAID, Chevy Chase, Maryland. Available at: www.usaidassist.org (accessed 15 May 2023).

Maluka, S., Chitama, D., Dungumaro, E., Masawe, C., Rao, K. *et al.* (2018) Contracting-out primary health care services in Tanzania towards UHC: how policy processes and context influence policy design and implementation. *International Journal for Equity in Health* 17(1), 1–13. DOI: 10.1186/s12939-018-0835-8.

Manongi, R.N., Marchant, T.C. and Bygbjerg, I.C. (2006) Improving motivation among primary health care workers in Tanzania: a health worker perspective. *Human Resources for Health* 4, 6. DOI: 10.1186/1478-4491-4-6.
Mbilinyi, C., Buma, D., Ngasa, S, *et al*. (2021) Advancing pharmacy practice in Tanzania: a descriptive report of pharmacy education and practice models in 3 institutions. *Journal of Health Care Organization, Provision, and Financing*. Published online 2021. DOI: 10.1177/0046958021999934.
McKinsey & Company (2004) *Acting Now to Overcome Tanzania's Greatest Health Challenge* (pdf). McKinsey & Company, New York.
Mkony, C.A. (2012) Emergence of a university of health sciences: health professions education in Tanzania. *Journal of Public Health Policy* 33(1), S45–S63. DOI: 10.1057/jphp.2012.51.
MOHCDGEC (2016) *Task Sharing Policy Guidelines for Health Sector Services in Tanzania (March)*. MOHCDGEC, Dar es Salaam, Tanzania.
MOHCDGEC (2019) *Staffing Levels for Ministry of Health and Social Welfare Departments, Health Service Facilities, Health Training Institutions and Agencies 2014–2019*. Ministry of Health and Social Welfare, Dar es Salaam, Tanzania.
MOHCDGEC (2020) *National Health Workforce Volunteering Guideline*. MOHCDGEC, Dar es Salaam, Tanzania.
MOHSW (2008) *Human Resource for Health Strategic Plan 2008–2013*. MOHSW, Dar es Salaam, Tanzania.
MOHSW (2009) *Assessment of the Pharmaceutical Human Resources in Tanzania and the Strategic Framework*. MOHSW, Dar es Salaam, Tanzania.
MOHSW (2013) *Mid Term Review of the Health Sector Strategic Plan III 2009–2015, Main Report*. World Health Group 59(Oct.). Ministry of Health, Dar es Salaam, Tanzania.
Mubyazi, G.M., Mushi, A., Kamugisha, M., Massaga, J., Mdira, K.Y. *et al*. (2007) Community views on health sector reform and their participation in health priority setting: case of Lushoto and Muheza districts, Tanzania. *Journal of Public Health* 29(2), 147–156. DOI: 10.1093/pubmed/fdm016.
Mujinja, P.G.M. and Kida, T.M. (2014) *Implications of Health Sector Reforms in Tanzania: Policies, Indicators and Accessibility to Health Services*. Economic and Social Research Foundation, Dar es Salaam, Tanzania.
Munga, M.A., Kilima, S.P., Mutalemwa, P.P., Kisoka, W.J. and Malecela, M.N. (2012) Experiences, opportunities and challenges of implementing task shifting in underserved remote settings: the case of Kongwa district, central Tanzania. *BMC International Health and Human Rights* 12(1), 1–12. DOI: 10.1186/1472-698X-12-27.
NEC CCM (2015) *Ilani ya CCM kwa ajili ya Uchaguzi Mkuu wa Mwaka 2015*. Available at: https://temco.udsm.ac.tz/images/stories/Election_Manifesto/ILANI_CCM_2015.pdf (accessed 19 May 2023).
Rutta, A.S.M., Francis, F., Mmbando, B.P., Ishengoma, D.S., Sembuche, S.H. *et al*. (2012) Using community-owned resource persons to provide early diagnosis and treatment and estimate malaria burden at community level in north-eastern Tanzania. *Malaria Journal* 11(May), 152. DOI: 10.1186/1475-2875-11-152.
Sirili, N. (2018) *Health workforce development post-1990s health sector reforms: the case of medical doctors in Tanzania*. PhD thesis, Umeå Universitet, Sweden.
Sirili, N., Kiwara, A., Gasto, F., Goicolea, I. and Hurtig, A.-K. (2017) Training and deployment of medical doctors in Tanzania post-1990s health sector reforms: assessing the achievements. *Human Resources for Health* 15(1), 1–12. DOI: 10.1186/s12960-017-0202-7.
Sousa, A., Scheffler, R.M., Nyoni, J. and Boerma, T. (2013) A comprehensive health labour market framework for universal health coverage. *Bulletin of the World Health Organization* 91(11), 892–894. DOI: 10.2471/BLT.13.118927.
Sue, K., Rosenberg, J., Weintraub, R., Goldsmith, J., Madore, M. *et al*. (2016) *Addressing Tanzania's Health Workforce Crisis through a Public–Private Partnership: The Case of TTCIH*. Cases Global Health Delivery Project. Harvard Business Publishing, Cambridge, Massachusetts, pp. 1–34.
Sukums, F. (2017) WISN + POA software capabilities map key user: LGAs key user. Unpublished report.
Titmuss, R.M. (1964) *The Health Services of Tanganyika: A Report to the Government*. Pitman Medical Publishing Company, London.
UDSM (2011) *Facts and Figures 2011/12–2016/17*. University of Dar es Salaam.
URT (2020) *United Republic of Tanzania National Human Resources for Health Strategy for 2020–2025 November 2020 (November)*. United Republic of Tanzania, Dodoma.
Waite, G. (1987) Public health in pre-colonial east-central Africa. *Social Science & Medicine* 24(3), 197–208.

WHO (2008) *Task Shifting Global Recommendations and Guidelines HIV/AIDS*. World Health Organization, Geneva, Switzerland.
Young, T.K. (1986) Socialist development and primary health care: the case of Tanzania. *Human Organization* 45(2), 128–134. DOI: 10.17730/humo.45.2.17p75666m4347g14.

Appendix: Organization of the Tanzanian Health System

In commitment to increasing health-care services to the rural population, following the transition of power from the British, Tanzania developed a multitier decentralized health system with a local first point of contact in the villages to increasingly specialized, more central facilities (Fig. A1). In this system, health-care services were divided into primary and hospital care, a system which continues to the present day.

Primary care includes community health posts, dispensaries, health centres and district-level services. Most village governments employ two or more health workers (one male and one female), known as village health workers (VHW). After a short training of three to six months, VHWs are expected to run a community health post, providing health education and care for minor ailments to families in their communities. Staff at the next level of referral, the dispensary, supervise the VHWs. Dispensaries are run by a clinical assistant aided by an enrolled nurse and cater for a population of between 6,000 and 10,000 people. They provide basic maternal and child health care, among others.

Supervising the dispensaries are health centres that serve populations of about 50,000. Clinical officers run health centres supported by enrolled nurses. In addition to preventive care, health centres provide reproductive health services and minor surgery.

Hospital care: As of 2021, there were 184 districts in Tanzania with populations ranging from 1.6 million people in Kinondoni to 50,634 in the sparsely populated district of Mafia. Most districts have government-run district hospitals, and a few rely on religious organizations to sponsor non-governmental hospitals to become designated district hospitals. The designated district hospitals, in turn, receive government incentives, including subsidies and other benefits. District hospitals offer outpatient and inpatient services not available at the health centre. Medical doctors, along with nursing officers, serve at this level.

Serving the region (collection of districts, ranging from three to eight) is the regional hospital. The regional hospital offers more specialized services and often features medical and surgical

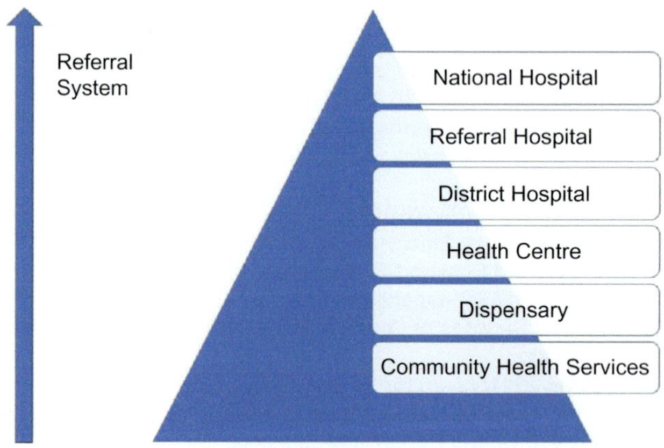

Fig. A1. Health-care organization in the United Republic of Tanzania. (From Maluka *et al.*, 2018.)

specialists. Above the regional hospitals are the national and specialized hospitals which provide referral health services and are also used as teaching hospitals. The staffing level for the health-care facilities has since been updated, with medical doctors now staffing the health-care centres and above. Table A1 shows the key health cadres' roles in Tanzania over the years.

Table A1. Key health cadres and their roles in Tanzania over the years.

Cadre	Period				
Roles and placement	1961–1967	1967–1980	1980–2006	2007–2021	2022–present
Medical doctors	Few in number Placed mainly in regional and tertiary hospitals	Increased in number following output from UDSM Slow reallocation to district hospitals	Increase in number of specialist and super-specialist medical doctors Specialist medical doctors allocated to tertiary and a few regional hospitals	Increased cadres and number of medical super-specialists Establishment of specialized hospitals, e.g. Jakaya Kikwete Cardiac Institute Medical doctors start manning health centres Health centres begin providing EmONc services	Reallocation of medical specialists to district hospitals
Assistant medical officers	The first medical cadre to provide EmONc Man district and regional hospitals	Increase in the number of training schools and, ultimately, number of AMOs	AMO specialization Increase in number of training centres for AMOs to five		
Dental officers	Assistant dental officers, who were upgraded from clinical officers, mostly placed at zonal hospitals and a few at regional hospitals	Return of dentists who had trained abroad Dentists mostly placed at tertiary hospitals	Establishment of dental training school Production of dental officers A few districts now have assistant dental officers	Increased production of dental officers Recruitment has dwindled	

Cadre	Period				
Roles and placement	1961–1967	1967–1980	1980–2006	2007–2021	2022–present
Nursing	Trained nurse and nurse midwife (certificate), mainly at district hospitals Registered nurses (diploma holders), mainly located at regional and tertiary hospitals	Specialization among trained and registered nurses in ENT, theatre and the like	Establishment of the nursing training school at Muhimbili		
Laboratory scientists	Laboratory assistant (certificate), mainly at district and lower levels	Production of laboratory technicians Laboratory technicians (diploma) manned district and regions	Production of laboratory technicians Laboratory technicians (diploma) manned district and regions	Production of laboratory scientist (degree holder)	
Pharmacy	Compounders who received short training course at the Central Medical Stores Mostly handled by other cadres (nurses, laboratory assistants) Start of the pharmacy diploma	Less than four pharmacists, who were trained abroad The start of the school of pharmacy degree course No pharmacist at the district level Pharmacy technicians placed mainly at regional hospitals and a few at the district level	Pharmacy technicians still manned district hospitals Pharmacists mainly manned regional hospitals and above Pharmacists' migration to private facilities	Pharmacists now placed at district level in large numbers	Increased production, although the uptake in the public sector has remained low
Physiotherapists					Reduced
Public health nurses					
Health promotion officers					
Health officers					

EmONc: Emergency Obstetric and Newborn care

The council health management team (CHMT) coordinates health-care services at the district level, including preventive, curative, rehabilitative, supervision and health promotion services. It comprises eight core members, including the district medical officer (leader), nursing officer, district health secretary and pharmacist. In addition, the CHMT has the mandate to add members, commonly referred to as co-opted members, as the need arises. The regional health management team (RHMT), led by the regional medical officer, performs a similar function at the regional level.

Public health programmes are led nationally by the MOHSW, frequently as vertical programmes, for example, the national AIDS control programme, reproductive and child health programme, TB and leprosy control programme, school health programme, and several others.

4 Primary Health-Care Financing and Resource Mobilization

Gemini J. Mtei[1]*, George M. Ruhago[2], Frida N. Ngalesoni[3], Ntuli A. Kapologwe[4,5], Maximillian Kassian Kazibure Mapunda[6] and Albino Kalolo[7]
[1]Abt Associates, Tanzania Public Sector Systems Strengthening Plus (PS3+) Project, Dar es Salaam, Tanzania; [2]Department of Development Studies, School of Public Health and Social Sciences, Muhimbili University of Health and Allied Sciences, Dar es Salaam, Tanzania; [3]Amref Health Africa, Dar es Salaam, Tanzania; [4]President's Office - Regional Administration and Local Government, Dodoma, Tanzania; [5]University of Dodoma, Tanzania; [6]World Health Organization, Dar es Salaam, Tanzania; [7]Department of Public Health, St Francis University College of Health and Allied Sciences, Ifakara, Tanzania

Abstract
Tanzania has been implementing health-financing reforms since independence, with the objective of increasing financial resources allocated for primary health care (PHC). Improvements have been made in planning, budgeting and financial allocation to increase efficiency by ensuring that available resources are used to delivery priority services. The introduction of DHFF and extension of core PFM systems to frontline PHC service providers are key steps towards the alignment between health-financing systems and core PFM systems. DHFF has improved predictability of funds availability and increased PHC provider autonomy to prioritize service delivery according to population needs. Moving forward, government reforms in health financing needs to focus more on expanding population coverage through prepayment schemes and adopt more strategic provider-payment mechanisms in existing public health insurance schemes and general government budget allocation.

4.0 Introduction

Tanzania's health-financing system is decentralized, mainly tax-based and funded through general government revenue collection, development partner support, pre-payment schemes, including social health insurance, private health insurance, the community health fund and direct out-of-pocket payments at the point of accessing services. Post-independence the government committed itself to providing free health services in all government health facilities and prohibited private practice (Jonsson, 1986; Kapologwe *et al.*, 2019). During the 1990s, health-financing reform was initiated in Tanzania, and the government introduced user fees for health-care services, following the World Bank and IMF Structural Adjustment Programs (SAP) policy. The reforms were expected to be a major catalyst in changing health-sector financing. However, the reforms did not reach the desired goal of increasing

*Corresponding author: gemini.mtei@googlemail.com

 Primary Health Care in Tanzania through a Health Systems Lens (eds N.A. Kapologwe *et al.*)
DOI: 10.1079/9781800623330.0004

funding for health services in Tanzania, rather there were increased inequalities and fragmentation in health-services delivery (Lugalla, 1995).

The government responded to the aftermath of the structural adjustment programme by strengthening health financing in Tanzania in the late 1990s and 2000s through the establishment of social health insurance, the National Health Insurance Fund (NHIF) for employees in the formal sector, improved Community Health Fund (iCHF) for the informal sector, insurance for workers in the urban informal sector (TIKA) and private insurance (Amu *et al.*, 2018).

This chapter provides a comprehensive account of the history of the health-financing reforms in Tanzania from the pre-independence period to the present day, focusing on the struggle endured in financing primary health care (PHC). The chapter further underlines the lessons learnt over time and the outlook of primary health-care financing in Tanzania.

4.1 Evolution of Health-Care Financing Reforms in Tanzania

The history of the struggle to finance primary health care in Tanzania is viewed through the reforms that took place at different periods in time, starting from the pre-independence period to the present day. Here we describe the reforms and their context in the struggle to improve primary health-care financing. A summary of the chronology of the reforms in PHC financing is presented in Fig. 4.1.

4.1.1 Primary health-care financing during the pre-colonial period, before 1880

Information on primary health-care financing during the period before the German and British colonization is scant. As in other African countries, this period is characterized by the existence

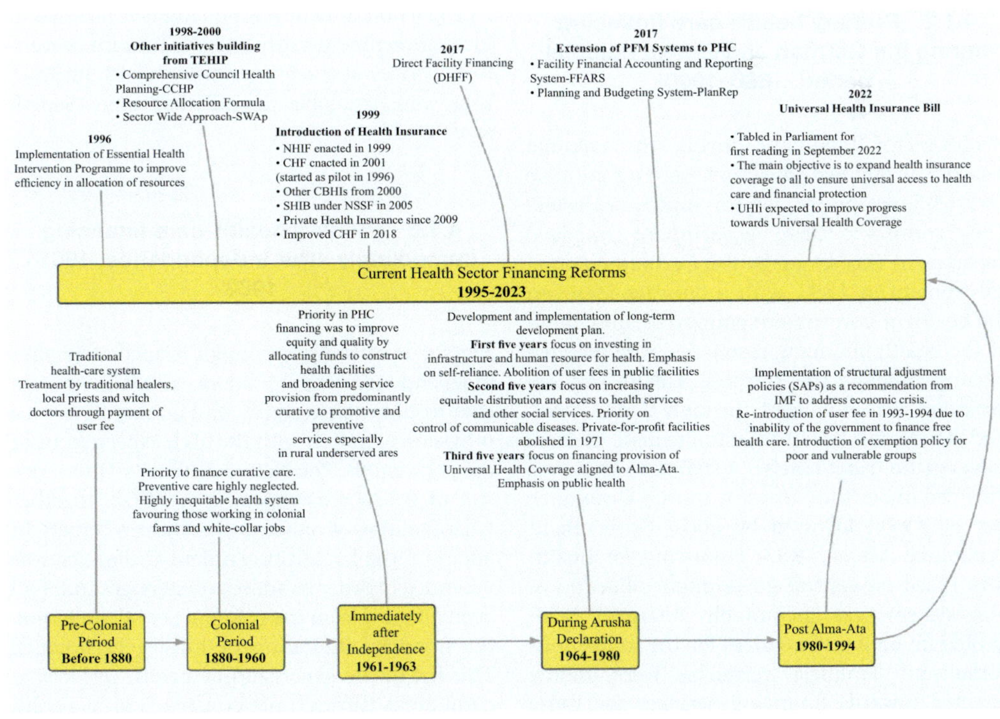

Fig. 4.1. Chronology of primary health-care financing reforms in Tanzania.

of a traditional health-care system documented to be one of the oldest and most diverse of all medicine systems (Mahomoodally, 2013). The traditional health-care system was organized around three core functions namely: (i) local healing using herbs and traditional remedies, (ii) religious healing whereby traditional religious practitioners (local priests) played a key role and (iii) the witch doctor or sorcerer who could either prevent people from experiencing illness (illness was conceived as invasion by evil spirits) or inflicting diseases or misfortunes on others for various reasons. During this time, patients paid user fees to traditional medical practitioners in terms of materials in the form of barter trade. Materials that had some monetary function were exchanged for health services, and these varied across tribes and included hoes, salt, cattle, goats, metal and labour (McCarthy, 1976). Moreover, healers offered alternatives payments whereby patients could compensate in kind or in work; and there was a possibility of payment on a credit basis.

4.1.2 Primary health-care financing during the German and British colonial period, 1880–1960

Health-sector financing during the colonial period was inclined towards financing curative care, while preventive care was mostly neglected. The country's first government medical department was set up by the German colonial government in 1891 with a curative focus on the health of government employees, and much of the health financing resources were directed towards fulfilling this purpose. Health-services provision was managed through a decentralized structure under the management of local leaders (the tribal chiefs), a structure that was provided under the Native Authority Ordinance Act of 1926, followed by Local Government Ordinance Act of 1953. Financing for health care relied on central government allocations. The system was inequitably financed, with limited financing of services for the indigenous community. Financial resources were mainly directed towards financing services for those serving the colonial economy in the farms or in white-collar jobs who lived in urban areas, while majority of the population, about 95% of whom lived in rural areas, were left with little or no health services (van Etten and Raikes, 1975; Mbilinyi, 1985; Semali *et al.*, 2007). Investment for health infrastructure and skilled personnel was also concentrated in urban areas, while rural localities were left underserved. The inequity in financing health-care services during this period were validated by German colonial secretary Bernard Dernburg, who wrote,

> A system of medical care for the blacks, even in the government sector of the medical services, does not yet exist. The introduction of such a system is our goal although the means to secure it will probably surpass the present capability of the protectorate. (Beck, 1977)

In the mid-1920s, the British administration introduced the dispensary system, which improved access to medical services in rural areas. However, management of rural health services was a legal mandate of the local authorities which by then did not have sufficient financial resources and the central government retained the management of service provision in other areas. A few years towards independence, a proportion of health financing was directed to local government authorities to finance preventive services at the few primary health facilities that were available during that time (Semali *et al.*, 2007).

4.1.3 Primary health-care financing immediately after independence, 1961–1963

The focus of the government immediately after independence was to adopt a health system that would ensure equity and quality in service provision to match with the high expectations of the population. The Native Authority Ordinance Act of 1926 was repealed in 1962, together with abolition of native authorities and chiefs. In addition, the Local Government Ordinance was amended in order to address challenges that had been adopted from the colonial period, including the financial limitation of local governments. This led to the expansion of health services to rural areas through the construction of health facilities and broadening services from predominantly curative to promotive and preventive services. These investments were funded using grants, credits, development aid and taxation. Most of these developments were reflected in the national development plans and implemented though the Ministry of Health annual plan and budget. Free health care was introduced in 1961 in an attempt to ensure equitable access to health care to all individuals (Kopoka, 2000; Mubyazi *et al.*, 2006). User fees, which existed during the colonial period, were abolished in all public health-care facilities and all health services were funded through general taxation.

4.1.4 Primary health-care financing during the Arusha declaration period, 1964–1980

The government developed the long-term perspective development plan to be implemented for the period 1964–1980. This long-term development plan was adopted to address challenges that were inherited from colonial structures during the early years of independence and it was used to guide investment in priority areas such as health (Semali *et al.*, 2007). These challenges included the inability of local governments to finance the rapidly expanding health services due to the limited revenue collection base and limited central government financial resources to subsidizing health-care financing across local governments. There was increasing investment in the construction of health infrastructure, including health centres, dispensaries and public toilets, through support from different sources, including through community support, but the local governments did not have the ability to maintain and keep them running. The long-term plan was executed through three consecutive five-year development plans.

Health financing in the first five-year development plan (1964 to 1969) was focused on investing in infrastructure and human resource for health, and the aim was to establish a regional hospital in each region, build 300 health centres to serve about 50,000 people each and supervise about eight dispensaries. Consequently, there was a need to increase enrolment of health-care workers and introduce new cadres to cater for the large demand of health-care workers (MOHSW, 1990). Administration was decentralized to districts which were given the mandate to collect tax revenue and finance provision of health services (PO-RALG, 2018b). Further, the Arusha Declaration was adopted in 1967, which insisted on self-reliance as a mechanism to ensure sustainable provision of public services, including health. The Arusha Declaration called for home-grown solutions to increase revenue space so as to provide adequate health services to all and reduce dependency on donor financing (TANU, 1967). During this period the average government health expenditure as a percentage of the total government expenditure was around 6.4%, ranging from 5.2 to 8.9% (Fig. 4.2).

The second five-year development plan was implemented from 1969 to 1974, with the aim of increasing equitable distribution and access to health services and other social services while emphasizing the control of communicable diseases. During this period the aim was also to complete some of the unfinished agenda of having a health centre for every 50,000 people and dispensary for every 10,000 people, with the government health expenditure targeted on this. During this period, private for-profit health-service provision was abolished in 1971 and user fees at voluntary/faith-based facilities were kept at a minimum (Kopoka, 2000) as a way of improving equity in access to health care. Services in public facilities continued to be provided free through general tax financing.

The third five-year development plan (1976 to 1981) intended to provide clean water and to establish universal health services. This plan was landmark in implementing the primary health care following the Alma-Ata Declaration in 1978, with a goal of health for all by 2000 (WHO, 2002). The objective of providing clean water signalled a focus on preventive medicine with huge health education campaigns such as ‘Mtu ni afya’ (Man Is Health), that emphasized maintaining personal hygiene and environmental sanitation as an approach to combat communicable diseases (Biermann and Wagao, 1986; Ngowi, 2009).

The implementation of third five-year development plan was heavily financed by foreign aid, which greatly increased the effectiveness of the annual health budget. Over 70% of the health development section of the 1973–1974 budget was derived from bilateral and multilateral aid,

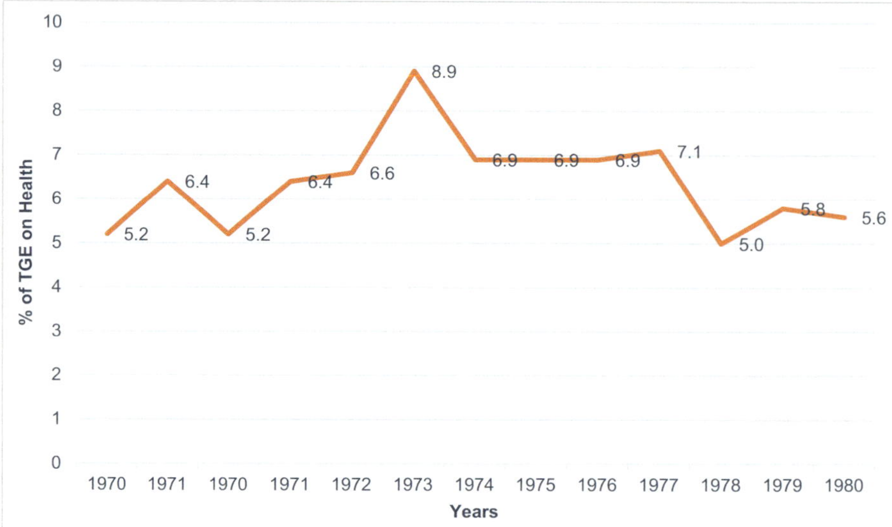

Fig. 4.2. Trend of government health expenditure as a % of total government expenditure (TGE) 1970–1980. (From Jonsson, 1986).

which saw support in the construction of dispensaries, rural health centres and schools for medical auxiliaries. Foreign aid was taken as a catalyst to speed up development, while building self-reliance (Chagula and Tarimo, 1975).

4.1.5 Primary health-care financing after the Alma-Ata declaration, 1980–1994

The period of the 1980s to the 1990s was characterized by a global economic crisis that led to the country adopting the structural adjustment policies (SAP) imposed by the International Monetary Fund. Countries globally were not able to provide free social services, including education and health, through government financing due to escalating health-care costs, limited government funds and increasing inefficiencies in the health sector (World Bank, 1993; Shaw and Ainsworth, 1995). Hence there was a call for the re-introduction of user fees and health insurance as alternative means to finance health care, in addition to improving efficiency in the use of scarce public resources (Shaw and Ainsworth, 1995). User fees were re-introduced in Tanzania in 1994, starting with higher level facilities. By 1996 user fees had already been also introduced to dispensaries and health centres (Kopoka, 2000). Exemption policies were in place for chronic illnesses and special groups; and waivers for those who could not afford to pay user fees. The introduction of user fees to a large extent imposed a hurdle to achieve the objective of access to health care for all which was the cornerstone of reforms that had been implemented since independence (Mmbuji *et al.*, 1996; Newbrander and Sacca, 1996). The exemption and waiver policy that was adopted in line with the introduction of user fees failed to provide effective access to the poor and those with catastrophic health conditions as there were no funds earmarked to finance exemption, hence this ended up undermining the quality-of-service provision.

4.2 Primary Health-Care Financing in the Current Health-Sector Reforms, 1995–2022

From 1995 the government embarked on health-sector reforms to address the shortcomings experienced during implementation of the SAP, with the aim of improving equity, efficiency, effectiveness and accessibility of services to communities. Several reforms were adopted in collection and allocation of resources to improve alignment with priority service delivery. The 1993 World Development Report (WDR), with a theme 'Investing in Health', insisted on the necessity of government spending to focus more on interventions that are more cost-effective, and which do more to help the poor (World Bank, 1993). More spending should be directed to low-cost but highly effective programmes such as the control and treatment of infectious diseases, instead of giving more attention to specialized care at tertiary facilities, which provide little gain for the money spent (World Bank, 1993). The report also argued for governments to promote diversity and competition in health financing and service delivery. Most of the reforms adopted in Tanzania during this period align with investment proposals put forward by the 1993 WDR, including the introduction of the Tanzania Essential Health Intervention Project (TEHIP), which implemented key reforms in planning and budgeting, the Health Sector Basket Fund, which established a collective pool for development partners as a sector-wide approach (SWAp) initiative, the introduction of health insurance, the implementation of direct facility financing and public financial management reforms.

4.2.1 Improving efficiency in resource use through the Tanzania Essential Health Intervention Project

The Tanzania Essential Health Intervention Project (TEHIP) was introduced in Tanzania in 1996 with the objective of testing the 1993 World Health Development Report hypothesis that major improvements in health outcomes could be realized by prioritizing allocation of available scarce resources based on cost-effectiveness and the burden of disease as a response to address inefficiencies in the use of scarce public resources (World Bank, 1993). TEHIP was introduced in Tanzania to support planning and budgeting process so that resource allocation and use will better be aligned with priority needs as measured by disease burden. It is important to note that TEHIP was introduced in the environment whereby priorities in planning and budgeting were mainly controlled by central government, while regions were at the frontline of managing delivery of services. Local government authorities had a very minimal part in priority setting during planning and budgeting. As a result, most priorities that were funded in plans and budgets were not aligned to disease burden at the local level and financing was not strategic enough to prioritize support to cost-effective interventions. In response to that, TEHIP introduced a district planning tool which was used by district health management teams (DHMT) to undertake problem analysis based on disease burden and use the information to develop plans and budgets. TEHIP supported the two districts where it was implemented to establish a standard essential health-intervention package based on disease burden and use this to prioritize allocation of financial resources through the planning tool. As part of its strategy to increase the resource envelope, the TEHIP project injected into the system an equivalent of about \$2 per capita to complement the government funds allocated for district plans. This injection expanded the district resource envelope to an equivalent of about \$12 per capita, which was the minimum spending level proposed by the WDR93 for the health system to provide essential health services (World Bank, 1993). Through TEHIP, the engagement of district management, especially DHMT in planning and budgeting, was improved and resources were better aligned to priority community needs. Results from TEHIP showed significant gains in health-outcome improvements in the two districts where TEHIP was implemented, especially in reducing mortality. This proved the WDR93 hypothesis that with a modest increase in resource envelope, major health-outcome gains could be realized if resources are targeted on the major diseases burden and a cost-effective approach is taken (de Savigny *et al.*, 2004). While governments across low- and middle-income countries are striving to expand fiscal space to finance health care, it is equally important to invest massive effort to improve efficiency in resource allocation, including introducing strategic purchasing. This balance between increasing health-resource mobilization and allocating resources efficiently, especially targeting primary health care, is also insisted upon in the recently published Lancet Global Health Commission on financing primary health care (Hanson *et al.*, 2022). The analysis of benefit incidence in Tanzania shows that PHC services in public facilities are more equitable compared to hospital services (Mtei *et al.*, 2012), hence allocating more financial resources to PHC would an appropriate way of improving equity in access to health care, especially among the poor.

There are three key messages that could be learnt from the TEHIP experience in relation to resource use. First, even with available scarce resources, country health systems can adopt more cost-effective approaches to improve delivery of services by prioritizing resource allocation to interventions that address high-burden diseases; second, it is possible to integrate government resources with other donors funds and develop joint plans and budgets to address priority intervention areas instead of each donor operating in a silo through vertical programmes; third, the focus in the health system should not only be on promoting resource allocation but also advocate for efficiency in resource allocation. The TEHIP implementation experience contributed to the scaling up of other key health-sector reforms, namely the introduction of SWAp through the formulation of health-sector basket funding (HSBF) and the introduction of the comprehensive council health plan (CCHP), which is a tool building on the initial TEHIP planning tool for developing council plans and budgets as explained below.

4.2.2 More health-system reforms building on the TEHIP initiative

Comprehensive council health planning

The comprehensive council health planning (CCHP) guideline was introduced in 1999 building on the TEHIP efforts on introducing a district planning tool and further consolidating health-sector resources, avoiding duplication and ensuring equity. This was in line with the aim of decentralization, by devolving planning and implementation of primary health-care services to council level (Maluka *et al.*, 2011). The CCHP has been revised from time to time to respond to the health-sector policy and strategic plans. CCHP fifth edition is the most recent edition. The CCHP guideline incorporates the essential health package to facilitate the districts and health facilities to efficiently allocate available resources, monitor implementation and ensure the allocated resources are utilized effectively. The CCHP includes objectives, strategies and costed activities to address health priorities and indicators to measure implementation progress. The planning guideline is built based on partnership in health-services delivery, including the communities utilizing the services, the council health management team (CHMT), council health boards, health-facility governing committees, the private sector and non-governmental organizations.

LGA resource-allocation formula

To ensure equitable resource allocation, the CCHP guideline provided the resource-allocation formula to be utilized in allocating central government and development funding for the health sector to local government authorities (LGAs), such as the block grant and health-basket fund. The resource allocation formula is designed as capitation-based, with risk adjusters for health-care needs proxied by the size of the population, burden of diseases proxied by under-five mortality and equity proxied by poverty incidence and capped land (MOHSW, 2011). The fifth edition of CCHP guideline in 2020 updated the allocation formula to accommodate the health-sector financing reforms, such as direct health facility financing (DHFF). The updated resource allocation formula enables allocation of resources to two levels: to councils and to health facilities. The updated resource allocation to the council includes population poverty, under-five mortality and capped land. Allocation for council hospitals considers workload and performance of the hospital, while that of lower health level facilities takes into consideration the output indicators such as health-service utilization, facility performance, catchment population and capped land (Ministry of Health, 2020).

Sector-wide approach and introduction of health-sector basket fund

The implementation of the TEHIP project improved evidence-based planning and budgeting; however, this process remained uncoordinated. There was a growing discontent between the government of Tanzania and development partners. The development partners suspected that the government was diverting budgets to other less-funded activities. On the other hand, the government indicted that development partners were by-passing the existing government systems and working more with NGOs, resulting in increased verticality. Available evidence on the vertical approach, compared to integrated health-service delivery, indicates that the former results in duplication of efforts, leading to inefficiencies; limited evidence exists on whether they have positive spill-over effects in improving health systems (WHO, 2018).

To increase coordination of the development partners' support, the government of Tanzania in collaboration with development partners, as part of the health-sector reforms, introduced the sector-wide approach (SWAp) initiative in June 1998 (Martinez-Álvarez, 2014). The reforms aim at increasing the efficiency of development aid, through country ownership and taking the lead in development partners' coordination and the delivery of quality essential health-service delivery through one comprehensive health plan (Brown, 2000). Under health-sector basket funding (HSBF), donors with common interests pool their funds together for health into one basket, and hence move away from a system whereby donors were individually directing their support to specific health projects (Burki, 2001; Mubyazi *et al.*, 2004). This approach therefore served as a fund-pooling mechanism that contributes to government efforts to strengthen primary health-care services. Despite long-time promotion of the SWAp, there is still a significant amount of money flowing through vertical disease programmes such as HIV/AIDS, TB and malaria. There are a significant amount of PEPFAR and Global Fund resources that are flowing through off-budget, and hence undermining the efforts of the government to align service delivery with the purpose of improving efficiency and equity in resource allocation. Parallel flows of resource across vertical programmes increase inefficiency in delivery of PHC due to duplication of financing. In most cases, frontline PHC providers need to handle multiple flows of resources that are not integrated in their spending guidelines and accounting procedures and are not aligned with facility priorities. Efforts are still needed from the government to establish measures that will improve alignment in the flow of funds across different sources, including donors' off-budget resources.

4.3 Health Insurance in Tanzania

The introduction of health insurance in Tanzania is in line with the implementation of the SAP that were initiated in the early 1990s with the purpose of addressing financing resource gaps and efficiency in use of public resources to improve availability of health services (World Bank, 1993; Shaw and Ainsworth, 1995). While user fees were introduced in the early 1990s, the introduction of health insurance or prepayment schemes started in 1996 with the pilot of the Community Health Fund (CHF) before it was formally enacted in 2001. In 1999, the National Health Insurance Fund (NHIF) was introduced as a health insurance scheme for public servants. Social Health Insurance Benefit (SHIB) was also introduced in 2005 as part of the National Social Security Fund (NSSF) to cater for the health-care needs of members. In addition, the Insurance Act was introduced in 1996, hence paving the way to establish private health insurance firms in parallel with other firms that provide general insurance. The following sections provide an overview of the current health insurance arrangements in Tanzania and their implication for financing PHC.

4.3.1 Community Health Fund (CHF)

The Community Health Fund (CHF) represents a prepayment scheme that was designed by the government of Tanzania in collaboration with the World Bank to cater for health financing for people in the informal sector, particularly those in rural areas. CHF started as a pilot programme in Igunga district in 1996, before it was enacted in 2001 through a CHF act that created the space for the implementation of CHF schemes across all districts in the country. The key objectives of CHF were to generate additional revenue so as to cover financial gaps, improving equity in access to health care, empowering household and community in participation in decision making and promoting cost sharing (Ministry of Health, 1999). The Council Health Service Boards (CHSBs) were given the mandate to manage the implementation of the scheme in each council. A counterpart scheme, TIKA, was also introduced in 2009 for the urban informal population with the same objectives as CHF. Membership to CHF is on voluntary basis and services were limited to one PHC provider of members' choice. There were variations in CHF contributions across districts and this was determined by the community through their local council bylaws. The government provided matching grants, equivalent to the amount of revenue contributed by members. Management of CHF funds was similar to the management of other funds at the council level, whereby CHF revenue had to be used according to council plans (Ministry of Health, 1999). In this case, CHF was not design as a health-insurance scheme at the beginning, but rather an alternative cost-sharing mechanism to generate revenue for financing health care across councils. While CHF was designed as a PHC scheme to enhance the provision of basic services closer to the community, there was not a clear purchaser–provider split and no provider-payment arrangements to reimburse facilities for services rendered to CHF members. In this case, there was no clear mechanism to address equity and variations in need across PHC facilities since CHF revenue was included in the general council budget, which by then was only prepared at the council level and facility plans and budgets were not visible in planning systems. Several studies that were conducted revealed a lot of challenges in implementation of CHF, including low uptake of membership across communities, hence leading to low enrolment countrywide. The main reasons for this low uptake include limited benefit package, non-portability of CHF card, poor quality of services, poor understanding of health insurance concept, low income, non-continuity in provision of care through referral system, less incentive to providers to improve quality and weak CHF management (Shaw, 2002; Mtei and Mulligan, 2007; Kamuzora and Gilson, 2007; Stomer *et al.*, 2012).

Other reasons include broad exemption policies. So many groups, services and specific diseases are exempt, and user fees for non-exempted services are so low, that some see very little incentive to join the CHF. Recognizing these challenges, the government through the Ministry of Health and President's Office - Regional Administration and Local Government (PO-RALG) decided to implement measures to improve the operation of CHF through improved CHF (iCHF), as an interim step while the country is preparing for a wider reform in its health insurance system (PO-RALG, 2018a).

4.3.2 Improved Community Health Fund (iCHF)

The Improved Community Health Fund (iCHF) was implemented as an interim step to improve the operation of Community Health Fund in Tanzania while the country is continuing with the process of improving the whole health-insurance system through the introduction of universal health insurance. The initiative was implemented through the Government Circular No. 1 of 2018 without changes in the CHF Act of 2001 (PO-RALG, 2018a). The improved CHF originated in early 2000 from different development partners' (such as SDC, GIZ and Pharm Access) initiative to pilot different modality that could improve the operation of CHF which proved to be successful (Kalolo *et al.*, 2018) . These partners selected different regions to pilot different designs of CHF, including through separation of purchaser and provider roles, introducing portability, provider payment mechanisms and harmonization of contributions. The pilots were implemented in selected regions, such as Dodoma, Morogoro, Shinyanga (under SDC), Mbeya, Tanga, Mtwara (under GIZ) and Arusha, Kilimanjaro, and Manyara (under Pharm Access) (Kalolo *et al.*, 2015). The piloted, improved CHF model changed the modality of enrolment from passive enrolment at health-facility level to active enrolment at the village level using enrolment officers. Further, a provider-payment mechanism was put in place to reimburse health facilities for the services that have been provided to CHF members. In addition, iCHF members were given choices of provider from which they can seek care, including faith-based facilities, elevation of pooling to region level and the iCHF card was made transferable within the region, meaning iCHF members can select the provider of their choice to seek care. In 2018 the government, after a thorough review of the success (Kalolo *et al.*, 2015, 2018) of pilot operations across regions, decided to scale up of iCHF across all regions. All key iCHF features that were implemented in pilot regions were adopted in the rollout of iCHF. These include elevation of pooling level in the region through the RAS office, portability of iCHF card, introduction of capitation payment arrangements, active enrolment of members at village level and enhancement of benefit packages to include selected services at the regional referral hospital (PO-RALG, 2018a). Access to district and regional hospitals requires a referral letter from primary health facilities. Administratively managed by NHIF, iCHF was viewed as an interim plan because the government has plans for universal health insurance. It is important to note that the implementation of iCHF was just a policy change though.

Financing of iCHF is through premiums from households and contributions from the national government. In the design of the scheme, households who are deemed too poor are exempt from premium payments. Premiums are per household of six and are set according to the geographical location of households (rural vs urban region) (Kapologwe *et al.*, 2017). The distribution of premium is as follows: 80% is allocated to capitation payments to hospitals and primary-care facilities, 10% commission for the officer who enrols a household, 9% for administration costs and 1% for reserves. Contributions from the national government comprise equal matching funds for each household premium contribution received at the regional level. However, there have been challenges in the disbursement of matching funds since none has been disbursed since the official rollout of iCHF in 2018. There are still challenges that exist under iCHF, including low enrolment due to limited knowledge of health insurance, poor quality of services, unclear understanding of iCHF package limitations at regional referral hospitals and incomplete purchaser–provider split as regions still have the mandate to oversee delivery of services across LGAs. Further, the exemption and waiver policy that still operates under iCHF creates less incentive for people to enrol in iCHF. In addition, the premium contribution set under iCHF does not generate enough to expand benefit packages under iCHF.

4.3.3 Other community-based health insurance schemes

In addition to the introduction of CHF and NHIF, other community-based health insurance (CBHI) schemes also emerged in the early to mid-2000s, to cater for health-care costs across different groups in the informal sector. The commonly known schemes include VIBINDO, which brings together workers in small-scale industries and petty business, and UMASITA, which covers wider informal sector groups. It is estimated that in 2007 there were about 12 CBHI registered schemes, with the current statistics showing 43 such schemes registered by the Tanzania Network of Community Health Funds (TNCHF) (PHRplus, 2006; Toutant, 2010). However, these schemes are currently inactive.

4.3.4 National Health Insurance Fund (NHIF)

In 1999, the government introduced a compulsory National Health Insurance Fund (NHIF) to cover health-services costs for formal public-sector employees (United Republic of Tanzania, 1999). The scheme officially started to collect funds from its members in 2001 (Ministry of Finance, 2001). It was initially introduced for central government employees, followed by all public sector workers in 2002 (NHIF amendment 2002) and later the scheme was allowed private membership where any other members of the public can subscribe in the scheme. For public servants it is mandatory, and employees contribute 3% of their monthly salary and the government contributes the same amount, which provides the contributing employee, spouse and up to four legal dependents with access to outpatient and inpatient care from accredited facilities. Contributions from members who are enrolling to NHIF on voluntary basis depends on the type of health-benefit package that they choose. The NHIF has different packages to suit different demands of the population.

The benefit package is comprehensive, covering consultations, medicines (including all generic medicine in the NEMLIT, cancer drugs, selective combination medicines and immune suppressants), diagnostic tests (including CT scans and MRI), OPD services, inpatient

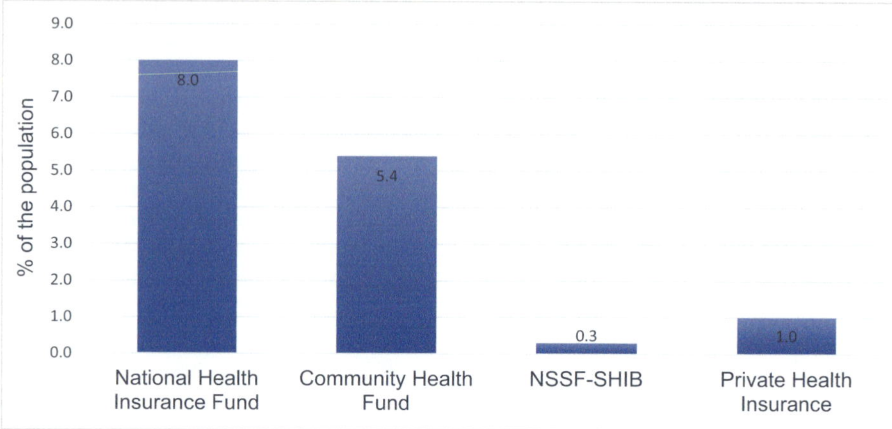

Fig. 4.3. Health insurance coverage in 2022. (From Ministry of Health, 2022.)

services, all surgical services, physiotherapy, dental services, issuance of reading glasses and orthopaedic appliances, such as collar supports, walking aids, walking prostheses and hearing aids. There are a few exclusions and limitations to the above benefits package, such as services provided by public-funded programmes like TB and leprosy services and immunizations, major epidemic events, public health programmes and socially disapproved acts.

All public health facilities get blanket accreditation to provide services for NHIF members. Non-government health providers (private facilities, diagnostics centres including imaging and laboratories, pharmacies, accredited drugs dispensing outlets [ADDOs] and specialized clinics), have to apply for accreditation based on the NHIF guidelines (McIntyre *et al.*, 2008; Mdee, 2009; Humba, 2011). Estimates as of 2019 indicate that NHIF coverage is about 9% of the total population, an increase from 7.1% in 2011 (Humba, 2011), 5% coverage in 2008 and 5.3% in 2009 (McIntyre *et al.*, 2008; Mdee, 2009). In 2022 NHF coverage had reached 9% of the population (Fig. 4.3).

4.3.5 Social health insurance benefit under NSSF

The social health insurance benefit for the members of the National Social Security Fund (NSSF) was introduced in 2005 (Salum and Manase, 2021). The scheme provides health-insurance benefits to members of NSSF, the majority of which are employees from private and parastatal organizations. Beneficiaries include spouse and up to four dependents who are below the age of 18 years. The SHIB benefits package includes inpatient and outpatient care from an earmarked facility. These services include hospitalization, consultation with clinical/medical officer/specialist or consultant, basic and specialized investigations, minor and major surgeries, drugs on the NEMLIT and referral to higher-level hospitals (Salum and Manase, 2021). Exclusions include services received free of charge from other government schemes, such as maternity care; immunization, treatment for TB and leprosy, cancer, HIV/AIDS, epidemics, mental illness, and injuries where a third party with insurance is involved; cosmetic surgery; services/ treatments for self-inflicted diseases; physiotherapy at home; medical examination for employment; therapeutic trials; and expensive specialized investigative procedures like DNA typing. SHIB uses capitation to reimburse service providers. Being voluntary, the SHIB scheme achieved only a low coverage of 2% of NSSF members by 2014, largely due to insufficient public information, limited access to accredited facilities and some members having access to other insurance schemes including private health insurance and NHIF (Salum and Manase, 2021).

4.3.6 Private health insurance

Private health insurance is a growing industry in Tanzania, though at a slow rate. The introduction of private health insurance is regulated under the Private Health Insurance Act of 2009. Private health insurance firms are urban-biased and mainly provide health-care coverage for private firms employees and few individuals (Mtei *et al.*, 2007). Only a few firms are pure private health insurance companies, as most insurance firms integrate health insurance (life insurance) with other types of insurance. Premium contribution to private health insurance is based on risk and there are a wide range of benefit packages from which members can select based on their ability to pay.

Overall, health insurance coverage remains very low at 14.7% of total population, leaving about 85% of the population without health insurance (Fig. 4.3). Relying on health insurance and other prepayment arrangements is the most sustainable way of guaranteeing access to health care without financial risk protection. Furthermore, health insurance is currently highly fragmented with small pools targeting different segments of the population. This fragmentation undermines the potential for cross-subsidization across people with different income levels and health risks. For example, CHF, which is a scheme targeting the informal sector, is only enrolling population groups that are considered to have low income, so does not pool enough resources to be able to cover an expanded PHC benefit package of good quality; while those in the formal sector who are considered to be middle- or higher-income earners are either covered through NHIF, SHIB or private health insurance with an expanded benefit package. This kind of health insurance arrangement creates inequities in access to health care. It is important for the health-sector reforms to consider improvements in pooling arrangements to reduce the degree of fragmentation.

4.4 General Health Sector Expenditure Pattern

Estimates from the National Health Account reports show that there has been a decrease in out-of-pocket payment from 47% in 2002/3 to 32% in 2019/20. This decrease was accompanied by an increase in donor financing from 27% in 2002/3 to 34% in 2019/20. Donors' contribution to the health sector was at the peak in the years 2005/6 and 2013/14 where it accounted

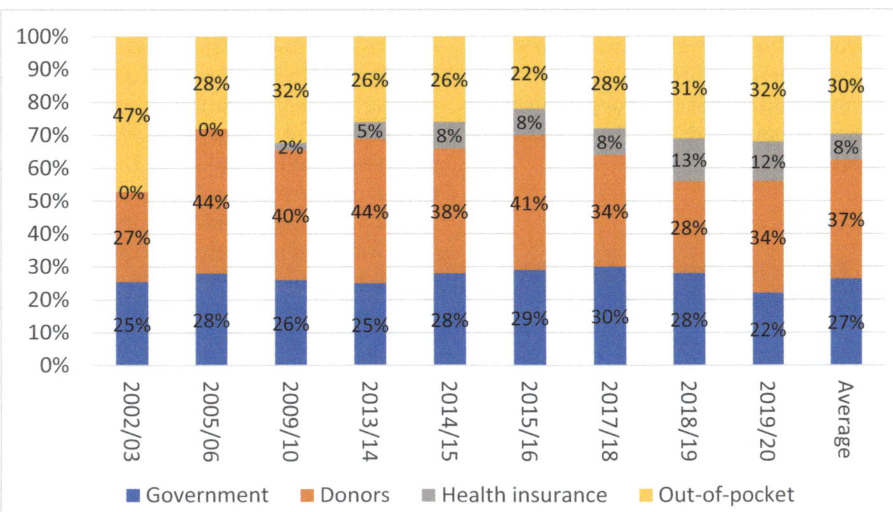

Fig. 4.4. Contribution of different sources in health-sector financing in Tanzania. (From National Health Accounts reports 2006, 2010, 2016, 2022.)

for about 44% of total health expenditure (THE) before starting to decline (Fig. 4.4). Government domestic financing to the health sector has decreased from 28% in 2002/3 to 25% in 2019/20. On average, donor financing played a significant role in financing the health sector for the analysed period of 9 years whereby it accounted for about 37% of THE, while out-of-pocket was the second major source of financing the health sector. Government contribution to the health sector accounted for only 27% of THE, while the health insurance contribution is at 8%. This implies that in general the health sector has a high level of dependence on external donor financing which poses a risk to sustainability in financing health care. In addition, the level of out-of-pocket payment is very significant, posing financial risk to the population when accessing health care. It is recognized worldwide that out-of-pocket payment is the most regressive way of financing health care as it poses the risk of driving a significant proportion of the population into poverty and leaving others without means to finance other basic necessities like food and shelter (WHO, 2000, 2010). Analysis shows that out-of-pocket payments are regressive and about 2% of the population in Tanzania incurs catastrophic health expenditure, while another 1% is falling below the poverty line due to direct out-of-pocket payments when accessing health care (Mtei *et al.*, 2012, 2014).

The continuous dominance of donors in THE indicates that a significant proportion of donor support is through vertical programmes rather than general budget support, a fact that might impose risk on financial cross-subsidization in the health sector.

4.5 Decentralization of Health Financing to PHC

The decentralization by devolution policy (D by D) was adopted in 1999, whereby the main objective was to give communities more authority and responsibility to manage delivery of health care and other public services. Through D by D, the council health management team (CHMT) was responsible for developing plans and budgets for health facilities and managing expenditures, including procuring inputs such as medicine and medical supplies for public primary health facilities. The revenue collection at PHC facilities was supervised by and deposited at the council health sector bank accounts (MOHSW, 2011). Health-facility staff, in collaboration with health-facility governing committees (HFGC), had responsibility for identifying health facilities' input needs and submitting to the council medical officer's office, and the latter had the responsibility of procuring these inputs and delivering to health facilities (Ministry of Health, 2022). This passive approach of managing primary health facilities' finances at the council level encountered several challenges, including delays in procurement of inputs and imbalances in the distribution of inputs across service providers. Further, health-facility staff and communities surrounding these facilities had limited knowledge and ownership of facility plans, budgets and expenditure decisions because most of these decisions were done at the central LGA management level and often not fully communicated to facilities, making it harder to deliver front-line services to patients and serve their communities (Kesale *et al.*, 2022).

As a result of these challenges, the government decided to further delegate decision making space, processes and management to primary health facilities for some inputs critical to deliver services at this level of health service provision. From 2011, public primary health facilities were allowed to open their own bank accounts and gradually were allowed to deposit their collections, starting with district hospitals. More primary health facilities started to manage funds in their own facility bank accounts following the introduction of the pay-for-performance (P4P) programme in Pwani in 2011 and later during the introduction of result-based-financing (RBF) in 2015. Having a bank account was one of the pre-conditions to receive RBF payments. It was during this time that NHIF also started to reimburse primary health facilities directly to their facility bank accounts for those facilities that had one (Binyaruka *et al.*, 2015).

4.5.1 Direct health-facility financing

In 2017, the entire health sector formally adopted direct health-facility financing (DHFF). A condition was put for all primary health facilities to open a bank account for them to receive health basket-fund (HBF) payments. The modality of HBF disbursement was changed from disbursing funds to LGAs and instead funds were disbursed directly to individual health facility bank accounts (Fig. 4.5). Adopting DHFF in disbursing HBF was a major step in the improvement of health financing for PHC, including adopting strategic purchasing in the disbursement of Central Treasury funds. Experience shows that adopting an improved provider payment in disbursing both public and private funds directly to frontline primary health facilities is a major step towards improvement of the quality of services. Funds need to flow directly to frontline service providers to give them autonomy to manage and allocate resource to produce priority community services according to needs (Barroy *et al.*, 2019; WHO, 2022). The shift of HBF to DHFF modality was a major revolution in public financial management (PFM) system in Tanzania as it proved that it is possible to improve the alignment between health-sector financing and PFM rules and regulations for the purpose of improving efficiency, equity and service delivery by introducing more strategic purchasing in the central budgetary system of the country (Kapologwe *et al.*, 2019; Kalolo *et al.*, 2021; WHO, 2022).

Following the adoption of DHFF policy to disburse HBF, a capitation payment formula was developed which is used to calculate payments for each individual primary health facility by the Ministry of Finance and Planning (MoFP). The capitation formula was designed to capture variations in needs, equity and performance across public primary health facilities (Ministry of Health, 2020). The first disbursement of HBF DHFF from the Treasury to facility bank accounts was in fiscal year (FY) 2017/18.

Further institutionalization of DHFF was realized with iCHF also adopting the capitation payment method to disburse funds directly to primary health facilities, a similar modality to HBF since 2018. In addition, all PHC facilities are receiving NHIF reimbursement directly to facility bank accounts. The adaptation of DHFF in primary facilities has strengthened primary health facilities' autonomy and accountability in planning, budgeting and expenditure, improved transparency in fund use and increased community ownership. DHFF has increased fund

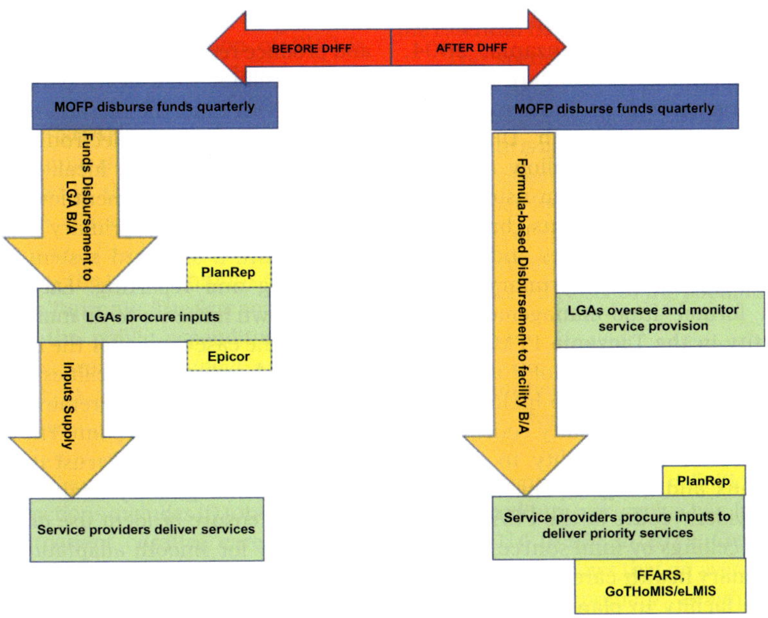

Fig. 4.5. Flow of health-basket funds before and after direct health-facility financing. (Prepared by author using DHFF Management Framework 2022.)

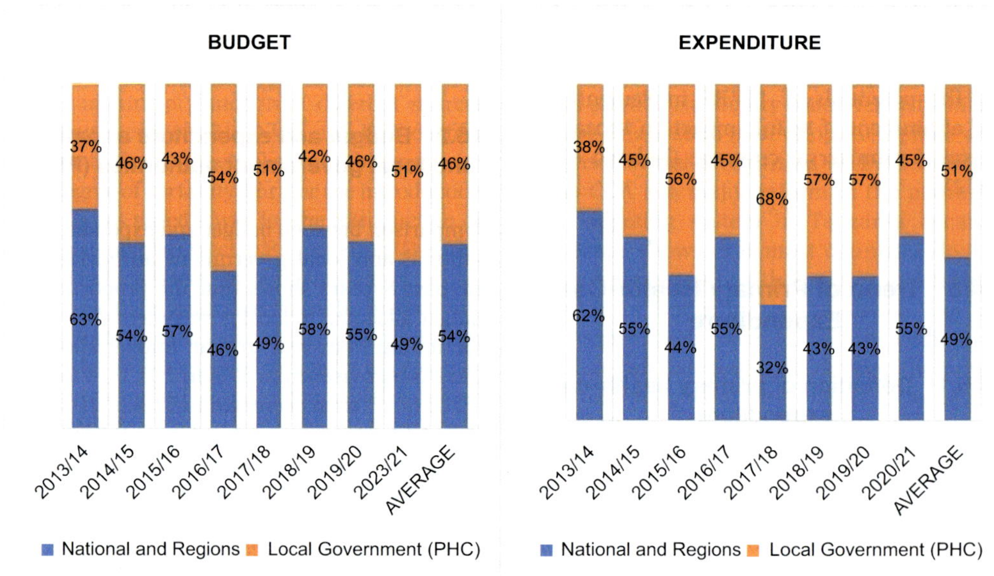

Fig. 4.6. Budget and expenditure at national and local government authorities. (Prepared by author using Ministry of Health Public Expenditure review [PER] Reports.)

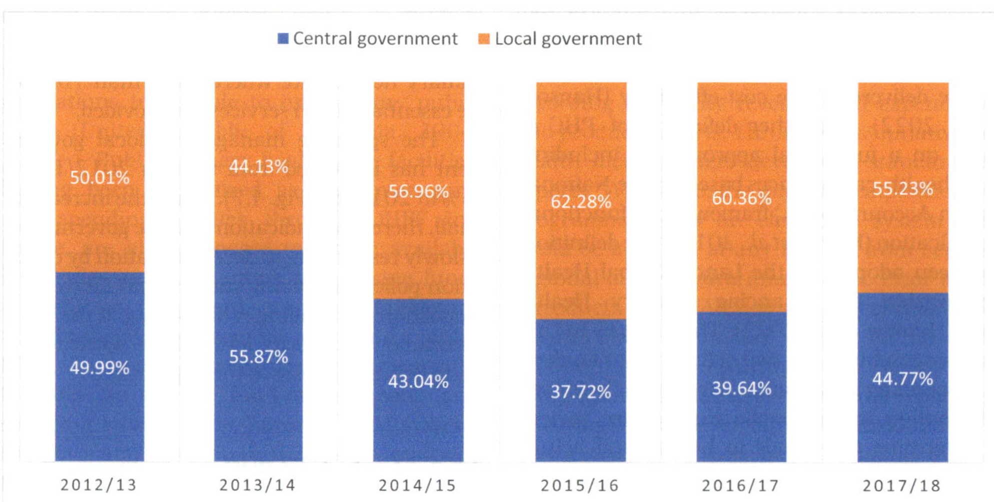

Fig. 4.7. Comparison in expenditure pattern between central and primary health care (local government authorities) in the health sector.

spent in sub-Saharan Africa was about $75. Per capita spending slightly increased to $18 in 2019 in Tanzania while the average in sub-Sahara increased to $83. Tanzania expenditure on PHC is even below some of the neighbour East African countries such as Kenya and Uganda (Fig. 4.8). In this case, Tanzania needs to increase priority in allocating and spending PHC funds to address

Countries	2016	2017	2018	2019
Botswana	133	276	274	267
Burkina Faso	35	37	31	32
Cabo Verde, Republic of	67	80	88	82
Central African Republic	19	26	50	34
Comoros	31	39	37	40
Congo	32	32	28	28
Côte d'Ivoire	52	56	58	61
Democratic Republic of the Congo	14	11	10	13
Eswatini	123	138	154	134
Ethiopia	19	19	19	21
Gabon	110	108	120	118
Ghana	54	54	61	
Guinea	31	25	27	32
Kenya	48	44	49	53
Liberia	47	34	30	33
Malawi	26	30	27	21
Mali	24	26	26	26
Mauritania	26	30	33	34
Mauritius	254	280	302	309
Mozambique	24	28	31	
Namibia	214	236	229	211
Niger	12	18	20	21
Nigeria	54	51	44	49
Sao Tome and Principe	86	99	97	91
Senegal	36	36	42	40
Seychelles	408	456	491	492
Sierra Leone		27	25	26
South Africa	220	250	264	257
South Sudan		19	19	15
Togo	30	32	32	30
Uganda	22	20	21	21
United Republic of Tanzania	**17**	**18**	**19**	**18**
Zambia	45	52	60	54
Zimbabwe		63	78	55
Sudan			28	22
Average sub-Saharan Africa	75	81	84	83

Fig. 4.8. Tanzania PHC spending per capita (spending in USD) in comparison with other countries. (From Hanson *et al.*, 2022. Ministry of Health Public Expenditure Review reports, FYs 2012/13–2017/18.)

health care needs of the large segment of the population. It is estimated that about 70% of essential population needs could be addressed if PHC services were to be improved.

4.7 Remaining Challenges in PHC Financing and Recommended Strategies to Address Them

4.7.1 Resource mobilization and pooling

General tax revenue and prepayment arrangements are the most reliable mechanisms to sustainably finance the provision of health care including PHC services. The analysis since independence shows that while Tanzania has made significant efforts to improve general tax financing and introduce health insurance schemes, the generated resources from these sources are not enough to sustainably provide PHC services effectively. General budget allocation to the health sector is still below the Abuja target of spending 15% of total government budget on the health sector. In addition, health insurance coverage and revenue generated from this financing source is still very low. As a result, there is still high reliance on out-of-pocket payments to finance health care, a financing arrangement that is highly inequitable (WHO, 2000, 2010). In addition, the country has high level dependence on external financing which is not a sustainable way of financing health care.

On top of having limited resources generated through general tax and health insurance and high dependence on external financing, there are inefficiencies in the way revenue mobilization is arranged. There is a high level of fragmentation in health insurance arrangements which undermines the opportunities for cross-subsidization. It is internationally acceptable that establishing bigger pools of revenue collection provides the opportunities to ensure equity in access to health care whereby health-care needs financing for those who are poor or have a low income can be cross-subsidized by those who are higher-income earners. But the current arrangements to a large extent fragment the population by income groups whereby CHF is mainly targeting low-income earners in the informal sector, who in most cases do not have sustainable income, while NHIF and other formal sector schemes are targeting those who could be considered as middle- or higher-income earners. Further, a significant proportion of donors' support goes through off-budget by direct funding of fragmented vertical programmes. This creates inefficiencies when allocating government resources as there is a risk of parallel funding of some interventions with what the donors are supporting through off-budget arrangements. Evidence shows that effective coordination of donors' financing through the establishment of robust public financial management systems, transparency and accountability standards for all development partners contributes to improving equity in access and quality of health-care provision (Logie *et al.*, 2008; Farmer *et al.*, 2013).

It is therefore necessary for financing reforms in Tanzania to focus on:

1. Increasing revenue generation through domestic taxation to sustainably finance health-care needs. The overall increase in general revenue generation will open space to increase allocation to PHC financing.
2. Addressing fragmentation in health insurance. Actions need to be taken to improve the size of pooling through harmonization of public health insurance pools. This will help to ensure that enough resources are generated and there is room for cross-subsidization. Deliberate actions need to be taken to allocate funds to pay premiums for the poor/indigents in health insurance schemes.
3. Improving development partners' coordination. It is necessary to establish a mechanism that will ensure effective coordination of development partners' financing in the health sector. The government needs to know the amount of available donor resources and for what interventions they will be used so that it can prioritize the available scarce public resources effectively. The government might need to clearly communicate the priorities for PHC so that donors can mobilize their external support towards these priorities.

4.7.2 Purchasing arrangement

Strategic purchasing is a core pillar for improving equity, efficiency and quality in provision of PHC delivery. The DHFF implementation is a major step towards introduction of strategic purchasing in the core PFM system. However, DHFF in the Treasury system is currently focusing on improving strategic purchasing under HSBF. More advocacy is needed to introduce strategic purchasing in the disbursement of other consolidated funds such as domestic funds allocated for OC (other charges, i.e. funds allocated to cover operation costs). It is important to adopt a formula-based allocation of OC directly to facilities to increase predictability and autonomy of PHC facilities. Strategic allocation of resources directly to PHC facilities is a more effective approach of putting people at the centre of health care which is supposed to be the priority of every health system as proposed in the World Health Report 2008 (WHO, 2008).

Further, NHIF management needs to introduce strategic purchasing in the National Health Insurance Fund (NHIF). Currently this scheme is using fee-for-service arrangements to pay providers, a method that has proved to be inefficient as it increases administration costs to both purchaser and providers (Langenbrunner *et al.*, 2009). Experience shows that adopting more strategic purchasing arrangements such as capitation or blended provider mechanism create more incentives to improve the quality of PHC service provision (Hanson *et al.*, 2022).

4.7.3 Public financial management

Alignment between the public financial management system (i.e. institutions, policies and processes that govern the use of public fund) and the health financing system (revenue collection, pooling and purchasing) is a key ingredient to facilitate progress towards achieving universal health coverage (Cashin *et al.*, 2017). The introduction of DHFF and extension of PFM systems to frontline PHC providers is a major step towards realization of this alignment. However, the challenge remains on ensuring effective implementation of DHFF and use of PFM systems at provider level. Procurement rules and regulations need to be simplified so as to not act as a barrier for effective use of DHFF resources at PHC. PFM rules and regulation should be revisited to increase autonomy and flexibility of PHC providers in reallocation of resources according to changing health-care priorities without passing through a heavily bureaucratic process.

It is also necessary to extend the internal audit function to PHC-provider level to make sure that effective internal checks are in place so that the facility will not spend money without following required regulations and procedures. Continuous capacity building is also required to ensure that PHC facility staff are conversant with the use of PFM systems to plan and budget, procure inputs, account for fund use and produce reports. Plans and budgets should be improved at the PHC level to make sure that they take into consideration emerging diseases such as NCDs. Primary care is the first point of contact, therefore, early diagnosis and management of NCDs and related risk factors will reduce anticipated complications that might lead to catastrophic health expenditures and premature deaths. The CHMT should incorporate mentorship support on financial management during their supportive supervision visit at PHC level.

Tracking of fund use also needs to be improved. There are several PHC financial and clinical data collection systems, such as GOTHOMIS, DHIS2, FFARS, PlanRep and openIMIS. However, the systems are disjointed, which impairs real-time data visibility as well as the integration of financial and clinical information. These systems need to be interoperable to facilitate tracking of fund use linked to health service outputs/outcomes.

4.7.4 Looking forward: Envisioned government strategies to address challenges in PHC financing

In its effort to improve the health-financing system, the government is currently in the process of making the law that will ensure everyone has enrolled in health insurance. The Universal Health Insurance (UHI) Bill (URT, 2022) was presented for the first time in Parliament in September 2022. Among key health-system financing improvements that are anticipated upon enactment of the UHI bill are:

1. The reduction in the fragmentation of health insurance by retaining only one public health insurance scheme.
2. The establishment of a standard minimum benefit package that will be equally accessible to everyone. This will help to remove the current existing inequalities in access to health care among public health insurance schemes (CHF/iCHF, SHIB and NHIF).
3. The establishment of a mechanism to enrol the poor into health insurance schemes through public financing. This will help to guarantee equity in access to health care. An effective identification process will be put in place so as to make sure that all those who qualify to be subsidized by the government are actually included in health insurance schemes.
4. Improving regulation of health insurance so as to safeguard the rights of health insurance members, contracted health facilities and health insurance schemes. The Tanzania Insurance Regulatory Authority will be the regulator of health insurance schemes, both public and private schemes.

It is anticipated that, if well implemented, the UHI law will be a major step towards achieving universal health coverage by guaranteeing access to needed health care and financial protection to the whole population. However, the government will need to secure sustainable financing sources to enrol the poor into health insurance schemes, otherwise it will be a challenge to guarantee access to health care for this population group.

4.8 Conclusion

A stable political economy and progress in health policy in Tanzania has resulted in more public resources being channelled to PHC as part of the implementation of the decentralization policy. Consequently, the fiscal decentralization has resulted in improved service delivery of PHC. The introduction and operationalization of the direct health-facility financing initiative has enhanced the flow of funds to lower-level health-service providers and has increased provider autonomy in planning and delivery of health services. DHFF has revolutionized public financial management systems in Tanzania as it proved that it is possible to improve the alignment between health-sector financing and PFM rules and regulations for the purpose of improving efficiency, equity and service delivery by introducing more strategic purchasing in the central budgetary system of the country. DHFF has led to increased accountability and governance in the health system at the PHC level, increased health-system responsiveness to patients who receive care in facilities and improved health-seeking behaviour and service utilization at primary-care providers.

Despite the observed improvements in financing for PHC, the amount of financial resources flowing to PHC is not sufficient to deliver required services. More effort is needed to increase financing through pooling arrangements and introduce strategic purchasing for PHC. The government needs to adopt innovative approaches to increase overall domestic resources so that more funds will be allocated for PHC.

Bibliography

Amu, H., Dickson, K.S., Kumi-Kyereme, A. and Darteh, E.K.M. (2018) Understanding variations in health insurance coverage in Ghana, Kenya, Nigeria, and Tanzania: evidence from demographic and health surveys. *PloS One* 13(8), e0201833. DOI: 10.1371/journal.pone.0201833.

Barroy, H., Piatti, M., Sergent, F., Dale, E., O'Dougherty, S. *et al.* (2019) Let managers manage: a health service provider's perspective on public financial management. *World Bank Blogs*. Available at: https://blogs.worldbank.org/health/let-managers-manage-health-service-providers-perspective-public-financial-management (accessed 11 May 2023).

Beck, A. (1977) Medicine and society in Tanganyika, 18901930; a historical inquiry. *Transactions of the American Philosophical Society* 67(3), 1. DOI: 10.2307/1006330.

Biermann, W. and Wagao, J. (1986) The quest for adjustment: Tanzania and the IMF, 19801986. *African Studies Review* 29(4), 89–104. DOI: 10.2307/524008.

Binyaruka, P., Patouillard, E., Powell-Jackson, T., Greco, G., Maestad, O. *et al.* (2015) Effect of paying for performance on utilisation, quality, and user costs of health services in Tanzania: a controlled before and after study. *PloS One* 10(8), e0135013. DOI: 10.1371/journal.pone.0135013.

Brown, A. and WHO (2000) *Current Issues in Sector-Wide Approaches for Health Development: Tanzania Case Study*. World Health Organization, Geneva, Switzerland.

Burki, O. (2001) *Sector-Wide Approach in Tanzania: The Health Sector Example*. Swiss Agency for Development and Co-operation, Bern.

Cashin, C., Bloom, D., Sparkes, S., Barroy, H., Kutzin, J. *et al.* (2017) *Aligning Public Financial Management and Health Financing: Sustaining Progress toward Universal Health Coverage*. World Health Organization, Geneva, Switzerland.

Chagula, W.K. and Tarimo, E. (1975) Meeting basic health needs in Tanzania. In: Newell, K.W. (ed.) *Health by the People*. World Health Organization, Geneva, Switzerland.

de Savigny, D., Kasale, H., Mbuya, C. and Reid, G. (2004) *Fixing Health Systems*. International Development Research Centre, Ottawa.

Farmer, P.E., Nutt, C.T., Wagner, C.M., Sekabaraga, C., Nuthulaganti, T. *et al.* (2013) Reduced premature mortality in Rwanda: lessons from success. *BMJ* 346, f65. DOI: 10.1136/bmj.f65.

Hanson, K., Brikci, N., Erlangga, D., Alebachew, A., De Allegri, M. *et al.* (2022) The Lancet Global Health Commission on financing primary health care: putting people at the centre. *The Lancet. Global Health* 10(5), e715–e772. DOI: 10.1016/S2214-109X(22)00005-5.

Humba, E. (2011) Pioneering social health insurance in Tanzania: the case of the National Health Insurance Fund (NHIF). In: *MMS Bulletin 120: Improving Access Through Effective Health Financing, Reader of the Swiss TPH's Spring Symposium*, UBS Training and Conference Centre, Basel, Switzerland.

Jonsson, U. (1986) Ideological framework and health development in Tanzania 1961-2000. *Social Science & Medicine* 22(7), 745–753. DOI: 10.1016/0277-9536(86)90226-1.

Kalolo, A., Radermacher, R., Stoermer, M., Meshack, M. and De Allegri, M. (2015) Factors affecting adoption, implementation fidelity, and sustainability of the Redesigned Community Health Fund in Tanzania: a mixed methods protocol for process evaluation in the Dodoma region. *Global Health Action* 8, 29648. DOI: 10.3402/gha.v8.29648.

Kalolo, A., Gautier, L., Radermacher, R., Stoermer, M., Jahn, A. *et al.* (2018) Implementation of the redesigned Community Health Fund in the Dodoma region of Tanzania: a qualitative study of views from rural communities. *The International Journal of Health Planning and Management* 33(1), 121–135. DOI: 10.1002/hpm.2403.

Kalolo, A., Kapologwe, N.A., Samky, H. and Kibusi, S.M. (2021) Acceptability of the Direct Health Facility Financing (DHFF) initiative in Tanzania: a mixed methods process evaluation of the moderating factors. *The International Journal of Health Planning and Management* 37(3), 1381–1401. DOI: 10.1002/hpm.3402.

Kamuzora, P. and Gilson, L. (2007) Factors influencing implementation of the Community Health Fund in Tanzania. *Health Policy and Planning* 22(2), 95–102. DOI: 10.1093/heapol/czm001.

Kapologwe, N.A., Kagaruki, G.B., Kalolo, A., Ally, M., Shao, A. *et al.* (2017) Barriers and facilitators to enrollment and re-enrollment into the community health funds/Tiba Kwa Kadi (CHF/TIKA) in Tanzania: a cross-sectional inquiry on the effects of socio-demographic factors and social marketing strategies. *BMC Health Services Research* 17(1), 308. DOI: 10.1186/s12913-017-2250-z.

Kapologwe, N.A., Kalolo, A., Kibusi, S.M., Chaula, Z., Nswilla, A. *et al.* (2019) Understanding the implementation of Direct Health Facility Financing and its effect on health system performance in Tanzania: a non-controlled before and after mixed method study protocol. *Health Research Policy and Systems* 17(1), 11. DOI: 10.1186/s12961-018-0400-3.

Kapologwe, N.A., Meara, J.G., Kengia, J.T., Sonda, Y., Gwajima, D. *et al.* (2020) Development and upgrading of public primary healthcare facilities with essential surgical services infrastructure: a strategy towards achieving universal health coverage in Tanzania. *BMC Health Services Research* 20(1), 218. DOI: 10.1186/s12913-020-5057-2.

Kesale, A.M., Mahonge, C.P. and Muhanga, M. (2022) The functionality of health facility governing committees and their associated factors in selected primary health facilities implementing direct health facility financing in Tanzania: a mixed-method study. *Health Science Reports* 5(3), e611. DOI: 10.1002/hsr2.611.

Kopoka, P.A. (2000) Provision of health services in Tanzania in the twenty first century: lessons from the past. In: *Workshop on Economic Policy Environment in Tanzania in the Twenty First Century: Lessons from the Nyerere Legacy on 30 March 2000*, Institute of Development Studies, University of Dar es Salaam. Available at: https://www.eldis.org/document/A28578 (accessed 4 July 2023).

Kumar, A.K.S., Chen, L.C., Choudhury, M., Ganju, S., Mahajan, V. *et al.* (2011) Financing health care for all: challenges and opportunities. *Lancet* 377(9766), 668–679. DOI: 10.1016/S0140-6736(10)61884-3.

Langenbrunner, J.C., Cashin, C. and O'Dougherty, S. (eds) (2009) *Designing and Implementing Health Care Provider Payment Systems How-To Manuals*. International Bank for Reconstruction and Development/World Bank, Washington, DC. DOI: 10.1596/978-0-8213-7815-1.

Logie, D.E., Rowson, M. and Ndagije, F. (2008) Innovations in Rwanda's health system: looking to the future. *Lancet* 372(9634), 256–261. DOI: 10.1016/S0140-6736(08)60962-9.

Lugalla, J.L. (1995) The impact of structural adjustment policies on women's and children's health in Tanzania. *Review of African Political Economy* 22(63), 43–53. DOI: 10.1080/03056249508704099.

Mahomoodally, M.F. (2013) Traditional medicines in Africa: an appraisal of ten potent african medicinal plants. *Evidence-Based Complementary and Alternative Medicine* 2013, 617459. DOI: 10.1155/2013/617459.

Maluka, S.O., Hurtig, A.-K., Sebastián, M.S., Shayo, E., Byskov, J. *et al.* (2011) Decentralization and health care prioritization process in Tanzania: from national rhetoric to local reality. *The International Journal of Health Planning and Management* 26(2), e102–120. DOI: 10.1002/hpm.1048.

Martinez-Álvarez, M. (2014) *Development Assistance for Health in Tanzania: Has the Sector Wide Approach Achieved the Principles of Aid Effectiveness?* London School of Hygiene and Tropical Medicine, London.

Mbilinyi, M. (1985) 'City' and 'countryside' in colonial Tanganyika. *Economic and Political Weekly* 20, WS88–WS96.

McCarthy, D.M.P. (1976) Media as ends: money and the underdevelopment of Tanganyika to 1940. *The Journal of Economic History* 36(3), 645–662. DOI: 10.1017/S0022050700099526.

McIntyre, D., Garshong, B., Mtei, G., Meheus, F., Thiede, M. *et al.* (2008) Beyond fragmentation and towards universal coverage: insights from Ghana, South Africa and the United Republic of Tanzania. *Bulletin of the World Health Organization* 86(11), 871–876. DOI: 10.2471/blt.08.053413.

Mdee, H.I.Z. (2009) Challenges and opportunities of community based health funds (CBHF) in the emerging social health insurance policy environment. In: *7th Community Health Financing Association of East Africa (CHeFA-EA) Regional Conference*, Entebbe, Uganda.

Ministry of Finance (2001) *Speech by the Minister for Finance Hon. Basil P. Mramba (MP), Introducing to the National Assembly the Estimates of Government Revenue and Expenditure for the Financial Year 2001/2002*. Ministry of Finance, Dar es Salaam, Tanzania.

Ministry of Health (1999) *Community Health Fund (CHF) Operations Guidelines*. Ministry of Health, Dar es Salaam, Tanzania.

Ministry of Health (2020) *Comprehensive Council Health Planning Guideline*, 5th edn. Ministry of Health, Community Development, Gender, Elderly and Children, Dodoma.

Ministry of Health (2022) *Direct Health Facility Financing Management Framework*. Ministry of Health, Dar es Salaam, Tanzania.

Mmbuji, P.K., Ilomo, P.A. and Nswilla, A.L. (1996) *Implementation of Health Service User-Fees in Tanzania: An Evaluation of Progress and Potential Impact*. Cost-Sharing Implementation Unit-MOH, Dar es Salaam, Tanzania.

MOHSW (1990) *Tanzania National Health Policy*. Ministry of Health, United Republic of Tanzania, Dar es Salaam, Tanzania.

MOHSW (2011) *Comprehensive Council Health Planning Guideline*, 4th edn. Ministry of Health and Social Welfare, United Republic of Tanzania, Dar Es Salaam, Tanzania.

Mtei, G. and Mulligan, J.-A. (2007) *Community Health Funds in Tanzania: A Literature Review*. Ifakara Health Research and Development Centre (IHRDC), Dar es Salaam, Tanzania.

Mtei, G., Mulligan, J.-A., Ally, M., Palmer, N. and Mills, A. (2007) *An Assessment of the Health Financing System in Tanzania: Report on SHIELD work package 1*. Dar es Salaam, Tanzania.

Mtei, G., Makawia, S., Ally, M., Kuwawenaruwa, A., Meheus, F, *et al.* (2012) Who pays and who benefits from health care? An assessment of equity in health care financing and benefit distribution in Tanzania. *Health Policy and Planning* 27 Suppl 1, i23–34. DOI: 10.1093/heapol/czs018.

Mtei, G., Makawia, S. and Masanja, H. (2014) Monitoring and evaluating progress towards universal health coverage in Tanzania. *PLoS Medicine* 11(9), e1001698. DOI: 10.1371/journal.pmed.1001698.

Mubyazi, G., Kamugisha, M., Mushi, A. and Blas, E. (2004) Implications of decentralization for the control of tropical diseases in Tanzania: a case study of four districts. *The International Journal of Health Planning and Management* 19 Suppl 1(S1), S167–S185. DOI: 10.1002/hpm.776.

Mubyazi, G., Massaga, J., Kamugisha, M., Mubyazi, J.-N., Magogo, G.C. *et al.* (2006) User charges in public health facilities in Tanzania: effect on revenues, quality of services and people's health-seeking behaviour for malaria illnesses in Korogwe district. *Health Services Management Research* 19(1), 23–35. DOI: 10.1258/095148406775322061.

Newbrander, W. and Sacca, S. (1996) *Cost Sharing and Access to Health Care for the Poor: Equity Experiences in Tanzania*. Management Sciences for Health, Boston, Massachusetts.

Ngowi, H.P. (2009) Economic development and change in Tanzania since independence: the political leadership factor. *African Journal of Political Science and International Relations* 3, 259–267.

PHRplus (2006) *Catalogue of Community Based Health Financing Schemes Tanzania*. PHRplus and CHeFA-EA, Bethesda, Maryland.

PO-RALG (2018a) *Community Health Fund Improvement Circular no.1 (Waraka Namba 1 wa Maboresho ya Mfuko wa Afya ya Jamii-CHF/TIKA)*. PO-RALG, Dodoma.

PO-RALG (2018b) *History of Local Governments in Tanzania*. PO-RALG, Dodoma.

Ruhago, G.M., Ngalesoni, F.N., Kapologwe, N.A., Kengia, J.T., Ngocho, J. *et al.* (2022) Strengthening financial management systems at primary health care: performance assessment of the Facility Financial Accounting and Reporting System (FFARS) in Tanzania. *Frontiers in Health Services* 2, 787940. DOI: 10.3389/frhs.2022.787940.

Salum, Z.M. and Manase, J. (2021) Employee awareness and perceived service quality of social health insurance benefit in Tanzania: evidence from Dar es Salaam NSSF members. *Universe International Journal of Interdisciplinary Research* 1, 89–99.

Semali, I., Tanner, M. and De Savigny, D. (2007) Health reform cycles in Tanzania: 1924–1994. *Tanzania Journal of Development Studies* 7(2). DOI: 10.4314/tjds.v7i2.47892.

Shaw, R.P. (2002) *Tanzania's Community Health Fund: Prepayment as an Alternative to User Fees*. World Bank, Washington, DC.

Shaw, R.P. and Ainsworth, M. (eds) (1995) *Financing Health Services through User Fees and Insurance: Case Studies from Sub-Saharan Africa*. World Bank, Washington, DC. DOI: 10.1596/0-8213-3396-8.

Stomer, M., Hanlon, P., Tawa, M., Macha, J. and Mosha, D. (2012) *Community Health Funds (CHFs) in Tanzania: Innovations Study*. Swiss TPH, Dar es Salaam, Tanzania.

TANU (1967) *The Arusha Declaration and TANU's Policy on Socialism and Self-Reliance*. Publicity Section, TANU, Dar es Salaam, Tanzania.

Toutant, R. (2010) *Tanzania Network of Community Health Funds: CEO Progress Report*. TNCHF, Dar es Salaam, Tanzania.

United Republic of Tanzania (1999) *The National Health Insurance Fund Act*. The United Republic of Tanzania, Dar es Salaam, Tanzania.

United Republic of Tanzania (2004) *The Public Finance Act, 2001, Act no.6 of 2001: Principal Legislation*. Government Printer, Dar es Salaam, Tanzania.

United Republic of Tanzania (2015) *Budget Act*. United Republic of Tanzania, Dar es Salaam, Tanzania.

United Republic of Tanzania (URT) (2022) Muswada Wa Sheria Ya Bima Ya Afya Kwa Wote Wa Mwaka 2022 (Universal Health Insurance Bill). In: *Special Gazette of the United Republic of Tanzania*, Government Printer, August 10, 2022 (Vol. 103).

van Etten, G.M. and Raikes, A.M. (1975) Training for rural health in Tanzania. *Social Science & Medicine* 9(2), 87–92. DOI: 10.1016/0037-7856(75)90099-2.

WHO (2000) *Health Systems: Improving Performance. The World Health Report 2000*. World Health Organization, Geneva, Switzerland.

WHO (2002) *Declaration of Alma-Ata, 1978*. World Health Organization, Geneva, Switzerland.

WHO (2008) *The World Health Report 2008: Primary Health Care Now More than Ever*. World Health Organization, Geneva, Switzerland.

WHO (2010) *Health System Financing: The Path to Universal Coverage*. Geneva, Switzerland.

WHO (2018) *Integrating Health Services: Brief*. World Health Organization, Geneva, Switzerland.

WHO (2022) Direct facility financing: concept and role for UHC. World Health Organization. Available at: https://apps.who.int/iris/handle/10665/351945 (accessed 11 May 2023).

World Bank (1993) *The World Development Report 1993: Investing in Health*. Oxford University Press, New York. DOI: 10.1596/0-1952-0890-0.

5 Health Commodities Supply Chain

Romuald Mbwasi[1]*, William Reuben[2], William Mfuko[3] and Zarina Shamte Madabida[4]

[1]Senior Lecturer (Supply Chain), St John University, Dodoma, Tanzania; [2]President's Office – Regional Administration and Local Government, Dodoma, Tanzania; [3]Consultant, Health Supply Chain, Dar es Salaam, Tanzania; [4]Expert, Industrial Pharmacy and Marketing, Dar es Salaam, Tanzania

Abstract

The development of the health commodity supply-chain system, particularly at primary health-care level is described. The chapter starts with the pre-independence period when there was an absence of even a rudimental health commodity supply system, and progresses through to the 1960s and 1970s when the country experienced a gradual move towards a strengthened supply system that targeted the primary health-care levels, including the creation of district stores to distribute health commodities to primary health facilities. In the severe economic crisis of the 1980s, Tanzania was hit by acute shortages of health commodities at all levels while in the 1990s the reform period gradually built a PHC supply-chain system which was more lower-level-facility oriented. This resulted in the introduction of a standardized commodity kit-system for primary health facilities, which later evolved into indent approaches and finally to the integrated logistic system (ILS). The ILS gave more decision-making power to the primary health facilities in terms of what and how much to order, based on needs and availability of funds. The chapter also describes major developmental and technical changes over the last 20 years which have strengthened the supply-chain system, characterized by the restructuring of the Central Medical Stores (CMS) to become a semiautonomous medical stores department, improving staff capacity, building on supply-chain management and warehousing facilities, the establishment of a logistic management unit at the MOH, the introduction of electronic management information systems (eLMIS), the establishment of the Tanzania Medicines and Medical Devices Authority (TMDA) for quality assurance and the setting up of a bottom-up-quantification system that primarily reinforces the role of lower-level facilities in managing their supplies. The chapter acknowledges the critical role international organizations and donors have played in building up a more reliable and effective health commodity supply system in Tanzania. It points out the importance of global technical innovations in shaping the future of supply-chain characteristics. The chapter includes a monitoring and evaluation (M&E) section which is critical for monitoring, maintaining and improving the performance of the health commodity supply system in the country.

5.0 Introduction

Besides the availability of trained and supervised health-care staff (physicians, nurses and other medical personnel), effective health-care service delivery is dependent on the availability and regular supply of health commodities (including medicines, diagnostic equipment and laboratory reagents, as well as a functional medical infrastructure including beds and medical utensils).

*Corresponding author: rmbwasi@gmail.com

 Primary Health Care in Tanzania through a Health Systems Lens (eds N.A. Kapologwe *et al.*)
DOI: 10.1079/9781800623330.0005

Consequently, one cannot talk about the evolution of primary health care (PHC) in Tanzania without tracking the development of supplies of health commodities in the health-care system. This evolution should clearly show how health commodities were made available to health facilities to meet patients' needs during the periods before independence (pre-colonial and colonial), between independence and the Arusha Declaration emphasizing rural development (1967), during the economic recession and structural adjustments in the 1970s and 1980s and during the health reform period (up to 2022). From here a projected vision will be described of how such services are expected to evolve in the foreseeable future, for example 30 years from today (2022).

In this chapter, we use the five supply-chain functions, namely:

1. selection;
2. quantification/forecasting;
3. procurement;
4. storage; and
5. distribution for use,

together with the conceptual framework shown in Table 5.1 to navigate the evolution of health commodities' supply in Tanzania.

Collectively considered and in a well-functioning health supply system these five key areas constitute access to the needed health commodities for improving health outcomes for a range of diseases prevailing in a country. In this context access to effective health commodities requires strong management support, which is comprised of: sustainable financing, reliable health and supply systems; geographical ease of access, and affordable product prices.

Selection is defined as the process of choosing rationally evidence-based health commodities with acceptable known profiles

Table 5.1. The evolution and improvement of the health commodity supply chain in Tanzania since Independence.

	1993–2023		
1961–1993	1993–2003	2004–2016	2016–2023
CMS era	**The Medical Stores Department (MSD) era**		
	Direct donor support to MSD	Donor-supported projects through implementing partners in collaboration with MSD	
Fragmented supply-chain functions	World Bank capitalization and Danida external management team	USAID, Global Fund (GF), Bill and Melinda Gates Foundation	USAID and Swiss Agency for Development and Cooperation
32 years	10 years	12 years	7 years
Multiple ministries responsible After the Arusha Declaration in 1967 only government imports From 1973 to 1997 state-owned NAPCO imports health commodities for the private sector	MSD established in 1993 through World Bank loan and started work in 1994 with foreign management team and counterparts until 2003. Great improvements through health cash and carry approach.	Improvements of supply chain through: • health commodity logistics • quantification • procurement processes • quality assurance and pharmacovigilance • warehousing and distribution • pharmaceutical and health-care waste management • establishment of TFDA and Pharmacy Council • rollout of the ADDO programme	Establishment of a logistics management unit (LMU) within MOH/PSU Expert staff hiring Rollout of the prime vendor system complimenting MSD
In the 1980s, Danida support with essential drug kits for dispensaries and health centres	Between 1998 and 2000 MOH with Danida support piloted the indent pull system in Morogoro to replace the push Essential Drug Programme (EDP)		

to be used in a health system. The health commodities must be suitable for treating prevailing health conditions, be of acceptable quality and effectiveness and be available in the market at affordable prices to most patients. *Quantification/forecasting*, modestly defined, is the estimation of what is needed. Often the quantified quantities must match the available funding. *Procurement* refers to the acquisition of the required/quantified health commodities from appropriate and capable suppliers. *Storage* refers to the accommodation of the procured health commodities at proper places and locations with appropriate temperatures and humidity, including an acceptable level of cleanliness and arrangement with appropriate inventory/stock management tools. *Distribution* refers to the proper transportation of the procured health commodities to health facilities for use. *Use* denotes the proper or rational use of the health commodities at health facilities and for patients.

For any supply chain to be effective, there must be a health commodity policy, law and regulation, including a management support system consisting of an appropriately skilled workforce, infrastructure, and standard operating procedures, among other requirements (USAID, 2011; Rushton *et al.*, 2014; JSI, 2017).

The ultimate aim of any health supply-chain effort, evolving, is to make available health commodities of acceptable quality, and effective, safe and affordable to the majority of the population accessing health-care services in any health facility in the country.

Inadequate availability of and access to essential health commodities are significant barriers to delivering critical health care in developing countries (Rao *et al.*, 2006). In recent reports (internal supply chain quarterly MOH reports), the availability of essential health commodities in most public health facilities was found to be improving. Improved availability of critical health commodities for the public sector requires building a robust logistics and supply-chain management system that includes all the elements briefly described earlier.

According to the World Health Organization (WHO, 2022), a reliable health supply system will do the following: integrate supply management into health-system development; develop an efficient mix of public–private partnerships; maintain medicines quality in distribution channels; and ultimately increase access to essential health commodities throughout the health commodities supply system.

In the next section, we will briefly cover the evolution of the related issues on health commodities access, availability, quality, effectiveness, affordability and rational use from a systems point of view. We will mainly focus on how, collectively considered, the six essential functions of the health supply chain evolved to improve the health commodities supply chain in the country.

5.1 Evolution of Health Commodities Supply System in Tanzania

The conceptual framework below (Fig. 5.1) will guide tracking the evolution of Tanzania's health commodities supply-chain system by a defined era or period in time.

5.1.1 Health supply chain during the pre-colonial and colonial periods, before 1885–1919

Traditional medicine healers, who prevailed predominantly before the introduction of modern medicines, used natural health commodities without any system but based on local availability. The commodities used lacked any assurance of safety, quality and effectiveness. Foreign occupancy and missionaries started to construct a physical health infrastructure for their curative services that used Western health

Fig. 5.1. Evolution of health commodities supply system in Tanzania.

commodities (Beck, 1985). Rudimentary health commodities supply chain functions emerged without specific training.

5.1.2 Health supply chain during the British era, 1919–1962

The British rulers attempted to set curative and preventive services at the community level by establishing dispensaries following the introduction of the native Authority Ordinance in 1926, and trained and employed dispensers and tribal dressers and established a central medical store for supplies (Table 5.1).

The evolution of the key functions of the public health commodities supply chain in Tanzania since independence, can thus be tracked over three sub-eras:

1. Central Medical Stores (CMS) era (1961–1993).
2. National Pharmaceutical Company (NAPCO, 1993–1997).
3. CMS transformation to MSD (as a semi-autonomous agency) and going forward (1993–to the present day).

This last period is further subdivided:

1. Functioning of the newly established MSD under the foreign executive management team (EMT) (1993–2003).
2. Overall supply-chain improvements through technical support from development partners:
    - the DELIVER Project (2004–2016);
    - the *Jazia* (Swahili for 'to top up') Prime Vendor System (from 2014, ongoing); and
    - Global Health Supply Chain-Technical Assistance-Tanzania (GHSC-TA-TZ) Project (from 2017, ongoing).

5.1.3 Central Medical Stores, 1961–1993

The procurement, storage and distribution of health commodities to government hospitals, health centres and dispensaries, as well the voluntary agency (faith-based) hospitals and dispensaries in Tanzania, has been carried out by a government-owned central unit, the Central Medical Stores (CMS).

In essence, until 1993 the CMS operated under four ministries: the Ministry of Health, the Ministry of Finance, the Central Establishment Office and the Ministry of Works (Ministry of Health, 1995). Under the Ministry of Health, CMS was organized as part of the pharmaceutical supplies section of the Hospital Services Department. A chief supplies officer headed the CMS and reported to the assistant chief medical officer of the Hospital Services Department. The Central Establishment Office undertook the implementation of civil service regulations. CMS as a government store was governed by the financial orders and stores regulations of the Ministry of Finance. The supervision and control of its buildings and facilities were under the Ministry of Works (MOW). CMS did not have the mandate to carry out direct procurement. The MOF did the procurement through its Central Tender Board.

During this period, CMS had poor performance due to multiple factors. These included poor product selection, quantification and procurement of health commodities, which were procured as branded products, whose purchases were influenced mainly by multinational pharmaceutical companies' medical representatives. By then, the concept of essential medicines, as we know it today, was non-existent. As a result, the health commodities' selection, procurement, storage, distribution and use were unguided and chaotic. Multiple procurements of similar products characterized this situation, often resulting in delayed port clearance and vast quantities of expensive branded products expiring on the shelves each year at CMS and the stores at the health facility.

In addition, the CMS being under four ministries caused immense administrative and management problems. The CMS's poor management of the health supply chain was further compounded by a lack of autonomy caused by operating under a highly politicized environment (with multiple interest groups that have competing interests influencing procurement, distribution and other supply-chain decisions for CMS).

Further, a politically oriented rather than technically oriented decision making process prevailed at that time; even if there was a generally agreed-upon technical solution to a problem, political considerations often blocked or obstructed technical solutions from moving forward.

Moreover, undercapitalization, inadequate managerial capability and underfunding from government, regional, district and central hospitals (Ministry of Finance, 1993) exacerbated CMS operations. This situation led to insurmountable inefficiencies that brought about constant leadership changes without any improvements in the operations of the CMS and the overall public health commodity supply-chain system in the country.

During this period, the local council collected supplies for primary health facilities from CMS, stored them at district stores and later distributed them to the primary health facilities. Usually, the responsible officer at the council, which could be the district medical officer or health officer, depending on who was available at that time, would determine the facility's needs or respond to the demands raised by the facility in charge.

5.1.4 The National Pharmaceutical Company, 1973–1997

The National Pharmaceutical Company (NAPCO) was established in 1973 as a parastatal organization under the umbrella of the Board of Internal Trade (BIT). Its main objective was to import health commodities (medicines and medical supplies), to supply the private sector and when deemed necessary to support CMS in acquiring health commodities for public health facilities.

NAPCO operated as a business company headed by a general manager under BIT. Besides being a wholesaler, it also operated retail pharmacies within six branches in Dar es Salaam, Mwanza, Mbeya, Dodoma, Moshi and Kigoma regions, from where patients could buy their medicines. In a way, the availability of drugs for cash relieved the pressure on public health facilities where services and medications were free.

Based on the government policies during that period, where private companies were not allowed to import pharmaceuticals, NAPCO was the sole importer, mainly serving the private sector, while CMS catered for public facilities.

At first, NAPCO operated efficiently and smoothly until 1978, when the country got involved in the war with Uganda. The war caused a severe deficiency of foreign currencies which heavily affected the performance of NAPCO. The importation of health commodities was drastically cut, resulting in scarcity of health commodities countrywide.

Further, the government ordered NAPCO to establish retail pharmacies at regional hospitals, to improve the availability of health commodities at the facility level for private purchase. However, NAPCO could not meet the demand from the facilities and the initiative failed. The NAPCO failure is an important lesson that needs to be taken into account when authorities are advocating the establishment of pharmacies for MSDs in hospitals, a repeat of history. This failure tells us that the involvement of government organizations into commercial business within the existing government rules, regulations and procedures may not work. Full commercial principles must be applied for such undertakings to succeed.

As crises mounted, to improve health commodities' availability in the country, the government liberalized the trade of health commodities, allowing private companies and individuals with foreign currency to import health commodities to support the health system. This move resulted in:

- Very stiff competition, as the number of suppliers increased, affecting the monopoly of NAPCO. The removal of the import monopoly, together with administrative and managerial issues, led to NAPCO closing its business in 1997.
- Compromised quality of multiple companies importing medicines through unregulated competition. At this time, the government did not have a competent regulatory authority to check on the quality of pharmaceuticals imported into the country. The responsibility of allowing pharmaceutical imports was vested in the Pharmacy and Poisons Board, which did not have any product registration system but approved imports without any mechanism for scientific evidence of effectiveness.

- The government triggering local production, which created two government-owned pharmaceutical manufacturing companies: the Tanzania Pharmaceutical Industry (TPI) and Keko Pharmaceutical Industry (KPI). However, both companies were also affected by foreign currency scarcity and operated far below capacity. Eventually 60% of their shares were sold to private individuals under the privatization policy. At the same time, the CMS was reorganized into a semi-autonomous organization leading to an 'eyes-on and hands-off' organization devoid of direct government control.

5.1.5 Tanzania's economic crisis, health-sector reforms and essential health commodities supply, 1978–1990

Tanzania's economic crisis

CMS challenges were further worsened by the economic crisis in the country between 1978 and 1990, triggered by the war to liberate Uganda and followed by the global recession. During this period, the government encountered difficulties financing and managing the rapidly expanding demand for health services. Structural adjustment measures (devaluation of the shilling, freezing staff recruitment and government spending, introducing cost-sharing measures in the education and health sector, among others) were imposed on Tanzania (Lugalla, 1995) by the IMF/World Bank, further aggravating the situation. At the end of the decade and further into the 1990s, a system that had promised improvement in health services could no longer do so. Attention to health-care services decreased as well, all together leading to an overall critical shortage of essential health-care services and commodities.

National drug policy, national essential drugs list and standard treatment guidelines

With a broader objective to improve the performance of the pharmaceutical sector, the government endorsed the first national drug policy (NDP), the standard treatment guidelines (STG) and the national essential drugs list (NEDLIT) in 1991. To further address the problem of the pharmaceutical sector, the government adopted a master plan for the development of the pharmaceutical sector (PSMP) in the country covering the period 1992 to 2000 (Ministry of Health, 1992), with the following main components:

- reorganization of the Central Medical Stores and the establishment of regional stores. However, the regional stores' plan was later abandoned in favour of zonal stores;
- changes in the drug distribution system from the 'push' kit system to a health facility inventory-based requisition 'pull' system;
- rational use of drugs through universal use of the NEDLIT and standard treatment guidelines; and
- increase in the local production of pharmaceuticals.

The PSMP provided a framework for the coordination of activities performed by various stakeholders (public, private, NGOs, donors and others). Implementation of the NDP and the PSMP was coordinated by the Pharmaceutical Services Unit (PSU) within the Ministry of Health.

The Tanzania essential drug programme and the kit supply system

To address the scarcity of health commodities at primary health facilities, as the result of the economic crisis, the government, in 1983, with the support of the Danish government through its agency Danida, launched the essential drug programme (EDP) to distribute EDP-kits to primary health facilities (dispensaries and health centres only). Hospitals continue to order from the CMS.

Under the EDP, two ration kits were used: a blue-coloured belt for health centres and a yellow-coloured belt for dispensaries. They were delivered every month. Each kit was expected to last a month, and, as they were already prepacked, the then CMS, later Medical Stores Department (MSD), only had to receive, store and distribute them up to the district headquarter level. The district would then later distribute them to primary health facilities with the aim to do so on the first day of each month.

Although district medical officers (DMO) had the mandate to redistribute dormant commodities to other health facilities with higher demand, that rarely happened because of transport and financial constraints. Nevertheless, the primary health-care system benefited from the kit system, because higher-level facilities could no longer divert kit contents for hospitals as was the case when they were supplied from council stores.

Details on the drug kit supply system, its contents and management, including advantages and disadvantages of the kit supply system, costs, relevance or pre-conditions to set up a kit supply system can be found in *The Logistics Handbook: A Practical Guide for the Supply Chain Management of Health Commodities* (USAID, 2011).

A study in 1998 found that almost all (99%) kits distributed arrived at their destination, pointing out that the advantage of a prepacked kit supply is that there is minimum loss during delivery (Pricewaterhouse Coopers Tanzania, 1999). Nevertheless, the standardized nature of the kits meant that, in some areas, certain commodities, especially drugs, were depleted at a faster rate, causing stock-outs or accumulated surpluses due to differences in demand and disease burden. Other reasons for more rapid depletion were miscalculation of the local needs and peak consumptions early in the month caused by an inflow of patients taking advantage of the delivered medications.

The kit system outlived the CMS and continued through the newly formed MSD.

Introduction of the indent supply system

In 2000, with the Danish government's support through its agency, Danida, the Pharmaceutical Service Unit (PSU) designed a new 'pull' system (Indent) to replace the drug kit system.

The Indent supply is a drug distribution system in which primary health facilities determine the health commodities quantities to be requisitioned from the MSD or the supplier. It is also sometimes called a 'pull' system, as opposed to the kit system, referred to as the 'push' system.

The Indent system was piloted in Morogoro region, covering all primary health-care facilities. The pilot result showed significant improvement in essential health commodities availability at the facility level compared to the ration kit, the push supply, system.

The Indent system expanded the list of essential medicines from 35 to 70 items. It allowed health facilities to specifically order individual medicines based on their local needs as long as the medicine was approved for that level of service.

For efficient delivery of these commodities to primary health facilities, the mode of delivery remained through a customized kit system. The customized kits were locally assembled by the MSD based on the orders submitted by the individual health facilities.

The system, however, did not include supplies for vertical programmes such as family planning and specific disease-control programmes (malaria, sexually transmitted infections (STI), tuberculosis, leprosy and HIV). These remained administratively and logistically independent within the MSD supply-chain system.

A detailed description of the Indent supply system can be found in referred sources (Management Sciences for Health, 2012).

Medical Stores Department (MSD) as a semi-autonomous entity, 1993–2022

In 1993, following the recommendation of the master plan for the pharmaceutical sector (MPPS, 1992–2000), developed as part of the health-sector reforms, it was finally decided to restructure the CMS, under one ministry, the Ministry of Health, with the view of converting it to an independent, efficient, autonomous and financially self-sustaining agency.

Before the establishment of the MSD, the Ministry of Finance implemented the recommendation of the MPPS (1992–2000) which was moved after the official establishment of MSD to the MOH by Parliamentary Act in 1993.

The MSD structure included a managing board of trustees to provide oversight and guidance on the operations of the new department. It also established an executive management team, which was required to operate the MSD for an interim period of 5 years. The MSD Regulations (1996) were prepared to guide further its operations in the interim and long term.

The primary role of the MOH remained in policy making and overall supervision of the pharmaceutical sector (private and public).

MSD interim period, 1993–2003

The MSD came into being in 1993 (Medical Stores Department Act, 1993), but operations effectively started in 1994 with the establishment of an external executive management team (EMT) of directors with similar numbers of local counterpart directors.

As specified in the MSD Regulations of 1996, during this interim period (1993–1998 and further extended to 2003), the director general and the other directors with their counterparts constituted the EMT of the MSD. The EMT responsibilities, meetings and decisions at these meetings were spelled out in the regulation.

During the ten years of the interim period, the MSD has been capitalized by the World Bank, with the expatriate EMT funded by Danida. MSD operations greatly improved, that is, health commodities' availability increased significantly as noted in several MOH internal performance reports, and the MSD became self-sustaining (as it operated under a cash and carry principle) to prevent capital drain. For example, at one point, the government granted the MSD 2 billion TZS for capitalization but the management returned the grant, indicating that the MSD was overcapitalized. Consequently, the MOH used the funds to procure CT scanners for Muhimbili and the Kilimanjaro Christian Medical Centre.

Upon the expiration of the interim period (1993–2003), operations of the MSD were characterized by frequent leadership changes that saw the slow decline of MSD operations to the extent of needing an infusion of new capital to make it operate as optimally as it had during the initial interim period of its existence. New capital could not easily be identified.

Some vital issues needed action to improve MSD performance during that phase. Questions about why MSD performance and efficiency declined after the departure of the expatriate EMT when it was built on a solid and stable financial base needed to be answered. In the opinion of the authors, the following three reasons might have contributed to a large extent to MSD's deteriorating performance:

- The fall of MSD was partly the result of operational changes. Upon the departure of the expatriate EMT, the MSD model of operation changed from business principles to a public organization model working on civil service principles. This pertains to abandoning a 'cash and carry' principle into the provision of credit facilities on ordered commodities. The credit facility relaxed the government's need to deposit money in a timely way at the MSD for public health facilities to procure their commodities for its facilities. Untimely payment of credits caused a tremendous erosion of MSD capital, resulting in a growing and accumulated delayed reimbursement arising from outstanding debts (i.e. the cost of their procurement, storage and distribution of commodities to health facilities). The debt was estimated at 200 billion in the FY 2017/18 (*The Citizen*, 26 October 2018), but at the time of writing this chapter, the debt is believed to have gone even higher.
- Failure to observe the MSD's legal semi-autonomous status, with the management directly answerable to the board of trustees and not to the sector ministry, sometimes subjected the MSD to decide on essential undertakings without critical analysis of its business impact. MSD operational principles were, on many occasions, violated by acting directly on directives from the sector ministry or higher authority. This attempt weakened the board's authority, making it incapable of managing the MSD effectively.
- The increasing demand for modern health services, the number of expanding primary health-care facilities and the employment of advanced medical treatment procedures in our tertiary hospitals are not critically analysed by decision makers at the government level. These changes have a tremendous impact on MSD future performance to meet all these demands and needs and to set up new strategies that could relieve pressure on the MSD. For example, the involvement of private suppliers in the spirit of PPP to some government officials is still taboo (unmentionable). It is better to realize now that, in the near future, the MSD may not be able to meet the national demand for health commodities. Therefore,

the need for other strategies, such as the prime vendor system (PVS), should be considered as alternatives to relieve the MSD.

5.2 Donor Support to Improve MSD and the Overall Health Commodity Supply Chain in Tanzania, 2003–2022

In terms of the improvement of the MSD and the entire health commodity supply chain in Tanzania, the country has benefited from a variety of projects funded by several donors. Key donors were the World Bank, Danida, the Bill and Melinda Gates Foundation, USAID, the Swiss Agency for Development and Cooperation and the Global Fund for HIV/AIDS, TB and Malaria.

Below follows a brief description of each of their projects, their achievements and challenges to support the supply chain.

5.2.1 World Bank

The World Bank Health and Nutrition Project, as part of the IMF structural adjustment approach, provided seed capital to the MSD following its establishment in 1993.

5.2.2 Danida

Danida supported several improvements in the health supply chain in Tanzania during the CMS era (1961–1993) and, as noted above, during the early years of the MSD (1993–2006). Danida supported the logistics of vaccines and supplies distribution for the whole country by providing vehicles to each district that carried vaccines and kits to primary health facilities, fuel for kerosine refrigerators that kept vaccines at health facilities and supported supervision activities within the districts.

Following the Indent system, supported by Danida, a new system for managing all health commodities, including those of the vertical programmes, was introduced through additional support from USAID and GFATM (The Global Fund). The system was called an integrated logistics system (ILS). It is briefly described below.

5.2.3 The integrated logistics system

The integrated logistics system (ILS) is a system for reporting utilization of health commodities and requesting resupply following specific guidelines which were widely distributed and used (Ministry of Health, 2013). The ILS also incorporates the various categories of supplies managed by different vertical programmes such as HIV/AIDS and malaria.

Each vertical programme had its own supply system, leading to fragmentation and overload of staff time, resulting in wide variations in effectiveness and efficiency. The ILS included all levels of facilities at PHC level, with different quantities and types of health commodities allowed to be kept and ordered. Under ILS, only the expanded programme of immunization (EPI), neglected tropical diseases (NTD), nutritional supplements and the National Tuberculosis and Leprosy Programme (NTLP) were excluded.

The ILS was piloted in Iringa and Dodoma in 2005 and was fully rolled out countrywide by 2009. The ILS introduced a new ordering system with different forms filled at all levels of health facilities.

The report and request (R&R) form was used (and continues to be used) for quarterly reporting and requesting order quantities of over 100 health commodities. The R&R document contains a fixed logarithm that needs data from the store's ledger and a physical inventory count to estimate quarterly consumption, which is subsequently used to estimate the quantities to order or required by the next quarter.

The completed R&R form is submitted to the district office for review by the DMO, though in most cases the activity is delegated to the district pharmacist. Any discrepancies identified in the order would be clarified and corrected before being sent to the MSD. Individual copies of R&R forms remain at the health facility, district office and the MSD. As previously mentioned, for the indent system, to ease the workload on the MSD due to packaging and delivery, the MSD divided the facilities into three groups (A, B and C), each placing orders quarterly but at different periods.

5.2.4 MSH SEAM project, 2000–2006

The Strategies for Enhancing Access to Medicines (SEAM) programme was funded by the Bill and Melinda Gates Foundation and implemented by Management Sciences for Health in Tanzania to improve access to essential medicines and vaccines in the developing world by fostering partnerships between the public and private sectors.

In collaboration with the MOHSW and relevant stakeholders, the project piloted and later rolled out nationwide the ADDO (accredited drug dispensing outlets) project to improve access to essential health commodities without prescription at drug outlets in peri-urban and rural areas. After 2006 these outlets continued to operate, but faced multiple challenges, such as providing far beyond the allowed set of essential health commodities and a lack of supervision and quality assurance, and operated only in urban areas. Details of the establishment, rationale and primary objectives of the ADDO project can be accessed through the Center for Pharmaceutical Management (2008).

Developed from concept to implementation in 2000, an alternative/complementary health commodity supply for the faith-based health facilities, based on the principles of public–private partnership, was developed by the SEAM project. Initially MSH approached the Ministry of Health with the concept of prime vendor, as an alternative to complementary to the MSD, but the parent ministry did not accept the idea.

The SEAM project then negotiated with Christian Social Services Commission and the Lutheran Church took on the idea. As a result, a prime vendor system started in the country's northern region. The faith-based health facilities used the system to obtain their requirement from competitively selected private suppliers in case the MSD could not provide. It worked for a number of years but with an improving MSD and due to internal operational issues the programme, though it continues to work, is weak and ineffective with only a few faith-based health facilities using the system. Nevertheless, using the same principles described later in this chapter, the government of Tanzania adopted a similar model to pilot and eventually roll out the *Jazia* (Swahili for 'top-up') Prime Vendor System in the country.

In close collaboration with the Tanzania Food, Cosmetics and Drug Authority (TFDA), which evolved into the TMDA (Tanzania Medicines and Medical Devices Authority), the SEAM project conceptualized and launched a nationwide port-of-entry assessment for pharmaceutical products, the Quality Assurance Programme. The intervention aimed at on-the-spot testing to ensure that essential health commodities entering the country were safe, efficacious and of acceptable quality. With these achievements, the MHS/SEAM project ended in 2006, leaving behind the above-noted improvements in the supply chain in the country.

5.2.5 The DELIVER pharmaceutical supply chain management (PSCM) project, 2004–2016

John Snow Inc. (JSI) was appointed to implement the DELIVER project to improve access to medicines and medical supplies by strengthening the public health supply chain through improvement in (i) health commodity logistics; (ii) quantification; (iii) procurement processes; (iv) quality assurance and pharmacovigilance; (v) warehousing and distribution; and (vi) pharmaceutical and health-care waste management. The end-of-project report details the project's achievements over the course of ten years (USAID, 2016). Highlights of the achievements are described in the following summary.

Policy

In collaboration with JSI, Danida and other stakeholders, the government of Tanzania developed supply chain and pharmaceutical priorities in the National Pharmaceutical Action Plan (NPAP 2017–2020) (Ministry of Health, 2016).

Capacity building

The project trained over 18,000 health-care workers representing all levels of the supply chain on various supply-chain functions. A total of 548 additional health-care workers and stock verifiers were trained in 24 regions on pharmaceutical waste disposal guidelines.

System strengthening

End-use verification data was developed, an instrumental performance-management tool for systems monitoring stock-out rates. For example, for artemisinin-based combination therapies for malaria stock-outs decreased from 24% in 2012 to 3% in December 2015 (USAID, 2016).

Logistics management unit

In collaboration with JSI and the Global Fund, the government standardized supply-chain management and hired 73 staff, who were placed in those units.

Management information system

Implementing an electronic logistics management information system (eLMIS), a web-based application for managing logistics data, created a more sustainable solution. Reporting rates from all sites between January and March 2016 increased to 93% for the integrated logistics system (ILS) and 95 and 92% for the antiretroviral (ARV) and laboratory logistics systems, respectively (USAID, 2016).

Quality assurance

This facilitated greater use of and sensitization to the pharmacovigilance system, resulting in a 76% improvement in the adverse drug reaction (ADR) reporting rate (USAID, 2016). The renovated laboratory at Muhimbili University of Health and Allied Sciences has enhanced capacity in research and development from which Tanzania and East Africa benefit.

Quantification

The project built local capacity and significantly increased the level of country ownership in the management of the quantification process. Achievements include 78% forecast accuracy rates for family planning in 2014, 94% accuracy rate for ARVs, and 95% for antimalarials in 2015.

Procurement

As of 2015, the project procured a total of $276 million-worth of health commodities: $205 million of antiretroviral therapy (ART), rapid test kits, and other HIV commodities; over $51 million of antimalarial commodities; and over $20 million of family planning and reproductive health commodities (USAID, 2016).

Warehousing and distribution

The optimal design and construction of the warehouse-in-a-box have nearly tripled the total number of pallet positions at the MSD. Optimized distribution routes improved access to life-saving health commodities and led to a 10% reduction in distribution costs.

These achievements are believed to have generated high impact and positive health outcomes for the Tanzanian health sector. The cited areas above contributed to strengthening supply chains, building capacity and ensuring health commodity security. Equipped with a vision for sustainability, innovation, and collaboration, the work during this period has produced systems and processes for high-performing supply chains, leading to greater availability of life-saving health commodities but not necessarily solving all the health commodity supply chain issues in Tanzania. More is yet to be accomplished to attain a skilled workforce with up-to-date tools to achieve a cost-efficient system. Given this background, the TA-TZ project took over from DELIVER in 2017 from the same donor and, implemented by a new partner GHSC, it aims to take the country to the next level of improved public-sector health commodity supply chain.

5.2.6 Jazia Prime Vendor System: A public–private partnership model to improve health commodity availability, 2014–2022

An assessment report of the MSD's performance in meeting health facilities' needs concluded there were major deficiencies and performance issues which called for the establishment of a supplementary or top-up system that was more efficient and transparent, with assured quality of health commodities and stabilization of prices. The supplementary supply system will only be used when the MSD fails to supply the requested health commodities (Wiedenmayer *et al.*, 2019).

Although in the early years after independence public health facilities were not allowed to procure health commodities from private suppliers, with the government change of policy in terms of the increasing role of the private sector in health services, participation and the introduction of the public-private partnership policy, in case of unavailability of health commodities at the MSD, public health facilities were allowed to purchase missing items from private health-commodity suppliers.

This direct purchase was limited to higher-level health facilities (district, regional and referral hospitals). The primary health facilities could only make purchases through the DMO office on their behalf and distribute the commodities to them. This approach did not reflect well the PHC principles, such as equity, active involvement in the determination of their needs and joint needs based on planning with the district health management teams.

Although purchases from private suppliers resolved critical shortages of vital health commodities that temporarily were not available at the MSD, the system faced a lot of challenges, such as:

- prolonged and bureaucratic procedures which had to be followed before the actual purchase of health commodities was made;
- unreliable quality of purchased health commodities from poorly prequalified suppliers;
- unstable prices of health commodities led to a great variation in prices of similar products from various suppliers;
- the widespread tendency of collusion between disloyal staff and suppliers, leading to erroneous prices to benefit individuals; and
- the increased tendency towards corruption as the system had poor transparency.

Following the multiple challenges encountered under the direct procurement from private suppliers through formal tendering (collection of three quotations), there was a need to develop a more effective and efficient, less bureaucratic and more transparent system, with much more stable prices and suppliers who were thoroughly prequalified. This led to the introduction of the prime vendor system.

This system is a complementary purchasing system from private suppliers whereby all public health facilities purchase health commodities missing at the MSD from competitively prequalified and appointed suppliers, called the prime vendors.

The system is known as the Jazia Prime Vendor System and it complements the system when the MSD has failed to supply some needed health commodities. There was only one prime vendor (PV) per region.

The Jazia Prime Vendor System is built within the regional administration, overseen, supported and managed by established administrative structures such as the regional administrative secretary (RAS), regional prime vendor coordination office, and regional and council health management teams. The Swiss Agency for Development and Cooperation (SDC) funded the initial stages through the Health Promotion and System Strengthening Project (HPSS) from 2014 to 2019. It was later rolled out countrywide by the government, with the support of various donor-funded projects including HPSS.

The selection of prime vendors follows a prequalification process first, then a tendering process for the prequalified suppliers only.

Bidders are evaluated on various criteria, after which the selected bidder enters into a contract with the region to supply health commodities for 3 years at fixed prices of agreed health commodities. These decentralized and structured private-sector purchases have improved accountability at primary health facility level through direct purchase of their needs from the approved vendor through the DMO office.

5.2.7 USAID/GHSC-TA-TZ project, June 2016–June 2021

To strengthen the health commodity supply chain in Tanzania, the TA-TZ project took over where DELIVER left off. TA-TZ officially ran operations in the country from June 2016 to June 2021 (and further extended to 2023) to compensate for years lost due to the COVID-19 pandemic and to prepare for the takeover by yet another USAID project called NextGen for the next 5 years.

As a continuation of DELIVER by different contractors, the TA-TZ project is designed to provide more specialized technical assistance to strengthen the country's health supply chain systems across various disease programmes.

The programme's goal supporting the development of an agile, robust, and sustainable health supply chain that will contribute towards improving medicines' availability and the health status of Tanzanians. In coordination with in-country and development partners, TA-TZ assists the government's health programmes and stakeholders by providing technical assistance across four objectives (Fig. 5.2).

The key stakeholders to this programme (in addition to USAID and CDC) include: the Ministry of Health (MOH), specifically the Pharmaceutical Services Unit (PSU), Diagnostics Service Section (DSS), Information, Communication and Technology (ICT) Directorate and vertical programmes, including the National AIDS Control Programme (NACP) and the National Malaria Control Programme.

The project has maintained continuity in supply-chain performance since taking over from the previous project (JSI|/DELIVER), sustaining or improving forecast accuracy, reporting rates, product availability and other key supply-chain metrics. Through these four objectives the project will be able to:

- strengthen central and local governance and accountability to the health commodity supply chain at these levels;
- improve the delivery of health commodities in the country and institutionalize the use of high-quality, accurate data;
- build capacity and a strong culture of collaboration among stakeholders; and
- be able to transition the logistics management unit (LMU) and other activities to government counterparts to accelerate and sustain efficient health commodities supply chain in the country.

The Holistic Supply Chain Review (Ministry of Health, 2017), conducted in 2017, has been the main driving force behind supply-chain achievements during this period (2016 to 2022). GHSC-TA-TZ was one of the key players in the planning and execution of the review, which the Global Fund funded. The review was accepted by all key public-sector health supply chain stakeholders, reflecting a shared vision for health supply chain challenges and priority areas for improvement. A costed National Pharmaceutical Action Plan was prepared to guide the implementation of priority recommendations of the review (USAID, 2018, USAID, 2019).

Through this programme, there has been improved stock availability through stock-outs

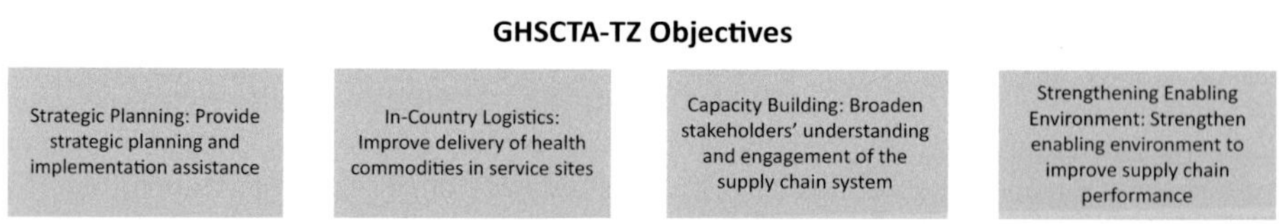

Fig. 5.2. GHSCTA-TZ health supply chain improvement objectives. (From USAID, materials are open source.)

reduction of key commodity groups. Specifically, health commodity stock-out rates were reduced to around 10%. Key to this achievement is the support the programme provided to the central-level quantification and the supply-chain processes at lower health-system levels through the LMU. The development and deployment of the eLMIS, which is embedded in the health-care ecosystem and firmly established as a vital part of the health-care environment, resulted in significant increase in access to health supply chain data (USAID, 2018).

The scaling up of the implementation of information management has seen an increase in the use of supply-chain data for decision making by stakeholders. This included the MSD supply-chain component of the results-based financing approach that incentivized MSD staff to improve their performance. These efforts have increased the potential for using data to improve supply-chain performance, for example:

- There is a general improvement in supply-chain data quality as health-system staff have become more familiar with the different technology platforms in the supply system.
- The ongoing effort to bring about interoperability between systems will also continue to improve data quality as more resources are invested in this purpose.
- A drive to invest in facility-level data reporting infrastructure through the eLMIS which allows direct capturing of 'dispensed to users' data, will further boost supply-chain data quality and availability of health commodities in the long term.

5.3 The Future Health Commodity Supply Chain in Tanzania

5.3.1 Background

With more advanced technologies, the future of the health commodity supply chain, like many areas in the health-delivery system, will achieve a more effective, efficient and patient-centred approach. As part of this evolution, Tanzania hopes to realize universal health coverage (UHC), which is set out in the fifth health sector strategic plan as a goal to be achieved by 2030. The authors present below a projection of what is likely to happen in the health supply chain, and what changes and actions we, as a country, need to pursue in order to prepare for this.

Given these technological changes and the current (2022) level of the health supply chain in Tanzania, what is the future of the health supply chain in Tanzania in the next 10–30 years?

Informed projections tell us that, in the coming ten or more years, an effective and efficient (low-cost and minimal waste) supply chain will prevail globally, including Tanzania. This transformation is due to the multiple effects of the fourth Industrial Revolution, which is currently ongoing as a result of a combination of advanced technologies, often referred to as 'industry 4.0 technologies or supply chain 4.0', which includes:

- the interconnection of computing devices via the internet (Internet of Things);
- analytics of large data sets;
- artificial intelligence and machinal routine handling;
- autonomous robotics and drone applications; and
- communication through satellites.

Combining many of these technologies, coupled with knowledge on management and application, will provide timely information for faster and better decision making to inform supply-chain actions. More importantly these technologies will eliminate the burden of supply-chain data collection and reporting currently imposed on the overburdened primary health-care staff.

5.3.2 Harnessing the power of the global fourth industrial revolution

Currently, the supply chain in Tanzania lacks quality supply-chain data to inform correct and timely decisions. The reason for this is that there is a disconnect between the reality on the ground and the data in the current system (e.g. eLMIS, among others) because of a lack of diligence by primary health facility staff to collect, provide and enter quality data. For example, to complete and forward a needed task, a common observation seen is the entering of a zero for 'stock values', apparently because facility staff do not want to count the physical stock.

Heavy reliance on primary health facility staff to collect data manually and semi-manually, manage and inform their stock levels, calculate order quantities and submit handwritten paper-based data to the district level or a nearby health facility with eLMIS, imposes significant responsibility on facility staff. The submitted data from over 7000 primary health facilities in the country also places a significant management burden on all upstream government of Tanzania and partner staff. These barriers create an effective cap on data quality that can be achieved with reasonable resource inputs.

It has been noted that systems with consistently higher data-quality management employ processes that shift facility-level data-gathering responsibilities to upstream entities (through informed push/mobile warehouse designs). Centralizing those functions through a data migration and management control tower approach would minimize the scope of the data-quality challenges that Tanzania is currently facing (USAID, 2018).

Accurate data and factual knowledge will be the basis for informed decisions and practical solutions. Health commodity purchases – in terms of what to buy, when to buy, what quantities to buy, et cetera, will cease to depend on guesswork (inaccurate forecasts and poorly functioning quantification data and planning models). With the adoption of technology that eases the data-collection burden, the entire health supply chain in the country should become technologically driven and more patient-centric.

With automated data collection, analysis and dissemination, the authors foresee that in the next 10 to 30 years, Tanzania's health supply chain will be technologically driven, that is, cutting-edge technologies will have become mainstream.

With the Internet of Things and health systems' interoperability, upstream and downstream supply chains in the country will be more connected than ever before. That means healthcare systems across Tanzania will have adapted to changes brought about by digitalization due to the fourth Industrial Revolution. It also implies that country supply chains will be interconnected with suppliers and other health services across the globe.

It is foreseen that the government of Tanzania, international agencies and private sector actors will have reorganized the healthcare delivery around signals due to extensive digitalization (the digital era). The data will be generated from patient populations and systems on a real-time basis. All health functions will be connected and interdependent.

The case study below paints the reality of what will happen regarding the supply of health communities to individual patients while they remain in their homes. It describes a situation encountered by a retiree, Mzee Hamza, living in downtown Dar es Salaam in Tanzania.

The moral of this story and its implication for PHC in Tanzania is that a digitalized delivery system, coupled with a drone system, can serve communities and patients who live in hard-to-reach areas in all seasons.

5.3.3 Initiatives and investments needed to align with the anticipated changes in supply-chain operations

The series of initiatives and investigations that the government, global funding agencies and private actors should undertake to build the capacity for future supply chains in Tanzania, as part of a long-term digital supply-chain strategy/roadmap, must include the following areas:

- building patient-centric supply chains – these will consist of building mechanisms for instilling a patient-centric culture in supply-chain functions, and clinical integration, whereby supply staff and clinicians work together;
- cross-unit/sector data partnerships – characterized by supply-chain integration: internal and external (end-to-end/down-up stream integration);
- capacity-building for new-era skills – invest in workforce training, entrepreneurial innovation and services, including investments in research and development;
- public–private market crossover – development of models for effective public–private supply-chain collaboration; and
- digitalization – collaborative data gathering, analytics and utilization.

Case study: Meet Mzee Hamza in the year 2030.

Mzee Hamza, a retired man, is waiting for the bus at Mlandizi outside Dar es Salaam. He reaches for his mobile and reviews the daily news. The day's events stream to Mzee Hamza on an advertising-supported video page. Absorbed in thoughts, he fails to notice how tired and thirsty he has become. A vibration on his wrist from his wearable glucometer alerts him that his blood sugar is higher than normal. He boards the bus and heads for home in Dar es Salaam. When he arrives home, Mzee Hamza takes out his 'at-home diagnostic test' gadget.

Within minutes, the test confirms a high blood-glucose level and recommends seeking further consultation with one of three local doctors currently available online. Mzee Hamza selects a doctor and calls for a video consultation.

Via the cloud, the doctor accesses Mzee Hamza's electronic medical record, including his vital health signs and genetic data. The doctor confirms his sugar levels, other allergies and the type of medication needed.

The doctor then transmits his prescription electronically to a local pharmacist.

Twenty minutes later, Mzee Hamza receives a notification that his medication is on the way, transported via drone.

When the medication arrives, Mzee Hamza hears his phone vibrating, alerting him of the arrival of his medicine.

He watches from his window as the drone lands near the front veranda of his small house in a densely populated and overcrowded part of Mbagala.

Before opening the package, Mzee Hamza carefully inspects the package to verify its authenticity.

Mzee Hamza's entire treatment experience is captured electronically and sent to a central system (an electronic data-control tower) that will inform future health-care planning.

A few days later, Mzee Hamza's sugar levels are normal, and he is healthier again.

As he returns to his daily routine, he pauses to consider the changes he has seen in the health-care system over the past 20 years.

He realizes that he no longer waits in long lines at the public health facility. He no longer worries about whether they have the correct diagnostics or medicines available or considers whether the health products he needs are of good quality. He is more confident in the quality of health-care services now than ever before, thanks to technological advances that have taken place in the country and globally in the last 10 to 30 years (adapted from Maeve and Prashant, 2017).

Fig. 5.3 provides an overview of where the country currently stands (baseline) and the projected future in achieving the goals of a digitalized health commodity supply chain.

5.3.4 Way forward

Moving forward, so as not to be left behind on the technological changes impacting on health supply chain, we in Tanzania need to take note of the facts:

- We are operating in an ever-changing environment.
- Our thinking, actions and ways of doing things must change.
- We need to align procurement and supply-chain management processes with the requirements of the fourth Industrial Revolution ecosystems.
- We can start with a baseline assessment of where we are currently (Figs 5.3 and 5.4) to develop strategies and prepare a realistic roadmap of actions and investments the country needs to make for the next 10 to 30 years.

Supply-chain advocates must take the lead to influence politicians to accept these anticipated changes and prepare for them.

5.4 Monitoring, Evaluation and Learning of the Supply-Chain System

5.4.1 Overview

The objective of logistics in pharmaceutical supply organizations is to make people, processes and systems work together to support the

over a particular time frame. Reports, in general, should be as concise as possible but, at the same time, they should include all vital information. The better the report structure, the easier and more accurate a performance evaluation can be. The report's objective could be as follows:

- to provide supervisors/managers with the necessary information to monitor activities;
- to keep a record of the history of supply-chain logistics activities;
- to provide an overview of how supply-chain logistics activities are arranged in the programme or field location, the key responsibilities and how well operations are managed;
- to identify what the current problems are and what pending activities are yet to be implemented; and
- to follow up and keep records on key performance indicators.

5.5 Best Practices

One of the critical parts of monitoring and evaluation is accurate data collection. Nevertheless, a good supply of data does not guarantee the achievement of the goals and objectives. In many cases, collected data is used to facilitate understanding past events rather than being used to drive future actions.

To benefit from the monitoring and evaluation activities, proper short-term, mid-term and long-term performance monitoring plans should be put in place. A measurement process must be put in place to ensure frequent, constructive reviews of defined measures and to develop a culture of measurement and improvement. All staff should be able to see how their performance affects the achievement of the organization's or health facility's overall goals and objectives.

When the progress of key performance indicators has continuously been tracked over a period, an organization and its teams can have clear visibility of the priorities of the organization or supply-chain system, which leads to easy identification of trends, strengths, weaknesses and opportunities. Having this information to hand allows the planners to learn and make better informed decisions.

KPIs should be carefully chosen, closely reflecting the organization's supply-chain system strategy and priorities. They should clearly and transparently communicate what is expected, what should be kept at the forefront of the mind and how the KPI should influence the execution of the day-to-day activities.

5.6 Lessons Learnt

With all the effort and resources put into improving the health commodity supply chain over many decades health commodity stock-outs remain a big challenge. Some of the key reasons include:

- insufficient funding of essential health commodities;
- inadequate staffing levels, compounded by the lack of appropriate technical skills (in pharmaceutical and supply-chain management) – at all levels of the supply chain (upstream and downstream); and
- inefficient and ineffective pharmaceutical and supply-chain information-management systems – that puts the burden of manual and semi-automated data collection and data quality accountability on the overburdened health-care staff at facility level.

5.7 Recommended Actions

Steadily, prospectively and simultaneously the government of Tanzania should endeavour:

- to increase funding for essential medicines, including those for specific disease programmes;
- to improve quality and quantity of pharmaceutical staff at all levels, with the appropriate technical skills (in pharmaceutical and supply-chain management) of the supply chain with prioritization of polytechnical staff (pharmaceutical technicians and assistants) to address supply-chain issues at primary health facilities; and
- to digitalize supply-chain data collection at all levels and thus remove the burden of data quality and collection from overburdened health-care staff.

Bibliography

Beck, A. (1985) Health care and society in colonial Tanzania: a new approach? *Reviews in Anthropology* 12(2), 109–113. DOI: 10.1080/00988157.1985.9977720.

Center for Pharmaceutical Management (2008) *Accredited Drug Dispensing Outlets in Tanzania Strategies for Enhancing Access to Medicines Program*. Prepared for the Strategies for Enhancing Access to Medicines Program. Management Sciences for Health, Arlington, Virginia. Available at: http://www.drugsellerinitiatives.org/publication/altview/addo-in-tanzania-strategies-for-enhancing-access-to-medicines-program-final-report/PDF/ (accessed 5 July 2023).

JSI (2017) *Supply Chain Manager's Management Handbook: A Practical Guide to Management of Health Commodities*. John Snow, Inc, Arlington, Virginia.

Lugalla, J.L.P. (1995) The impact of structural adjustment policies on women's and children's health in Tanzania. *Review of African Political Economy* 22(63), 43–53. DOI: 10.1080/03056249508704099.

Maeve, M. and Prashant, Y. (2017) *Designing Global Health Supply Chains for the Future*. The William Davidson Institute, University of Michigan, Ann Arbor, Michigan.

Management Sciences for Health (2012) *MDS-3: Managing Access to Medicines and Health Technologies*. Management Sciences for Health, Arlington, Virginia.

Medical Stores Department Act (1993) p.111.

Medical Stores Department Regulations (1996).

Ministry of Finance (1993) "*Letter of Undertaking for the Establishment of the Central Medical Stores as an Autonomous Government Agency.*" Government of Tanzania, Dar es Salaam, Tanzania.

Ministry of Health (1992) "*The Pharmaceutical Master Plan (1992–2000).*" Government of Tanzania, Dar es Salaam, Tanzania.

Ministry of Health (1995) *Pharmaceuticals and Medical Supplies Sector Study: Finance Study*. Government of Tanzania, Dar es Salaam, Tanzania.

Ministry of Health (2013) *Integrated Logistics System Guidelines*. Government of Tanzania, Dar es Salaam, Tanzania.

Ministry of Health (2016) "*National Pharmaceutical Action Plan (NPAP 2017–2020).*" Government of Tanzania, Dar es Salaam, Tanzania.

Ministry of Health (2017) "*Holistic Supply Chain Review of Tanzania.*" Government of Tanzania, Dar es Salaam, Tanzania.

Pricewaterhouse Coopers Tanzania (1999) *Tanzania Public Expenditure Review: Health and Education. Financial Tracking Study*. Government of Tanzania, Dar es Salaam, Tanzania.

Rao, R., Mellon, P. and Sarley, D. (2006) *Procurement Strategies for Health Commodities: An Examination of Options and Mechanisms within the Commodity Security Context*. USAID, Arlington, Virginia.

Rushton, A., Croucher, P. and Baker, P. (2014) *The Handbook of Logistics and Distribution Management*, 5th edn. Kogan Page, London.

USAID (2011) *The Logistics Handbook: A Practical Guide for the Supply Chain Management of Health Commodities*. USAID, Arlington, Virginia.

USAID (2016) *Health Logistics in Tanzania: Timeline of Accomplishments for Supply Chain Interventions, Supply Chain Management System*. USAID, Arlington, Virginia.

USAID (2018) *Midterm Review Final Report: Global Health Supply Chain Program Technical Assistance – Tanzania (GHSC TA-TZ)*. USAID, Arlington, Virginia.

USAID (2019) *Annual Report: Global Health Supply Chain Program Technical Assistance – Tanzania (GHSC TA-TZ)*. USAID, Arlington, Virginia.

WHO (2022) WHO work on supply systems. Available at: https://www.who.int/teams/health-product-policy-and-standards/medicines-selection-ip-and-affordability/medicines-supply (accessed 12 May 2023).

Wiedenmayer, K., Mbwasi, R., Mfuko, W., Mpuya, E., Charles, J, *et al.* (2019) JAZIA prime vendor system-a public-private partnership to improve medicine availability in Tanzania: from pilot to scale. *Journal of Pharmaceutical Policy and Practice* 12(1). DOI: 10.1186/s40545-019-0163-4.

6 Health Management Information and Evidence in Primary Health Care in Tanzania

Felix Sukums[1]*, Chacha Marwa[2], Mackfallen Anasel[3], Desderi Wengaa[4], Erick Kitali[5], Innocent Mboya[6], Oresto Michael Munishi[7], Leonard Katalambula[8], Antony Kapesa[9], Maryam Amour[10], Claud Kumalija[11] and James Tumaini Kengia[12,13]

[1]Directorate of Information and Communication Technology (ICT), The Muhimbili University of Health and Allied Sciences, Dar es Salaam, Tanzania; [2]Mbeya Medical Research Centre, National Institute for Medical Research, Tanzania; [3]School of Public Administration and Management, Mzumbe University, Morogoro, Tanzania; [4]Directorate of Digital and Information Systems, USAID/PS3 Plus Activity, Abt Associates Inc., Tanzania; [5]Directorate of Information and Communication Technology, President's Office – Regional Administration and Local Government, Dodoma, Tanzania; [6]Department of Translational Medicine, Lund University, 202 13 Malmo, Sweden; [7]Department of Strategic Information, International Centre for AIDS Programs, Jangid Plaza, Ali Hassan Mwinyi Road, Dar-es-Salaam, Tanzania; [8]University of Dodoma, Tanzania; [9]Catholic University of Health and Allied Sciences, Mwanza, Tanzania; [10]Department of Community Health, Muhimbili University of Health and Allied Sciences, Dar es Salaam, Tanzania; [11]Health Management Information System Unit, Ministry of Health, Dodoma, Tanzania; [12]Directorate of Health, Social Welfare and Nutrition Services, President's Office – Regional Administration and Local Government, Dodoma, Tanzania; [13]University of Dodoma, Tanzania

Abstract

Health information system (HIS) refers to a data collection and management system that supports the use of health information for planning, management and decision making. Robust HISs are required for the proper management of health data to produce and share high-quality health information for informing planning and decision making at different levels of the health system. This chapter presents the evolution of health information, the adoption of digital technologies and the evolution of primary health care (PHC) research and evidence in Tanzania. The evolution documentation covers four periods: before 1961, between 1961 and 2000, between 2001 and 2012 and between 2013 and 2022. Furthermore, the evolution of health information and evidence in PHC is organized around WHO's six building blocks. The chapter documents different developments,

*Corresponding author: fsukums@muhas.ac.tz

 Primary Health Care in Tanzania through a Health Systems Lens (eds N.A. Kapologwe *et al.*)
DOI: 10.1079/9781800623330.0006

achievements, challenges and lessons regarding the adoption of HIS digital technologies, and the use of different sources for evidence-based decisions for better PHC.

6.0 Introduction

This chapter describes the evolution of health information and evidence in the Tanzanian health system systems, focusing on the PHC level. The chapter describes various sources of routine and non-routine health information, the evolution of data collection and management, the evolution of PHC research conduct and the generation of evidence to inform the planning, management, delivery, monitoring and evaluation of PHC.

Robust HISs are required for the proper management of health data to produce and share high-quality health information for informing planning and decision making at different levels of the health system (AbouZahr and Boerma, 2005; Nutley and Reynolds, 2013). Managing the available health-care data allows health systems to create holistic views of patients, personalize treatments, improve communication and enhance health outcomes. At any level of the health system, specifically at PHC, HIS should be capable of capturing, analysing, integrating and sharing health data across the PHC level. In addition, HIS should facilitate data or information exchange at different health system levels.

With regards to digital health systems, different terminologies have been used over time to define the use of digital technologies in the health-care system, such as ICTs for health, HIS, eHealth and digital health. For instance, the World Health Organization (WHO) defined eHealth (electronic health) as using ICT for health; digital health as 'the use of digital, mobile and wireless technologies to support the achievement of health objectives. Digital health describes the general use of ICTs for health and includes both mHealth and eHealth'. Similarly, digital health includes eHealth, mHealth and telemedicine, in the widespread use of digital technologies for health-care and health-related purposes in a wide range of settings in health-care settings and public health (WHO, 2019).

Moreover, emerging digital technologies, such as robotics, 3D printing, drones and the Internet of Things (IoT), have led to the growing use of different digital devices by health professionals, health managers as well as clients (ECLAC, 2021). The use of digital solutions for health information management, such as electronic health records (EHRs), has transformed and facilitated the treatment of many classes of patients. The ever-increasing volumes of digital data relating to health-care treatment and patients have demanded advancements in big data analytics and AI-based innovations in improving decision making in the management of different health systems and public health (Sakr and Elgammal, 2016).

As indicated in the Tanzania Digital Health Strategy 2019–2024, digital technologies have great potential to facilitate timely availability and accessibility and the use of high-quality health information for the provision of better-quality health-care services, and thus digital health information systems should respond to the demands and needs of stakeholders, including clients, health professionals, health managers and policy makers through user-centred design to ensure responsive, resilient and inclusive health systems (MOHCDGEC, 2019).

6.1 Concepts of Health Information and Evidence

6.1.1 Health information systems

The health information system (HIS), as one of the six building blocks, is essential for health-system strengthening as it is a cornerstone of informed decision making. HIS facilitates the following four key functions: (i) data collection or generation, (ii) compilation or collation, (iii) analysis and synthesis, and (iv) communication or dissemination and use (WHO, 2008a).

Even though the terms HIS and health management information system (HMIS) are interchangeably used, HMIS is facility-based or institution-based service records or community-based routine HIS (RHIS). HMIS supports numerous clinical and administrative procedures and functions. HIS can refer to both paper-based and digital information systems. HIS involves both routine (mostly institution-based data sources) and non-routine data sources (Stansfield *et al.*, 2006).

6.1.2 Routine health information

Routine health information refers to data regularly collected and reported during health-service delivery in a health facility and community, especially in patient management, facility management, disease surveillance and monitoring of service provision and resource use (AbouZahr and Boerma, 2005; WHO, 2007; Glèlè Ahanhanzo *et al.*, 2015). The sets of health data collected are mainly statistics on health services, epidemiological data and administrative and financial data. Data in RHIS are primarily the significant sources of health information for evidence-based planning and decision making in the health sector in a country (AbouZahr and Boerma, 2005; MOHCDGEC, 2017a).

Electronic medical record (EMR) systems are key individual and administrative records systems at a health facility or service delivery points (Shortliffe, 1999). EMRs are digital versions of paper-based patient charts or registers. The systems capture a wide range of patient records, including demographics, medical history, medications, allergies, immunizations, vital signs, physical examination findings, laboratory tests, radiological images, photos, prescriptions, billing, payments and insurance information (Stein *et al.*, 2013). EMRs are more valuable than paper records because they enable health-care providers to manage data quality better, easily access and share patient information, track patient information over time, monitor patients' health status and improve health-care quality (Manca, 2015).

6.1.3 Non-routine health information

The non-routine health information sources include household and other population-based surveys, censuses, civil registration and vital statistics systems, disease surveillance systems, health facility surveys and administrative data systems (MOHCDGEC, 2017a). The non-routine health information collected from demographic and health surveys (DHS), health demographic sentinel surveillance (DSS) systems and other non-routine surveys complement routine health information. Disease-specific surveys contribute to non-routine health information. The DSS provided sentinel data for health policy and planning and to monitor the impact of health reforms (Mwageni *et al.*, 1998).

Other HISs implemented in Tanzania include registries for health facilities, health workers, clients and disease registries, and also civil registration and vital statistics, surveys and community data collection through paper and electronic registers and many other advancements that are shared by the Tanzania Government ministries, agencies and departments.

6.2 Evolution of Health Information Systems

This section presents the evolution of health information and digital technologies over time to improve PHC. The section will cover four periods: before 1961, between 1961 and 2000, between 2001 and 2012 and between 2013 and 2022. The discussion revolves around the WHO's six building blocks: leadership and governance, health information, health services delivery, health workforce, health planning and financing and health commodities. The aim is to document different developments, including achievements, challenges and lessons in the health sector as far as health information and digital technologies are concerned. Table 6.1 summarizes some of the significant HIS milestones achieved in Tanzanian PHC.

6.2.1 Evolution of HMIS Before 1961

In the period before 1961, Tanganyika was mainly dependent on research studies to gather health information and understand health statuses such as the prevalence of diseases, morbidity and mortality. There were no formalized health-information systems in health facilities

Table 6.1. HIS-related developments in PHC.

Year	Initiative or achievement
Before 1961	Health information was mainly dependent on research studies to gather and understand health statuses, such as the prevalence of diseases, morbidity and mortality.
1960s	Introduction of first health information system, called 'Kalamazoo', which dealt with only morbidity and mortality data (Mungwabi, 2006).
1980s	Over 46 data-collection tools were introduced through the first health-sector reform in 1982.
1989–1992	Inception of health management information systems (HMIS), including formulation of MTUHA paper-based tools.
1993	Launch and roll-out of the first version of HMIS/MTUHA.
1993–1995	MTUHA software in bDASE.
1994–1997	HMIS tools were introduced throughout the country while it transitioned through various significant milestones.
1996–1999	MTUHA major revision, software not compatible. Launch of the second version of HMIS/MTUHA. The MTUHA system was initially introduced in dispensaries and health centres. Introduction of a computer-based HIMS in district hospitals. HMIS tools were upgraded to accommodate hospital data, this addition was called Hospital MTUHA.
2000–2004	Lapse of funds to maintain and scale HIS.
2008–2010	Adoption and piloting of District Health Information System Version 2 (DHIS2) in Tanzania.
2009–2010	Introduction of specific course on health information management and financing (CMT 04212) was introduced as part of clinical assistant (CA) and clinical officer (CO) curricula to equip CO and CA students to use MTUHA tools, manage patient records and prepare and submit various reports to the relevant authorities.
2011	A five-year MESI was launched in order to enhance evidence-based decision making across the Tanzanian health sector.
2013	Government launched an eHealth Strategy (2013–2018) focusing on prioritizing the implementation of electronic medical records systems in district hospitals.
2013	Completed the national roll-out of the DHIS2 in all districts.
2013	The data dissemination and use (DDU) strategy was developed.
2016	Guidelines and standards for integrated health facility electronic management systems (iHFeMS).
2017	Launch of the Tanzania Health Data Collaborative (THDC) for coordinated actions to address the prevailing challenges in data and systems.
2019	Launch of the Digital Health Strategy (2019–2024) providing strategic direction in implementing digital health initiatives across the health sector.
2022	Launch of the PHC Digital Transformation Roadmap (2022–2026) providing guidance on mobilizing resources and the digitalization of PHC services.

and at the community level. As indicated in a report to the government on the health services of Tanganyika, most statistics, for example, the prevalence of diseases, morbidity and mortality, were obtained through studies. It was, therefore, difficult to have a precise assessment of priorities in the country's health needs (Titmuss, 1964).

Before and immediately after independence, computerization was not possible due to the absence of computers, and later even when computers became available, there was still a lack of basic computer literacy, technical support and supporting infrastructure such as electricity. In the early 2000s, the government started promoting the automation of some basic functions in hospitals and began using computers for record keeping. The improvement in using computers was partly due to the tax-free policy for computer importation and the increasing availability of electricity in big cities (Elovaara *et al.*, 2006).

6.2.2 Evolution of HIMS between 1961 and 2000

After Tanganyikan independence in 1961

In the 1960s, the journey to a formal health-information system began. The first HIS was called 'Kalamazoo' and it dealt only with morbidity and mortality data (Mungwabi, 2006). This system, therefore, was easy to manage and easy to orient and it was even easier to understand the filled-in data. As days went by, managers demanded more data, different definitions of the elements and even increased frequencies in reporting some data.

In 1980, a new information-management system started under what was then called the 'essential drugs programme'. This system was relatively more inclusive of other data, and therefore, the HMIS now having changed, contained more data.

In the early 1980s, vertical health programmes (VHP) started to flourish in Tanzania, from reproductive and child health (RCH) to expanded programmes of immunization (EPI) and others. As the number of these VHP increased, the number of health information needs also increased. Each VHP designed its HIMS(s). The systems were then visibly chaotic. The need for an integrated system became imperative, and stakeholders began to chart the way out.

A report to the government about health services in Tanganyika indicated that there was insufficient data regarding various disease patterns and health-service delivery indicators on which conclusions about the causes of high infant and child mortality can be based. This implied that there was no reliable HIS, for instance, disease surveillance, mortality recording and vital statistics and routine data recording on health services provided at the community and health facility levels. Furthermore, a review conducted in 1991 reported that inadequate informational management skills among District Medical Officers (DMOs) and Regional Medical Officers (RMOs) were one of the factors affecting the planning and management of PHC in Tanzania (MOH, 1991).

Health information management in the Alma-Ata declaration in 1978

The Alma-Ata Declaration in 1978 indicated that information is one of the critical operational aspects of PHC (WHO and UNICEF, 1978). Furthermore, the conference's objectives included exchanging experience and information on the development of PHC within the framework of comprehensive national health systems and services. This implied that health-information systems at PHC are vital foundations to obtain the required health information.

Furthermore, the conference stressed the need for technical and operational aspects, stating, 'PHC requires the development, adaptation, and application of appropriate health technology that the people can use'. By implication, this technology included ICT.

The conference also agreed and recommended that governments use simple and relevant information systems to support planning, implementing, budgeting for, monitoring, supervising and evaluating the delivery of PHC services, including better allocation, distribution and use of health resources and the improvement of managerial processes and capabilities. This should align with the development of health indicators for planning, implementing, monitoring and evaluating PHC, including community engagement and self-health care. The conference further called for promoting PHC among countries through sharing health information, experience and expertise. Furthermore, the conference called for an integrated approach to health-information exchange at all levels of health systems.

The planning, provision and supervision of PHC, as well as referral services, require high-quality information. However, due to limited organizational and technical capacities for information management in PHC, only minimum required data/information should be collected at the PHC and higher levels (WHO and UNICEF, 1978). The conference recommended starting with qualitative information rather than gathering precise quantified data. It further elaborated on the need for diverse information requirements at different levels and emphasized an incremental approach to information collection and management. Similarly, the conference proceedings emphasized data minimization during information sharing. Design, implementation and use of HMISs, including data collection, analysis and use, should be integrated into PHC rather than as an isolated business (WHO and UNICEF, 1978).

Establishment of the HMIS in the late 1980s and its first roll-out in 1993

Since its establishment in the 1980s, the HMIS has transitioned through various significant milestones. Several studies reported that the health system was being overburdened with over 46 data-collection tools which had been introduced through the first health-sector reform in 1982. Health workers reported lack of time to collect all the necessary information and were additionally challenged by the lack of technical expertise on how to manage and use the information that they had collected.

In response to this feedback from the health system, the HMIS was introduced with the aim of creating a routine data system that would be easier to use, manage and maintain. In efforts to introduce formal health information management practices, the government of Tanzania, in collaboration with different partners, developed the first version of HMIS which was launched in 1993. The first version entirely used the English language, and it was soon realized upon testing that the users had limited command of the English language. This necessitated the change from English to Kiswahili, the national language. Thus, the HMIS in Kiswahili is known as Mfumo wa Taarifa za Uendeshaji wa Huduma za Afya (MTUHA).

The first HMIS edition was published officially in 1993. It was piloted in all primary health facilities, dispensaries and centres in only two districts, Mbeya Rural and Mafinga. The paper-based HMIS version was later rolled out to all dispensaries and health centres in the country (Mahundi *et al.*, 2011).

Computerization of the MTUHA system

The computerization of MTUHA registers started in the same year, 1993, up to 1997. This system, for PHC, had 12 books serving all the data needs, including registers, tally sheets and report forms. At each administration level, there were MTUHA-focused persons or MTUHA officers. The ministry implemented a national computer database known as MTUHA Programme (MTUHAPROG). This proprietary HMIS was implemented in all regional medical offices in Tanzania. In early 2000, MTUHAPROG was developed on the Microsoft Access 97 database-management system and aimed to computerize important routine health data reported by health facilities at the district level (Sukums *et al.*, 2021). However, it was difficult to modify MTUHAPROG due to ownership of the source, which necessitated payment of a fee to make changes. MTUHAPROG was replaced by a national roll-out of DHIS version 1.3 in hospitals and districts.

Upgrading to HMIS second edition in 1997

HMIS/MTUHA was introduced in 1993 and has been revised two times, in 1997 and 2013. The first version of district health information software (DHIS) was adopted and piloted in Tanzania in the year of 2002, with DHIS 1.3, and transitioned to DHIS 1.4 later. The second roll-out was implemented in 1997 when HMIS tools were upgraded to accommodate hospital data, this addition was called Hospital MTUHA. Health facilities used paper-based reporting to the districts, and the districts captured these reports into their software. By the end of 1997, all facilities in Tanzania were implementing the MTUHA system except the four national referral hospitals and five specialized hospitals. The system was installed in computers in all 117 districts in Tanzania in order to facilitate health-data management and other administrative activities at DMO offices.

The stand-alone architecture of the two versions of HMIS had challenges in updating the software and data sharing. The challenges included the high operational costs due to the nationwide travel required for installing and maintaining the system, supportive supervision, troubleshooting and data submission (Sukums *et al.*, 2021). For instance, data from the systems was sent to the Ministry in Microsoft Excel sheets either as e-mail attachments or discs for entry into the national database.

6.2.3 Evolution of HIMS between 2001 and 2012

Health-information governance during the health-sector reforms, 1999–2006

The Joint External Evaluation of the Health Sector in Tanzania, 1999–2006, indicated that the Health Sector Strategic Plan 2 (HSSP2) prioritized improving central support systems such as health-management information systems and information and communication technology (COWI and Goss Gilroy Inc, 2007). The evaluation report shows that efforts were made to strengthen HMIS and were implemented in facilities owned by faith-based organizations and the private sector. Some of the HMIS-related weaknesses discussed include unreliable data and insufficient capacity for data management and use across the health sector. The report also indicated a need for a comprehensive framework for monitoring and evaluation. There was also a lack of clear roles and interrelationships between the HMIS, sentinel surveillance surveys, national census data and specific studies.

The baseline conditions in 1999 showed weak HMIS. The report indicated that a health-information officer (data management and analysis) should be a member of council health management teams (CHMTs) as per strengthening council health services. Also, a special section in the Health Information and Research Section (HIRS) of the Ministry of Health and Social Welfare (MOHSW) was recommended to systematically catalogue studies and results for improving the evidence base of policy making and planning.

The HMIS unit was established under the HIRS section of the Policy and Planning Division of the MOHSW. The HMIS unit was responsible for processing and analysing routine data from all health facilities. The HIRS section also conducts surveys together with the National Bureau of Statistics and has a National Sentinel Surveillance Unit (integrated into the MOH in 2002 after the completion of the Adult Morbidity and Mortality Project). Based on information collected through these various systems, the section prepares all information required for the JAHSR, the MKUKUTA, GBS and the MDGs. It compiles the Annual Health Statistical Abstract (COWI and Goss Gilroy Inc, 2007).

The Joint External Evaluation of the Health Sector in Tanzania, 1999–2006, also made the following health information-related recommendations:

1. There should be an exchange and sharing of information between regional hospitals in each zone and between referral hospitals in the country.
2. The monitoring and evaluation function of the MOHSW should be strengthened.
3. There should be a strengthening of routine and non-routine health information through HMIS and extensive surveys, such as the census, DHS, DSS, civil registration and vital statistics, respectively.

Reduction of funding and disintegration of HMIS between 2004 to 2008

The resources donors allocated to maintain the HMIS dwindled between 2004 and 2008. The system became corrupted and disintegrated after donor funding was redirected to the basket-funding modality. Within the basket funding, support to the HMIS was accorded lower priority than delivering direct clinical health services. Since the HMIS faced challenges and operated in a disintegrated manner, vertical programmes, such as those dealing with tuberculosis (TB), human immunodeficiency virus (HIV) and the expanded programme on immunization (EPI), established their parallel systems to routinely monitor and report the data required by the government and development partners. HMIS, therefore, continued to operate at a suboptimal level. Despite the disintegration of the MTUHA, all councils maintained data collection and reporting uncoordinatedly.

From 2004 to 2008, the HMIS disintegrated and experienced a low-performance period, including low usage of the HMIS due to the system's disintegration. Over the years, pressure on the MOHSW and other health-service providers for evidence-based decision making and proof of results mounted.

Commitment to strengthen the HMIS through the HSSP III in 2009

In 2009, a need to strengthen the HMIS was emphasized by stakeholders through the Health

Sector Strategic Plan 2009–2015 (HSSP III). The effort to rejuvenate the HMIS was undertaken by establishing and implementing the M&E Strengthening Initiative (MESI) from 2010 to 2015.

This national guiding document identified and committed the government and stakeholders to strengthening monitoring and evaluation, including the HMIS, as a key area of focus within the health sector. HSSP III 2009–2015 recommended the establishment of the monitoring and evaluation section, whose main roles would include, among other things, the creation of a more robust, locally owned and integrated HMIS. This would increase the availability of strategic information that would aid decision making for improving health outcomes in the country.

The Government of the United Republic of Tanzania, with technical assistance from international development partners, developed and implemented MESI to improve HIS in the country. HMIS was revised and remained a robust tool for documenting and sharing health information at the individual facility level. At the moment, all facilities in PHC use MTUHA to document all activities at the facility. Routine data are currently collected by 17 MTUHA books that comprise registers, tally sheets and summary forms.

1. Registers, that are used for patient identification with services provided at different clinics or units in a facility (e.g. OPD, IPD, laboratory, dental). Various programmes have specific registers, such as the expanded programme of immunization (EPI), antenatal care (ANC), family planning (FP), TB, HIV/AIDS et cetera, where each patient is recorded on a line and continuity of service to each patient can be followed and tracked.
2. Tally sheets are summary forms where necessary conditions and services that do not need follow-up are recorded with a mark and no patient identification.
3. Reports (summary forms) contain the selected indicators (as per services provided), which can be used to inform action at the facility or are sent to the district for further use.

Every health facility is required to fill 15 HMIS registers, namely: book 1: HMIS guidelines; book 2: facility and hospital summary book; book 3: community book; book 4: ledger; book 5: out-patient register; book 6: antenatal care register; book 7: child register; book 8: family planning register; book 9: diarrhoea treatment book; book 10: monthly report book; book 11: dental register; book 12: labour and delivery book; book 13: postnatal register; book 14: in-patient register; book 15: human resource register; and an additional two books which are: (i) laboratory register; and (ii) gender-based violence (GBV) forms.

The data systems that are used all over the country by all districts are presented in Table 6.2. Some of the data systems are used by all health facilities in Tanzania. Some health centres use others, but the positive thing is that all systems have already been rolled out to all councils in Tanzania. The plan is to enrol the same on all facilities, including health centres and dispensaries.

Health planning and financing

There are several digital solutions which are used at PHC level for efficient health planning and financing. These solutions include PlanRep and billing modules in EMR.

PlanRep – originally referred to as the Local Government Planning, and Reporting Database – was first developed and introduced in Tanzania over a decade ago under the Local Government Reform Programme. It was meant to simplify and standardize the preparation of local government authority (LGA) planning, budgeting and reporting processes in support of the decentralization by devolution policy (D by D). PlanRep links the strategic and annual planning process with expenditure tracking and implementation monitoring.

In 2006, in addition, the district burden of disease assessments and district health accounts under the Tanzania Essential Human Interventions Project (TEHIP) were incorporated into the new PlanRep2 planning guidelines and software in order to enhance the potential use of information for planning at the council level. Through the TEHIP project, Tanzania implemented health demographic sentinel surveillance (DSS) systems with sentinel surveillance sites in

Table 6.2. Existing health-data systems according to the health/health-related function.

Component/function	Reporting tools	Format	Disease/domain
Health management and routine data management	HMIS/MTUHA registers	Paper	All
	Patient management tools Eight tools (5 recordings and 2 reporting): CTC 1 CTC 2 Pre-ART registers ART registers Cohort analysis register Cross-sectional reports Cohort analysis	Paper	HIV/AIDS
	DHIS2	Digital	All
	DHIS-ETL	Digital	TB
	CTC 2 database	Digital	HIV
	CTC 3	Digital	HIV
Health operations management	GoT-HOMIS	Digital	All
Health workforce	HRHIS, TIIS, LAWSON, professional councils' databases, WISN/POA, biometric attendance	Digital	N/A
Inventory management	eLMIS (report and request), integrated logistics system (ILS)	Digital	All
	CTC pharmacy module	Digital	HIV/AIDS
	Ledgers and dispensing registers	Paper	All
Financial management/ budgeting and planning	Facility financial accounting and reporting system (FFARS)	Digital	N/A
	PlanRep GePG	Digital Digital	N/A N/A
	CCHP using PlanRep 3	Digital	N/A
Health insurance	National Health Insurance Fund	Digital	All
Disease surveillance and reporting	eIDSR, IDWE	Digital Paper	Communicable diseases
ePRS Client registry Health-facility registry	Digital web-based and mobile apps	Digital	Administration
OpenSRP/Unified Community System	Community-based HIS	Digital	All, HIV

several districts. The DSS collected longitudinal information on the population's demographic, household, socio-economic (education, occupation) and environmental (source of drinking water and sanitation facility) characteristics. Verbal autopsies were conducted on all registered deaths using specific standard questionnaires to determine the causes of death.

Over the years, PlanRep has been improved and extended to reflect developments in planning and financing at the local government level. In the health sector, for example, the development of the meso and macro versions allowed for aggregation and scrutinization of both budgets and reports at regional and national levels, respectively, to facilitate monitoring of local authority health spending in line with national priorities.

6.2.4 Evolution of HIMS between 2013 and 2022

Leadership and governance

Strong leadership and governance is a cornerstone for ensuring proper coordination, investment, implementation, monitoring and evaluation of HIS. Similarly, leadership and governance require a well-functioning HIS for evidence-based planning, policy formation and decision making at the PHC level. There is also a need for a strong digital health and data governance at the PHC level.

Ensuring strong leadership and governance of digital technologies, data systems and digital transformation is paramount in the digital era. It is the role of digital health leadership and governance structures to ensure that the data systems or digital health interventions are developed and implemented to allow seamless, sustainable and secure data and information exchanges at all levels of the health systems.

Launch of the national e-Health strategy in 2013

In 2013, the e-Health Strategy 2013–2018 was launched as a guide to the deployment and use of ICT in the health sector (Darcy *et al.*, 2014). Since then, several strategic initiatives have been implemented to improve health-care service provision and data management and use for informed decision making in policy making, planning and implementation of health interventions. The MOHCDGEC planned to ensure that, by 2020, all hospitals and at least 25% of primary health facilities utilized ICT applications for administrative, financial and clinical operations and ensured interoperability among the digital health systems.

In 2016, the government produced guidelines and standards for iHFeMS (MOHCDGEC, 2016), with a strong focus on improving the efficiency of administration and revenue-management business processes in large health facilities covering district hospitals. The guidelines document has helped implement other HMIS systems for general guidance and reference on functional and non-functional requirements for developing and implementing hospital information systems.

In the same year, national guidelines on data quality assessment (DQA) were developed to ensure the management, availability, accessibility and visibility of high-quality health information across the health sector. All these documents provide operational guidance and standards in health-data management, including data collection, analysis, quality control, sharing and use for informing practice.

Health data collaborative for improved evidence-based decisions

In 2017, the Tanzania Health Data Collaborative (THDC) coordinated actions to address the prevailing challenge in data and systems (MOHCDGEC, 2017b). THDC aimed at harnessing the collaboration and partnership of government agencies with its partners and stakeholders, including in-country health-development partners, civil society and the private health sector, to improve coordination and harmonization of health data-related investments and initiatives. The initiative aimed to improve further and harmonize the information and data systems in Tanzania to increase efficiency and improve outcomes of the investments made to a single monitoring and evaluation framework for the tracking goals of the Health Sector Strategic Plan 2015–2020 (HSSPIV) and sustainable development goals (SDGs). THDC has prioritized adopting digital solutions and enhancing data governance and use across the health sector, including in PHC.

Launching of the national digital health strategy in 2019

In 2019, the government of Tanzania launched the Digital Health Strategy 2019–2024 to provide strategic direction in implementing digital health initiatives across the health sector

(MOHCDGEC, 2019). Thereafter, the Tanzania Digital Health Investment Road Map was revised and aligned with the new digital health strategy (Watts, 2020). The refreshed roadmap includes 37 costed investment recommendations, two of which are to enhance health-service delivery through investments to digitalize hospitals and PHC. Among other things, the strategy strives to utilize digital technologies to improve efficiency, accessibility (including telehealth), patient safety and quality and continuity of care.

PO-RALG, in collaboration with stakeholders at the national and PHC level, is finalizing the development of the PHC Digital Transformation Roadmap 2022–2026 (PO-RALG and MOH, 2022) to coordinate and mobilize resources for implementing the digitalization of PHC services.

Roles of PHC organs in digital health governance

Leadership and governance during the planning, implementation and use and maintenance of HMIS and digital health solutions at PHC are of critical importance in ensuring the successful adoption and use of the systems and data generated from the systems. Different actors at the PHC and secondary and tertiary levels have various roles and responsibilities in ensuring the visibility and use of quality data at the service delivery points or decision making stations. For instance, health workers at different levels are responsible for data collection, collation, storage, curation, analysis and dissemination and use for various health-care provision purposes and resources management, planning and decision making aspects.

The Tanzania Digital Health Strategy 2019–2024 streamlined governance structures at national and subnational levels to ensure effective management of digital health initiatives and systems and increased data use (MOHCDGEC, 2019). However, the functioning of these structures is more observed at the national level. The less effective digital health governance structures at lower levels of health systems are setbacks to the overall efforts and investments in PHC digitalization. The previous strategy did not stipulate digital health governance structures to guide the development of digital health at the PHC level. In the current strategy, the digital health governance structure includes the CHMTs, institutional digital health committees and health facility digital health committees. However, there are no functional digital health governance structures at the PHC level, thus slowing the overall efforts and investments in PHC digitalization.

At the primary level, members of RHMT and CHMT are responsible for health information management apart from their overall responsibility for coordinating, supervising, monitoring and coordinating health-service delivery. Health management teams at different levels are responsible for the regular performance and data reviews to ensure the availability and utilization of quality data for improving better health-care delivery to Tanzania, especially in rural and underserved communities and populations. Regional and council health management teams ensure quality data is collected, managed and used for better PHC in Tanzania. Furthermore, health facilities are responsible for daily performance management and supervision of the use of health information systems available in their respective facilities by making sure health workers are capable of capturing, managing, analysing and using data at the service delivery points. MOHCDGEC and PO-RALG provide HIS guidelines, including standards and procedures for data management and use (MOHCDGEC, 2017a).

While the ministry's role is to provide strategic oversight to ensure the roadmap for digitalization of PHC responds to the broader health-sector goals of increasing quality, access and equity of health services through the use of digital systems and data, PO-RALG is focused on developing, evolving, implementing and rolling out the health operations management information system (i.e. GOTHOMIS) for PHC facilities in collaboration with different stakeholders, including development and implementing partners.

Evolution of DHIS2/HMIS

DHIS was adopted by MOHSW in 2008 and was later piloted in Pwani region. Before rolling it out to the rest of the country, the ministry revised all its HMIS paper tools. The process was finalized in 2011. The significant steps of the DHIS2 adoption, piloting and national roll-out are summarized in Fig. 6.1. Data from the forms

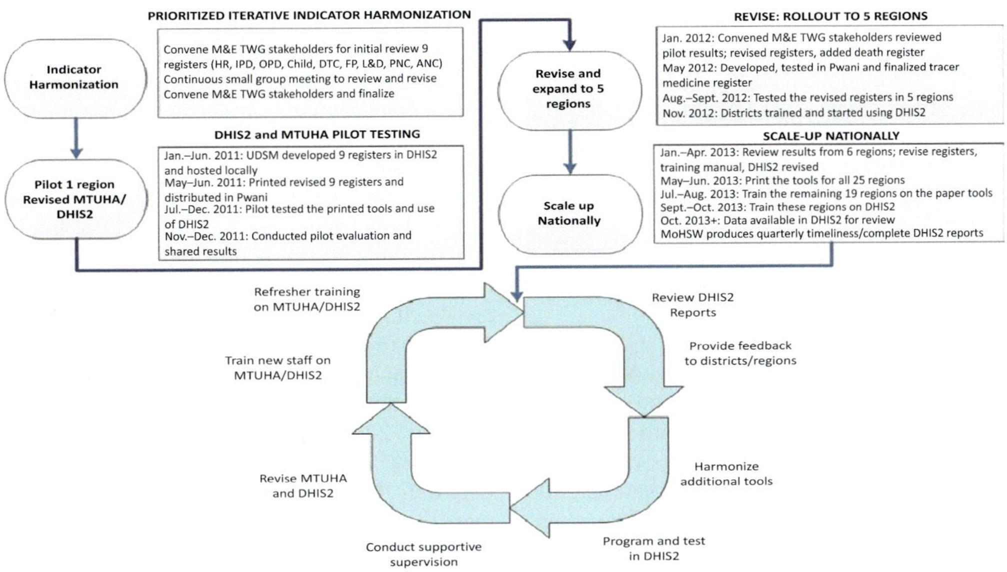

Fig. 6.1. Major steps of DHIS2 adoption, piloting and national roll-out. (Copyright © Ministry of Health, Tanzania.)

are congregated at the facility or district level and fed into the DHIS2. Once entered into the DHIS2, the data is accessible to all levels within the health system and is used for making sound, evidence-based decisions related to service provision and management at all levels of the health sector.

In 2013, the third version of HMIS was introduced when a set of registers, tally sheets and summary forms was introduced; this went hand in hand with the roll-out of DHIS. Before 2013, there were 12 HMIS booklets, and in 2018 this was improved and the number of books increased to 17, into which data has to be entered manually. The system covers all health programmes and health-care services. Regardless of ownership, it requires all health facilities to use the system and report to the district health authorities monthly. The overall goal of the HMIS system is to optimize the performance of health services at all levels of administration through the timely provision of necessary and sufficient information required by the health managers to monitor, evaluate and plan their activities. Its success requires an integrated, decentralized, functional and reliable system (Mboera *et al.*, 2001).

Implementation of eHealth strategy, 2013–2018

The government of Tanzania regularly conducts mapping of data-health systems or digital-health solutions and initiatives across the health sector. In 2018 the implementation of Tanzania's first eHealth strategy was assessed. The assessment revealed the increase in the maturity level of digital technologies had shifted the focus of collecting and reporting from aggregate data to client-level data and hence improved data usability at all levels of the health system. A total of 169 health-related data systems operational in Tanzania were identified in assessment conducted in 2020 (Kikoba *et al.*, 2019; MOHCDGEC, 2019). Some of the systems have national coverage, while others are institutional, others at a specific geographic location or programme-based, and some of them are at the piloting phase, while others are operational. However, the implementation was found to be less coordinated and fragmented, and with limited interoperability. There were limited digital health solutions at the PHC level.

Moreover, at the PHC level, digital health systems are expected to address health-system challenges related to the management of health facilities, service delivery, health workforce, health information systems, health commodities and technologies, and health financing and financial management. Table 6.2 presents some of the systems used within PHC and linkages to disease-specific, subnational- or national-level data systems.

Revolution of health commodities-related HIS

Different digital solutions have been implemented to improve the management of the health supply chain across the health sector. The MOH, in collaboration with partners, customized an open-source platform named OpenLMIS and implemented an electronic logistic management information system (eLMIS), which was later integrated with an EPICOR 9-based enterprise resource planning (ERP) system at the Medical Stores Department (MSD). The EPICOR 9 EPR covers procurement, financial management, warehousing and inventory management.

The eLMIS is an information system designed to manage data on medicines and medical supplies. The system starts with the health facility in charge of government-owned and faith-based facilities filling in a paper-based requisition and report (RR) form that serves a dual purpose of reporting available stocks while requesting a re-supply of stocks for the next quarter. The RR forms are sent to the district, on a quarterly basis, where the district pharmacist (DP) enters the data in a computer-based system known as the eLMIS. The frequency of reporting has now been changed from quarterly to monthly. Data entered in the system includes the quantity of medicine and medical supplies available at the end of the quarter, the quantity used in the respective quarter and the quantity requested for the next quarter.

The system allows primary health facilities to order and receive health commodities through RR forms. The eLMIS is a centralized web system, thus allowing data entered at PHC level to be immediately accessed by officials at district levels, the MSD and the Pharmaceutical Supplies Unit of the MOH and officials at PO-RALG. At the MSD, a logistics management unit (LMU) processes the RR forms and converts them to orders used to prepare delivery packages. Since 2018, the eLMIS has been integrated with EPICOR, software used by the MSD for various functions including procurement, stock management, financial management, warehousing and distribution of medicines and medical supplies.

In some PHC facilities, different HIS were deployed to facilitate the management of information about health commodities and general health supply-chain management. eLMIS, based on OpenLMIS, was rolled out countrywide in 2014 for the managing, requisition and reporting of health commodities. The ILS Gateway, based on CommCare Supply, was used to gather data on 22 tracer commodities from more than 4500 facilities, feeding this data into the national eLMIS. eLMIS was used to manage more than 6000 service-delivery points and supports requisitioning supplies for all programmes, including malaria, TB, HIV/AIDS, laboratory commodities, essential medicines and vaccines and some other essential supplies. ILS Gateway installed on a mobile device was used by facilities for managing their inventory. The system facilitated alerting on stock-outs, calculating reorder amounts, managing requisitions, tracking of orders, notifying upcoming deliveries and ensuring compliance with supply-chain standard operating procedures.

The immunization and vaccine development (IVD) programme uses its system, the vaccine information management system (VIMS), which is a web-based source of data on commodities, cold-chain assets and routine immunization. Most PHC facilities used paper-based reporting forms in which data were entered into the VIMS by the district immunization and vaccination officers (DIVO). Immunization data is also reported through HMIS forms and entered into the DHIS2, which is linked to the VIMS through the HIM. VIMS was implemented to improve the requisition and distribution of vaccines and cold-chain drugs. VIMS is used at the council level for entering data from health facilities which are collected using either the paper-based system or integrated with the Tanzania Immunization Registry (TImR).

Moreover, the IVD programme has implemented the Tanzania Immunization Registry for managing immunization cases and commodities at health facilities, which is expected to be within the VIMS. The TImR is a tablet-based mobile application deployed in over 3700 primary health facilities in 15 regions as of December 2020 (Secor *et al.*, 2022). Its introduction aimed at improving the tracking of vaccines and children of vaccination age and the management of defaulters. It also aimed at reducing the data collection burden on health workers through the use of barcodes to retrieve up-to-date information.

There were also plans to integrate all vertical programme data requirements at health facilities into the improved GoTHoMIS at the government-owned PHC facilities. The government and its partners are striving to improve demand-driven forecasting, delivery, distribution and consumption of required commodities across the health sector. The integration of different systems will enable health facilities, districts, health programmes and institutions to order the correct amounts of drugs and other commodities in a timely manner. EMRs and other client-level data systems at the point of care (POC) should be capable of tracking and showing the quantity of drugs/commodities utilized, as well as stock levels in each POC, so that demands can be generated and automatically submitted to the national eLMIS. This will minimize or eliminate frequent stock-outs and expired medicines, which used to be a common problem and is currently being faced by some health facilities.

Private and faith-based PHC facilities have a range of hospital information systems with varied functionalities related to inventory management, stocks and supplies and dispensing. The PHC facilities also use parallel laboratory systems such as Labnet and DAISA, which have some components of health commodities.

The National AIDS Control Programme (NACP) CTC2 pharmacy module is an MS Access-based system used in many facilities to manage dispensing and stocks of ARV and OI drugs, linked to the NACP CTC2 database. The NACP CTC2 database itself is in use in more than 3000 facilities, but not all of those use the CTC2 pharmacy module.

The ILS Gateway facilitated communications between facilities and the MSD on stock levels. It focuses on 20 priority 'tracer commodities' rather than all products. These 20 commodities include family planning, malaria, laboratory and some other essential supplies. It allows reporting by facilities on basic phones by structured SMS. It was used by over 4800 facilities which are all low-level 'ordering' facilities (non-ordering satellite facilities and hospitals are excluded). The ILS Gateway transport module was also implemented and used to assist in management and communication during the delivery of commodities from warehouses to health facilities by drivers.

The limitations of the logistics systems included limited coverage of the systems and increased workload due to the parallel use of paper-based requisition and report form reported monthly to the district pharmacist (DP) who enters the data into the eLMIS.

Service delivery

IMPLEMENTATION OF ELECTRONIC MEDICAL RECORDS. Since 2015 the government of Tanzania has made a tremendous change in electronic medical records (EMRs). It started with the development of GoT-HOMIS in 2015 by PO-RALG in collaboration with MOHCDGEC, Mzumbe University and Kibaha Education Center (KEC). GOTHOMIS is an electronic information system intended to collect and report individual-level clinical information (basic patient-level clinical data set) for both hospitals and PHC facilities, and to support health facilities in service delivery management. PO-RALG and MOHCDGEC, in collaboration with the PS3 project, made significant improvements to the systems. The focus is to enrol all health facilities in Tanzania in it, in order to move from paperwork to electronic data collection, management, analysis and decision making. The introduction of GOTHOMIS Lite to address issues like centralization, deployment to low-resources settings, the addition of missing modules and integrations with other systems through Muungano and OpenHIM have also been implemented.

GOTHOMIS captures registration (regular/emergency), clinical and investigations data across patient-visit episodes. With a centralized repository of the data at the national level, GOTHOMIS makes it possible to have a complete patient profile and medical record whenever a patient visits any health facility across the country. The availability of centralized data is also an indispensable ingredient for data analysis, research and decision making at a facility, at LGA, regional and national levels. As of July 2022, more than 1462 facilities were using GoTHOMIS.

DIGITAL SOLUTIONS FOR COMMUNITY HEALTH SERVICES. The strategy emphasized the enhancements in the use of digital solutions to engage community health workers for improved provision of community-based health services and promote community engagement. Tanzania has, over time, implemented several digital solutions for primary and community health care. The initiatives include needs assessment for digitalization of PHC facilities and community health services, covering ICT infrastructure and hardware, human resources and training needs, and assessment of existing digital implementation status.

Different partners have been supporting the government in leveraging the Open Smart Registers Platform (OpenSRP) community digital platform to improve community health-care delivery and referral systems for HIV, RMNH, malaria, TB, family planning, nutrition and gender-based violence in Tanzania. The use of OpenSRP aligns with the government's priorities of extending mHealth platforms and fostering sustainability and interoperability with existing systems such as EMRs at health facilities and DHIS2. OpenSRP mobile application has been used by community health workers (CHWs) and volunteers for various purposes, for example, patient registration and tracking, surveillance activities in their community, household visits, school visits, community and facility workflow management and decision support system et cetera. In 2022, the government has adopted the OpenSRP as a unified community system (UCS) to be used for all community-based digital health interventions.

DIGITAL SOLUTIONS FOR HEALTH PROMOTION. Tanzania has been using digital platforms for community health, client feedback and health promotion-related interventions since the 2010s. The mHealth platform was established to host several solutions, including mHealthPPP and other programmes for a range of services to inform, educate and remind clients about health issues using SMS. There is a need to further integrate this information, education and communication messaging services in one platform, expand beyond SMS to leverage the growing use of smartphones by clients, and also leverage client data to personalize content, through linking with point-of-service systems. In this area, the Afya Maoni project electronically collects client feedback. There is a need to strengthen and scale this work as a comprehensive client feedback and feedback response system.

HEALTH WORKFORCE. Like many sub-Saharan African countries, Tanzania faces a serious shortage of human resources for health (HRH). Adequately dealing with the human resource challenge requires accurate and up-to-date information on the current supply and status of health workers in the country.

The government has been striving to use digital solutions or systems for human resource information management to effectively address staffing shortages and the skills-mix imbalance, and to use e-learning systems and other digital solutions for the provision of pre-service and in-service education, including continuing professional development.

To address the human resource and information systems crisis, the Tanzanian MOHSW revised its HRH Strategic Plan in 2008. One of the prioritized activities was establishing a comprehensive human resource for health information system (HRHIS) and the training institution information system (TIIS), to capture information from both the public and private sectors to facilitate effective planning, production, recruitment and retention of human resources in Tanzania (Ishijima *et al.*, 2015). The systems were developed and tailored according to the needs of the government, allowing for better planning, production, recruitment and retention of human resources in health.

To enhance the optimal allocation of the health workforce in 2015, the MOH, in collaboration with implementing partners, developed the prioritization and optimization analysis (POA) and workload indicators for staffing needs (WISN). Additionally, the health workforce allocation optimization tool (WAO) was developed to support the recruitment and allocation of health workers to health facilities. The systems have been integrated with other systems such as human capital management information systems (HCMIS), professional council databases and training institution regulators (Tanzania Commission for Universities [TCU] and National Council for Technical Education – Vocational Education Training [NACTEVET]) to support real-time data available to inform policy and decision making.

The tools use an evidence-based approach and health indicators to drive health workforce optimization and allocation decisions. This has improved the management and allocation of the workforce in Tanzania based on need and maximizes employee satisfaction by deploying workers to their preferred working stations. There are ongoing efforts to ensure all health workforce-related systems exchange data for easier access to quality workforce data.

Health planning and financing

In 2017, the PlanRep system went through a process of transformation. Key features were added to the system to help deliver the wider system goals of accountability, transparency, efficiency and equity (Ruhago *et al.*, 2022a). One of the most significant improvements is the extension of the system to the lower local government (LLG) level, through the inclusion of facility-level data. This has enabled LGAs to progressively incorporate the plans and budgets of service providers, facilitating analysis of activities and spending at those lower levels, and more directly reflect the outputs of the opportunities and obstacles to development (O&OD) process. Additionally, other key improvements of PlanRep included an overall system design of the technology itself. Instead of being a stand-alone, desktop-based software prone to version issues, the new PlanRep is housed on the government's central server and is accessible via the web from anywhere, anytime. Its technology platform also creates the opportunity for additional enhancements and the integration of key systems.

In 2017, PO-RALG and the MOH, in collaboration with PS3 and other partners developed FFARS, a unified system of accounting and reporting used to capture expenditures of different sectors (such as health and education) at the facility level (Ssennyonjo *et al.*, 2022). This software records budget disbursement and expenditure and generates reports at facility, council, regional and ministry level.

FFARS was transformed from the existing manual templates of all public expenditures into an electronic system that could be accessed at any locality from the central, regional or local government level. All health facilities in Mainland Tanzania were using electronic FFARS (6000 + facilities with a 99% + system use rate) as of July 2022, and all responsible ministries can access information on how facilities are spending funds on a daily basis. The commitment of health facilities and schools to use FFARS and improve their financial management was reflected in the effort of facilities without connectivity to travel to a connected site to enter their FFARS data into the system (Ruhago *et al.*, 2022b). To address this connectivity problem, a mobile FFARS version was developed to facilitate ease of use, especially in remote areas where there are no or limited computers and internet connectivity or local area network (LAN).

Health-information exchange through integration and interoperability

Interoperability is the ability of different information systems, devices and applications to access, exchange, integrate and cooperatively use data in a coordinated manner, within and across organizational, regional and national boundaries, to provide secure and seamless portability of information and optimize the quality of life of individuals and populations globally through open standards and interoperable digital solutions or systems (Nsaghurwe *et al.*, 2021).

The government promoted data exchange among systems through an interoperability layer, instead of peer-to-peer integration. Tanzania's Digital Health Investment Roadmap (2017–2023) articulated the vision of the government through MOH and PO-RALG with a number of digital health investments that include harmonization and connection of digital health systems through putting in place enterprise architecture, including governance, guidelines and standards for interoperability (MOHCDGEC, 2019).

The Muungano Gateway at PO-RALG and the health information mediator (HIM) at the MOH are the mechanisms used to facilitate interoperability or sharing of information between all local government systems hosted at PO-RALG

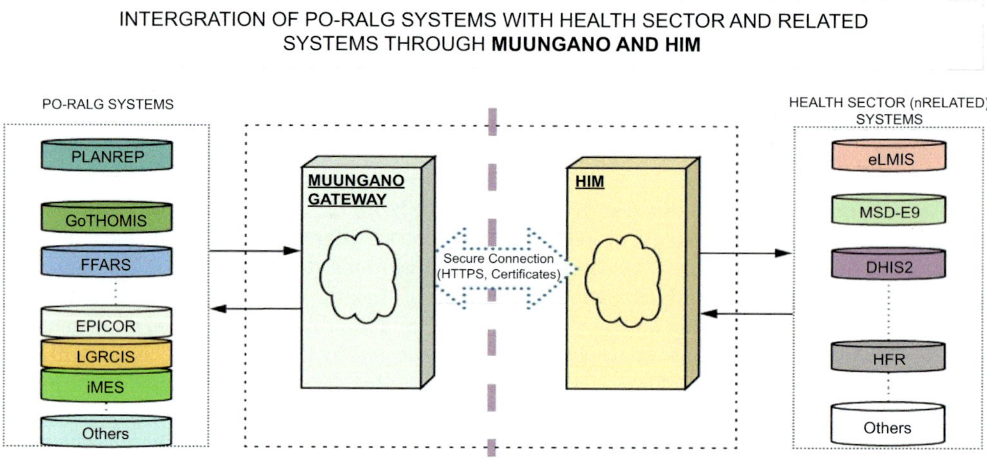

Fig. 6.2. Systems connected to the Muungano Gateway and HIM. (Copyright © PO-RALG, Tanzania.)

and all health systems hosted at the MOH. Fig. 6.2 illustrates the systems' connectedness, information exchange and the types of transactions among the systems through the Muungano Gateway and HIM exchanged by them.

Data-quality assessment and improvement

According to Heywood and Rohde (2001), information use is made more accessible if it is ritualized. Routines are set up as part of the 'information culture'. Despite having the data systems that have the capability of data analysis, the studies (Nutley and Reynolds, 2013; Anasel *et al.*, 2019) indicated that the data is rarely assessed, analysed and used for informed decision making, especially at lower levels of health systems where frontline health workers, nurses and clinical officers have responsibilities for data-related tasks and service delivery (MOHCDGEC, 2017c; PO-RALG and MOH, 2022). There is a significant relationship between the availability of data systems and data use. Also, it assumed that data systems available within health-care units would be used to guide every decision made, action taken and change made in that health unit and influenced by outside policies, norms and regulations (Heywood and Rohde, 2001).

The data systems mapping indicates that the identified systems have capabilities for data synthesis and visualization or exchanging data with other data systems, which are among the important attributes supporting data analysis and use. However, there are limited data-use practices among stakeholders at different levels of the health sector (Anasel *et al.*, 2019). Tanzania's national guidelines for health data quality assessment (DQA) were developed in 2016 in order to promote health-data improvements in Tanzania in the past 15 years, particularly after the introduction of DHIS2. Data quality audits conducted by a variety of programmes and funders have highlighted concerns about the quality of the data collected through routine health-information systems (MOHCDGEC, 2017c). As per the national DQA guidelines, the council level and PHC facilities are responsible for DQA during data collation or aggregation and validation from health facilities before entering them into the national DHIS2 or respective national systems.

The government has been building capacity to ensure health data quality. Key good data quality being worked on include timeliness, completeness, currency, consistency and accuracy. Data quality has been improving over time in line with the increase in data systems. The overall trend of the six performance indicators shows a level of uniformity of data in DHIS2.

Despite the improvement of data quality, there were a non-uniformity of data in DHIS2 and those in the HMIS tools (registers and or, in its absence, tally sheets), which may lead to improper decision making relating to health-service provisions to the community. It is therefore paramount that all key players involved in data management (health-care providers and HMIS focal at LGAs) closely and actively work together to further improve the uniformity of data from HMIS Tools and DHIS2 as well as other data systems and improve the overall quality and use of data across the health sector as per the national DQA guidelines.

6.2.5 Capacity building on data quality and use for informed actions

Capacity building on the design, deployment and use of HMIS is equally important and an ever-changing agenda to cope with technological advancements in digital health. There are ongoing efforts to improve pre-service and in-service training to be responsive to ever-changing technologies, the diverse information needs of communities and health professionals and health systems in general, to produce competent human resources for HMIS and information management.

Between 2009 and 2010, the MOH developed a course on health information management and financing (CMT 04212) for different cadres of health workers, for example, clinical assistants/officers (CA/CO cadres) at the PHC level. The course focused on different aspects of HMIS, the introduction of MTUHA/HMIS, the use of HMIS data-collection tools, reporting forms, medical records filing and numbering systems, recording HMIS/MTUHA ledger and community registers, as well as electronic patient record systems. Furthermore, as part of continuing professional development, training health-care workers and managers to use data for policy, advocacy and monitoring health and social service programmes is imperative in evidence-based planning and decision making.

The value of health information is not recognized, thus information use in PHC is shallow due to several barriers. There are organizational, technical and individual factors which hinder the proper adoption of health-information systems, data management and information at the point of data collection, service delivery and across PHC. PO-RALG, in collaboration with partners, implemented a data-use and quality-improvement (QI) initiative in which technology-enabled situation rooms (Fig. 6.3) for data review were created in selected regions and councils, leveraging Tanzania's integrated monitoring and evaluation system (iMES) platform for data analytics, data visualization (for example, dashboards and display), and institutionalizing a sustainable approach for data review and use by decision makers (Data for Implementation, 2022).

6.2.6 Supportive supervision

The MOH implemented a digital Afya supportive supervision information system (AfyaSSS) for planning and conducting technical and managerial supervision and assessments to improve the quality of supportive leadership conducted at different health-system levels. It coordinates and links all types of supervision for coherent and consolidated action plans for quality improvement. The digital solution aims to support health managers in PHC in managing supportive supervision to improve data use for evidence-based actions at all

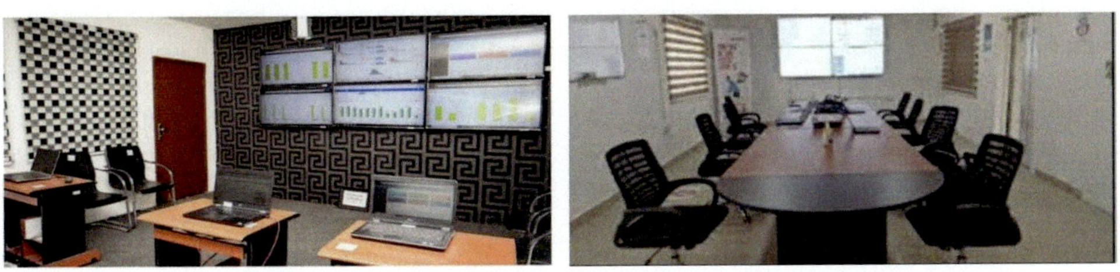

Fig. 6.3. Promoting data use – meeting rooms equipped with computing facilities and internet infrastructure to visualize and display data from different sources. (Copyright © PO-RALG, Tanzania.)

levels, and coordinate and harmonize supportive supervision. AfyaSSS addresses several challenges in PHC, including limited coordination of supervisory visits and assessments and their subsequent data and reporting systems, inadequate provision and implementation of feedback from supervision and challenges for councils to manage and use supervision-related data across all facilities and types of supervision.

6.3 Evidence From Research Relevant to PHC Reforms

PHC research refers to research done to foster evidence-based approaches that focus on improving the availability, access and quality of PHC services. Most of the research conducted in PHC settings is often considered 'implementation research' aimed at tapping into issues surrounding the PHC system to change the routines of practitioners and adopt the better ones (van Weel, 2007). Drawn from Beasley *et al.* (2007) and Peters *et al.* (2013), six categories of primary health-care research in the African context have been suggested:

1. Basic studies that help develop the research tools for PHC.
2. Clinical studies that focus on the burden of disease and the clinical processes involved.
3. Health-services research that focuses on the way PHC is organized and the processes involved.
4. Health-systems research that taps into a policy level and may look at the relationship between health policies, political dimension and social or economic systems.
5. Educational research that focuses on the development of educational programmes for PHC and continuing professional development.
6. Implementation research that seeks to explore and quantify the feasibility of research interventions and the delivery of health-care services for informed decision making.

The bulk of PHC research in Tanzania begins at the district, health facility and community levels. However, some research studies may touch on higher levels depending on the theme, such as considerations on equity, multisectoral collaborations and relevant technology that directly impact PHC, which can correctly be referred to as PHC research.

6.3.1 Relevance of PHC research

PHC research can be used to improve the understanding of local health problems and their management. Furthermore, it helps to improve the entire health-care system, effectively use health-care resources, address the needs of patients and communities, strengthen self-efficacy (van Weel and Rosser, 2004) and understand the levels or patterns of self-care and other healthcare-seeking behaviours. It needs to be emphasized that PHC research is more applicable where the majority of health problems in the population are located (van Weel and Rosser, 2004).

Health research therefore is an integral component of a PHC system that entails gathering evidence to improve health outcomes of the populations and provide avenues for designing and implementing interventions tailored towards disease prevention and control to enable the systems to respond better – and faster – to the challenges of a changing world (Beasley *et al.*, 2007; WHO, 2008b).

Primary health-care research is essential to provide information and evidence to inform evidence-based practice, planning, monitoring and evaluation, and consequently developing better health systems and sound policies. Community-directed research methods, such as understanding the community's beliefs, knowledge, perceptions, attitudes and practices towards health services, are necessary for generating anthropological or ethnographic evidence that can also be utilized to integrate the delivery of multiple PHC interventions of community approaches. Data is the most important component of research undertakings. Research that informs PHC must therefore use the PHC data to identify the problem and develop feasible solutions, policies and practices. To obtain quality data for research, it is empirical to ensure that the HMIS is robust and functional.

Therefore, PHC research must be multidisciplinary to be able to create a strong, resilient and robust primary-care system and policies that can provide both excellent clinical and population-based care through evidence-based decisions inferred specifically at the primary-care level.

6.3.2 Evolution of PHC research (description of PHC research priorities over time)

The role of systematic research in public and global health has been documented since the 17th century by the work done by John Graunt and William Farr in health research, statistics and epidemiology. Disparities in investment in health care between infectious diseases control and public health during colonial rule were common in Tanganyika, as was the case elsewhere. Investment in health care by colonial government was in the interests of the empire. Health priorities were set to control epidemics that existed for the care of European settlers, the colonial army and local productive labour (Young, 1986). Research efforts during colonial rule was only limited to disease surveillance, therapeutic trials, infectious and parasitic diseases, nutrition deficiency and other issues that resulted in maximizing productivity, with no focus on PHC (Heller, 1949, Heller, 1954).

Nevertheless, the rampant disease conditions stirred scientific work, which was a significant entry into health research introduced by German colonial rule, notably by some of the most renowned scientists throughout history. These included Robert Koch, who discovered mycobacterial tuberculosis bacilli as the cause TB, and Gustav Giemsa, who developed the malaria Giemsa stain from then Tanganyika Central Pathology Laboratory at the current Ocean Road Cancer Institute (ORCI) premises in 1877/78 (Mwaluko *et al.*, 1991). It was from this laboratory that Robert Koch, as well as researching TB, also conducted research in the fields of infectious diseases epidemics including malaria, blackwater fever, sleeping sickness and relapsing fever. He received the Nobel Prize in December 1905 for his investigations and discoveries on TB. Such research was very important to inform practices and treatment of individual patients.

Despite such achievements in scientific research, poor understanding of public-health research resulted in research proposals being dismissed and deemed not in the interest of the colonial administration at the time. It has been recorded that, in late 1938, a wealthy British patron, Champion Russell, wrote to the Colonial Office offering a donation of £1000 for an integrated health campaign in British Africa that would address chronic and infectious diseases as well as sanitary improvements for the local communities, a form of PHC research. Well-summarized by Helen Tilley (Tilley, 2016), Russell said: 'I appeal for a government experiment in a district selected by them – which would 'try out' the results of having a healthy population – as it were, on a laboratory scale.... It seems evident that the prevention of disease should be seriously tackled.'

Motivated by the presence of young graduates from Makerere College Medical School and the foreseeable need for the tested intervention that could help the community, Russell went on to propose that 'the idea would be to have a model district, which might be eventually of use as a practice ground for young sanitary officers who have left Makerere and Mulago, before taking up a career.' The outcomes, he argued, would result in 'less incidence of disease ... a lower death rate, improved physique – greater intelligence, more inclination to work, [and] more enterprise.' Equally important, the data gathered would lead to new insights, 'under present conditions in Africa', about disease distribution, susceptibility, and immunity. 'Such an experiment in health is a scientific necessity.' Russel's proposal was unequivocally rejected by colonial medical directors in Uganda, Kenya and Tanganyika. However, his suggestions stirred discussions 10 years later, leading to increased grants towards public health and medical research through what became the Colonial Development and Welfare Act of 1940 (Paterson, 1939; Tilley, 2011, 2016).

Infectious diseases of importance, such as African trypanosomiasis, malaria, yellow fever, syphilis, measles, poliomyelitis, tuberculosis and zoonotic diseases were the major African health concerns that needed to be addressed by interventions at the community level.

Therefore, research works were key to understanding the patterns and trends of diseases of major concern in the communities leading to the formation of appropriate interventions. This was the basis of establishment of some of the research centres.

In 1922 the Sleeping Sickness Service Unit in Tabora was established under the leadership of Dr Frank Apted, responsible for medical surveillance and treatment of sleeping sickness cases (Human African trypanosomiasis) under German colonial rule.

The British colonial government appreciably expanded research work in Tanganyika under the oversight of the East African High Commission and established the East African Medical Survey (1947) on lymphatic filariasis in Malya, and the Filariasis Research Unit (1948) in Mwanza, which were merged in 1954 to form East African Institute for Medical Research.

Under the British Colonial and Welfare Scheme (1949), an East African Malaria Unit (EAMU) was established in Ubwari (Mbweni), northern Tanzania by Captain Dr Bagster Wilson. In 1951, the unit was moved to Amani in the East Usambara Mountains and was renamed East African Malaria Institute (EAMI); it became operational later in 1954 and renamed the East African Institute of Malaria and Vector-Borne Disease (EAIMVBD) (Graboyes, 2017).

Notably, before independence many health services in Tanganyika were established in the urban areas (mostly for the affluent white population), except for a few religious organizations' hospitals scattered in the rural areas (Beck, 1977; MOH, 1990, 2003), a fact that underpins the role of non-state actors in public health in the colonial era. In 1957, the Swiss Tropical Institute Field Laboratory (STIFL) was established in Kilombero by a Swiss zoologist, Dr Rudolf Geigy, under the Swiss Tropical Institute. In the same year, the African Medical and Research Foundation (AMREF) was also established, after the idea of improving the health of Africa's disadvantaged was raised by three colleagues, Sir Michael Wood, Dr Thomas Rees and Sir Archibald McIndoe, back in 1956 from Ol'Orien farm on the slopes of Mt Kilimanjaro where they lived. From its headquarters in Nairobi, Kenya, AMREF was actively providing support for mobile health services and offering surgical intervention in mission hospitals in Tanganyika, as well as offering avenues for health research (AMREF, n.d.)

The first research on PHC immediately after independence was done by Richard M. Titmuss a British professor who was working in Tanganyika before independence. His Excellence Mwalimu Julius Kambarage Nyerere, the first president of Tanganyika, commissioned him to investigate health care in Tanganyika at the time and to give his recommendations. Professor Titmuss produced a report titled, 'The Health Services of Tanganyika – a Report to the Government'. In his report, he highlighted the need for research in public health to be able to appropriately respond to the health needs of the local community. He stated that:

> It would be unwise and inappropriate, even if it were feasible, to transport to Tanganyika an entirely western pattern of health services. For efficiency and economy, the services must meet the special needs of the people in their local circumstances. Priorities must then be indicated by the analysis of these needs. Much will also depend on the manpower or skills available and locally acquired.... It is necessary to build a health service adaptable to these varied conditions, which must, for a considerable time, make the most economical use it can of scarce skills, while endeavouring to bring the greatest benefit to as large a proportion of the population as possible.

Therefore, Professor Titmuss recommended establishment of a central unit to study disease incidence, distribution and trends, both epidemic and endemic and even further the development of medical research institutions, independently and in cooperation with the universities, common services organizations and international research foundations (Titmuss, 1964).

Following such recommendations, the East African Medical Research Commission (EAMRC) was established in 1967 under the East African Common Services Organization (EACSO) through the enactment of Act No. 14 of 1962, which was signed on behalf of the East African Common Services, with the advice and consent of the East African Central Legislative Assembly, by H.E. Julius Nyerere, the president of Tanganyika, Hon. W.F. Coutts, the governor-general of Uganda, and Hon. Malcolm MacDonald, the governor of Kenya.

Among others, major objectives of the EAMRC were to recruit and train indigenous research personnel from the member states and oversee the establishment of the five specialized research institutions hosted by each of the three member states and operated across the entire East African region. The EAMRC was mandated to coordinate, set health research priorities and submit research programmes, annual reports and financial statements to the EACSO. Two institutions were in Tanganyika, which continued from before independence, namely the East African Institute for Medical Research and the East African Institute of Malaria and Vector-borne Diseases. Other institutions were the East African Virus Research Institute (Uganda); the East African Trypanosomiasis Research Organization (Kenya); and the East African Leprosy Research Centre (Kenya). In 1968, the EAMRC established a Tuberculosis Investigating Unit (now the National Tuberculosis Reference Laboratory) in Dar es Salaam. In 1970 Helminthiasis Research Units were established by the EAMRC at Bombo Hospital in Tanga (now NIMR Tanga Medical Research Centre) and the Isamilo Research Centre (now NIMR Mwanza Medical Research Centre).

The establishment of the research centres by the EAMRC helped to push forward the agenda for research in Tanganyika. Most of the established research centres conducted research focusing on infectious diseases that were of major concern at the time in particular areas, such as malaria in Tanga and schistosomiasis in Mwanza, and this research directly informed PHC on diseases. A better understanding of diseases that mostly affected the community had a considerable impact in formulating primary health-care interventions.

Following the collapse of the East African Community (EAC) in 1977, all the institutions established under the EAC could no longer function under the EAMRC. The government of the United Republic of Tanzania, therefore, decided to re-organize the health research centres into a national institute. In 1979, Parliament Act No. 23 established a parastatal organization under the MOH, known as the National Institute for Medical Research (NIMR), which became fully operational in 1980 with the mandate to coordinate, carry out and promote health research designed to alleviate disease among the people of Tanzania. NIMR was empowered to take over all health-research institutions in the country which, until the demise of the EAC, were administered by the EAMRC and given the mandate to train local personnel for carrying out scientific research of medical problems among others.

6.3.3 PHC research development after the Alma-Ata declaration, 1978–1994

The Alma-Ata Declaration (1978) best promoted PHC as a means to address health problems in communities, fostering equitable access to promotive, preventive, curative, palliative and rehabilitative health services. Likewise, medical research had to be adjusted and NIMR had the responsibility as the instrument of the MOH to conduct research that will inform PHC structures in the country. The declaration identified PHC as the key to the attainment of the goal of health for all. Achievement of this goal demands a sustainable investment in community-oriented PHC research activities that are well aligned with the health-system structure. However, NIMR had taken over research centres from which little attention was given to PHC research.

Following the nationalization policy in the late 1960s and early 1970s, the stage was set for the integration of STIFL into a government agency, which was achieved in 1991 when it became NIMR Ifakara Centre. Notably, most of the research that informed PHC at the time continued to be conducted from the Ifakara Centre with the oversight of NIMR.

In 1996, the Ifakara Centre was expanded to the Ifakara Health Research and Development Centre (IHRDC) and established as a registered trust operating under the MOH in 2004 to conduct household surveys, clinical trials and translational research to inform reforms in the health sector. Most of the research work to support PHC was conducted during this period. Later, in 2008, IHRDC was renamed as the Ifakara Health Institute (IHI) and became an independent research organization.

Historically, both IHI and NIMR conducted household surveys, clinical trials and translational research specifically tailored towards improving PHC, including malaria vector control, insecticide-treated nets (Font *et al.*,

2001), malaria vaccines and treatment. Malaria research was done mostly from the NIMR Amani and Tanga centres which continue to be the hub for malaria research, while NIMR Mwanza Centre focused on helminths and later on HIV research. NIMR Muhimbili Centre and later NIMR Mbeya Centre became pivotal for TB research in the country. Research conducted in these centres provided vital evidence that helped to improve tremendously PHC delivery tackling infectious diseases burdening the community.

6.3.4 Trends in health-research priorities in Tanzania and their contribution to PHC research

National health research priorities are driven by the annual scientific conference organized by NIMR that brings together local and international scientists who disseminate their research findings for consumption. Research priorities are set from the consensus based on the key findings and discussions resulting from the meeting. These have been divided into three main groups, namely biomedical, health systems and social determinants of health. However, the country's health-research priorities have been evolving, mainly around infectious diseases under the biomedical group (NIMR, 2006, 2015). Notably, most of the research on infectious diseases is conducted in primary health facilities and hence has direct or indirect contribution to improvement of PHC. Research on vertical programmes, for example, malaria, HIV, tuberculosis and helminths, have been conducted from primary facilities and hence utilize PHC structures to improve access to health care.

Priorities for PHC research have been evolving, as pointed out earlier, from a basic sciences focus to a more diverse involvement of health-systems research. The strengthening of health-system research was composed of research on service delivery, health policy, HIS, essential health-intervention packages, decentralization and reproductive and child health, which are key components of PHC that have occurred mostly since 1990s, undertaken by IHI and NIMR. Intervention research in malaria prevention and ITNs, HIV interventions, maternal and child health, as well as research on human resource for health which had direct impact on policy change, could be good examples of the health systems and PHC research (Font *et al.*, 2001).

6.3.5 Translating research findings into policy and action

Collaboration between PHC clinicians, academic departments and research institutions among others is essential in order to translate research to action and educate future primary-care professionals and researchers, including in the use of interventions that are implemented through community health-care workers. However, at the roots of PHC research and evidence utilization are the health facilities that are expected to utilize the findings for planning and improving practice. Hospital management teams and councils' health-management teams can utilize research findings for planning, setting indicators for performance monitoring and monitoring disease trends.

In spite of that, long-standing deadly diseases, such as malaria, HIV, TB and newly emerging infectious and non-infectious diseases, may be more effectively addressed through global, regional and local knowledge-sharing and cooperation (WHO, 2008a). However, all need to be informed by PHC research, ranging from problem diagnosis, designing context-specific solutions and uncovering bottlenecks to implementation of PHC interventions or initiatives.

PHC research by itself is hugely diverse and it is difficult to draw a line between non-PHC research and PHC research. However, it's agreed that PHC research must provide evidence that will feed in to improve at least one of the health-systems building blocks. As pointed out earlier, despite the fact that most of the research has been disease-oriented and little of it focused on PHC and community interventions, in most cases, the output of such research work contributed to improvement of care. In an effort to provide quality health services in limited settings, research in PHC has transcended to assessing the use of digital technology, including clinical decision support systems or algorithms (CDSS or CDSAs) in PHC settings. Therefore, PHC facilities have been upfront, safe to say, providing a conducive environment for trials of various innovations incorporated in improving health and health-care delivery interventions due to their close proximity to the community.

Capacity for research in PHC has been lacking for long time (Montorzi *et al.*, 1990) despite the fact that, through research work, research centres have been involved in building capacity to health-care workers in PHC over time (Freyvogel, 1979). Taking the health system lens, some PHC research focuses on specific building blocks in order to guide reforms in the specific blocks. Moreover, different research studies have been conducted in the country to assess the factors associated with access, quality, satisfaction of service and improving capacity towards the universal health coverage vision to inform reforms (Gilson *et al.*, 1994; Marmot *et al.*, 2008; WHO, 2013). Studies on responsiveness and expanding services in primary health facilities (Kapologwe *et al.*, 2020), health-care financing and supply chain that guide the delivery of equipment and essential medications (Mwencha *et al.*, 2017) and the importance of the workforce in PHC (Manzi *et al.*, 2012) are all necessary to inform the PHC systems and structures.

6.3.6 Source of the PHC research data for decision making

Data generated from research is an important element of any health-care system to feed into decision making processes and it is a starting point from which meaningful information can be derived. Since independence, research and academic institutions have been conducting research that informed practices and PHC policies in the country. Unreliable data sources and a lack of readily available data necessitate collecting raw data each time the research question is addressed. A good HIS, be it primary or secondary data, remains critical for a successful health system and research. Data collected from reliable sources using appropriate methods will always facilitate the generation of meaningful information, which in turn can be used to make informed decisions. Ideally, HMIS should be the primary source of readily available data to facilitate PHC research.

Data used in the decision making model can be explained in six steps from data availability (Fig. 6.4). Available data must provide information that can be used as evidence for decision making. However, data must make sense to be

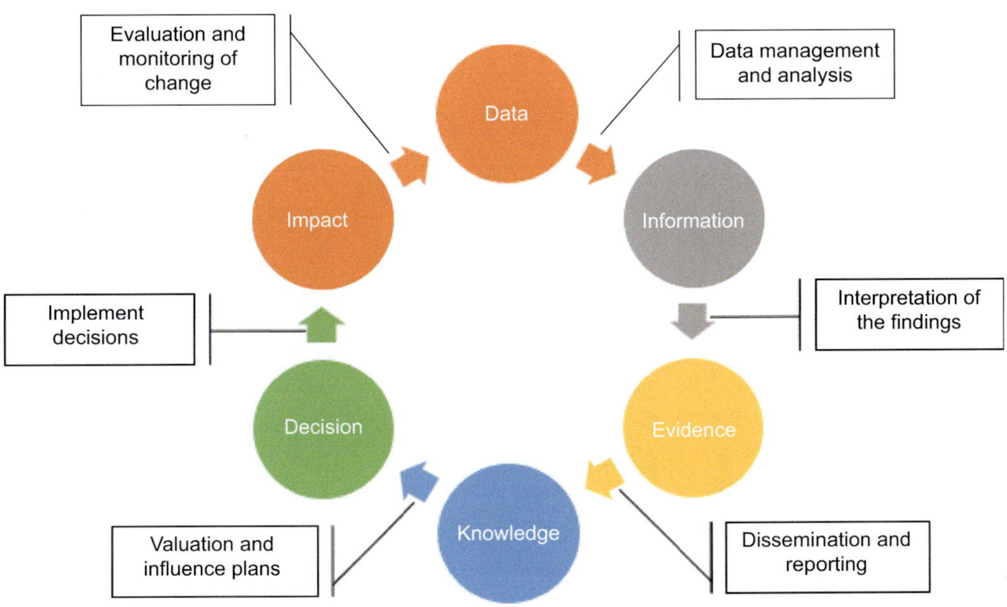

Fig. 6.4. Decision making model using research findings. (Adapted from the WHO framework.)

reasonably interpreted. The role of data management is to ensure that quality data is used for analysis. Health-data aggregation must therefore undergo a quality check before analysis to guarantee the validity and accuracy of all analysed data; such will ensure accurate user findings. Knowledge generated from research evidence needs to be weighed between different options before being taken for decisions. Considerable research done in other settings using either similar or different methodologies widens the scope of knowledge and is essential to validate the generalizability of research findings before implementation or adoption as policy. It is essential to evaluate the impact of the interventions or policies and monitor changes influenced by practices adopted due to research evidence. New interventions or policy uptakes can also be implemented in PHC through implementation research which generates data that facilitates systematic modification of the current practices. In the course of monitoring, more careful recording of findings should be done, resulting in more data. However, the process might need to be smoother, and conflicting factors must be given attention at some stages. Policy and decision makers such as the ministry, programmes and governing bodies need to be informed based on the evidence obtained at the implementing levels to guide decision making processes for implementable policies; this is the role of research.

6.4 Lessons Learnt on Evidence for Decision Making at PHC

6.4.1 Lessons learnt on HIMS and data use

Achievements in HIS

Tanzania has made remarkable progress in leveraging digital health to transform the health system, thus doing away with the paper format (Fig. 6.5). Health-data quality improvements have been achieved in the past 15 years, particularly after the introduction of DHIS2. The government has invested in data management and use capabilities through various implementation of strategic initiatives, including continuous data review and auditing. In 2019, health-data quality was reported to have improved to 92% from 45% in 2016 (MOH, 2021).

The desired state is that data systems of the HIS would provide specific information to support the decision making process at each level of the health system. The use of automated analysis

Fig. 6.5. HMIS archives in paper format. (Images provided by PO-RALG.)

tools could improve local data use (Hoxha *et al.*, 2022). However, data analysis and use capabilities are limited to support data usage due to various reasons, especially at the point of data collection and the government engaging in health-data collaborative strategies to further prompt data use for informed decision making at the PHC level.

Increase efficiency and cost-effectiveness

Before 2017, plans and budgets for PHC facilities were drawn up by experts at LGA HQ. The process was lengthy, taking more than three months. The improved PlanRep revolutionized the process in terms of efficiency, transparency and accountability. Improved PlanRep (since 2017) reduced the annual plan preparation time from an average of three months to only 2 weeks. The significant time saved was in planning, costing, budget assessment and scrutinization at all levels (LGA, RS, sector ministry, PO-RALG and MOFP). Currently, every process is done remotely (electronically).

The improved PlanRep increased transparency and accountability. Cost reduction has been noticed after the introduction of the improved PlanRep system. The decrease was more than 50%, mainly in stationery, transport and subsistence allowances – the cost of these three items was at a peak during budget assessment, scrutinization and submission.

At the PHC level, FFARS has significantly improved tracking of all PHC facility expenditures (over and under expenditure), while the use of GoTHOMIS by health facilities revolutionized financial management due to a drastic increase in revenue collection and improved financial reporting. Furthermore, deploying digital technology can avoid system data fragmentation and increase efficiencies.

Challenges affecting health information management and use in PHC

Despite the efforts of implementing HIS, the data systems are still not delivering on their promises to facilitate informed local decision making. There is still a limited trust in the data produced due to various data-quality issues. There are frustrations in implementing HIS, data collection, analysis and use at the PHC level.

Some of the challenges hindering PHC digital transformation include limited human and financial resources for PHC digitalization, insufficient and unreliable ICT infrastructure, weak digital health governance structure, absence of legal frameworks on digital health and data protection, inadequate digital-related knowledge and skills, limited compliance with digital health and data standards and systems interoperability (PO-RALG and MOH, 2022). Therefore, it is crucial to equip health facilities with quality and reliable infrastructures such as computer systems, tablets and biometric register machines (MOHCDGEC, 2017c).

Currently, data is limited for routine planning, management and service delivery decision making at central, subnational and facility/community levels. This results in misallocation of health resources, poor targeting and under-performance of health programmes and ineffective and inefficient services, as well as the inability to even recognize and address performance challenges – short-term wastage of funds due to development and maintenance costs of parallel systems, long-term wastage of funds due to the difficulty of legacy integration of existing unplanned systems and not enough funding to go around to support the platforms that do exist.

Data from MOHCDGEC shows that only 50% of 6828 facilities have computerized data-collection systems, yet depend on paper-based data collection. Double-entry data is commonly used; data are first entered in papers and then transferred to computers/systems. Currently, Tanzania is in the transition from paper-based medical records to electronic records whereby all health-care facilities are expected to digitize individual health data and streamline them to the centralized database to make it easier for health-care workers and other key stakeholders to access health records (MOHCDGEC, 2017c). To achieve this vision, more infrastructure must be improved in establishing electronic data management.

6.4.2 Lessons learnt and the future of PHC research

The challenge of developing research in primary care can be met only by creating a strong infrastructure for PHC research in the country.

This should include strengthening research departments and institutions, improving interaction among researchers in fields related to PHC, improving training programmes for PHC researchers, developing more practice-based primary-care research networks and increasing local funding for research in primary care. A greatly increased commitment of international organizations both within and outside primary care is needed, particularly the funding bodies (Beasley *et al.*, 2007).

Community participation is a foundational principle of PHC for improved health outcomes, equity, service access, relevance, acceptability, quality and responsiveness (Bath and Wakerman, 2015). Community engagement in PHC research is similarly essential to successfully implementing PHC interventions designed from research evidence. Therefore, patients are the main stakeholder for PHC research, and CHWs, HCWs in primary facilities, local leaders and NGO/FBOs are among other key stakeholders in designing and conducting research (De Maeseneer *et al.*, 2003; Bath and Wakerman, 2015).

Coordination and linkage of all PHC research nationwide is key to identifying implementation challenges and setting priorities to ensure a sustainable and equitable health-care provision. The country should therefore aim towards linking data from cross-sectional surveys (whether population- or hospital-based), cohort studies, clinical trials, registers, HMIS, health insurance and other administrative data (Wellcome Trust, 2015) to facilitate holistic and multidisciplinary research.

Ideally, the linked data needs to be individualized to assess specific risk factors at the individual level whenever possible. Unique identification of individuals during health-service delivery and research activities is essential for attaining continuity of care but also tracking during research work, for example, cohort studies (Maret-Ouda *et al.*, 2017) in routine HMIS data. However, the confidentiality of data should be ensured following proper legal and ethical requirements, with lessons learned from countries with the successful linkage of multiple data sources from vital national statistics, population-based surveys and hospital registers.

6.5 Conclusion and Recommendations

Improving availability, accessibility and use of high-quality health information is among the priorities of universal health coverage, particularly through PHC in Tanzania. The country has made notable progress in transforming health-information management and use, the adoption of digitalization of PHC services, health data governance and overall PHC digital transformation. PHC digital transformation and the Tanzania Digital Health Strategy 2019–2024 are striving to deal with existing organizational, individual and technical challenges. The existing challenges include uncoordinated digitization and digitalization of HIS across the health sector, limited digital skills and motivation and inadequate ICT infrastructure and facilities. Health workers are overwhelmed with multiple parallel HIS, thus wasting their time, losing their focus on patient care and leading to poor data quality and limited data-sharing and use. The challenges hinder appropriate use of HIS, health information and evidence for efficient delivery of PHC.

The introduction of various data systems or digital solutions at the PHC level has tremendously transformed the performance of the health system in terms of improved planning and financial management, as well as efficiency and cost-effectiveness. Digitalization of all PHC services facilitates data use and collection at the POC and the retrieval and access of any needed information, and expedites its utilization at higher levels of the health system.

Learning of the previous and current implementation of HIS should inform the adoption of the solutions to avoid challenges by aligning technologies to the needs of the health system, ensuring system thinking and understanding of the ecosystem, and developing a shared understanding of the importance and adoption of emerging digital technologies among the different players, the role of accountability in the use of digital health solutions in a patient-centred way to improve health outcomes, while streamlining stakeholders' and partners' digital health priorities with national, regional and international priorities and streamlining efforts and resources and responsive health systems.

Adopting emerging technologies is imperative in addressing most PHC and other health system challenges: artificial intelligence (AI), machine learning (ML), drones, blockchain, and big data analytics. Some of the use cases in the health supply chain include the use of drones for the delivery of medicines/supplies in remote areas and the use of artificial intelligence (AI) and machine learning (ML) in areas for data analytics to support decision making for commodities forecasting, distribution and inventory management. Furthermore, big data analytics, ML and AI can be used for predictive and prescriptive analytics, for example, forecasting demands for medicines/supplies. Internet of Things-based sensors can support decision making, for example, measuring things such as location, movement, temperature, humidity, et cetera, while blockchain can facilitate the efficient and secure tracking and tracing of drugs. The emerging technologies should be implemented in an ethical, appropriate, responsible, explainable and human-centred manner.

PHC development requires evidence from research. Throughout history, health research has shaped PHC in different aspects. Contributions towards understanding infectious diseases and their preventive and management interventions, service delivery, information management and resource allocation must be acknowledged. However, more research activities tailored to PHC are needed to continue providing evidence that can support or influence improvements in PHC in Tanzania. Evidence-based reforms and system adjustments will always prove effective in attaining UHC. Therefore, expanding collaboration between government sectors that oversee PHC, such as PO-RALG and institutions that conduct research, remains key to addressing the specific research needs of PHC.

Moreover, the need to properly document all PHC research activities and related operations/interventions happening in the country calls for the establishment of a 'Journal of Primary Health Care in Tanzania'. Collaboration between the academic, research and available primary health-care structures in the country is instrumental and should be encouraged to sustain the operationalization of this journal.

A health system resource centre has been established at PO-RALG to archive all the country's best practices and hold all the information relating to health and other social welfare issues. This centre ensures that the regional and district-level information systems are interoperable and provide quality data. It is also a platform for data dissemination, ensuring accessibility and utilization of data for sharing best practices, policy and decision making across the country. Therefore, this can be emulated in some other African countries and inspire local leaders in the HMIS sector to do their best. All in all, it is essential to know that no matter how much the government loves to share its data, data security must be given its weight. The WHO is advocating for health-data collaboration, and it is high time for all African countries to embrace this initiative.

Bibliography

AbouZahr, C. and Boerma, T. (2005) Health information systems: the foundations of public health. *Bulletin of the World Health Organization* 83, 578–583.

AMREF (n.d.) Our Founders – Amref Health Africa. Available at: https://amref.org/our-history/founders/ (accessed 27 April 2023).

Anasel, M., Swai, I. and Masue, O. (2019) *Creating a Culture of Data Use in Tanzania: Assessing Health Providers' Capacity to Analyze and Use Family Planning Data*. Measure Evaluation, Chapel Hill, North Carolina.

Bath, J. and Wakerman, J. (2015) Impact of community participation in primary health care: what is the evidence? *Australian Journal of Primary Health* 21(1), 2–8. DOI: 10.1071/PY12164.

Beasley, J.W., Starfield, B. van Weel, C., Rosser, W.W. and Haq, C.L. (2007) Global health and primary care research. *The Journal of the American Board of Family Medicine* 20, 518–526. DOI: 10.3122/jabfm.2007.06.070172.

Beck, A. (1977) Medicine and Society in Tanganyika, 1890-1930: a historical inquiry. *Transactions of the American Philosophical Society* 67(3), 1–59. DOI: 10.2307/1006330.

COWI and Goss Gilroy Inc (2007) *Joint External Evaluation of the Health Sector in Tanzania, 1999–2006*. Ministry of Foreign Affairs, Koege, Denmark.

Darcy, N., Elias, M., Swai, A., Danford, H., Rulagirwa, H. *et al.* (2014) eHealth strategy development: a case study in Tanzania. *Journal of Health Informatics in Africa* 2. DOI: 10.12856/JHIA-2014-v2-i2-107.

Data for Implementation (2022) *Data.FI Semi-Annual Performance Report 2022: October 2021–March 2022 (Translating Data for Implementation [Data.FI])*. USAID, Washington, DC.

De Maeseneer, J.M., van Driel, M.L., Green, L.A. and van Weel, C. (2003) The need for research in primary care. *The Lancet* 362(9392), 1314–1319. DOI: 10.1016/S0140-6736(03)14576-X.

ECLAC (Economic Commission for Latin America and the Caribbean) (2021) *Digital Technologies for a New Future*. United Nations, Santiago.

Elovaara, P., Igira, F.T. and Mörtberg, C. (2006) Whose participation? Whose knowledge? Exploring PD in Tanzania-Zanzibar and Sweden. In: *Proceedings of the Ninth Conference on Participatory Design: Expanding Boundaries in Design*, Vol. 1. Association for Computing Machinery, New York, pp. 105–114. DOI: 10.1145/1147261.1147277.

Font, F., Alonso González, M., Nathan, R., Kimario, J., Lwilla, F. *et al.* (2001) Diagnostic accuracy and case management of clinical malaria in the primary health services of a rural area in south-eastern Tanzania. *Tropical Medicine & International Health* 6(6), 423–428. DOI: 10.1046/j.1365-3156.2001.00727.x.

Freyvogel, T.A. (1979) Collaboration suisse au développement de la santé publique en Tanzanie. *Sozial-Und Präventivmedizin SPM* 24(2–3), 137–140. DOI: 10.1007/BF02094147.

Gilson, L., Alilio, M. and Heggenhougen, K. (1994) Community satisfaction with primary health care services: an evaluation undertaken in the Morogoro region of Tanzania. *Social Science & Medicine* 39(6), 767–780. DOI: 10.1016/0277-9536(94)90038-8.

Glèlè Ahanhanzo, Y., Ouendo, E.-M., Kpozèhouen, A., Levêque, A., Makoutodé, M. *et al.* (2015) Data quality assessment in the routine health information system: an application of the Lot Quality Assurance Sampling in Benin. *Health Policy and Planning* 30(7), 837–843. DOI: 10.1093/heapol/czu067.

Graboyes, M. (2017) *The Experiment Must Continue: Medical Research and Ethics in East Africa, 1940–2014*. Ohio University Press, Athens, Georgia.

Heller, H.S.L. (1949) Colonial medical research. *BMJ* 2(4622), 330–331. DOI: 10.1136/bmj.2.4622.330-a.

Heller, H.S.L. (1954) Colonial medical research. *The Medical Journal of the South-West* 70, 91–94.

Heywood, A. and Rohde, J. (2001) *Using Information for Action: A Manual for Health Workers at Facility Level*. The Equity Project, Arcadia, Pretoria, South Africa.

Hoxha, K., Hung, Y.W., Irwin, B.R. and Grepin, K.A. (2022) Understanding the challenges associated with the use of data from routine health information systems in low-and middle-income countries: a systematic review. *Health Information Management Journal* 51, 135–148.

Ishijima, H., Mapunda, M., Mndeme, M., Sukums, F. and Mlay, V.S. (2015) Challenges and opportunities for effective adoption of HRH information systems in developing countries: national rollout of HRHIS and TIIS in Tanzania. *Human Resources for Health* 13, 1–14.

Kapologwe, N.A., Kibusi, S.M., Borghi, J., Gwajima, D.O. and Kalolo, A. (2020) Assessing health system responsiveness in primary health care facilities in Tanzania. *BMC Health Services Research* 20(1), 104. DOI: 10.1186/s12913-020-4961-9.

Kikoba, B., Sukums, F., Abel, Z., Shidende, N., Kijuu, Y. *et al.* (2019) Assessing how health data systems support data use in the Tanzanian health system. In: *Presented at the 12th Health Informatics in Africa Conference (HELINA 2019)*. Available at: https://www.researchgate.net/publication/341459483_Assessing_How_Health_Data_Systems_Support_Data_Use_in_the_Tanzanian_Health_System (accessed 12 May 2023).

Mahundi, M., Kaasbøll, J. and Twaakyondo, H. (2011) Health information systems integration in Tanzania: tapping the contextual advantages. In: *2011 IST-Africa Conference Proceedings*, IEEE, New York, pp. 1–11.

Manca, D.P. (2015) Rebuttal: Do electronic medical records improve quality of care? Yes. *Canadian Family Physician Medecin de Famille Canadien* 61(10), 846-847, 850-851.

Manzi, F., Schellenberg, J.A., Hutton, G., Wyss, K., Mbuya, C. *et al.* (2012) Human resources for health care delivery in Tanzania: a multifaceted problem. *Human Resources for Health* 10, 3. DOI: 10.1186/1478-4491-10-3.

Maret-Ouda, J., Tao, W., Wahlin, K. and Lagergren, J. (2017) Nordic registry-based cohort studies: possibilities and pitfalls when combining nordic registry data. *Scandinavian Journal of Public Health* 45(17_suppl), 14–19. DOI: 10.1177/1403494817702336.

Marmot, M., Friel, S., Bell, R., Houweling, T.A.J. and Taylor, S. (2008) Closing the gap in a generation: health equity through action on the social determinants of health. *The Lancet* 372(9650), 1661–1669. DOI: 10.1016/S0140-6736(08)61690-6.

Mboera, L.E.G., Rumisha, S.F., Magesa, S.M. and Kitua, A.Y. (2001) Utilisation of health management information system in disease surveillance in Tanzania. *Tanzania Journal of Health Research* 3(2), 15–17. DOI: 10.4314/thrb.v3i2.14213.

MOH (1990) *National Health Policy*. Ministry of Health, Dar es Salaam, Tanzania.

MOH (1991) *Planning and Management of Primary Health Care in Tanzania: A Manual for District Health Teams*. Ministry of Health, Dar es Salaam, Tanzania.

MOH (2003) *National Health Policy: United Republic of Tanzania 2003*. Ministry of Health, Dar es Salaam, Tanzania.

MOH (2021) *Tanzania Health Sector Strategic Plan V*. Ministry of Health, Dar es Salaam, Tanzania.

MOHCDGEC (2016) *Guideline and Standard for Integrated Health Facility Electronic Management Systems*. Government of the United Republic of Tanzania, Dodoma.

MOHCDGEC (2017a) *DHIS 2 Functions and Data Use for Health Information System Strengthening: Training Manual*. Government of the United Republic of Tanzania, Dodoma.

MOHCDGEC (2017b) *Tanzania Health Data Collaborative*. Government of the United Republic of Tanzania, Dodoma.

MOHCDGEC (2017c) *Tanzania Digital Health Investment Road Map 2017–2023*. Government of the United Republic of Tanzania, Dodoma.

MOHCDGEC (2019) *Tanzania Digital Health Strategy 2019–2024*. Government of the United Republic of Tanzania, Dodoma.

Montorzi, G., Mboera, L., IJsselmuiden, C. and De Haan, S. (1990) *Tanzania, an Assessment of the Health Research System*. A country report of the AHA. Council on Health Research for Development, Geneva, Switzerland.

Mungwabi, H.N. (2006) An investigation of efficacy of the document- based health management. *University of Dar Es Salaam Library Journal* 8(1), 32–48. DOI: 10.4314/udslj.v8i1.26645.

Mwageni, E., Momburi, D., Juma, Z., Irema, M. and Masanja, H. (1998) *Tanzania Essential Health Interventions Project: Adult Morbidity and Mortality*. Ministry of Health, Dar es Salaam, Tanzania.

Mwaluko, G.M., Lukmanji, Z. and Kasele, H.A. (1991) *Health and Disease in Tanzania*. HarperCollins Academic, London.

Mwencha, M., Rosen, J.E., Spisak, C., Watson, N., Kisoka, N. *et al*. (2017) Upgrading supply chain management systems to improve availability of medicines in Tanzania: evaluation of performance and cost effects. *Global Health, Science and Practice* 5(3), 399–411. DOI: 10.9745/GHSP-D-16-00395.

NIMR (2006) *Tanzania Health Research Priorities, 2006–2010*. National Institute for Medical Research, Dar es Salaam, Tanzania.

NIMR (2015) *Setting a National Agenda for Health Systems Research for Tuberculosis, Malaria and Neglected Tropical Diseases in the United Republic of Tanzania*. National Institute for Medical Research, Dar es Salaam, Tanzania.

Nsaghurwe, A., Dwivedi, V., Ndesanjo, W., Bamsi, H., Busiga, M. *et al*. (2021) One country's journey to interoperability: Tanzania's experience developing and implementing a national health information exchange. *BMC Medical Informatics and Decision Making* 21(1), 139. DOI: 10.1186/s12911-021-01499-6.

Nutley, T. and Reynolds, H.W. (2013) Improving the use of health data for health system strengthening. *Global Health Action* 6, 20001. DOI: 10.3402/gha.v6i0.20001.

Paterson, A.R. (1939) Paterson to Secretary of East African Governors Conference April 13, 1939. CO 847/16/2.

Peters, D.H., Tran, N.T. and Taghreed, A. (2013) *Implementation Research in Health: A Practical Guide*. World Health Organization, Geneva, Switzerland.

PO-RALG and MOH (2022) *National Primary Health Care Digital Transformation Roadmap*. Government of the United Republic of Tanzania, Dodoma.

Ruhago, G.M., Kapologwe, N.A., Ngalesoni, F.N., Kengia, J.T., Kibusi, S.M. *et al*. (2022a) Cost-efficiency analysis of the improved web-based planning, budgeting, and reporting system (PlanRep) in Tanzania. *Frontiers in Health Services* 1, 15. DOI: 10.3389/frhs.2021.787894.

Ruhago, G.M., Ngalesoni, F.N., Kapologwe, N.A., Kengia, J.T., Ngocho, J. *et al.* (2022b) Strengthening financial management systems at primary health care: performance assessment of the Facility Financial Accounting and Reporting System (FFARS) in Tanzania. *Frontiers in Health Services* 128, 787940. DOI: 10.3389/frhs.2022.787940.

Sakr, S. and Elgammal, A. (2016) Towards a comprehensive data analytics framework for smart healthcare services. *Big Data Research* 4, 44–58. DOI: 10.1016/j.bdr.2016.05.002.

Secor, A.M., Mtenga, H., Richard, J., Bulula, N., Ferriss, E. *et al.* (2022) Added value of electronic immunization registries in low-and middle-income countries: observational case study in Tanzania. *JMIR Public Health Surveillance* 8, e32455.

Shortliffe, E.H. (1999) The evolution of electronic medical records. *Academic Medicine* 74, 414–419.

Ssennyonjo, A., Osoro, O., Ssengooba, F., Ekirapa-Kiracho, E., Mayora, C. *et al.* (2022) The government budget: an overlooked vehicle for advancing strategic health purchasing. *Health Systems and Reform* 8(2), 2082020. DOI: 10.1080/23288604.2022.2082020.

Stansfield, S.K., Walsh, J., Prata, N. and Evans, T. (2006) *Information to Improve Decision Making for Health*, 2nd edn. The World Bank, Washington, DC.

Stein, H.A., Stein, R.M. and Freeman, M.I. (2013) Office efficiency and public relations. In: Stein, H.A., Stein, R.M. and Freeman, M.I. (eds) *The Ophthalmic Assistant*, 9th edn. Elsevier Saunders, London, pp. 79–97.

Sukums, F., Simba, D., Kumalija, C., Asiimwe, S., Pothepragada, S. *et al.* (2021) Avoiding pitfalls: key insights and lessons learnt from customizing and rolling out a national web-based system in Tanzania. *The Electronic Journal of Information Systems in Developing Countries* 87(6), e12193. DOI: 10.1002/isd2.12193.

Tilley, H. (2011) *Africa as a Living Laboratory: Empire, Development, and the Problem of Scientific Knowledge, 1870–1950*. University of Chicago Press, Chicago, Illinois. DOI: 10.7208/chicago/9780226803487.001.0001.

Tilley, H. (2016) Medicine, empires, and ethics in colonial Africa. *AMA Journal of Ethics* 18(7), 743–753. DOI: 10.1001/journalofethics.2016.18.7.mhst1-1607.

Titmuss, R. (1964) *The Health Services of Tanganyika: A Report to the Government*. Lippincott Williams & Wilkins, London, pp. 27–29. DOI: 10.1097/00005650-196401000-00006.

van Weel, C (2007) Research in primary care: how to live-up to its needs? *Primary Health Care Research and Development* 8(01), 1. DOI: 10.1017/S1463423607000011.

van Weel, C. and Rosser, W.W. (2004) Improving health care globally: a critical review of the necessity of family medicine research and recommendations to build research capacity. *The Annals of Family Medicine* 2(suppl. 2), S5–S16. DOI: 10.1370/afm.194.

Watts, G. (2020) The Tanzanian digital health agenda. *The Lancet Digital Health* 2(2), e62–e63. DOI: 10.1016/S2589-7500(20)30005-4.

Wellcome Trust (2015) *Enabling Data Linkage to Maximise the Value of Public Health Research Data: Full Report*. Wellcome Trust, London.

WHO (2007) *Everybody's Business: Strengthening Health Systems to Improve Health Outcomes: WHO's Framework for Action*. World Health Organization, Geneva, Switzerland.

WHO (2008a) *Framework and Standards for Country Health Information Systems*. World Health Organization, Geneva, Switzerland.

WHO (2008b) *The World Health Report 2008: Primary Health Care Now More than Ever*. World Health Organization, Geneva, Switzerland.

WHO (2013) *The World Health Report 2013: Research for Universal Health Coverage*. World Health Organization, Geneva, Switzerland.

WHO (2019) *WHO Guideline: Recommendations on Digital Interventions for Health System Strengthening*. World Health Organization, Geneva, Switzerland.

WHO and UNICEF (1978) *Primary health care: report of the International Conference on Primary Health Care, Alma-Ata, USSR, 6–12 September 1978 / jointly sponsored by the World Health Organization and the United Nations Children's Fund.* World Health Organization. Available at: https://apps.who.int/iris/handle/10665/39228

Young, T.K. (1986) Socialist development and primary health care: the case of Tanzania. *Human Organization* 45(2), 128–134. DOI: 10.17730/humo.45.2.17p75666m4347g14.

7 Health-Service Delivery

Harrieth P. Ndumwa[1], Jackline E. Ngowi[1], Amani Kikula[1]*, Belinda J. Njiro[1], Castory Munishi[1], Bakari Salum[2], James Tumaini Kengia[2,3], Abel Makubi[4] and Bruno F. Sunguya[1]

[1]Muhimbili University of Health and Allied Sciences (MUHAS), Dar es Salaam, Tanzania; [2]President's Office – Regional Administration and Local Government, Dodoma, Tanzania; [3]University of Dodoma, Tanzania; [4]Ministry of Health, Dodoma, Tanzania

Abstract

Primary health-care (PHC) service delivery in Tanzania has transformed from the medical services which existed in colonial times and provision by Christian missionary organizations to service delivery which is now guided by national health policies. There has been a shifted to an emphasis on providing high-quality PHC. The evolution of PHC service delivery has been influenced by development and strategic plans and national health polices guided by national priorities, and the political and economic environment in Tanzania. The organization of PHC service delivery cuts across both facility and community levels. Initially, PHC service delivery at the community level aimed at promoting key health issues such as sanitation, nutrition and reproductive health, but has now become the target for vertical programmes together with health promotion and preventive efforts. The government has been attempting to strengthen PHC service provision through infrastructure, policy and governance improvements over the years with the aim to attain universal health coverage (UHC).

7.0 Background of Service Delivery in Tanzania

7.0.1 Historical perspective in health-service delivery

Health-service delivery during the pre-independence era

During the pre-independence era and up to the 1930s, the health system of Tanganyika consisted of two distinct sectors: the medical services operated by the colonial state and the voluntary sector, which consisted of Christian missionary organizations. Medical services were mainly based in urban areas and areas of economic interest (Jennings, 2015), while the voluntary sector had limited resources, though it met most health needs of the people of Tanganyika (Jennings, 2018) (Fig. 7.1). The health of the natives was only considered when their diseases also threatened the colonial members of society, as in the case of malaria and plague (Bruchhausen, 2003). Between the 1930s and the 1940s, the public–private model was developed and established through cooperation between the colonial state medical sector and the voluntary sector, and this helped in addressing the challenges of health-service delivery through the voluntary sector, including the underfunding which resulted from

*Corresponding author: amanikikula@gmail.com

 Primary Health Care in Tanzania through a Health Systems Lens (eds N.A. Kapologwe *et al.*)
DOI: 10.1079/9781800623330.0007

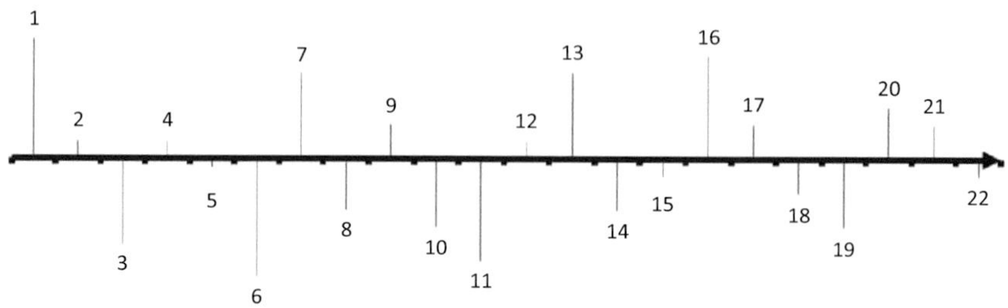

Key:
1. State-operated and voluntary Christian missionary medical services
2. Public–private cooperation was established (pre-independence)
3. Hospitals: 98; health centres: 22; dispensaries: 975
4. Only 30% of pregnant women had access to ANC services
5. Facility delivery was only 11% (independence era)
6. Arusha Declaration, which put emphasis on access to PHC and free medical care for all under the principle of universal access
7. Nationalization of some church-owned hospitals, ArushaDeclaration
8. Expanded programmeof immunization (EPI) was established as a vertical programme
9. Hospitals: 149; health centres: 240; dispensaries: 2644
10. Development of guidelines for implementation of PHC
11. Private-for-profit services abandoned, FBO and parastatalorganizations authorized to own HFs (Alma-Ata Declaration)
12.Standard treatment guidelines (STG) and the national essential medicine list for Tanzania (NEMLIT) first published
13. Tanzania Development Vision 2025
14. First health-sector strategic plan (plan of work)
15. National health policy and health-sector reforms document
16. National health-care intervention package introduced
17. Traditional and Alternative Medicine Act was formulated in 2002
18. The national strategy for growth and the reduction of poverty (NSGRP)
19. Primary health-care service development programme (PHSDP)
20. BRN initiative
21. Establishment of star-rating assessment for PHC health facilities
22. District hospitals: 178; health centres: 920; dispensaries: 7242 (HSR – Asthana)

Fig. 7.1. Timeline of key events related to PHC.

the colonial state barely allocating funds for missionary health-care facilities (Jennings, 2018).

Health-service delivery during and after independence

Following the independence of Tanganyika in 1961, and the subsequent birth of 'Tanzania' in 1964, the government placed social welfare, including education and health, at the centre of its development vision. After independence, the Tanzanian government continued to invest in basic health services (which were later known as primary health services) as a potential tool in fighting diseases and improving the quality of life of the majority of people (Ministry of Health, Community Development, Gender, 2007). During this period, the emphasis was on curative services, with minimal efforts relating to preventive services. By December 1961, the country had 98 hospitals, 22 rural health centres and 975 dispensaries serving the entire population. Only 30% of pregnant women received antenatal care, with only 11% of all children being born in health facilities (Ministry of Health, Community Development, Gender, 2007).

Delivery of primary health-care services during the 1964–1977 period

The 1967 Arusha Declaration placed emphasis on access to PHC for all to attain its objectives (TANU, 1967). Voluntary agencies were considered as critical partners in delivering health services, especially in maternal and child health. Some of the church-owned hospitals, such as the Lutheran hospital in Kilimanjaro (currently, Kilimanjaro Christian Medical Centre – KCMC), were nationalized and health services were funded by the state from 1967 but ownership was retained. In 1977, the private for-profit ownership was abandoned, and authorized organizations, namely faith-based and parastatal organizations, were permitted to own and expand their health facilities (Jennings, 2015). During this period, Tanzania was leading the global health agenda in focusing on PHC and this led to the Alma-Ata Declaration in 1978 (Birn and Krementsov, 2018). Improvements in health-care delivery were noted at the end of the third phase of the five-year development plan, when there were a total of 149 hospitals, 240 health centres and 2644 dispensaries in the country, enabling 95% of the rural population to reside within 10 kilometres of the nearest health facility, and around 72% of the people being within a 5-kilometre radius of a health centre. The health centres and dispensaries provided PHC services to the population. The MOH in the 1970s, recognizing the lack of preventive measures, established the Directorate of Preventive services. The Expanded Programme on Immunization (EPI) (the name was later changed to the Immunization and Vaccine Development Programme) was started as a vertical programme responsible for vaccine supply-chain management and distribution.

Delivery of primary health-care services during the 1978–1994 period

During the 1978–1994 period, delivery of PHC services was influenced mainly by the 1978 Alma-Ata Declaration. In 1983, the MOH developed guidelines for the implementation of the PHC programme in Tanzania. In 1990, the national health policy and health-sector reforms proposal programme documents were developed to guide provision of health services based on the principles of PHC suggested in the Alma-Ata Declaration. During the period 1991–1994, health-sector reforms were proposed to address several service-related challenges relating to health-services delivery, including PHC services. The suggested reforms included the following: the provision of cost-effective health services and public health packages; strengthening the referral system; improving health services infrastructure; promoting the public–private mix; integrating vertical health programmes; promoting the use of research findings to improve delivery of health services; and improving the availability of medicines, other medical supplies and medical equipment.

Delivery of primary health-care services from 1995 to the present day

The delivery of PHC services during the 1995 period onwards was guided by the national health policy of 1990 which decentralized the health-care system, leaving the MOH with the main role of setting health policy guidelines. Sixty years post-independence, in December 2021, the network of primary health facilities had reached 7242 dispensaries, 920 health centres and 178 district hospitals.

7.0.2 Policy context on PHC service delivery

While the content of the policies were developed to cater for a variety of the country's contexts, the health sector and particularly the PHC system has been influenced and directed by these policy changes.

The Tanzania development vision 2025 (Vision 2025)

The Tanzania Development Vision 2025, which was published in 1999, aimed at achieving a high-quality livelihood for all Tanzanians by the year 2025. To attain its objectives, Vision 2025 focused on access to quality PHC for all; a quality reproductive health service for all individuals of appropriate ages; a reduction in infant and maternal mortality rates by three-quarters; and the participation of the community in the delivery of health services (Vice President's Office, 2005).

The five-year development plans

The 1969–1974 health plan aimed to develop preventive and rural health services within the country, as a result of which maternal and child health control measures gained much success. While the 1975–1980 development plan was structured to accommodate donor funding on preventive and other disease control programmes, the 5 year development plan (FYDP I, 2011/12–2015/16) aimed to mobilize Tanzania's resources in order to improve the provision of basic services (United Republic of Tanzania, 2011). For the health sector, FYDP

surveillance and early identification through integration with the community.

7.1 Current Arrangements for Delivery of Primary Health Services in Tanzania

The provision of primary health services is categorized as facility based and community based within the district or council health system. The facility-based health system delivers primary health services through a network of public and private dispensaries, health centres and hospitals. At the health facility level, primary health services are delivered mainly by health professionals. Community health workers and other health professionals deliver community health and social welfare services at the community level.

7.1.1 Hierarchy of PHC service delivery in Tanzania

Community health services

The evolution of community health-service delivery and current practices are well described in Chapter 8.

Dispensaries

Dispensaries evolved from the upgraded village health posts which were initially present in Ujamaa villages to provide basic health-care for the community. Currently, dispensaries form the base of the health-facilities pyramid, offering outpatient and maternal and child-care services. The health policy directs every village to have a dispensary for an average population of 5,000–10,000. Tanzania has a total of 12,318 villages with 7045 dispensaries, of which 5295 (75.2%) are public-owned. The coverage of a dispensary for every village is still under 60%, with variations between different geographical areas (Boex *et al.*, 2015).

Health centre

Advocacy for the establishment of health centres began in 1938 with the first one established in 1950, under the slogan, 'A dispensary must become a health centre' (HC). Originally HCs were responsible for providing community-level services on a preventive basis, and later they adopted the curative role. Since then, HCs have become the referral level for dispensaries and provide a slightly broader range of services than dispensaries, including in-patient care and emergency caesarean delivery. They cater for an average population of between 25,000 and 50,000. Current health policy is to have a health centre for every ward, but currently the coverage is only 24% of the required number of wards of target wards (Kapologwe *et al.*, 2020).

The district/council hospital

According to the health policy, every council/district is required to have one council/district hospital, which usually provides services to an average of 250,000 people. A district that does not have a public district hospital can enter into a service agreement (contractual agreement) with a hospital run by a faith-based organization, whereby it becomes a designated district hospital. In some circumstances a council/district might have more than one district hospital, depending on geographical or population dynamics. To date, there are 142 operational government hospitals, and some other council-designated hospitals serving as hospitals at the level of district/council.

7.1.2 Government effort in provision of primary health care

Since independence in 1961, Tanzania emphasized the objective of achieving PHC for all by working on initiatives to increase coverage and access to health among all communities. Training village medical helpers and setting up of first aid posts began in 1969. Tanzania Mainland had 233 active first-aid posts. Later on, the plan shifted from having one dispensary per village to having one primary health unit per village, hence dispensaries served a purpose of providing services to several villages. Thus, the Alma-Ata Declaration (1978) was only a confirmation of programmes which already existed in Tanzania policies and a confirmation of the programme which had already been envisaged in the Tanzanian politics of African socialism. The declaration called for 'urgent and effective national and international action to develop and implement PHC throughout the world'. It underlined the utility of universal accessibility, community participation and undermined inequality in health care (Alma-Ata 1978–2018) (WHO, 1978). By 1978/1979 there were 2600 dispensaries, 239 health centres and 67 district hospitals, of which 17 were designated district hospitals. At that time, 72 and 93% of the population were living within 5 kilometres and 10 kilometres of the health facility respectively (Young, 1986). Beginning in 1980, Tanzania faced an economic crisis which significantly affected the accessibility and functioning of the health sector and other social services. To respond to the crisis, the first health-sector reform was established in 1993 to solve the problem of underfunding and improve accessibility in primary health services (COWI *et al.*, 2007).

Twenty years after the declaration, a total of 72% of Tanzanians were living within 5 kilometres of health facilities and 93% lived within 10 kilometres of a health facility. The ultimate aim was the achievement of the social goal of 'health for all' by 2000. As demonstrated in the declaration, preventive services were pioneered and made available at all levels of PHC under the belief that 'It is better to prevent a person from getting the disease than treat them when they acquire the disease' (World Health Organization & Alliance for Health Policy and Systems Research, 2017). The health policy enlightened the goal of the declaration that every village would be able to manage its own health services by 2000, with maximum community involvement in planning, implementation and health services management, depending on central government for commodities support only. Following the decentralization policy, districts were able to make their own decisions, independent of referring to central government. Despite having invested in PHC and the establishment of PHC, some parts of the population had poor access to PHC services, with some living more than 10 kilometres from the nearest health facility (World Health Organization & Alliance for Health Policy and Systems Research, 2017).

The government then established the reform programme, Primary Health Services Development Programme (PHSDP), commonly known as Mpango wa Maendeleo wa Afya ya Msingi (MMAM) in Kiswahili, which aimed to improve accessibility of PHC services by ensuring that every village has a dispensary and every ward has a health centre. In ensuring provision of quality health services at primary health facilities, the Tanzanian government introduced a quality improvement framework in health care that started in 2004, with a second phase in 2011–2016, and a star-rating system for primary health facilities implemented in 2014, to grade the performance and quality of maternal health services. The system was a part of the Big Result Now campaign that was adapted from a Malaysian government campaign. It was organized in a way that meant that primary health facilities were rated on a scale of 0 to 5, based on studied quantity and quality indicators of health-service delivery (Ministry of Health and Social Affairs and PO-RALG, 2014; CGTN, 2018; Renggli *et al.*, 2018). Also, national guidelines for infection prevention and control (IPC) in health-care facilities were developed in 2004 and a second edition in 2018, with ongoing implementation to guide improvement of IPC practices and safety of the services to patients and health-care workers within PHC and beyond (Hokororo *et al.*, 2021).

The government, in collaboration with other stakeholders, has directed efforts towards improving access to primary health services in the country, through renovating health centres, dispensaries and district hospitals, building new health-care centres at district hospitals, health centres and clinics and the placement of medical equipment and staff at facilities under construction/renovation, as well as other facilities providing health services in the country (Fig. 7.2; Table 7.2). Up to December 2020, a total of 102 hospitals, 487 health centres and 1198 dispensaries had been built in the country. In the same period, a total of 12,865 employees were hired and distributed to various centres providing health services; the prime vendor system (PVS) and an improved community health fund (iCHF) were established and started working in all 26 regions of Mainland Tanzania. The procedure for sending money directly to health centres, direct health facility financing (DHFF) has been

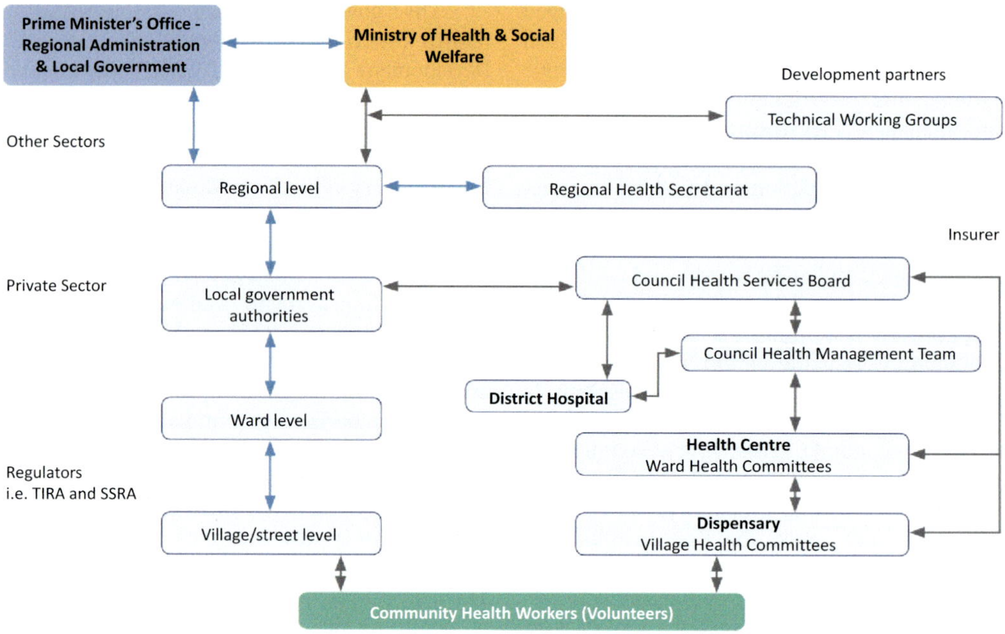

Fig. 7.2. Key PHC organizational structures and decision making bodies in the United Republic of Tanzania.

established at 5175 government health centres, and an improved community health fund (iCHF) has been established and started working in all 26 regions of Mainland Tanzania.

7.1.3 Challenges in the provision of primary health care

Despite the developments in the provision of quality PHC services to the majority of the population, there are still areas that do not receive the same balance of services due to geographical restrictions, distance from district headquarters and poor infrastructure. Some facilities are located 50 kilometres or more from the council or a neighbouring centre that provides emergency services and caesarean sections for pregnant women, and the road infrastructure is poor. Areas along the borders face challenges in accessing health services due to increased interaction with neighbouring countries. Difficult and poor working environments also lead to a further shortage of health-care workers in these settings. Some of these include: Kigoma region areas, such as Kasulu council, Katavi region, for example, Mpimbwe council, Mpanda councils et cetera; Mtwara region in Tandahimba and Nanyamba councils; and Kagera region in Ngara, Karagwe, Kyerwa and Misenyi councils. Due to the shortage of health centres, some of them serve between 30,000 and 80,000 people, with no adequate infrastructure to serve such large number of people. Other areas are inaccessible to any health-care centre; examples of such areas include the Butiama DC council at Karia (37,308) and Kyanyari (42,125) clinics; Pandambili Ward Kongwa council (82,392); Nkome Clinic in Geita DC council (65,000); and Lushamba Ward in Buchosa council.

There were still problems in terms of the quality of services delivered in some facilities, with only about one-fifth (20%) of facilities rated at three stars and above. Social accountability is also low; analysis of the star rating assessment (SRA) showed that less than one-third (30.4%) of PHC facilities were socially accountable (Yahya and Mohamed, 2018).

Despite efforts at ensuring wide coverage of primary health services across the country,

Table 7.2. Service package for primary health facilities.

Level of a facility	Services offered
District hospitals	Outpatient department (OPD), inpatient department (IPD), care and treatment clinic (CTC), antenatal clinic (ANC), TB/leprosy services
	Emergency major operations
	Clinics – NCD
	Emergency caesarean operation
	Oral health services
	Minor surgery
	Immunization services
	Family planning services
Health centres	OPD, IPD, CTC, TB/leprosy, ANC services
	Emergency caesarean operation
	Minor surgery
	Basic oral health services
	Immunization services
	Family planning services
	TB/HIV services clinics
Dispensaries	Basic OPD, ANC services
	Emergency oral health services
	Minor surgery
	Immunization services
	TB/HIV services clinics
	Family planning services
	Outreach and mobile services

equipment and supplies were inadequate and unsatisfactory and delivery systems to respective health facilities were a challenge due to the poor transportation system. Supplies are still dependent on importation from other countries and vertical programmes which pose a challenge considering the feeble economic system. Utilization of some services is still inadequate; specific groups such as older people, women and adolescents are underutilizing the available services. While 98% of all women have made at least one clinic visit, only 15% made their visits before the fourth month of pregnancy (Moshi, 2021). Also, a decline in attendance rates was reported, from 64% in 2005 to 36% in 2010 (World Health Organization & Alliance for Health Policy and Systems Research, 2017). Up to 2019, no geriatric services were provided in PHC facilities, other than the exemption policy which was only available in some parts of the country.

Population growth and urbanization in Tanzania have had a significant impact on improving the health of the population, which has resulted in an increase in average life expectancy. However, a disproportionate improvement has been observed where life expectancy has increased by 13 years in rural areas, compared with a three-year increase in urban areas. Urban populations in Tanzania have higher under-fives mortality and maternal mortality than rural areas, and studies indicate that urban populations are at an increased risk for specific health problems, including cholera, diabetes and road traffic accidents. Despite the fact that urban residents have better access to health services and improved availability of essential health-prevention measures compared to rural residents (the so-called 'urban advantage'), higher health-service coverage in cities has not been translated into improved health outcomes in a number of areas, including nutritional status of women of reproductive age (WRA), use of family planning (FP), anaemia in WRA and low birth weight. HIV/AIDS is also significantly higher for urban females. Moreover, adolescent girls are the most vulnerable and they epitomize the apparent HIV and AIDS urban paradox. A risky urban environment interplays with gender and age to compound the adolescent girls' vulnerability.

Dar es Salaam, which is projected to be a megacity by 2025, is home to about five million people, with a population growth of 7%, more than twice the national growth rate of 3%. With this rate of urbanization, some parts of the city areas effectively share the characteristics of slums and this has highlighted a need to re-examine urban health, particularly due to its unusually poor health indicators (NBS, 2013; Ministry of Health and Social Welfare, 2015; MOHCDGEC, 2021).

Out of 615 primary health facilities located in Dar es Salaam, 36 are hospitals, 63 are health

Table 7.3. Urban–rural comparison of selected health outcome indicators in Tanzania. From HSSP V, 2020.

Themes	Indicator	Urban	Rural	Slums
General population	Life expectancy (years)	60	62	44–46
	HIV/AIDS (%)	7.2	4.3	–
	Unimproved latrines (%)	21	73	83
	No latrines (%)	2	13	14
Child health and nutrition	U-5 mortality/1000 live birth	71.2	65.9	97
	Low birth weight (%)	9.1	5.8	–
	Stunting (%)	24.7	37.8	46–56
	Diarrhoea (%)	14.1	11	60
	Prelacteal feeds (%)	12	14.5	91
Maternal health	Maternal mortality (rate)	432	336	–
	Overweight (%)	42	21	–

centres and 516 are dispensaries (Health facility registry Tanzania, 2022). However, the growth rate of the city is outpacing the capacity of these facilities, as reflected by the poor health indicators on reproductive, maternal, newborn, child and adolescent health outcomes (Table 7.3). Furthermore, ownership of facilities has a unique distribution in this region, with 80% being privately owned, in contrast to the national average of 30% private ownership of facilities. This defeats the existing geographical accessibility to services in the city, with limitations placed on poor households. Poor performance of key health indicators is evidence of the mismatch between increased population-pressure mismatch and health-system development.

At this moment in time, health indicators of the urban poor are not always better than those of the rural poor. In urban areas, most health services are provided by private health facilities. Urbanization and industrialization will require new approaches in health-care delivery to meet the preventive, diagnostic and curative services within this setup, creating new joint ventures, and new relations between governmental and private providers. The PHC arm needs to take special care to accommodate this unique situation for all the expanding cities in the country. Another special account should be considered in the streamlining of health-service coverage that is fragmented within the country, where fragmentation in programmatic alignment of the health services is in existence.

7.1.4 Success of PHC service delivery

The Tanzanian health workforce situation (locally trained human resources for health) is one of the areas where success has been recorded, especially for rural health-care services. Since the establishment of the PHSDP between 2007 and 2017, there has been an increase in geographical accessibility with the construction of new facilities and the improvement of existing ones. However, only about 70% of the health facilities provide delivery care. An average of 72% of the Tanzanian population lives within 5 kilometres of a health facility, with some remaining discrepancies, ranging from 25% in Kagera region to 100% in Dar es Salaam, with the general service readiness of the facilities rated to be 42 (Ministry of Health, 2013). Current coverage of health-care services at primary health-care level is as high as 90%, with most of the population accessing the services within 10 kilometres. This indicates success in reducing home deliveries for women and reducing the first delay, that is, seeking health care per demand. The decentralization approach introduced in the health-care system in the 1990s empowered primary health-care facilities at district hospitals, health centres and dispensaries to autonomously have a wide range of decision making choices. This has raised their capacity in addressing health needs and preferences (Moshi, 2021). Decentralization in LMICs has also helped to improve the functionality of health facility governing committees (HFGCs), although with varying functionality depending on several factors namely, 'the context and decentralization type, members' awareness of their roles, membership allowance and availability of resource to the facility in which HFGCs operate to produce the desired outcomes' (Kapologwe *et al.*, 2019; Kesale *et al.*, 2022a). Introduction of direct health facility financing (DHFF) in the fiscal year 2017/18 (Kalolo *et al.*, 2022) helped to improve functionality and accountability of HFGCs (Kesale *et al.*, 2022a) and improvement of critical services such as maternal health services (Tukay *et al.*, 2021).

7.1.5 The road ahead for PHC service delivery

Strengthening prevention and treatment services at community level and in health-care facilities is an important step towards achieving universal health coverage and building resilient health systems that can effectively adapt and respond to changing population health needs within the country. Increasing expertise, particularly in the areas of rehabilitation care, geriatric care, NCDs and medical supply, to match the level of care at the respective primary health facilities will regulate unnecessary referrals to tertiary hospitals for patients who require a primary health-care level of treatment. Innovative solutions to the existing problems and the growing population demands need to be in place, together with implementation of the policies which currently exist to ensure adequate service delivery and quality even in the face of financial constraints (Bustreo *et al.*, 2019). Various countries have developed different models of networks which involve public primary health facilities and other stakeholders in the provision of services. For example, the layered on top model, in which one PHC organization incentivizes public health activities for multiple private providers. Another example is the district organization model in which district hospitals contract other facilities to provide a defined package of services appropriate to their level, which is practised in Thailand (World Health Organization & Alliance for Health Policy and Systems Research, 2017). The requirement for coordinating health programmes to have equitable investment across PHC is of great importance moving forward to achieve comprehensive service delivery at the PHC level within the country.

7.1.6 Innovations in PHC service delivery

Tanzania has been improving its provision of PHC with the adoption of digital technology and innovative solutions for some of its public health challenges, including adolescent health and sexual and reproductive health. Ongoing developments in the use of evidence-based information and technology, such as Tanzania's eHealth strategy and investments in fibre optic cables across Tanzania, have provided an enabling environment for progress and presented new opportunities for young people from both rural and urban areas. The advancements in e-consultation that evolved during the COVID-19 pandemic should be an area that PHC should build on to improve service delivery (Mold *et al.*, 2021). The increase in mobile phone use over the last few years in Tanzania has led to about 40% of the population having access to internet. Like other African countries, access to these technologies will only continue to grow, especially as connectivity improves in rural areas. Initiatives being made in frontier technologies, such as artificial intelligence (AI) and machine learning, are transforming the delivery and accountability of services. For example, Tanzania is taking integrated management of childhood illness (IMCI) into its next phase, using AI to support improvements in case-management algorithms and hence quality of care. An IMCI-derived decision-support protocol has shown how using mobile technology at the point of care not only improves clinical care but also increases the likelihood a child will receive correct treatment at home (Bustreo *et al.*, 2019).

7.2 Lessons From the Past

To provide high-quality PHC, there is a need for organized health-service delivery backed by a strong system and adequate human resources, infrastructure, drugs and supplies. Tanzania, among many other countries who pioneered PHC, has excelled moderately in fulfilling its population health-demands despite its many obstacles (World Health Organization & Alliance for Health Policy and Systems Research, 2017; Wandwalo *et al.*, 2022).

Tanzania has significantly lowered death rates in younger age groups over the last ten years, surpassing the millennium development goal for child mortality. Infant and under-five mortality rates decreased by almost a half between 1999 and 2010. Despite this progress, Tanzania's health outcomes are still worse than predicted given the country's level of development (Ogbo *et al.*, 2019; Kisenge *et al.*, 2020).

The fragmentation of vertical and horizontal health programmes has been posing a challenge in delivering services at PHC level and hence there is a need to integrate them and redefine the functioning of PHC (Donev *et al.*, 2013; World Health Organization & Alliance for Health Policy and Systems Research, 2017; Kapologwe *et al.*, 2022). To better utilize the available decision making authority within the framework of decentralization, it is essential to vest power to the districts in areas such as recruitment of trained health staff and formulation of job descriptions among others (World Health Organization & Alliance for Health Policy and Systems Research, 2017).

The financing of health care in the United Republic of Tanzania has been facing difficulties owing to challenged resources. The donor proportion of total health spending is still large, and despite development partners' sector-wide strategy, vertical financing streams still persist, particularly for priority disease management programmes. Furthermore, hefty out-of-pocket expenditures make health financing extremely regressive, putting the poor at a significant financial disadvantage, and the policy on waivers and exclusions has been poorly implemented. The existing health insurance plans, including community health funds, are affected by adverse selection and the low number of policy holders, leading to a negative impact on the utilization of PHC services in the country (World Bank, n.d.; P4H Network, 2016/2017; Piatti-Fünfkirchen and Ally, 2020).

A discrepancy in terms of availability of services at PHC level still exists. An assessment done in 2012 by SARA found that less than 25% of dispensaries are fully up to standard. And even with improved access there is still a concern of affordability and quality of services offered (Piatti-Fünfkirchen and Ally, 2020). The improvement in access and availability of PHC in rural areas also needs to go hand in hand with improvement of quality of the service.

UHC is the future of Tanzania's health-care system because it is a key driver of economic development and is critical in breaking the vicious cycle of poverty which has an enormous impact on the health of the people. As we strive towards UHC, the country is working on improving the social determinants of health, such as education, unemployment, and job insecurity, working conditions, early childhood development, housing, basic amenities and the environment. Addressing the social determinants of health is a primary approach to achieving health equity as they account for 30–55% of health outcomes. When the social determinants are improved, most people will live a healthy life and thus reduce pressure to the health-care system (Atashbahar *et al.*, 2022).

As stated in the Alma-Ata Declaration of 1978, PHC is key to the attainment of the goal of 'Health for All'. Thus, in the road to UHC, Tanzania starts with a strong commitment to PHC that provides the services needed which is the most equitable and sustainable strategy in achieving health for all. Tanzania has to deploy practical, scientifically sound and socially acceptable methods and technology and make them universally accessible to individuals and families through their full participation and at a cost that the community and the country can afford (P4H Network, 2016/2017).

Tanzania has to build a strong health-care system that is responsive to the current dynamics in demographics and disease trends. For example, the health system moving towards the future needs to be responsive to the health needs of the youth which, as per 2012 census, formed 50.1% of the population (MOHCDGEC, MOH, NBS, OCGS and ICF, 2016), needs to be ready to cater for the increasing elderly population (Maluka, 2013; Akinyemi *et al.*, 2014; Frumence *et al.*, 2017; Amani *et al.*, 2020) and the growing burden of NCDs (Roman *et al.*, 2019).

Putting it all together, service delivery at PHC level and the progress to attaining UHC needs to go hand in hand with good governance and leadership (see Chapter 2), health financing (see Chapter 4); health information systems (see Chapter 6); facility infrastructure, medicines and medical supplies (see Chapter 5) and a competent, motivated and equitably distributed workforce that is aligned with population and community health needs (see Chapter 3).

Bibliography

Akinyemi, R.O., Izzeldin, I.M.H., Dotchin, C., Gray, W.K., Adeniji, O. *et al.* (2014) Contribution of noncommunicable diseases to medical admissions of elderly adults in Africa: a prospective, cross-sectional study in Nigeria, Sudan, and Tanzania. *Journal of the American Geriatrics Society* 62(8), 1460–1466. DOI: 10.1111/jgs.12940.

Amani, P.J., Tungu, M., Hurtig, A.-K., Kiwara, A.D., Frumence, G. *et al.* (2020) Responsiveness of health care services towards the elderly in Tanzania: does health insurance make a difference? A cross-sectional study. *International Journal for Equity in Health* 19(1), 179. DOI: 10.1186/s12939-020-01270-9.

Atashbahar, O., Sari, A.A., Takian, A., Olyaeemanesh, A., Mohamadi, E. *et al.* (2022) The impact of social determinants of health on early childhood development: a qualitative context analysis in Iran. *BMC Public Health* 22(1), 1149. DOI: 10.1186/s12889-022-13571-5.

Birn, A.-E. and Krementsov, N. (2018) "Socialising" primary care? The Soviet Union, WHO and the 1978 Alma-Ata Conference. *BMJ Global Health* 3(Suppl 3), e000992. DOI: 10.1136/bmjgh-2018-000992.

Boex, J., Fuller, L. and Malik, A.A. (2015) *Decentralized Local Health Services in Tanzania: Are Health Resources Reaching Primary Health Facilities, or Are They Getting Stuck at the District Level?* Urban Institute, Washington, DC. Available at: https://www.academia.edu/44668593/Decentralized_Local_Health_Services_in_Tanzania_Are_Health_Resources_Reaching_Primary_Health_Facilities_or_Are_They_Getting_Stuck_at_the_District_Level (accessed 16 May 2023).

Bruchhausen, W. (2003) Practising hygiene and fighting the natives' diseases: public and child health in German East Africa and Tanganyika territory, 1900–1960. *Dynamis* 23, 85–113.

Bustreo, F., Mshinda, H., Hinton, R., Hausmann-Muela, S. and Tanner, M. (2019) Commentary: primary health care in Tanzania – Leading the way through innovation. *EClinicalMedicine* 13, 12–13. DOI: 10.1016/j.eclinm.2019.07.010.

CGTN (2018) *Tanzania Introduces Rating System for Healthcare Facilities*. CGTN Africa, Nairobi, Kenya. Available at: https://africa.cgtn.com/tanzania-introduces-rating-system-for-healthcare-facilities/ (accessed 16 May 2023).

COWI, Goss Gilroy Inc and EPOS (2007) *Joint External Evaluation of the Health Sector in Tanzania: 1999–2006, Health (San Francisco)*. Ministry of Foreign Affairs, Copenhagen.

Dominicus, D.A.R. and Akamatsu, T. (1989) Health policy and implementations in Tanzania. *The Keio Journal of Medicine* 38(2), 192–200. DOI: 10.2302/kjm.38.192.

Donev, D., Kovacic, L. and Laaser, U. (2013) The role and organization of health care systems. In: Burazeri, G. and Zaletel-Kragelj, L. (eds) *Health: Systems, Lifestyles, Policies*, Vol. 1. Jacobs Verlag, Lage, Germany, pp. 3–14. Available at: https://www.researchgate.net/publication/257830385 (accessed 16 May 2023).

Frumence, G., Nyamhanga, T., Anaeli, A. and Talebian, S. (2017) Facilitators and barriers to health care access among the elderly in Tanzania: a health system perspective from managers and service providers. *Journal of Aging Research And Healthcare* 2(1), 20–31. DOI: 10.14302/issn.2474-7785.jarh-16-1354.

Hokororo, J., Eliakimu, E., Ngowi, R., German, C., Bahegwa, R, *et al.* (2021) Report of trend for compliance of infection prevention and control standards in Tanzania from 2010 to 2017 in Tanzania mainland. *Microbiology & Infectious Diseases* 5(3), 1–10.

Jennings, M. (2015) The precariousness of the franchise state: voluntary sector health services and international NGOs in Tanzania, 1960s – mid-1980s. *Social Science & Medicine* 141, 1–8. DOI: 10.1016/j.socscimed.2015.07.018.

Jennings, M. (2018) Cooperation and competition. In: Greenwood, A. (ed.) *Beyond the State*. Manchester University Press, Manchester, UK, pp. 153–173. DOI: 10.7765/9781784996789.

Kalolo, A., Kapologwe, N.A., Samky, H. and Kibusi, S.M. (2022) Acceptability of the Direct Health Facility Financing (DHFF) initiative in Tanzania: A mixed methods process evaluation of the moderating factors. *The International Journal of Health Planning and Management* 37(3), 1381–1401. DOI: 10.1002/hpm.3402.

Kapologwe, N.A., Kalolo, A., Kibusi, S.M., Chaula, Z., Nswilla, A. *et al.* (2019) Understanding the implementation of Direct Health Facility Financing and its effect on health system performance in Tanzania: a non-controlled before and after mixed method study protocol. *Health Research Policy and Systems* 17(1), 11. DOI: 10.1186/s12961-018-0400-3.

Kapologwe, N.A., Meara, J.G., Kengia, J.T., Sonda, Y., Gwajima, D. *et al.* (2020) Development and upgrading of public primary healthcare facilities with essential surgical services infrastructure: a strategy towards achieving universal health coverage in Tanzania. *BMC Health Services Research* 20(1), 218. DOI: 10.1186/s12913-020-5057-2.

Kesale, A.M., Mahonge, C. and Muhanga, M. (2022a) Effects of decentralization on the functionality of health facility governing committees in lower and middle-income countries: a systematic literature review. *Global Health Action* 15(1), 2074662. DOI: 10.1080/16549716.2022.2074662.

Kilonzo, G.P. and Simmons, N. (1998) Development of mental health services in Tanzania: a reappraisal for the future. *Social Science & Medicine (1982)* 47(4), 419–428. DOI: 10.1016/s0277-9536(97)10127-7.

Kisenge, R.R., Rees, C.A., Lauer, J.M., Liu, E., Fawzi, W.W. *et al.* (2020) Risk factors for mortality among Tanzanian infants and children. *Tropical Medicine and Health* 48(1), 43. DOI: 10.1186/s41182-020-00233-8.

Luhanga, C. and Ntabaye, M. (2001) Geriatric oral health issues in Africa: Tanzanian perspective. *International Dental Journal* 51(3 Suppl), 219–227. DOI: 10.1002/J.1875-595X.2001.TB00870.X.

Maluka, S.O. (2013) Why are pro-poor exemption policies in Tanzania better implemented in some districts than in others? *International Journal for Equity in Health* 12(1), 1–9. DOI: 10.1186/1475-9276-12-80.

Ministry of Health (2013) *Tanzania Service Availability and Readiness Assessment (SARA) 2012 Final Report July 2013*. Ifakara Health Institute, Dar es Salaam, Tanzania.

Ministry of Health, Community Development, Gender (2007) *The United Republic of Tanzania Ministry of Health and Social Welfare, Mpango Wa Maendeleo Wa Afya Ya Msingi (MMAM) 2007–2017, Primary Health Services Development Programme (PHSDP) 2007–2017*. Ministry of Health and Social Welfare, Dar es Salaam, Tanzania.

Ministry of Health and Social Affairs and PO-RALG (2014) *Program-for-Results Information Document (PID) Concept Stage*. Ministry of Health and Social Affairs and PO-RALG, Dodoma.

Ministry of Health and Social Welfare (2015) *Health Sector Strategic Plan July 2015–June 2020 (HSSO IV)*. 2020(July), 99. Ministry of Health and Social Welfare, Dodoma.

MOHCDGEC (2020) *The Second Guidelines for Provision of Oral Health Services in Tanzania*. Ministry of Health, Dar es Salaam, Tanzania, pp. 30–31. Available at: https://mercuryfreedentistry.files.wordpress.com/2020/06/tanzania-guidelines.pdf (accessed 17 May 2023).

MOHCDGEC (2021) *Tanzania Health Sector Strategic Plan 2021–2026*. Ministry of Health, Dar es Salaam, Tanzania.

MOHCDGEC, MOH, NBS, OCGS and ICF (2016) *Tanzania Demographic and Health Survey and Malaria Indicator Survey 2015–2016*. MOHCDGEC, MOH, NBS, OCGS and ICF, Dar es Salaam, Tanzania and Rockville, Maryland. Available at: https://dhsprogram.com/pubs/pdf/FR321/FR321.pdf (accessed 16 May 2023).

Mold, F., Cooke, D., Ip, A., Roy, P., Denton, S. *et al.* (2021) COVID-19 and beyond: virtual consultations in primary care-reflecting on the evidence base for implementation and ensuring reach: commentary article. *BMJ Health Care Inform* 28(1), e100256. DOI: 10.1136/bmjhci-2020-100256.

Mosha, H. (2006) Provision of oral health care services in Tanzania: implementation status (2005). *Tanzania Dental Journal* 12(1), 30–34. DOI: 10.4314/tdj.v12i1.37543.

Moshi, F.V. (2021) Prevalence and factors which influence early antenatal booking among women of reproductive age in Tanzania: an analysis of data from the 2015-16 Tanzania demographic health survey and malaria indicators survey. *PloS ONE* 16(4), e0249337. DOI: 10.1371/journal.pone.0249337.

NBS (2013) The United Republic of Tanzania 2012 population and housing census. *Population Distribution by Administrative Area* 255, 2130852.

Nicks, B.A., Sawe, H.R., Juma, A.M. and Reynolds, T.A. (2012) The state of emergency medicine in the United Republic of Tanzania. *African Journal of Emergency Medicine* 2(3), 97–102. DOI: 10.1016/j.afjem.2012.06.002.

Nyamuryekung'e, K. and Kahabuka, F. (2022) Accessing oral healthcare within a context of economic transition. In: Agrawal, A. and Kosgi, S. (eds) *Healthcare Access*. Intech Open, London. DOI: 10.5772/intechopen.94675.

Ogbo, F.A., Ezeh, O.K., Awosemo, A.O., Ifegwu, I.K., Tan, L. *et al.* (2019) Determinants of trends in neonatal, post-neonatal, infant, child and under-five mortalities in Tanzania from 2004 to 2016. *BMC Public Health* 19(1), 1243. DOI: 10.1186/s12889-019-7547-x.

P4H Network (2016/2017) *Universal Health Coverage (UHC) in Tanzania: Evaluating the Potential of a Public Private Partnership (PPP) in Health Financing System*. Available at: https://p4h.world/en/documents/universal-health-coverage-uhc-in-tanzania-evaluating-the-potential-of-a-public-private-partnership-ppp-in-health-financing-system/ (accessed 6 October 2022).

Piatti-Fünfkirchen, M. and Ally, M. (2020) *Tanzania Health Sector Public Expenditure Review*. World Bank, Washington, DC. DOI: 10.1596/34620.

Poulsen, S., Fubusa, F., Gemba, P.M., Lema, P.A., Mosha, H.J. *et al.* (1999) Distribution of dental therapists and assistant dental officers trained under the Tanzania-Danida Dental Health Programme 1981-1993. *Odonto-Stomatologie Tropicale = Tropical Dental Journal* 22(86), 19–22.

Renggli, S., Mayumana, I., Mboya, D., Charles, C., Maeda, J. *et al.* (2018) Towards improved health service quality in Tanzania: An approach to increase efficiency and effectiveness of routine supportive supervision. *PLoS ONE* 13(9), e0202735. DOI: 10.1371/journal.pone.0202735.

Roman, W.P., Martin, H.D. and Sauli, E. (2019) Cardiovascular diseases in Tanzania: the burden of modifiable and intermediate risk factors. *Journal of Xiangya Medicine* 4, 33. DOI: 10.21037/jxym.2019.07.03.

TANU (1967) *The Arusha Declaration and TANU's Policy on Socialism and Self-Reliance*. TANU, Dar es Salaam, Tanzania.

Tukay, S.M., Pasape, L., Tani, K. and Manzi, F. (2021) Evaluation of the direct health facility financing program in improving maternal health services in Pangani district, Tanzania. *International Journal of Women's Health* 13, 1227–1242. DOI: 10.2147/IJWH.S333900.

United Republic of Tanzania (2011) *Tanzania Five Year Development Plan 2011/2012–2015/2016: Unleashing Tanzania's Latest Growth Potentials*. Government of Tanzania, Dodoma. Available at: https://www.tralac.org/files/2012/12/5Year_development-plan.pdf (accessed 16 May 2023).

United Republic of Tanzania (2021) *National Five Year Development Plan 2021/22–2025/26: Realising Competitiveness and Industrialisation for Human Development*. The United Republic of Tanzania, Ministry of Finance and Planning (June), Dodoma, p. 321.

Vice President's Office (2005) *The United Republic of Tanzania National Strategy for Growth and Reduction of Poverty (NSGRP) Vice President's Office*. Government of Tanzania, Dodoma.

Wandwalo, E., Kamara, D.V., Yassin, M.A., Morrison, L., Nwaneri, N.B. *et al.* (2022) Enhancing Tuberculosis Case-Finding: A Case of Quality Improvement Initiative in Tanzania. *Tropical Medicine and Infectious Disease* 7(6), 97. DOI: 10.3390/tropicalmed7060097.

WHO (1978) Declaration of Alma-Ata. World Health Organization, Geneva, Switzerland. Available at: https://www.who.int/publications/i/item/WHO-EURO-1978-3938-43697-61471 (accessed 29 April 2023).

WHO (2015) *Global Database on the Implementation of Nutrition Action (GINA) National Nutrition Programme. 000(2011)*. World Health Organization, Geneva, Switzerland.

WHO*et al.* (2015) *Universal Health Coverage: Lessons to Guide Country Actions on Health Financing*. World Health Organization, Geneva, Switzerland. Available at: https://resourcecentre.savethechildren.net/pdf/uhc_and_health_financing.pdf/ (accessed 17 May 2023).

World Bank (n.d.) *Tanzania Overview: Development News, Research, Data*. World Bank, Washington, DC. Available at: https://www.worldbank.org/en/country/tanzania/overview (accessed 16 May 2023).

World Health Organization & Alliance for Health Policy and Systems Research (2017) Primary Health Care Systems (primasys): Comprehensive Case Study from United Republic of Tanzania. World Health Organization, Geneva, Switzerland. Available at: https://apps.who.int/iris/bitstream/handle/10665/341165/WHO-HIS-HSR-17.39-eng.pdf?sequence=1&isAllowed=y (accessed 17 May 2023).

Yahya, T. and Mohamed, M. (2018) Raising a mirror to quality of care in Tanzania: the five-star assessment. *The Lancet Global Health* 6(11), e1155–e1157. DOI: 10.1016/S2214-109X(18)30348-6.

Young, T.K. (1986) Socialist development and primary health care: the case of Tanzania. *Human Organization* 45(2), 128–134. DOI: 10.17730/humo.45.2.17p75666m4347g14.

8 Community Health Within Primary Health Care

Eric van Praag[1]*, Elihuruma M. Nangawe[2], James Tumaini Kengia[3,4] and Ntuli A. Kapologwe[4,5]

[1]Consultant, Health Systems and Community Care, Dar es Salaam, Tanzania; [2]PRAXIS in Health and Development – Policy, Systems, Strategies, QI and Capacity Development and Applied Research, Dar es Salaam, Tanzania; [3]President's Office – Regional Administration and Local Government, Dodoma, Tanzania; [4]University of Dodoma, Dodoma, Tanzania; [5]President's Office – Regional Administration and Local Government, Dodoma, Tanzania

Abstract

Community-based care as an essential component of PHC was defined at Alma-Ata in 1978 and reconfirmed through WHO/UNICEF in 2018, reflecting on principles of involvement, equity and comprehensiveness. In this chapter we describe how these development principles had already been embraced within Tanzania Health policies before and were maintained after 1978. The chapter identifies how far the implementation of these principles at the grass-roots level enabled sustainable change for health development.

Key events which stimulated community care approaches were: the villagization policy in 1967; basic health services in 1974; PHC declaration 1978; faith-based outreach and bottom-up activities in the 1970s and 1980s; a PHC unit in the MOH in 1983; and facility-based financial resources for community care in 2005. Events which hampered community care were the structural adjustment demands from the IMF and the specific disease control approaches by donors, the structural reforms by government to favour infrastructure and training, the commercialization of service delivery and self-care favouring cure above prevention, all hindering community systems strengthening to address felt needs.

Opportunities are identified, such as innovative digitalization of information sharing, evidence of community approaches for political and administrative recognition of workers and resources at community level and innovative financing strategies.

8.0 Summary

In the history of Tanzania's development several key events over time enabled or sometimes set back the evolution of community care (Table 8.1). The sections in this chapter describe the context and the effects of these events in detail at the community level of the PHC system. In the section on the future of community health key lessons learned are presented and suggestions made for specific actions to maintain the rich, but also challenging, history for community systems-driven health care. Tanzania's villagization policy is highlighted to set a formal structure for community care based on principles of engagement and basic health services, building on the community-owned

*Corresponding author: eric.vanpraag@gmail.com

 Primary Health Care in Tanzania through a Health Systems Lens (eds N.A. Kapologwe *et al.*)
DOI: 10.1079/9781800623330.0008

Table 8.1. Important periods where specific decisions about community care were implemented.

Period	Key developments
Independence 1961 to the Arusha Declaration 1968	Villagization and village health workers
Arusha Declaration to the Alma-Ata Conference 1978	Village health structures and faith-based outreach community services
Alma-Ata to structural adjustment 1980	Community-based driven approaches supported by Ministry of Health and projects
Structural adjustment to landmark community-based health programme stakeholders meeting in Bagamoyo 2012	Funding PHC declines, health-sector reforms with minimal community care and selective interventions from donors emphasizes only disease-specific home-care within communities
Bagamoyo meeting onwards	CBHP policy and operational guides reviving integrated community care, social accountability gaining ground

village health posts. Early successful initiatives through community outreach services by faith-based hospitals stood out clearly. In the Alma-Ata section Tanzania's lead role in defining PHC is highlighted. This led to the establishment of two major structures for community care. The first structure was the creation of the PHC unit in the MOH in 1983, resulting in the production and dissemination of PHC guidelines which emphasized community involvement. The second structure was the decentralization by devolution policy, which led to the formation of annual Council Comprehensive Health Plans in 1999 mandating the local government authorities (LGA) to plan and allocate resources for community care. The challenges section describes the setback to community care due to a lack of resources resulting from structural adjustment policies. The setback was also due to the more vertical point of view on PHC taken by the donor community supporting implementing partners to focus their resources in a top-down manner for fragmented interventions at community level at the expense of long-term community strengthening of health systems. The revival of community care began with the 2012 Bagamoyo stakeholders' meeting on community health worker (CHW) initiatives, which was led by the pioneering Helen Semu of the health promotion section of the ministry and was consolidated in the Health Sector Strategic Plan IV, formulated in 2015 and resulting eventually in the national policy and operational guidelines for community-based health services in 2020 and 2021 respectively.

8.1 Tanzania's Initiatives in Community Health

Community health is an integral part of every health system worldwide. Since Tanzania's independence in 1961, the call by the founding father Mwalimu Julius Nyerere to fight poverty, diseases and ignorance has guided national development policies to focus on the community as the ultimate resource for development, as was highlighted at the Arusha Conference and formalized in the second five-year development plan (1969–1974) (van Etten, 1976).

Historically, the implementation of the Arusha Declaration of 1967 brought people together from isolated hamlets into *Ujamaa* (African socialism) villages and ensured a functional hierarchical structure through ten cell leaders for each ten households reporting to a village chairperson to allow communal work, easier information flow and reporting and access to public services. Preventive medicine and health education were considered as equally important as curative services. In 1969 a health policy guideline was issued by the Ministry of Health to direct voluntary village health workers (VHW) and traditional birth attendants (TBA) to carry out prevention and care services for communities. The management of these roles was placed under the direct responsibility of district medical officers. The village focus for health care was further highlighted in the National Health Policy of 1970 and operationalized through the decentralization policy in 1972, making the district administration through the regional and district development directors directly responsible for the development of these basic health services (BHS) (Mwaluko *et al.*, 1991). Community health as part of BHS was promoted through establishing village health posts and training VHWs and rural development workers to emphasize preventive services (Chagula and Tarimo, 1975). Meanwhile health promotion auxiliaries, which in small numbers had been available since the pre-independence era and were responsible for sanitation at clinics and hospitals, were formalized by the MOH and used successfully as vaccinators at community level during the smallpox eradication campaign between 1968 and 1977, in the *Mtu ni Afya* (a person is health) campaign of 1973 and in the *Chakula ni Uhai* (food is life) campaign of 1976, during which radio programmes and wide distribution of posters and materials were used to educate communities. Community education focused on communicable diseases, prevention and nutrition through functional literacy techniques. Training of auxiliaries was regulated and certified as a new cadre called health assistants, supervised by health inspectors. These health inspectors were eventually called health education officers and in 1974 they were posted to operate under the responsibility of district hospitals as per the decentralization policy overseeing all environmental and educational aspects of health beyond medical care. Their tasks were to educate the public and to maintain hygiene and sanitation standards of public places like markets, bars, health facilities and primary schools in the community (Chagula and Tarimo, 1975). The numbers of health inspectors were small, varied by region and never reached coverage beyond the communities around health centres and hospitals (MOH, 1983).

Throughout the 1960s and the 1970s, these BHS activities were part and parcel of the national health development and formed the basis of the Tanzanian primary health care (PHC) experiences highlighted at the Alma-Ata Conference in 1978 to shape the defining of and the global commitment to PHC (Nhonoli, 1979).

The BHS gained importance over time and should be seen as complementing traditional health systems, which have always been widespread in Tanzania. Traditional health services have been provided by a wide range of traditional healers and practitioners as well as TBAs.

8.1.1 Traditional birth attendants

The MOH formally recognized the contributions of TBAs in 1980 and regulated their services through a national syllabus, with training in various districts with support from World Vision since 1985. In total about 5000 TBAs were trained nationwide (Safe, 1989). As the emphasis shifted away to facility maternal care, the formal support and training halted during the late 1990s. Services by TBAs as a community resource, however, continued throughout the country until the present day, although the emphasis nowadays is on TBAs' role to refer mothers for assisted deliveries in facilities in a timely manner.

8.1.2 Traditional health practices

Demand for traditional healing practices has always been deeply rooted in Tanzanian society. Local healers using roots and herbs, traditional priests addressing spirits and sorcerers removing evil spells, all have been a community source of health care. This was the only health resource up to late in the 19th century, at which time medical missionaries established the first hospital and some first aid posts providing 'Western medicine' in Tanzania (Mwaluko *et al.*, 1991). Popularization of Western medicine was enhanced with the introduction of injections for yaws, sexually transmitted diseases and malaria with a rapid visible effect from the 1940s onwards through the 20th century (Kilama *et al.*, 1974). Formal appreciation of traditional medicine started in 1968 with a right for traditional practitioners to practice (Mbwambo *et al.*, 2007) and in 1974 when the Muhimbili Medical Centre (MMC), in collaboration with the MOH, established a traditional medicine research unit to study the effectiveness of herbal products, which in 1991 was upgraded to the Institute of Traditional Medicine (Goergen *et al.*, 2001). In the 1980s, traditional healers organized themselves into local and national associations and collaborated with the formal health services at ministerial level, and some opened outpatient units within hospitals. The possibility of harmful practices in particular as a result of removing evil spells and possible delays in receiving effective disease management has always been a concern, hence the passing of a parliamentary act to regulate traditional medicine practices and the establishment of a unit of traditional medicine in the MOH under the Department of Clinical Services in 1989.

8.1.3 Social welfare

Commitment to health-related social welfare issues at community level came traditionally from faith-based hospitals with their care homes in the community for orphans and the poor, as well as disability care through running of leprosarias, which later become care centres or villages accommodating all disabilities. By the end of the 1990s, 16 such villages were running with the support of the German Relief Association (GLRA, 2020), and these exist to the present day (Kayombo, 2013).

Social welfare committees at village level were promoted by national departments of social welfare based at various ministries over time and functioned provided there were funds to support them. Social welfare officers were trained and deployed by the government to work at district facility level. During the 1980s there was a rapid growth of community-based organizations that dealt with health-related welfare issues because the structural adjustment programme reduced government funding and local district support, while faith-based and external supported projects maintained the response to demands from the community.

8.1.4 Community health initiatives

The health section of the second five-year development plan (1969–1974) stipulated that by the year 2000 every *Ujamaa* village should have a health post from which a male and a female VHW operated. The plan elaborated the move to *Ujamaa* villages in the first national health policy of 1970 and the first national health plan (1972–1980). The community was to contribute towards the refurbishing of a health post which could be a unit in any existing government facility and provide support to the VHW, while the office of the district medical officer was responsible for training, supervision and the provision of a bicycle (Magari *et al.*, 1991). New skills-based cadres were created for the most peripheral facilities, such as MCH aides and rural medical aides (RMAs) to guide the village health committees which included the VHWs and other community-based development workers. The number of RMA posted in rural areas increased between 1972 to 1982 from 578 to 4776, while MCH aides increased from 700 to 3282 (MOH, 2013). TBAs and traditional healers were to be registered and recognized for their services. This resulted in several community-based healthcare activities which involved village health workers who worked together with the nearest, but often still hard-to-reach, dispensaries where either an MCH aide, an RMA or a nursing assistant or health assistant were available. These initiatives were overseen by the nearest hospital, where a medical doctor, a public health nurse and a health inspector were participating. This was task shifting in the real sense and operated through outreach activities for supervision and mobile clinics in hard-to-reach villages. Actual performance depended a lot on commitment, the availability of local resources and project support.

Dioceses and mission hospitals took the lead in operationalizing the community-care component of BHS through regular outreach activities from their facility to communities in the district. The outreach activities received assistance from the village health workers in the community. For all designated faith-based facilities, their outreach activities were coordinated and supported by the government administrative health services in the district (Christian Medical Board of Tanzania, 1985).

All these initiatives were aligned to the national health policy of 1970 and the national health plan (1972–1980). In practice, construction was rarely finalized, but VHWs were available, involved and supported when any event occurred or when any long-term project took off.

For example, the Hanang Village Health project was started in 1975 in Babati by the Medical Missionaries of Mary in close coordination with district health authorities and handed over to them gradually after 1983. A total of 84 villages out of 104 in the district were covered with one or more VHWs in villages often without a dispensary or health post. Training was spread out over a period of 2 years, and involved local teachers and covered medical, nutritional and hygiene aspects in an integrated manner (Heggenhougen *et al.*, 1986).

The Mvumi Hospital Community Health project started in 1974, initiated by a medical missionary and emphasizing nutritional screening, health education, disease prevention and sanitation, supported by a nutritional rehabilitation unit with intensive mobile outreach activities. Many managerial and resource issues aggravated by cholera epidemics affected the mobile clinics over time, but in 1981 Dr Matomora adapted and revived the project through a focus on communities by listening to and learning from local leaders, running awareness seminars and building community activities through resource persons like traditional birth attendants and community health promoters. Establishing a continuous dialogue was found to be the key to success (Matomora, 1989) and was further refined in the Maasai Health Services community health workers project with the following lessons learned on community participation: (i) project staff must resist the role of expert and maintain that of facilitator to continuously involve community members; (ii) the pace of the project must be in step with the communities' understanding and readiness to accept it ; (iii) the role of the CHW must respond to the urgently felt need for curative services and maintain the balance with the need for preventive services including family planning and the long-range need for social change; and (iv) the project must respect the traditional social norms and in the Maasai case the patriarchal structure of the ethnic groups served (Nangawe, 1990).

KCMC Hospital's community health agenda promoted community-based nutritional rehabilitation in its regular seminars from around 1980, attended by health professionals from all twenty regional peripheral district hospitals and faith-based health facilities, with a focus on the linking of a nutritional rehabilitation unit in the facility with the VHWs for early detection, referral and follow-up for support and education (Urio *et al.*, 2014).

8.1.5 Commitment and initiatives from the medical faculty

During the 1970s the Muhimbili Medical Centre (MMC), which was the first medical school in Tanzania, committed to community care for its future doctors, by developing a specific comprehensive and practical community-health curriculum for medical undergraduates. With a solid base in behavioural sciences and family health, the second-year students implemented nutritional surveys among suburban communities and in their fourth year they attended a residential field training at the rural teaching unit of MMC in Bagamoyo (BTU) where they lived for a period of 8 weeks and rotated weekly at various facilities within the district to understand community needs, practiced relevant responses and learned the PHC facility and community duties of a district medical officer (Mpanju and Geverdinck, 1991).

8.2 The International Conference on Primary Health Care

In 1978 in Alma-Ata, the WHO and UNICEF organized the first global conference on health for all member states. PHC was defined, formalized and accepted as the solid basis for future health-care development to reach 'Health for All' by the year 2000. The Alma-Ata Declaration facilitates the harmonization of facility- and community-based systems when it states that 'Primary Health Care refers to the essential health care that is based on scientifically sound and socially acceptable methods and technology, which make universal health care accessible for all individuals and families in the community. It is through their full participation and at a cost that the community and the country can afford at every stage of their development in the spirit of self-reliance and self-determination'. Article VII.7 clearly identifies a role for CHWs and community-health-related development workers as it states: 'PHC relies, at local and referral levels, on health workers, including physicians, nurses, midwives, auxiliaries and community workers as applicable, as well as traditional practitioners as needed, suitably trained socially and technically to work as a health team and to respond to the expressed health needs of the community' (WHO, 1978).

Tanzania participated substantially at the Alma-Ata Conference through the presence of the then director of Preventive Services, Dr E. Tarimo, and Professor A.M. Nhonoli, the Director General of MMC. The case study of Tanzania detailed by Dr Chagula and Dr Tarimo in the landmark book *Health by the People* (edited by Ken Newell), published just prior to Alma-Ata, set an example of PHC by a few countries to many others on how to embark at national level on the development and at local level showing initial implementation successes of a PHC strategy benefitting communities. It spearheaded the 'Health for All' approach by massively expanding front-line health services and involving communities in their own health development (Chagula and Tarimo, 1975).

Inspired by the global momentum, after his return from Alma-Ata Professor Nhonoli wrote a book called *Primary Health Care Delivery in African Countries*, setting out his vision of PHC, in which he called on his professional colleagues to change attitudes, to put community health first supported by the formal health system and driven by the VHW cadre eventually as employed workers based at health posts (Nhonoli, 1979). His community-driven approach was certainly incorporated by many faith-based hospitals which were reviewed at the Tanzanian Churches Consultation on PHC organized by the Christian Medical Board of Tanzania (CMBT) in 1985 in Dodoma. The programmes already in existence for more than 5 years, such as the Hanang Village Health programme, the Mvumi Community Health Programme and the Maasai Health Services project, were presented as sustainable examples of PHC programmes. Trust, confidence building with local community members, training and motivating dispensary staff were key factors that drove community engagement for key felt health needs such as maternal, child health and nutrition, as well as safe water, sanitation and hygiene. The Dodoma Consultation was opened by Dr Chiduo, who was by then the minister for health, and was addressed by the then minister of state, Gertrude Mongella, both reaffirming Tanzania's governmental commitment to PHC to achieve Health for All by the year 2000. CMBT continued to support community-based health care until the late 1990s, collaborating with OXFAM and AMREF to train trainers, facilitators and facility staff following the lessons learned from the Dodoma Consultation and covering various districts and dioceses in nine regions of Mainland Tanzania.

After the Alma-Ata Conference in 1978, a major boost for PHC came from the Ministry of Health where, with support of the Danish International Development Agency (DANIDA), a national programme was established in 1982 with the task of coordinating and setting up training sites and promoting PHC. PHC was formally adopted as a strategy by the government in 1983. A secretariat was established in the MOH and guidelines for the implementation of PHC in Tanzania were published, along with the development of training guidelines which were widely distributed at all training institutions with support of AMREF, and aimed at improving access to health services (Christian Medical Board of Tanzania, 1985). A manual for district health teams on planning and management of PHC was developed and widely distributed as well (Magari *et al.*, 1991). PHC committees were established at village, district and regional level and by 1988 over 2000 out of the planned 16,000 VHWs were trained (Magari *et al.*, 1991). Sectors other than health took a lead in promoting PHC as well. A good example is the HESAWA project in the Lake Zone from 1985 to 2002, initially led by the Ministry of Water, later by the Ministry of Community Development in collaboration with the MOH and the Planning Commission. The focus was on safe water supplies and income generation; ventilated pit latrines at school and household levels; school health promotion and disease screening; and community hygiene education. VHWs were pivotal as the local facilitators with local water use groups linked to the community PHC committees. UNICEF assisted with implementation through SIDA support in a phased approach over 17 years to reach 600 villages in 30 districts. PHC principles such as multi-sectoral teamwork, integration of services and involving community structures were key. With donor support dwindling and coordination between different ministries often unclear the project failed to sustain itself (Rautanen *et al.*, 2006).

The PHC strategy emphasized the dual focus on service delivery at the most peripheral facilities, emphasizing maternal and child health and immunizations, as well as community care. It reflected key principles of PHC, such as involving communities structurally, establishing village PHC committees and collaboration with trained TBAs and VHWs for preventive and environmental aspects, as well as early and facilitated referrals (MOH, 1983, 1990; Mwaluko *et al.*, 1991).

Various evaluation reports, case studies and publications from these community-care initiatives during the 1970s and early 1980s in Tanzania describe the crucial roles these community resource people such as VHWs and TBAs play in getting communities involved in their own health and nutritional improvements, even if only small scale and with a support mechanism and a collaborative local government structure. In Muheza district the integration between community efforts and the local government structures stood out (Ebrahim *et al.*, 1988). In Mvomero Diocese, the community had the ability to respond effectively towards health and nutrition issues through sustained involvement (Matomora, 1989). In the districts mainly populated by the Maasai it was power given to women in such a strong patriarchal society which made reproductive health services feasible and acceptable (Nangawe *et al.*, 1987). The training of VHWs and TBAs was shown to be very effective if these community resource people were chosen from their communities and trained as close as possible to their communities (Nangawe *et al.*, 1985). In Kilombero, a more practical and local training curriculum was compared with the more centrally led national training using the same learning objectives and their community workers were found to be as effective and more competent to provide services the community really needs and were considered more acceptable (Mayombana *et al.*, 1990). All these projects identified as major challenges the need to scale up financial resources at the local level, the lack of practical local training, limited local capacity in leadership and time-consuming trust building between authorities and projects. A further analysis from these experiences showed that operationalizing decentralization with responsibilities, authority and financing are core to expanding community-care efforts (Christian Medical Board of Tanzania, 1985; Heggenhougen *et al.*, 1986; Gilson *et al.*, 1994).

All together these experiences reflect a wealth of knowledge and learning on the cornerstone role of community health systems in achieving Health for All by the year 2000.

8.3 Challenges of PHC Implementation at Community Level

Throughout Africa the health sector responded to the global economic decline in the late 1970s with structural adjustment measurements calling for the reduction of public spending, freezing of employment to improve efficiencies. Structural adjustments in Tanzania were made mandatory in order to receive IMF loans for budget support in 1984 and this had a direct effect on funding levels, on staffing, on the balance in favour of curative medicine vs support for prevention, and on the balance in favour of support for facility-based services vs strengthening community health care. Health-sector reforms developed during the 1990s became the key strategic response to reprioritize health-care delivery with limited resources. Privatization of health-service delivery was granted in 1991 and cost sharing of public services was introduced in 1993, making it very hard for the poor and vulnerable community members to obtain basic services (Maluka and Chitama, 2017). Various reasons for the reform were identified. First, there was the global economic downturn, which was felt in Tanzania. The proportion of GDP allocated for health declined from above the 7% around the mid-1970s to around 4 to 5% in the late 1980s/early 1990s. Second, as mentioned above the structural reform demands resulted in an abrupt freezing of new employment for government workers, including the professional staff at the peripheral health facilities. Third, there was the emphasis by the donors of shifting towards selective diseases with biomedical interventions focusing less on the PHC principles and more on technical and financial support only to medical or health interventions with short-term visible, cost-effective and measurable results which can be accounted for. Although selective PHC was meant as a temporary strategy (Warren, 1990) to address the heaviest disease burden until the time health systems became robust enough to integrate the interventions, the mode to operationalize it became very externally controlled and vertical as the preferred way for many bi- and multilateral agencies (Jonsson, 1986). Verticalization at community level was further strengthened by the establishment through donor-funded projects of disease-specific planning and supervision committees such as ward multisectoral AIDS committees, most vulnerable children committees, village multisectoral AIDS committees and ward multisectoral nutrition committees, which overlapped strongly with or even overtook the original village PHC committee structures as the former were supported and thus better funded.

However, a very insightful research project, Tanzania Essential Health Interventions Project (TEHIP), working through government district planners, tested a variety of health financing and management tools at district service level through an inclusive bottom-up planning process by local health officials and communities, expanding successfully from two districts into two regions between 1993 and 2006. The project identified a set of priority interventions according to the felt burden in the area and did challenge the vertical disease-selective implementation. Their community voice tool, using participatory research methods, identified local health needs and local solutions which fed into the district planning process. They concluded that, by building trust with local authorities and communities over time, an integrated approach does function in a mutually satisfactory and sustainable way. Implementation of these planning processes eventually covered two regions, but further expansion did not materialize due to lack of resources.

The step-by-step implementation of the health-sector reform during the late 1990s aimed to strengthen decentralization and a sector-wide approach at the district level, adapted further the TEHIP planning tools (Maluka and Chitama, 2017). This would allow LGAs to better plan and allocate direct facility support within the district through the annual council comprehensive health plan (CCHP). Direct facility support was fully implemented from 1999 onwards, including the allocation of 5% of that budget for community-care activities. Local fundraising was allowed, as free health services were abolished and cost-sharing introduced. Council health service boards (CHSB) and health facilities governing committees (HFGC) for district hospitals, health centres and dispensaries were established in 1999 (Kessy, 2014; Maluka and Bukagile, 2016). These committees were responsible for the planning and accountability of funds received, including overseeing the 5% community-support allocation. However few districts used these funds for outreach services or AD hoc allowances to promote community involvement through regular PHC village committee meetings or regular remunerating multi-purpose V/CHWs. The first health sector programme of work (1999–2002) acknowledged these hardships and called for a model community approach to mitigate the cost-sharing for those unable to pay and support CHWs. This model was established in Igunga district with support from the World Bank, but resources could not be mobilized for continuing implementation (Mtei and Mulligan, 2007). Instead community health care became more dependent on vertical, specific disease-control projects with their own service-delivery model supported by a donor (MOH, 1999).

Through subsequent health-sector reviews, the few comprehensive and integrated community health programmes revealed several sustainability gaps, including the absence of formal recognition and support of health committees and of CHWs. There were also inadequate coordination mechanisms among many fragmented initiatives, inadequate supervision and linkages between community and facility and poor community involvement or participation in planning and support. The mid-term review of HSSP III (2009–2015) in 2013 revealed the strong presence of vertical programmes in the MOH and the 'thinking in silos' hindering coordination, collaboration and integral reporting at facility and community level. The review noted that, due to the structural adjustments, reforms had prioritized facility-level PHC over community-based health systems (MOH, 2013).

Examples of these vertically managed projects at community level included the community-based distributors of family planning from 1986 onwards and the home-based care volunteers supported by specific disease control programmes like those for TB and HIV/AIDS. Evaluation reports do acknowledge and report the supportive role of community volunteers. The community component of

Fig. 8.1. Fragmentation of services affecting community health planners and workers. (Courtesy of Bram and Peter Petit, drawing from 1995 in Huduma ya Afya Msingi [HAM] Newsletter.)

these separate vertical projects did successfully address the social and health effects of dense family sizes by raising awareness and promoting family planning, and also introducing palliative care for HIV/AIDS, as well as promoting patient groups to facilitate treatment access and income generating, but its fragmented and partner-driven approach made it difficult, if not impossible, to integrate into the wider health-system management and into existing local structures (van Praag *et al.*, 2009; Mwai *et al.*, 2013), as illustrated also in Fig. 8.1.

Nevertheless, maternal and infant mortality rates remained very high, in addition to the burden of preventable communicable and non-communicable diseases. Rapid urbanization, the ageing of the population, changing of lifestyles and (re)emerging epidemics further complicate the ways to address the burden of disease and how to involve communities. Healthy ageing and school health are just two examples of neglected health issues within the current selective donor approaches that could benefit immediately from a community-driven approach responding to felt needs. Nevertheless, we should aim for a harmonized model whereby community-based health care and facility care within villages and urban neighbourhoods are seen as an integral part of PHC to reflect the meaning of community participation and ownership in a practical operational sense (UNICEF, 2016). The call for harmonization is not new and has already been highlighted in a special issue of *Social Science and Medicine* in 1989 looking at experiences with community health care ten years after Alma-Ata, with studies from Tanzania, Kenya and Ethiopia and an editorial from UNICEF demonstrating the advantages of community-based health programmes (CBHP). The authors state: 'PHC is neither cheap nor simple and CBHP is an integral part of that' (Mburu and Boerma, 1989).

8.4 Evidence of the Effectiveness of the Role of CHWs in Community Health Care from Tanzania and Eastern/Southern Africa

Systematic reviews have reported on the role and outcomes of CHW on sub-Saharan African countries and elsewhere in reaching 'Health for All' at the community level. Evidence of the effectiveness of community-based interventions implemented at the local level by CHWs to improve health of mothers, neonates and children under 5 years of age was presented in a mega review of over 700 studies of which 49% were from sub–Saharan Africa (Perry *et al.*, 2017).

The roles of CHWs in specific disease-control studies was systematically assessed through several studies from sub-Saharan Africa describing the roles and outcomes of CHWs in HIV care. CHWs contributed substantially to improving access, uptake and quality of HIV services as well as dignity, quality of life and retention in care. Their involvement in clinics helped to reduce waiting times, streamline patient flows and reduce workload. Comparing facility-based care with community-based care through CHWs no difference in mortality was seen. CHWs were reported as facing challenges such as lack of recognition, poor remuneration and non-involvement in decision making which will limit sustainability and integration in the broader health system (Mwai *et al.*, 2013).

Although methodologically challenged, evidence from reviews of several studies in sub-Saharan Africa suggests that that adding CHWs can be cost-effective, as was shown for reproductive, maternal, newborn, child and adolescent health (RMNCH) interventions, TB control and malaria control, with additional benefits in coverage and equity in service delivery (Vaughan *et al.*, 2015).

Good performance of CHW was significantly linked to factors like the mix of financial and non-financial incentives, frequent supervision, continuous training community involvement, strong coordination, frequent communication with the nearest health professionals and clear roles and responsibilities outlined in a systematic review of 144 studies globally, of which 83 were from sub-Saharan Africa (Kok *et al.*, 2015).

Evidence of the effectiveness of CHWs in PHC was studied in Tanzania in 1983 through a widely quoted and truly controlled community-based study in Bagamoyo district (Mtango and Neuvians, 1986). This study compared villages with CHWs trained in general PHC and villages without but which received the intervention later and it showed a significant reduction of mortality in the under-fives by CHWs through promotive and basic curative service interventions to manage under-fives with acute respiratory illnesses with antibiotics and effective referrals. A Cochrane review considered this paper as meeting all global criteria to be evidence-based of the effectiveness of CHWs.

Almost 30 years later a study on the feasibility of CHWs implementing broader under-five health-care management packages showed that community case management by trained CHWs of childhood illnesses is very feasible in the current context of primary health care in Tanzania, including the way they would assess, classify and treat sick children using an algorithm adopted from the integrated Community Case Management (iCCM) for malaria, pneumonia, and diarrhoea). These CHWs had undergone nine months of basic training and a specific refresher training on the algorithm. Implementing the iCCM protocol was as good as what medical professionals would do. However, bottlenecks found for scaling up were the need for reliable supply and functional supervision (Baynes *et al.*, 2018; PMO, 2018).

Also in the area of health promotion and education there is Tanzanian evidence from cluster randomized community studies that villages with CHWs trained through the national one-year course with an additional one-week workshop on early childhood development did achieve much better child development scores than in families in villages without CHWs (Baynes *et al.*, 2018). Effectiveness, acceptability and feasibility of CHWs if supported within an committed project was shown to be high in follow-up studies in Morogoro (LeFevre *et al.*, 2015) and in Mkuranga district (Kema *et al.*, 2012). Diagnostic tools like HIV rapid testing, TB sputum collection and rapid malaria antibody testing can be safely and effectively done, as has been shown in various parts of the country as part of the vertical disease control programmes over decades, and evidence has accumulated to justify the concern that top-down approaches do not work and may result in a lack of programme ownership and sustainability (Mubi *et al.*, 2011). As a result, participatory approaches have increasingly become popular. An example of such an approach is hereby presented. Working with AMREF, Mkuranga district significantly gained experience and improved its community participatory approaches in health development. AMREF's model of community-based health care (CBHC) approaches was used to implement integrated water and sanitation, child survival and reproductive health programmes/outcomes. The project established functioning village health and water committees. A 45% increase in the utilization of services was reported. Adequate nutrition status among children rose from 67.9 to 81%. Attendance of antenatal clinics rose from 35 to 70.2%. A total of 117 shallow wells, 21 boreholes and 25 rainwater harvesting systems were established (Kema *et al.*, 2012).

In summary, studies relevant to Tanzania's context show that CHWs have been proved to reduce the burden of communicable diseases in the community through enhanced health-promotion and disease-prevention education and were effective in bridging the gap between the community and the nearest health facility.

8.5 Revival of Community-Based Health Programmes in Tanzania

Specific national strategic support for community health systems beyond outreach services from facilities was absent in the earlier three- to five-year strategic plans since 1999 due to the challenges of operationalization of decentralization to village level, the serious shortage of qualified supervisory staff at the peripheral level and the continuing verticalization and fragmentation of specific disease-control programming. TEHIP tested innovations in decentralization embracing integrated, decentralized financing and participatory planning and showed the feasibility and acceptability of such a non-fragmented approach and developed relevant tools (de Savigny *et al.*, 2004). The vertical disease approach was still mentioned as a major issue in the report of the mid-term review of HSSP in 2013 and thus was hindering participatory driven community-based health programmes which were initiated decades ago (MOH, 2013). However, the HSSP IV 2015–2020 calls specifically on the health and social sector to 'achieve active community participation through a CBHP by revitalizing primary health care and social welfare' (MOHSW, 2015).

Opportunities existed for community integral approaches as guided by the national poverty reduction strategy of 2000 to 2015 and as well the efforts by the Tanzania Social Action Fund (TASAF). TASAF stimulated economic independence of poor and vulnerable households at village through safety nets by providing conditional cash transfers and establishing savings and loans groups, reaching one million households by 2017 to enable income, schooling and free access to public health services. It appears the opportunity to maximize effectiveness and efficiency was not optimally exploited (ISPA, 2017). Developing partners supporting a broader integrated community developmental vision, such as World Vision, UNICEF, BRAC, Care International, Jane Goodall Institute and Pathfinder, did achieve sustained but small-scale successes whereby CHWs facilitate the creation of saving groups, addressing environmental issues through agricultural and livestock education as well as sanitation and reproductive health promotion (Leisher and Hess, 2017). All these projects are time bound and will eventually face the crucial question of how communities and LGAs can take the lead to expand this with minimal inputs from partners in a well-coordinated manner.

In August 2012 the Ministry of Health and Social Welfare convened a broad stakeholders' meeting in Bagamoyo, to map and analyse ongoing community health activities and support mechanisms of CHW schemes. The meeting agreed on a common nomenclature, confirming that community health workers and coordination and support are essential to achieve universal health coverage (UHC) while recognizing CHWs as the critical link between communities and facilities. It called for formal coordination and operationalization under LGAs' leadership, with technical and financial support including incentives or a remuneration package from communities, local authorities and implementing partners. Valuable lessons were learned from organizations like AMREF, Jhpiego, and FHI and research institutions like MUHAS and IHI. The meeting served to revive interest and indicate a way forward on community health in the health sector, with the health promotion section (HPS) of MOHSW providing policy as well as technical leadership (MOHSW, 2012).

To address the constraints of supporting communities identified at the Bagamoyo meeting, the community-based health programme (CBHP) of the HPS put in place a technical team that facilitated production of National CBHP Policy Guidelines of 2014, the National Costed Community-Based Health Programme Strategic Plan 2015–2020, and the Community-based Health Programme Implementation Design 2017.

In February 2015, a Directorate of Health, Social Welfare and Nutrition Services was established at the President's Office - Regional Administration and Local Government (PO-RALG), the operational arm of the government, intended to strengthen PHC implementation through LGAs. This establishment confirmed that PHC was felt again to be the right direction Tanzania had embarked on since signing off the Arusha Declaration of 1967 and the basic health services expansion of the 1970s (MOHSW, 2011, 2015).

At the global level, community ownership through participation in planning and implementation of health care was confirmed and expressed in the Heads of State Declaration at the Global Conference on PHC in Astana, Kazakhstan in 2018 celebrating the 40th anniversary of the Alma-Ata Declaration, which was attended by senior officials from MOHCDGEC and PO-RALG. The declaration reconfirmed the strong commitment and advocacy for PHC as an integrated and comprehensive approach to reach UHC and attainment of the social development goals by 2030 (WHO, 2018).

During the period from 2017 to 2020 the government put mechanisms in place to make CHW a formal, professional, government-certified cadre trained under government staffing regulations and paid at least the minimum wage. One-year training courses were put in place at over 60 public and private health colleges and employment through the Public Service Commission was in its final phase of development. Over 12,000 CHWs were trained using a competence-based curriculum. However, funding for the coverage of salaries for all villages and urban neighbourhoods, even in a phased manner, could not be guaranteed, hence the need for an adaptation of the 2014 policy guide which called for a government salaried cadre.

8.5.1 The role of local leadership over time in guiding community care systems

The earliest examples of leadership in health affairs at community level were the village health committees, led by the village chairman, in which the VHWs are members. With the establishment of a PHC unit in the ministry a hierarchical reporting and support chain was established with district PHC teams, ward PHC teams and village PHC committees.

The involvement of health-related volunteers in decision making and ownership was a true reflection of the PHC principles, although externally funded projects were often the driving forces in the processes. With privatization and direct financing at peripheral facilities as a result of health structural reforms since the 1990s, decision making power was shifted to other bodies. These bodies included the health facility governance committees, which were guided at council level by district health boards, and council social service committees, and were involved in the annual comprehensive council health plans and budgets for the allocation of funds to implement community-care activities beyond the facilities as outreach support. The functionality of village-managed community health structures was eroded over time due to the lack of specific government and project support given to such community health structures, for example to village health committees. An evaluation of Mukaranga district in 2002 found that many communities were not aware of their CHWs or the functioning of village health committees (Mubyazi *et al.*, 2017). The actual revival of village (or *mtaa*) leadership and ownership in health or social welfare could not be reflected in the latest health-sector strategic plan V. Nevertheless, efforts are ongoing to institutionalize social accountability between facilities and communities by giving communities a stronger voice in their own health affairs.

8.5.2 Contemporary national policy guidance

The most recent Tanzania 2020 policy guidelines for community-based health and social welfare is directed towards establishing functional community-based services with a voluntary CHW cadre. This cadre should have a standardized incentive package that will work within the community under the technical supervision of the nearest health facility, while collaborating with and involving the existing community health structures. Project- or disease-specific health volunteers will qualify as CHWs as well, after specific refresher training under the umbrella of LGAs to eventually deliver a comprehensive package of health interventions at community level. The aim of the policy is to achieve healthy, empowered communities that contribute to socio-economic development. The policy is guided by a set of principles as follows:

- equity and social justice with regard to gender, religion, ethnicity and other social characteristics helps address the needs of categories that face a risk of marginalization;
- complementarity of roles between CHWs and social welfare agents and multilevel partnerships to optimize resources;
- rights and obligations of clients and providers contributing to quality assurance and quality improvement;
- attention to vulnerable and special groups to assure universal care;
- focus on integration in the management and delivery of health services so that clients receive a continuum of preventive and curative services, according to their needs over time and across different levels of the health system;
- tasks and roles based on knowledge and evidence-based results of experiences and studies within Tanzania;
- integrity, transparency and performance accountability of deployed and retained agents in respective communities (hamlets, villages);
- inclusion and participation of all stakeholders and communities and pooling of resources under the framework of the local government system (URT MOHCDGEC, 2020).

8.5.3 Consensus on operational aspects and implementation

As a result of intensive discussions between all stakeholders through the task force (which was later called the Technical Advisory Committee of CBHP), standard operational guidelines were finalized in 2021 and launched by the MOH in March 2022 and include the processes of training, nomination, financial support, ways to involve communities and a standardized service delivery package (MOH, 2021). Consensus was reached on several long-standing issues, such as voluntarism, capacity building, nomination and community involvement. The issues are detailed below.

Volunteerism

Although volunteer CHW programmes may appear to be cheap because there is no salary, volunteers cannot be held accountable if they do not perform, and as such programme effectiveness cannot be ensured. Also, high attrition rates are likely, which means not only that frequent training of new volunteers is required but also that it is difficult to keep track of volunteers and to judge their usefulness and commitment. Hence, retention is the single most critical predictor of success of a CHW programme, yet retention is only assured when CHWs are supported and financially compensated. The operational guide therefore calls for LGAs and donor-funded projects to provide a standardized and regular incentive commensurate to the work CHWs do.

Mechanisms still vary between councils and between partners, including: performance-based incentive mechanisms, as was tried in nine regions through results-based financing; utilization of the dispensary facility funds from cost-sharing, basket-fund support and incomes from the improved community health fund (iCHF) and National Health Insurance Fund (NHIF); bonuses from registering families on iCHF; and ad-hoc incomes of LGA by implementing special events and campaigns such as saving and credit cooperative organizations (SACCOS).

Capacity building

Experiences with the one-year training courses and earlier comparative studies showed that field-based and practical skill-based training of CHWs is more effective than national training far away from where the CHW comes from (Nangawe, 1990). Competency-based training is now standardized, with a national curriculum comprised of six stand-alone modules of two–four-week duration, nationally approved and responding to public health issues in Tanzania. The first 'basic principles' module is obligatory for a CHW to be certified and to start working. Clear reporting and supervisory structures within PHC are outlined and will require that both CHWs and their technical supervisors are well motivated and function harmoniously within the same integral primary health-care system.

Nomination and community involvement

It is widely accepted that the CHW should originate from the society that he or she serves and is familiar with. In other words, they should be one of the community owned resource persons (CORPs), together with traditional healers, extension officers, peer leaders for youth or representatives of patient groups. Short of that, it may become very difficult to be able to keep them. This is because non-owned CHWs will miss a sense of belonging and understanding to that particular society and they will always be striving to look for areas where they can prosper further. Clear procedures to put these principles into practice are outlined in the operational guide.

Community engagement as a policy and as a strategy is acknowledged as the engine oil of a car which is essential for the car to function well. However, actual running of the strategies at the community level remains a challenge. Several partners show the clear feasibility of involving community perspectives and functionality of health committees run by communities, such as the social accountability projects of Sikika and UNICEF adolescents' health project in Mbeya and Songwe (UNICEF Tanzania, 2021), with the usual sustainability concerns regarding when support for projects will end. LGA-driven community involvement takes place through the health facility governing committees which are in place in most councils, as incomes are now being generated by all peripheral health facilities. However, a bottom-up planning approach through health committees supported through this facility income generation must be assessed and reported. Using different approaches, which maximizes the community participation, has been shown to be feasible and remains intact beyond the project duration as shown in neighbouring countries.

Pending consensus building

SERVICE PACKAGE. The service package on what village health workers, or now CHW/Vs or VHW, are supposed to do has evolved over time. After the Arusha Declaration, the two village health workers at the village health post were supposed to treat minor illnesses and simple complaints and provide first aid for accidents and emergencies (Chagula and Tarimo, 1975; Nhonoli, 1979), while the health auxiliaries based at the peripheral facilities were to promote sanitation, provide education and participate in campaigns. With the formation of a PHC programme in 1983 and the launching of a national training guidelines for VHW, the focus on a team of CORPs in the community became stronger, responding to most community-based public health needs and reflecting multisectoral collaboration. The VHW, later called the CHW, was the pivot of this team. Actual delivery of a service package still depended heavily on a supportive project in the district or region through NGOs or faith-based hospitals. A controlled study in Bagamoyo, which showed that villages with a trained CHW had lower infant and child mortalities than villages without, was proof that the combined curative and preventive efforts resulted in a change (see Section 8.4).

With the graduation of CHWs following the one-year national course, the delivery package remained the same and includes basic curative services and promotional and educational functions provided by CHWs, supported by all CORPS. However, the practical inability to formally employ CHWs resulted in incorporation of these broadly trained CHWs for each project-specific disease or health issue usually with a strong preventive or supportive mandate such as home-based-care CHWs for HIV, TB sputum collectors and nutritional health promotors. Only few projects, such as Solidarmed in Ulanga and Connect in Kilombero, were able to support the iCCM model approach for infants and children as a true basic curative and preventive mix and promoted by UNICEF and WHO, as discussed in Chapter 6.

At the revival community health meeting in Bagamoyo in 2012, the debate on the legality of non-professionals handling prescription medication for life-saving events came up, with strong proponents and opponents. The task-shifting policy guidelines of 2016 by the MOH only mentioned curative functions of CHWs being rapid testing for HIV and malaria, as well as refills for chronic conditions (MOHCDGEC, 2016).

CHW supervisors, or should the introduction be prioritized in hard-to-reach areas first? Second, if the MOH and PO-RALG decide to continue with a voluntary cadre, how can incentives to compensate CHWs for their efforts be made in a standardized and sustainable way? Globally, the guidance is very clear. A panel of experts stated in the Bulletin of WHO: 'As was made clear in the Alma-Ata Declaration and as is valid today, CHWs, whether hired by the formal health system or selected and supported by communities, cannot be left to serve on their own. CHW programmes need be comprehensive rather than vertical and they should rely on both the community and the formal health system for supplies, communications and referrals' (Tulenko *et al.*, 2013).

The MOH and PO-RALG are debating the possibility of a salaried CHW supervisor as a first step, pending available resources. A total of 16,582 villages or urban neighbourhoods need to be covered. Availability may not be an issue as, by early 2018, 12,000 community health workers had graduated from the one-year training course, and a mapping exercise in 2015 estimated there were around 40,000 skilled and active community-health volunteers nationwide. Current readiness needs to be explored to see how many of them are still available and ready to serve as CHWs. The recurring costs, if covered by the government, would be far above the expenditure of any PHC cadre within a given fiscal year. Hence the need for innovative solutions to consider with stakeholders for co-funding options with interested donors.

How to finance the current incentive system is another debate among government and non-government stakeholders. Fragmentation and the lack of standardization have led to a wide variety of incentive practices. District-level representatives of PO-RALG, implementing partners and their guiding bodies in the MOH and donors have not agreed on how to deploy and reward CHWs and other CORPS with a standardized allowance and operational package. Even with potential financial resources available at the local level through direct facility funding, the lack of such a harmonized vision has hindered decision making by local authorities. In addition, prioritizing funding operational costs between community and facility often end up in 'either or' situations, pitting the need for facility functioning against the needs for community health systems to function. The way forward is an approach whereby budgets are not skewed towards facility operations. Revenues from facility-based health financing are to be used for community care plans as well, whereby trained CHWs and CORPS collaborate with the nearest facilities where trained supervisory technical staff such as a certified nurse and/or clinical officer, as well as a district-based CBHP coordinator, are all enabled to plan and guide this collaboration. Direct financing has been a step forward towards local ownership and dealing with the risks of ad-hoc demands due to external pressures by councils to divert community care funds.

Partnerships with development partners are emerging to support a voluntary cadre with regular basic incentives, travel, communication expenses and working tools, whereby harmonization with existing partnerships with a more selective disease approach needs to be discussed and reflected in integrated plans. Some local councils are pioneering this further at district level, with UN partners and local NGO projects such as UNICEF in districts in Mbeya, Songwe and Kigoma, SolidarMed in Ulanga district, the Benjamin Mkapa Foundation (BMF) in Chemba district and AMREF in Misungwi district.

Another funding option is for CHWs or CORPS to generate income themselves through bonuses by promoting and registering households for community health-insurance schemes, such as the iCHF. In turn the insurance provider can incentivize the CHW for the number of families registered (Pharmaccess Group, 2017).

8.6.2 Enhancing the quality of community-based PHC through social accountability

One approach to make both service users and service providers more responsible for access to and quality of service provision is through the promotion of social accountability at the community level. Social accountability is about efforts to change values and norms related to health seeking and services delivered through local, joint problem identification and being accountable for local solutions. Such an approach will eventually transition single-disease or health-issue donor- and project-driven community care to a more integrated and comprehensive needs-based community care, as felt by community members and their direct providers themselves.

Various tools have been developed to put social accountability into practice, and the one mostly used in Tanzania is the community score card (CSC). The process is based on the involvement of existing community structures, such as health committees and their members and available community-based resource personnel, through dialogue, initially among themselves and later together, to prioritize and thus score the issues and the solutions. Implementation is guided by joint accountability, an integral approach and a notion that change is possible even within current constraints. Experiences from CARE Tanzania, AMREF, Sikika, BMF, Health Promotion Tanzania (HDT), Jhpiego and GIZ, all of which piloted the use of CSCs through local councils, enabled an effective and regular dialogue between communities, community-care providers and staff at the nearest facility. Recently, the Ministry of Health has finalized a CSC facilitators' guide for comprehensive and integrated community-based health programmes (MOH/HPS, 2022b), as well as a guide on community engagement (MOH/HPS, 2022a).

The CSC process works through focused, guided and standardized discussions based on a scoring of people's expressed health and access issues, identifying sets of local solutions over which the community would have control and make both provider and user accountable (Fig. 8.3). With external project support and facilitation, all these initiatives were enthusiastically received and led to a higher sense of ownership and demand for quality care. The roles of village health committees or facility finance governing committees were instrumental, as both sides were involved and actively participated. The question of sustainability remains a challenge, as local councils, through their annual CCHP budgets, could not always guarantee continuous support.

Implementing a community score card using facilitated discussions between health facility staff, village representatives and the CHW is a method to improve the quality of health services and empower communities, which should be a priority in community health-care planning by LGAs. This social accountability monitoring approach through CSC is successfully implemented by Sikika in 11 districts.

8.6.3 Strengthening community platforms for health

Over time we have seen that the capacity within and between communities to contribute to their own health varied widely. Traditional healers

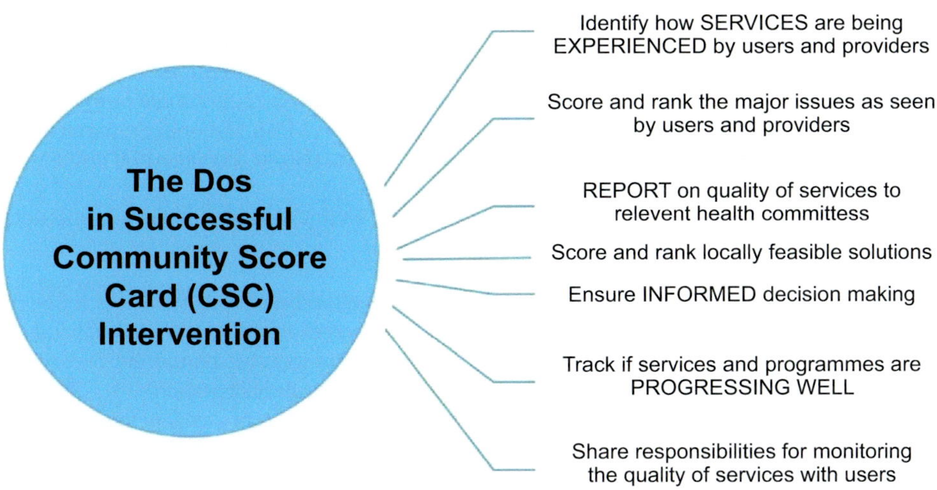

Fig. 8.3. Consideration for implementing a successful community score-card intervention. (Adapted, with permission, from Sikika, 2020.)

and TBAs were the earliest examples, followed by the VHW and later CHWs, with locally available workers in health-related fields such as agriculture, livestock, sanitation, education and social welfare. Recently, a further expansion occurred through various patient or youth groups or the elderly, with their peer leaders being present in the community. Currently these cadres exist, but the question is how to mobilize them into a platform to be utilized in a structural way. The most peripheral formal structure is that of the office of the village or urban neighbourhood (*mtaa*) leadership, with an elected chairman, appointed executive secretary and its own voluntary development and health and social welfare committees. In reality, the operational decision making bodies are at the ward level with the ward development committee, and at the facility level with the health-governing financing committees, which are all based on incentivized meetings through monetary means. Community representatives are members of these committees, but health-related community workers are optional members. With the expanding human resource for health, such a platform could be utilized for bottom-up planning and execution. Currently, one may find included in these committees (because of various funded projects), social welfare assistants, para-social or legal workers, treatment expert groups for chronic illnesses such as diabetes, HIV, disabilities, and TB, youth clubs with their peer leaders and the private sector through ADDO dispensers, and, in addition, the agricultural and livestock sectors through their extension workers and the informal sector through faith-based groups. All these are in fact CORPS and could have a much more effective role to play if coordinated and oriented well, with sustainable support from income generation through direct-financing mechanisms and from partners.

Broadening of community platforms

Village health platforms involving the private sector and CHWs can contribute to improve the quality of care by CHWs guiding households to team up with the ADDO and to explore how to best advise household members on what they can obtain from the ADDO. Self-care through directly approaching drug outlets is an increasingly common, but also a costly and risky practice, particularly in urban areas with a high density of drug outlets which are often not accredited. CHWs, after short orientation course linking up with ADDO providers through a digital platform, have the potential to assist household members to get value for money from the ADDOs and thus reduce the risk of unnecessary drug intake, as has been shown in Kibaha (Haroun *et al.*, 2022).

Pairing community youth leaders with CHWs

Council health managment teams (CHMTs) in Mbeya and Songwe regions, in collaboration with BMF and Restless Development, and with support from UNICEF, have initiated an approach of pairing of community-based youth peers with CHWs under the guidance of village health committees to identify and address specific adolescents' health issues, both in-school and for adolescents out of school. This project is ongoing and due for evaluation in 2023 (UNICEF Tanzania, 2021).

The national research agenda

To learn from and understand better local social norms for shaping the enabling environment as a prerequisite for a sustainable community health system, implementation research is needed on how communities can make better decisions for improving their health. Recently the National Institute for Medical Research (NIMR) published a research priority agenda for health development in Tanzania. One of the eight priority areas mentions community care in detail (NIMR, 2022). Future proposals being aligned to the NIMR National Research Agenda will help to search for potential funders and approvals.

The National Research Agenda stipulates it is vital to:

- understand and address factors influencing sloth and impediments in applying PHC principles (equity, community participation, intersectoral collaboration);
- analyse current engagement methods between community platforms for health and development;
- use applied health research (rapid ethnographic studies, rapid appraisals to measure communities' benefits on quality of life);

- study the potential of a household as a change agent to produce health (NIMR, 2022).

Improved efficiency through digital solutions

With the rapid growth of the utilization of mobile phones, often smart phones, there is an opportunity at all levels of a PHC system to enhance both the efficiencies and effectiveness of their work (Bustreo *et al.*, 2019). Many projects have taken advantage of this trend and use the relevant software to enable the cadres at the community and nearest-facility level to communicate, report and learn better. A good example is in promoting financial social protection through health insurance. Social protection is key in the current situation of uncontrolled marketing of health care which makes low-income groups highly vulnerable to vast expense in public and private health care and self-care through drug outlets. CHWs have a key role in promoting the iCHF and advising on the dangers of uncontrolled self-care and self-medication and several pilots are ongoing on how digital platforms can enhance subscription to iCHF by CHWs (Pharmaccess Group, 2017).

In addition, the functioning of CHWs can benefit further applications for self-learning, for facilitation referrals, data collection, rapid reporting, surveillance and to document their achievements, Examples are the data collection at household level for neglected tropical diseases (Madon *et al.*, 2014), communications to drug outlets (Haroun *et al.*, 2022) and family planning coverage reporting (Kyamanywa *et al.*, 2021). Challenges for sustainability still exist as there is still a low coverage of these new applications and continuous coverage of charge and bundle costs.

8.7 The Way Forward

It is crucial to plan ahead for action while learning lessons from the past. The following should be prioritized:

- commit to community-owned planning and implementation for improving health while complementing facility-based service delivery and appreciating differences in urban and rural needs;
- balance available resources for facility support with equal attention to community support;
- use available selected disease-oriented project resources to promote an integrated approach through local government mechanisms to ensure a revival of PHC principles such as local ownership, meaningful involvement and multisectoral teamwork;
- standardize rewards and incentives for community volunteers based on efforts made and ensure a fixed monthly minimum;
- develop implementation research to compare efficiencies, effectiveness, accountability and feasibility of community care in different contexts.

Acknowledgements

The authors wish to thank the following for their advice on this chapter: Ahmed Hingora, Jarl Chabot, Japhet Killewo, Leon Bijlmakers, Anosisye Kesale, Amani Kikula, Hassan Mshinda, Grace Mwanjela-Mwasuka, Elly Engelkes, Don de Savigny and Gabriel Upunda.

Bibliography

Baynes, C., Mboya, D., Likasi, S., Maganga, D., Pemba, S. *et al.* (2018) Quality of sick child-care delivered by community health workers in Tanzania. *International Journal of Health Policy and Management* 7(12), 1097–1109. DOI: 10.15171/ijhpm.2018.63.

Bustreo, F., Mshinda, H., Hinton, R., Hausmann-Muela, S. and Tanner, M. (2019) Commentary: primary health care in Tanzania - leading the way through innovation. *eClinicalMedicine* 13, 12–13. DOI: 10.1016/j.eclinm.2019.07.010.

Chagula, W.K. and Tarimo, E. (1975) Meeting basic health needs in Tanzania. In: Newell, K.W. (ed.) *Health by the People*. World Health Organization, Geneva, Switzerland.

Christian Medical Board of Tanzania (CMBT) (1985) *Tanzania Churches Consultation on PHC Dodoma*. AMREF, Nairobi.

de Savigny, D, Kasale, H, Mbuya, C and Reid, G. (2004) *Fixing Health Systems: the Issue, the Research, the Lessons*. IDRC, Ottawa.

Ebrahim, G.J., Kaingo, A. and Twaha, A. (1988) Learning from doing: progression to primary health care within A national health programme. A case study from Tanzania. *Journal of Tropical Pediatrics* 34(1), 4–11. DOI: 10.1093/tropej/34.1.4-a.

Gilson, L., Alilio, M. and Heggenhougen, K. (1994) Community satisfaction with primary health care services: an evaluation undertaken in the morogoro region of Tanzania. *Social Science & Medicine (1982)* 39(6), 767–780. DOI: 10.1016/0277-9536(94)90038-8.

GLRA (2020) *Tanzania, 60 Years Anniversary*. German Leprosy and Tuberculosis Relief Association, Dar es Salaam, Tanzania.

Goergen, H., Bruchhausen, W. and Kuelker, K. (2001) *The History of Health Care in Tanzania*. GTZ and National Museum of Tanzania, TPL, Dar es Salaam, Tanzania.

Haroun, Y., Sambaiga, R., Sarkar, N., Kapologwe, N.A., Kengia, J. *et al.* (2022) A human centred approach to digital technologies in health care delivery among mothers, children and adolescents. *BMC Health Services Research* 22(1), 1393. DOI: 10.1186/s12913-022-08744-2.

Heggenhougen, K., Vaughan, P., Muhondwa, E.P.Y. and Rutabanzibwa-Ngaiza, J. (1986) *Community Health Workers: The Tanzanian Experience*. Oxford University Press, Nairobi.

ISPA (2017) *Assessment of TASAF PSSN in Tanzania Using the ISPA-PWP tool*. EU/ILO, February, ILO, Dar es Salaam, Tanzania.

Jonsson, U. (1986) Ideological framework and health development in Tanzania 1961–2000. *Social Science & Medicine (1982)* 22(7), 745–753. DOI: 10.1016/0277-9536(86)90226-1.

Kayombo, E.J. (2013) Impact of training traditional birth attendants on maternal mortality and morbidity in Sub-Saharan Africa. *Tanzania Journal of Health Research* 15(2), 134–142. DOI: 10.4314/thrb.v15i2.7.

Kema, K.M., Komwihangiro, J. and Kimaro, S. (2012) Integrated community based child survival, reproductive health and water and sanitation program in Mkuranga district, Tanzania: a replicable model of good practices in community based health care. *The Pan African Medical Journal* 13(Suppl 1), 11.

Kessy, F.L. (2014) Improving health services through community participation in health governance structures in Tanzania. *Journal of Rural & Community Development* 9(2), 14–33.

Kilama, W., Nhonoli, A.M. and Makene, W. (1974) Health care delivery in Tanzania. In: Ruhumbika, G. (ed.) *Towards Ujamaa: Twenty Years of TANU Leadership*. East African Literature Bureau, Nairobi, pp. 191–271.

Kok, M.C., Dieleman, M., Taegtmeyer, M., Broerse, J.E.W., Kane, S.S. *et al.* (2015) Which intervention design factors influence performance of community health workers in low- and middle-income countries? A systematic review. *Health Policy and Planning* 30(9), 1207–1227. DOI: 10.1093/heapol/czu126.

Kyamanywa, H.W., Sheiza, R., Musoke, R., Magiri, D. *et al.* (2021) Integrating technology in diseases and epidemic control: a reliable means of mentorship, linkages, timeliness in data collection, reporting and planning of community interventions. In: *First Annual Health Promotion Conference: Health Promotion Services in Tanzania: Challenges and Opportunities in Behavioural Changes during Epidemics August*, MOHCDGEC, Dodoma.

LeFevre, A.E., Mpembeni, R., Chitama, D., George, A.S., Mohan, D. *et al.* (2015) Profile, knowledge, and work patterns of a cadre of maternal, newborn, and child health CHWs focusing on preventive and promotive services in morogoro region, Tanzania. *Human Resources for Health* 13, 98. DOI: 10.1186/s12960-015-0086-3.

Leisher, C. and Hess, S. (2017) *Tanzania Project Outcomes in the First Five Years, Tuungane Project, Kigoma*. Pathfinder International, Watertown, Massachusetts.

Madon, S., Amaguru, J.O., Malecela, M.N. and Michael, E. (2014) Can mobile phones help control neglected tropical diseases? Experiences from Tanzania. *Social Science & Medicine (1982)* 102, 103–110. DOI: 10.1016/j.socscimed.2013.11.036.

Magari, F., Malangalila, E.G., Mukoyogo, S.M. and Nyoni, C.J. (1991) *Planning and Management of Primary Health Care in Tanzania, A Manual for District Health Teams*. Ministry of Health, Dar es Salaam, Tanzania.

Maluka, S.O. and Bukagile, G. (2016) Community participation in the decentralised district health systems in Tanzania: why do some health committees perform better than others? *The International Journal of Health Planning and Management* 31(2), E86–E104. DOI: 10.1002/hpm.2299.

Maluka, S.O. and Chitama, D. (2017) *Primary Health Care Systems (PRIMASYS): Comprehensive Case Study from United Republic of Tanzania*. World Health Organization, Geneva, Switzerland.

Matomora, M.K.S. (1989) A people-centred approach to primary health care implementation in Mvumi, Tanzania. *Social Science & Medicine* 28(10), 1031–1037. DOI: 10.1016/0277-9536(89)90385-7.

Mayombana, C., Jenkins, J., de, D., Tayari, S., Lubomba, G. *et al*. (1990) Training of VHW in Tanzania, a comparison of two approaches. *Tropical Doctor* 20, 63–67.

Mburu, F.M. and Boerma, J.T. (1989) Community-based health care 10 years post Alma Ata. *Social Science & Medicine* 28(10), 1005–1006. DOI: 10.1016/0277-9536(89)90382-1.

Mbwambo, Z.H., Mahunnah, R.L.A. and Kayombo, E.J. (2007) Traditional health practitioner and the scientist: bridging the gap in contemporary health research in Tanzania. *Tanzania Health Research Bulletin* 9(2), 115–120. DOI: 10.4314/thrb.v9i2.14313.

Mpanju, W. and Geverdinck, I. (1991) *Presentation at Association for Medical Schools in Africa*. AMSA, Kampala.

MOH (1983) *PHC Review*. Ministry of Health, Dar es Salaam, Tanzania.

MOH (1990) *National Health Policy 1990*. Sera ya Afya, Wizara ya Afya, Jamhuri ya Muungano wa Tanzania.

MOH (1996) *Health Sector Reform: Plan of Action 1996–1999*. Ministry of Health, Dar es Salaam, Tanzania.

MOH (1999) *Health Sector Reform: Programme of Work 1999–2002*. Ministry of Health, Dar es Salaam, Tanzania.

MOH (2013) *Mid Term Review of HSSP III 2009–2015*. Ministry of Health, Dar es Salaam, Tanzania.

MOH (2021) *National Operational Guideline for Community based Health Services*. MOH-HPS Printing Press, Dar es Salaam, Tanzania.

MOHCDGEC (2016) *Task Sharing Policy Guidelines for Health Sector Services in Tanzania*. MOHCDGEC, Dar es Salaam, Tanzania.

MOH/HPS (2022a) *Guideline on Community Engagement (Draft)*. Ministry of Health, Dodoma.

MOH/HPS (2022b) *Guideline on Community Score Cards for Integrated Care*. Ministry of Health, Dodoma.

MOH PHC Coordinating Unit (1983) *Guidelines for the Implementation of the Primary Health Care Programme in Tanzania*. Ministry of Health, Dar es Salaam, Tanzania.

MOHSW (2007) *Health Policy, Dar es Salaam 2007*. Wizara ya Afya na Usitawi wa Jamii Sera ya afya, Dar es Salaam, Tanzania.

MOHSW (2011) *Hali ya Afya na Ustawi wa Jamii katika miaka hamsini ya Uhuru 1961–2011*. MOHSW, Dar es Salaam, Tanzania, p. 28.

MOHSW (2012) Report of the Stakeholders' Meeting on Community Health Workers' Initiatives: 'Exploring Sustainable Ways for Promoting Community Health in Tanzania'. MOHSW, WHO, UNICEF, USAID, Dar es Salaam, Tanzania.

MOHSW (2015) *Health Sector Strategic Plan July 2015–June 2020 (HSSP IV): Reaching all Households with Quality Health Care*. MOHSW, Dar e Salaam, Tanzania.

Mtango, F.D. and Neuvians, D. (1986) Acute respiratory infections in children under five years. Control project in bagamoyo district, Tanzania. *Transactions of the Royal Society of Tropical Medicine and Hygiene* 80(6), 851–858. DOI: 10.1016/0035-9203(86)90241-5.

Mtei, G. and Mulligan, J.A. (2007) *Community Health Funds in Tanzania: A Literature Review*. CREHS, IHA, Ifakara, Tanzania.

Mubi, M., Janson, A., Warsame, M., Mårtensson, A., Källander, K. *et al*. (2011) Malaria rapid testing by community health workers is effective and safe for targeting malaria treatment: randomised cross-over trial in Tanzania. *PloS ONE* 6(7), e19753. DOI: 10.1371/journal.pone.0019753.

Mubyazi, G.M., Mushi, A.K., Shayo, E., Mdira, K., Ikingura, J. *et al*. (2017) Local primary health care committees and community-based health workers in Mkuranga district, Tanzania: does the public recognize and appreciate them?. *Studies on Ethno-Medicine* 1(1), 27–35. DOI: 10.1080/09735070.2007.11886298.

Mwai, G.W., Mburu, G., Torpey, K., Frost, P., Ford, N. *et al*. (2013) Role and outcomes of community health workers in HIV care in sub-Saharan Africa: a systematic review. *Journal of the International AIDS Society* 16(1), 18586. DOI: 18586.

Mwaluko, G.M.E., Kilama, W.L., Mandara, M.P., Murru, M. and Macpherson, C.N.L. (eds) (1991) *Health and Disease in Tanzania*. Harper Collins Academic, London.
Nangawe, E.M. (1990) Experiences from the Maasai Health Services Project, Tanzania. Chapter 7. In: Streefland, P. and Chabot, J. (eds) *Implementing Primary Health Care, Experiences since Alma Ata*. Royal Tropical Institute, Amsterdam, The Netherlands.
Nangawe, E.M., Sitayo, E.O., Rowberg, E., McGinn, T. and Van Wie, W. (1985) The training component of the maasai health services project, Tanzania. *International Quarterly of Community Health Education* 6(2), 115–129. DOI: 10.2190/H7BG-4788-31VA-C04L.
Nangawe, E.M., Shomet, F., Rowberg, E., McGinn, T. and Van Wie, W. (1987) Community participation: the maasai health services project, Tanzania. *International Quarterly of Community Health Education* 7(4), 343–352. DOI: 10.2190/JPLM-XVKT-DXLW-LJE6.
Nhonoli, A.M. (1979) *Primary Health Care Delivery in African Countries*. University of Dar es Salaam, Dar es Salaam, Tanzania.
NIMR (2022) *Fifth National Research Agenda of NIMR 2021/2022–2025/2026*. NIMR, Dar es Salaam, Tanzania.
Perry, H.B., Rassekh, B.M., Gupta, S., Wilhelm, J. and Freeman, P.A. (2017) Comprehensive review of the evidence regarding the effectiveness of community-based primary health care in improving maternal, neonatal and child health: 1. rationale, methods and database description. *Journal of Global Health* 7(1), 010901. DOI: 10.7189/jogh.07.010901.
Pharmaccess Group (2017) *Improved CHF (iCHF) Model Implemented in Kilimanjaro and Manyara Regions*. Pharmaccess Group, Dar es Salaam, Tanzania.
PMO (2018) *Tanzania National Multisectoral Strategic framework for HIV/AIDS 2018/19–2022/2023*. PMO, Dar es Salaam, Tanzania.
Rautanen, S.L., Seppala, O. and Skytta, T. (2006) Health through Sanitation and Water Program (HESAWA). In: *Tanzania, Evaluation Study*. SIDA Evaluation 06/36, Stockholm.
Safe, J.A. (1989) *Ripoti Fupi Inayohusu Wakunga wa Jadi*. Wizara ya Afya, Dar es Salaam, Tanzania.
Sikika (2020) *Community Score Cards: A Comprehensive Report of Interventions from 11 Districts in Tanzania*. Sikika, Dar es Salaam, Tanzania.
Tulenko, K., Møgedal, S., Afzal, M.M., Frymus, D., Oshin, A. *et al*. (2013) Community health workers for universal health-care coverage: from fragmentation to synergy. *Bulletin of the World Health Organization* 91(11), 847–852. DOI: 10.2471/BLT.13.118745.
UNICEF (2016) *Health Systems Strengthening Approach*. UNICEF, New York.
UNICEF Tanzania (2021) *Operational Guidance on Implementing Community Based Working Relationships to Promote Adolescents Sexual and Reproductive Health and Rights within the GRREAT Initiative, Mbeya and Songwe Regions*. UNICEF, Dar es Salaam, Tanzania.
Urio, E.M., Jeje, B. and Ndossi, G. (2014) Community based nutrition rehabilitation in Tanzania: challenges and lessons learned. In: *International Symposium on Understanding Moderate Malnutrition in Children for Effective Interventions, IAEA CN-217/ Compilation of abstracts*, p. 44pp. DOI: 10.52439/IARG6699.
URT MOHCDGEC (2020) *Policy Guideline for Community Based Health and Social Welfare Services, towards a Sustainable Community Health and Social Welfare Services, Leaving No One Behind*. United Republic of Tanzania, MOHCDGEC, Dar es Salaam, Tanzania.
van Etten, G.M. (1976) *Rural Health Development in Tanzania*. van Gorkum BV, Assen, The Netherlands.
van Praag, E., Swai, R., Mpangile, G. and Mwanga, F. (2009) Implementing the continuum of care for HIV: lessons learned from Tanzania. In: Marlink, R.G. and Teitelman, S.J. (eds) *From the Ground Up: Building Comprehensive AIDS Care Programs in Resource-Limited Settings*, Vol. 3. EGPAF, Washington, DC, pp. 29–42.
Vaughan, K., Kok, M.C., Witter, S. and Dieleman, M. (2015) Costs and cost-effectiveness of community health workers: evidence from a literature review. *Human Resources for Health* 13(7), 1. DOI: 10.1186/s12960-015-0070-y.
Warren, K.S. (1990) Tropical medicine or tropical health: the Heath Clark lectures, 1988. *Reviews of Infectious Diseases* 12(1), 142–156. DOI: 10.1093/clinids/12.1.142.
WHO (1978) *Alma-Ata, Primary Health Care*, Health for All Series, no. 1. World Health Organization, Geneva, Switzerland.
WHO (2018) *Declaration of AstanaGlobal Conference on PHC, Astana Conference*. WHO/HIS/SDS/2018.61, Geneva, Switzerland.

9 Achieving Health-Systems Resilience in Tanzania

Albino Kalolo[1,2*], James Tumaini Kengia[3,4], Ntuli A. Kapologwe[3,4], Don de Savigny[5] and Japhet Killewo[6]

[1]Department of Public Health, St Francis University College of Health and Allied Sciences, Ifakara, Tanzania; [2]Centre for Reforms, Innovation, Health Policies and Implementation Research (CeRIHI), Dodoma, Tanzania; [3]President's Office - Regional Administration and Local Government, Dodoma, Tanzania; [4]University of Dodoma, Tanzania; [5]Swiss Tropical and Public Health Institute, Basel, Switzerland; [6]Department of Epidemiology and Biostatistics, Muhimbili University of Health and Allied Sciences, Dar es Salaam, Tanzania

Abstract

The contemporary challenges of the health system require a system that is resilient and responsive to shocks if the desired health outcomes are to be attained. A resilient health system should have a capacity to proactively foresee, absorb and adapt to shocks and structural changes in a way that allows it to sustain required operations, resume optimal performance as quickly as possible, transform its structure and functions to strengthen the system and (possibly) reduce its vulnerability to similar shocks and structural changes in the future. This chapter puts forward the struggles to achieve health-system resilience in Tanzania. Examples of actions that shaped resilience in the health system are provided, together with propositions that a resilient health system should be built on the foundations of emergency preparedness, change management, realigned relationships, involvement at all levels, motivation and foresight. Subsequently, the chapter provides suggestions for the future outlook on health-system resilience.

9.0 Introduction to Health-System Resilience

There is growing consensus that contemporary challenges to the health system require a system that is resilient and responsive to all types of shocks so that positive health outcomes are attained. The fourth Global Symposium on Health Systems Research in Vancouver, Canada, in 2016, had as its main theme 'Resilient and responsive health systems for a changing world' and one of the important subthemes was 'Enhancing health-system resilience: absorbing shocks and sustaining gains in every setting' (van de Pas *et al.*, 2017). Since then, there has been a growing interest among researchers, academics and policy makers in this subject, in particular trying to understand how to make health systems more resilient to address threats and shocks in the system. Currently, health-system resilience has become a buzzword when analysing health systems (Fridell *et al.*,

*Corresponding author: Kaloloa@gmail.com

DOI: 10.1079/9781800623330.0009

2019; Biddle *et al.*, 2020; Forsgren *et al.*, 2022; Ghebreyesus *et al.*, 2022).

Defined as 'a capability of health systems to succeed under varying conditions', health-system resilience has been operationalized as a concept that is not only focusing on capacity to absorb adverse events and recover, but also focusing on planned interventions against known challenges in the health-care system in any given setting (Kruk *et al.*, 2017; Biddle *et al.*, 2020; Iflaifel *et al.*, 2020). Operational definitions that foster a more consistent understanding of the concept have been adapted and include: 'health system resilience is the ability to prepare for, manage (absorb, adapt and transform) and learn from shocks' (Thomas *et al.*, 2020). In this definition, shock is an unexpected, sudden and extreme change that affects a health system, and is thus different from the predictable and enduring health-system stresses. Shocks can emanate from within the health system or outside the health system and impact the resources available to the system and the demands on the system (Hanefeld *et al.*, 2018). Examples of shocks include extreme weather events, floods, refugee and migration crises, infectious disease outbreaks, financial crises and conflicts.

The outbreak of Corona Virus Disease 2019 (COVID-19) is a recent example of a disaster that has caused severe shocks to health-care systems globally. On 19 October 2021 the World Health Organization (WHO) launched its position paper, 'Building Health Systems Resilience for Universal Health Coverage and Health Security during the COVID-19 Pandemic and Beyond,' to reinforce commitments for countries to be better prepared and make their health systems resilient against all forms of public health threats for sustained progress towards both UHC and global health security (Brown *et al.*, 2022; Ghebreyesus, 2020; Ghebreyesus *et al.*, 2022). To achieve this, the WHO (2021) insisted on building capacities on essential public health functions that improve, promote, protect and restore health systems by:

- building a strong primary health-care system as a foundation for bringing health services closer to communities;
- all-hazards emergency risk management that strengthens the ability of countries to prevent and tackle health emergencies, and can surge to meet the additional health-security demands imposed by health emergencies;
- engaging the whole of society so that all sectors work together towards achieving universal health coverage by 2030.

A resilient health system should have the capacity to proactively foresee, absorb and adapt to shocks and structural changes in a way that allows it to sustain required operations, resume optimal performance as quickly as possible, transform its structure and functions to strengthen the system and (possibly) reduce its vulnerability to similar shocks and structural changes in the future. This will be possible if the health system is built with the following foundations: (i) emergency preparedness, whereby financial investment and resources are made available towards resilience; (ii) change management, whereby health systems deliberately change to cope with stress; (iii) realigned relationships, whereby there is mutual trust, engagement and collaborations between actors; (iv) motivation; and (v) foresight, whereby there are strategies for long-term infrastructure, the human resources and other health-system inputs to enhance functioning of the system at all times.

During any crisis such a system should be able to: (i) identify where support measures are needed most based on changes in population-level health outcomes as detected by surveillance systems; (ii) distribute resources (human workforce, finances, commodities and other materials) through all possible means, even when the standard supply-chain system is not functioning; and (iii) forge relationships with a broad range of actors (public and private) to work together to identify and fill needed gaps.

Rogers and colleagues explain that the resilience of a health system addresses three main capacities: absorptive, adaptive and transformative (Rogers *et al.*, 2021). The absorptive capacity relates to the capacity of a health system to continue to deliver the same level (access, quality and equity) of health-care services and protection to populations despite the shock using the same level of resources and capacities. Adaptive capacity is the capacity of the health-system actors to deliver the same level of health-care services with fewer and/or different resources, which requires making organizational adaptations. The transformative capacity describes the ability of health-system actors to transform the functions and structure of the health system to respond to a changing environment.

9.1 The Threats to PHC and Health-System Resilience

Shocks regularly challenge the health-care system. Some are known and only require careful planning, analysis, execution and evaluation of the planned interventions (reforms), whereas some challenges are not yet known and present as humanitarian emergencies or disasters. Catastrophes that have challenged the world over time include: (i) Economic crises: economic crises are common in low/middle-income countries. (ii) Outbreaks of infectious diseases: this has been persistently presenting with emerging and re-emerging diseases. (iii) Transitions (demographic, epidemiological and nutritional) present challenges in terms of making the health system cope. For instance, with demographic transitions specifically in urban areas, it becomes challenging to plan for health services. Epidemiological and nutritional transitions challenge the health-care system with an increasing burden of communicable and non-communicable diseases. (iv) Political and civil unrest is an important shock in health systems of conflict-afflicted countries. (v) Natural hazards and disasters, such as famine, earthquakes, energy crises and other major emergencies are common in many settings, particularly in low- and middle-income countries.

Responding to the shocks requires that health-system hardware (inputs to the system such as the human workforce, financing and health commodities) and software (such as coordination, communication and partnerships) are strong, capable of learning, and can transform. Furthermore, the political and governance context of a given country plays an important role in ensuring a resilient health system. Moreover, the health sector is dependent on other sectors, which are also required to contribute in making the health system resilient.

In striving forward to reach universal health coverage, specifically using a primary health-care approach, strategies to enhance health-system resilience have been designed across settings. These strategies are usually aligned with the health-system building blocks, in that, for each component, there are specific strategies that have proven effectiveness. Box 9.1 (modified from Thomas *et al.*, 2020) provides a summary of recommendations from the literature.

9.2 History of the Struggle to Achieve Health-System Resilience in Primary Health Care in Tanzania

9.2.1 Role of leadership and governance in health-systems resilience

Resilient leadership and governance practices are needed for better health-system performance in different settings and conditions. Practices that embrace visionary policies, participatory decision making, a learning culture, effective communication and systems are critical in making sure that health systems can absorb the shocks and disruption that may occur as a result of unforeseen events like disasters and disease outbreaks. In the course of creating a resilient health system through leadership and governance structures, several aspects need to be considered. The WHO's Africa Region meeting deliberated four thematic areas that must be considered for sustained leadership and governance for a robust and resilient primary health-care system. The thematic areas are:

- Multisectorality/intersectorality: Practices that promote participation of all stakeholders from different sectors in addressing health-system challenges are required for a resilient primary health-care system. For example, approaches like Health in All policies (HiAP) and One Health have been implemented to promote resilience as threats and shocks to the health system can be tackled by different sectors.
- Moving from fragmentation to integration: Leadership and governance practices that help primary health care move from fragmentation to integration are seen as the stride forward to make health systems

Box 9.1. Strategies to strengthen health system resilience.

Building block (s)	Strategies
Leadership and governance	Effective and participatory leadership with strong vision and communication Coordination of activities across government and key stakeholders Organizational learning culture that is responsive to crises Effective information systems and flows Surveillance enabling timely detection of shocks and their impact Giving equal attention to top-down and bottom-up participatory approaches to governance Creating realistic, clear, and transparent health targets and indicators to measure the achievement of health-system resilience
Health financing	Ensuring sufficient monetary resources in the system and the flexibility to reallocate and inject extra funds Ensuring the stability of health system funding through counter-cyclical health-financing mechanisms and reserves Adequate purchasing power, flexibility and reallocation of funding to meet changing needs Comprehensive health coverage Available and accessible budget for crises
Health commodities and technologies	Improving local governance and access to health commodities Improving local use of technology
Human workforce	Appropriate level and distribution of human resources Ability to increase capacity to cope with a sudden surge in demand Motivated and well-supported workforce
Service delivery	Alternative and flexible approaches to delivering care Active involvement and use of community resources
Health-information systems	Improving surveillance through emergency operation centres and incident management systems Linking health-management information systems to broader forecasting trends Forecasting longer-term system shocks Integrating health information with other sectors

resilient. Such practices are in line with the horizontal approach of primary health care and does away with selective approach that may be a temporary solution to tackle pressing public health challenges while preparing for resilient and sustainable systems.

- Ensuring implementation and knowledge exchange is an important aspect of health-system resilience and this can be achieved in a learning health system. A learning health system is a closed loop that melds current evidence and health-system experience to promote continuous improvement.

- Rethinking resilience and embracing anti-fragility: While resilience is about recovery after performance degradation as a result of a shock, anti-fragility is defined as a performance gain when exposed to adversity. When there are shocks such as epidemics, governments are often under increased pressure to act quickly and at scale. By reimagining how they work, they can create resilient societies and public services for the next normal. Resilience can be achieved by more resilient societies, more resilient governance operations and more resilient core capabilities of the public sector, in relation also to provision of health services. The health-care system becomes anti-fragile if it learns to maintain an acceptable impact to all stakeholders as the system and environment change over time.

While addressing the four thematic areas, the following are important principles that need to be adhered to:

- Maintaining ethics during a health crisis: Responding to crises in an ethical way is an important principle for sustainability and institutionalization of approaches that are geared to build resilience; for example, despite a disaster, abiding by the patient rights established by the WHO that include: (i) receiving high-quality care and treatment, (ii) equitable access to healthcare services and information, (iii) confidentiality of information, (iv) informed consent, (v) self-determination and independence, (vi) access to health education, and (vii) the right to complain and demand compensation.
- Strengthening health-system capacity: Approaches that are geared to strengthening the health-system capacity at facility, outreach and community level have a significant role in ensuring resilience and anti-fragility. The number of resources and inputs in the health system define its capacity. Strengthening health-system capacity is of paramount importance for everyday resilience, as well as resilience during crises.
- Operationalizing strategies to cope with a health crisis: Putting forward clear strategies that are to be implemented to cope with shocks in the health system is one of the important steps in the stride forward to mount resilience. Leadership and governance practices that rely on strategies can do better in coping with crises and sustaining operations beyond the crises. Achieving readiness and health-system resilience is a continuous process of establishing, strengthening and maintaining a multisectoral response while constructing an infrastructure that can be applied at all levels, including primary health care. Achieving this requires political commitment and strong policies and policy direction. This should be in line with the WHO primary health care operational framework, which stipulates the importance of fourteen levers to be used at the PHC level. The PHC operational framework levers are as follows: political commitment and leadership; governance and policy frameworks; funding and allocation of resources; engagement of community and other stakeholders; modes of care; physical infrastructure; medicines and other products; engagement with other private sector providers; purchasing and payment systems; digital technologies for health; systems for improving the quality of care; primary health care-oriented research; monitoring and evaluation; funding and allocation of resources; governance and policy frameworks; and engagement of communities and other stakeholders (WHO and UNICEF, 2020).
- Engaging multisectoral stakeholders during a health crisis: Multisectoral engagement and implementation of some inclusive policies strategies like the Health in All policies (HiAP) (and the One Health strategic plan are needed for leveraging resources and for making sure that all important stakeholders are engaged in responding to the health threats and shocks, hence making the health system more resilient.
- Redesigning institutions to cope with a health crisis: One of the important steps in building resilience is the revitalization

of the PHC system to provide services that are up to the expectations of communities. Primary health systems which include all essential public health functions, elements and the capacities of related societal systems are the foundation for responding to health threats and shocks and must be strengthened. In order to make a strong primary health-care system, the Tanzanian government established the Department of Health, Social Welfare and Nutrition Services as an institution which, among other things, is responsible for the designing of infrastructure and capacity building for coping up with any health crisis.

In Tanzania, the leadership and governance practices before independence were mainly characterized by decisions that are ad hoc and were based on the goodwill of the colonial government. After independence and up to the present day, practices have been changed and have been on the side of strengthening resilience of the health systems. Grounded on the visionary and participatory principles and ensuring effective communication during shocks and crisis, leadership and governance practices after independence can be summarized into key policies that were vital in strengthening resilience: (i) directives of the Arusha Declaration in 1967; (ii) decentralization policy of 1978 and subsequent amendments; (iii) health-sector reforms in the 1990s; (iv) formulation of the national health policy and subsequent strategic plans. In addition, to implement the policies, a Directorate of Health, Social Welfare and Nutrition was established at PO-RALG to oversee the implementation of primary health-care services. With a growing burden of shocks from infectious and non-infectious diseases and natural disasters, there is a need to further strengthen the primary health-care system.

9.2.2 Information and evidence

Surveillance and response

Surveillance and response systems are needed for the collection of data that can be generated to produce evidence and knowledge. The existing passive and active surveillance system can be used as an infrastructure predictor for unforeseen events which may disrupt the primary health-care system. The routine and sentinel surveillance systems need to be well equipped to capture all data and information needed for detection, prevention and response to health threats and for translating such information into evidence and knowledge for decision making at the primary health-care level. Tanzania's primary health-care system for so many years has been used as a backbone of the event-based surveillance system and also is used for collection of samples for surveillance of certain diseases like polio and measles (Mghamba *et al.*, 2004; Rumisha *et al.*, 2007). There are systems like integrated disease surveillance and response (IDSR), which are used for routine reporting of various disease events which are of public health interest. Through IDSR the aggregated data at the district level are submitted at the regional and national level for disease surveillance and monitoring purposes.

Evidence-based policy making

Having policies that are in keeping with the predicted or unforeseen disruptions or crisis is an important component that can be used to contain the disrupted health system and get back to normal within a short time. Evidence synthesis and policy analysis, specifically using a policy analysis triangle, can help to build a resilient health system (O'Brien *et al.*, 2020). Policy analysis can be done using the policy triangle framework, that contains: context (why there is a need for the said policy for health-system resilience); content (what is the policy mainly about in the context of health-system resilience); process (how was the policy brought forward and implemented at the PHC level); and who are the actors (who participated in and influenced the formulation and its implementation). Crises often open the policy-making window, making it possible to institute long-awaited policies that were not politically feasible in earlier times. The establishment of the National Institute of Medical Research in 1979 was an important step in ensuring that research evidence is at the forefront in policy making and decision making in the health system, specifically so the primary health care system (Magesa *et al.*, 2011). Since then, there has been an intensification of research activities and efforts to translate research evidence in policy and practice. For example, NIMR has collaborated with local and international institutions to look for solutions to existing problems as well as emerging problems (Ikingura *et al.*, 2001; Magesa *et al.*, 2011).

9.2.3 Health workforce

Human resources for health (HRH) have always played a critical role in the provision of health services. During the colonial period, the health workforce was concentrated in limited administrative areas important to serve the colonial interest. With limited available medical officers, in 1918, the German government started training medical auxiliaries, mostly Africans, a move that would later be scaled up by the British (Hartwig, 1979). Furthermore, during the British colonial period, the need to reorganize health care, propelled by the Pridie Report, emerged and led into the establishment of training for inspectors and rural medical aides in 1949 to bring a balance between curative and preventive service. However, the intention was not achieved due to the preference for hospital-led services by the authorities (Hartwig, 1979; Young, 1986).

Contrary to the pre-independence era, after independence, following an acute shortage of medical staff with only 12 African doctors out of the 400 registered, many non-African doctors left the country. This created an acute shortage of medical doctors. Changes in political ideology to improve services in rural underserved areas necessitated the need to reorganize and design strategies to address the increasing demand for health manpower (Bech, 2013). Following Titmuss's report (Titmuss, 1964), which recommended the need for training more rural health professionals and integrating them within the existing system, several policy responses and innovations were adopted aiming at addressing the HRH shortage by setting strategies to increase HRH supply by engaging the private sector, designing curricula, training and recruiting mid-level cadres and improving recruitment practices, as well as enhancing HRH retainability in hard-to-reach areas. In 1967, during the Arusha Declaration, there was dedicated effort at training mid-level cadres, followed by a growth in the supply of physicians, medical assistants and rural medical aides in Tanzania from 1971 to 1980 (Bech, 2013; Gottlich, 2018). However, despite promising efforts in stabilizing the human-resource workforce crisis, in 1970, as a result of economic stagnation due to the international oil crisis of 1973 and 1979, the breakup of the East African Community (EAC) in 1977, the war in Uganda in 1978 and the decline in agricultural production that resulted in the 1986 structural adjustment programmes (SAPs) of the World Bank, the effect on HRH was a freeze in hiring and civil service wages, downsizing of employment, the resumption of private practice and the introduction of cost sharing. The HRH crisis persisted over time and culminated in 1996 when the government of Tanzania declared a health workforce crisis that was exacerbated by the emigration of skilled workforce to other countries in search of greener pastures (Kwesigabo *et al.*, 2012; Bech, 2013). To address the health workforce shortage, the government embarked on several interventions, including allowing the establishment of private medical training institutions, increasing enrolment of students in health-care universities and legal interventions such as a compulsory requirement for recruits to work in rural areas for not less than 2 years, partial decentralization of recruitment processes and increasing salaries for public health workers (Mkony, 2012; Sue *et al.*, 2016) and also the establishment of the Centre for Distance Education (CDE) by the Ministry of Health in 1997 to allow for continued training of staff while they are at their workplaces.

Due to a critical shortage of staff in the regions and local government authorities (LGAs) following the employment freeze in the aftermath of SAPs, the President's Office of Public Service Management (POPSM) issued a directive for a decentralized recruitment process where districts would identify their needs and hire new employees for around ten years from 2005 to 2010. In 2006, the deployment system changed to a partially centralized system to address issues of an equal distribution of health-care workers and the challenges of the recruitment system in the LGAs. In 2011, due to unequal health workforce distribution, MOHSW's fully started conducting the recruitment process through its Department of Administration and Human Resource Management, and in recent years there has been centralized recruitment by five key players – MOH, PO-RALG, POPSM, the Ministry of Finance (MOF), and Public Service Recruitment Secretariat (PSRS) – with a different mandate.

In 2008, the government launched a second five-year HRH strategic plan that, among other things, emphasized the need for partnership creation and recognition of the importance of mid-level cadres to address the HRH shortage. HRH strategic planning continued to be a tool for setting priority strategic investment areas for addressing HRH issues comprehensively (URT, 2014). Curbing the ever-increasing shortage of HRH necessitated designing an innovative approach with an incentive package to motivate staff to work in rural areas. One of the successful models is the Mkapa Fellows programme under the Benjamin Mkapa Foundation (BMF), in which health-care workers are recruited and deployed to hard-to-reach areas. The BMF provides extra incentives, including staff housing, additional allowances and covering the employment costs for the first 3 years before the government absorbs them into the public health system.

Although there has been some improvement in increasing HRH availability since independence, Tanzania still suffers a chronic shortage of HRH and moreover an issue distributing those who are well trained to serve in hard-to-reach areas. Task shifting (Manongi *et al.*, 2006), task sharing (Hermann *et al.*, 2009) and integration of services have become some of the contemporary solutions for addressing the HRH shortage and to improve efficiency, performance and effectiveness.

In Tanzania, different stakeholders have been engaged in making sure that PHC teams are capacitated in leadership and management. For example, the Primary Health Care Institute (PHCI) in Iringa has played a pivotal role over time in building capacity in primary health care across the country. In addition, the Centre for Educational Development in Health, Arusha (CEDHA) has for many years trained and capacitated the PHC workforce to gain skills and competencies in leadership and management to allow them to be resilient in their leadership roles at the PHC facilities.

9.2.4 Health-system financing

Health financing in Tanzania has evolved over time, with key reforms aimed at diversification of sources of financing and improvement in efficiency for utilization of services. In particular post-independence health services provision and financing mechanisms have been evolving based on the National Health Policy of 1990, revised in 2007. The government of Tanzania aimed at financing the health sector to facilitate the provision of equitable, quality and affordable health services consistent with the vision statement provided in the health policies through central government budget, health insurance, both public and private, grants, credits, development aid from development partners and user fees. Contrary to the post-independence era, during the colonial period, health-financing resources were directed towards financing services that were meant for those serving the colonial economy in urban areas, while the majority of the population in rural areas were left with few or no health services (van Etten and Raikes, 1975).

Immediately after independence, the changes in political direction necessitated the need for increasing financing of the health sector for the expansion of health services to rural underprivileged areas and broadening the services from a curative focus to include promotive and preventive services. These investments were funded using grants, credits, development aid and taxation. The government also introduced a policy of free health care in 1961, which was an attempt towards achieving universal access to health-care services. User fees, which existed during the colonial period, were abolished in all public health-care facilities and all health services were funded through general taxation (Kopoka, 2000).

The investment in the post-independence era resulted in improving the health-sector performance from 1964 to 1980 (Honest, 2009). However, during the period of the 1980s to the 1990s, due to the global economic crisis, Tanzania was forced to adopt the structural adjustment programme (SAP) (Biermann and Wagao, 1986). To curb the severe shortage of funding, the government re-introduced a cost-sharing system that is, user-charges for health services as part of SAP with exemption policies for chronic illnesses and special groups, and waivers for those who could not afford to pay user fees. The cost-sharing policy resulted also in the introduction of a national health insurance fund (NHIF), community health funds (later improved community health fund, iCHF), social health insurance benefit under NSSF and private health insurance (Mtei and Mulligan, 2007; Kengia *et al.*, 2013; Kalolo *et al.*, 2018).

From 1995, the government embarked on health-sector reforms to address issues experienced during the implementation of the SAP. Most of the reforms adopted in Tanzania during this period aligned with proposals put forward by the 1993 World Development Report (WDR), including the introduction of the Tanzania Essential Health Intervention Project (TEHIP), which implemented key reforms in planning and budgeting, including a health sector basket fund which established a collective pool for development partners, the introduction of health insurance, the implementation of direct facility financing and public financial management reforms. TEHIP was introduced in Tanzania to support planning and budgeting processes so that resource allocation and use would be better aligned with priority needs as measured by disease burden, and hence improve efficiency in resource allocation and use (de Savigny *et al.*, 2002). The TEHIP implementation experience later contributed to the introduction of the sector-wide approach (SWAp) in June 1998 (Martinez-Álvarez, 2014), the formation of health-sector basket funding (HSBF) in the early 2000s and the introduction of the comprehensive council health plan (CCHP) in 1999 (Maluka *et al.*, 2011) and PlanRep, which is a tool building on the initial TEHIP planning tool for developing council plans and budgets (Lea, 1993). The reforms aimed at increasing the efficiency in utilization of development aid and to avoid duplication of effort (Brown and WHO, 2000). CCHP continued to be an important resource-allocation tool at the level of the council until around 2017 when further fiscal decentralization through direct health facility financing (DHFF) started with the introduction of a health-facility planning tool (Kapologwe *et al.*, 2019). It is worthwhile noting that parallel to the SWAp arrangement, there existed financing mechanisms through vertical programmes and projects directed to specific diseases with high burden, such as AIDS and TB (Ngadaya, 2022) and immunization services (Vaughan and Walt, 1984). With a reducing funding envelope from external funding agencies, mobilizing local resources is becoming inevitable (Mori *et al.*, 2022).

9.2.5 Health commodities and technologies

Tanzania's public supply-chain system has evolved positively over the years from essential drug program (EDP) kits, 'the push system', to an integrated logistics system (ILS), the 'pull system'. All these developments have significantly improved the efficiency and performance of the public sector supply chain. However, the availability of health commodities, and especially essential medicines, has remained uneven. Several factors, both internal and external, are attributed to the uneven availability of health commodities, including inadequate financing, operational inefficiencies, lack of adequate HRH and poor coordination of donations and donor-funded commodities, among others.

Over recent financial years (2016/17, 2017/18 and 2018/19), the government has shown a huge commitment to health by increasing the budget allocation and timely disbursement of funds for health commodities (Piatti-Fünfkirchen and Ally, 2020). Furthermore, apart from central government funding in coping with budget deficit, health facilities have various other sources of funds which can be used to procure health commodities. These funds are known as complimentary or cost-sharing funds and include user fees (UF), community health funds (CHF), the National Health Insurance Fund (NHIF) and other health insurance funds. The recent holistic supply-chain review (HSCR), conducted in 2017 (Ruhago *et al.*, 2022), observed that these complimentary funds are increasingly becoming a significant part of funds available to cover health commodities' financial needs. Important also is the direct health-facility financing initiative that allowed facilities to make their own choices based on local public health needs (Kapologwe *et al.*, 2019). To complement the

Medical Stores Department (MSD) functions, the government, with development partners, have developed a complementary model for supply of health commodities known as the prime vendor system, which is currently in operation to support the delivery of health commodities, hence minimizing stock-outs in public health-care facilities (Wiedenmayer *et al.*, 2019). With progress made in routine and vertical programme supply chains, challenges nevertheless exist in emergency and crisis situations, making the preparation of contingency plans of paramount importance. In the recent COVID-19 pandemic, evidence has shown a scarcity in resources for health commodities in particular for low- and middle-income countries (McMahon *et al.*, 2020).

9.2.6 Health-service delivery under crisis

Emergence of complex health problems

'Complex or wicked' are terms used to describe some of the most challenging and complex issues of our time, many of which threaten human health. A wicked problem (Fig. 9.1) is a problem that is difficult or impossible to solve because of incomplete, contradictory

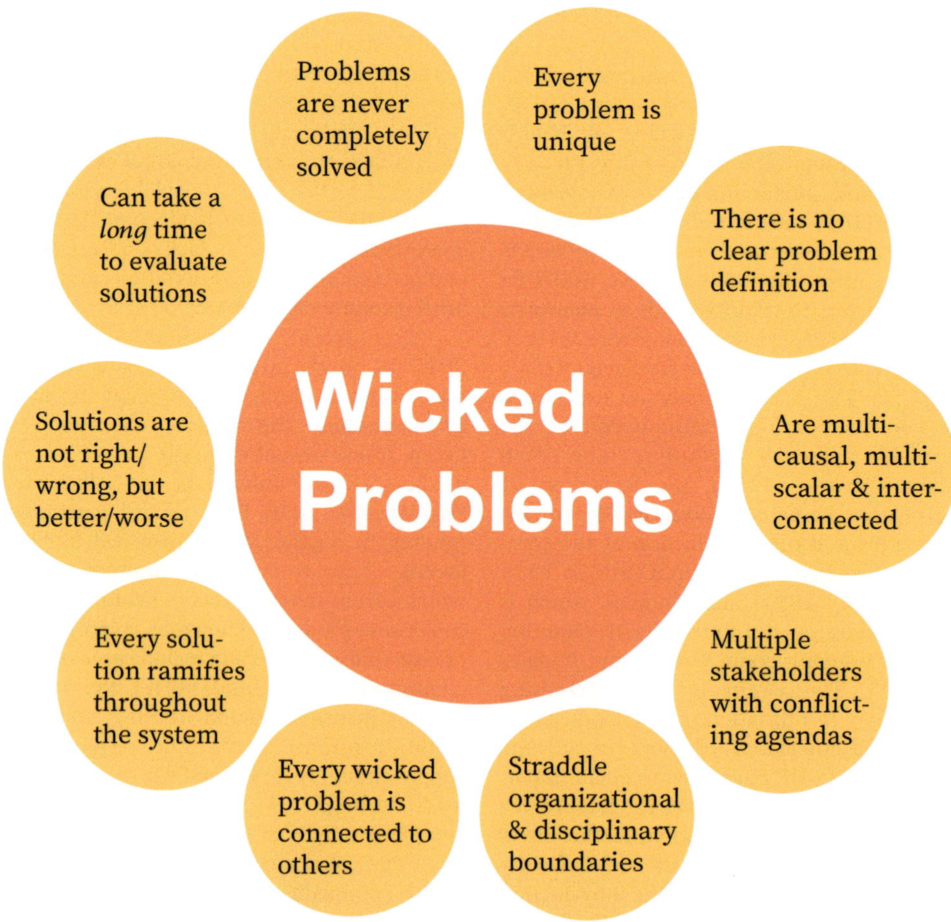

Fig. 9.1. Visual summary of the complexity of wicked problems. (From Transition Design Seminar, Carnegie Mellon University, 2016, https://transitiondesignseminarcmu.net/wp-content/uploads/2016/12/Wicked-problems-flower.png, based on Rittel and Webber, 1973.)

and changing requirements that are often hard to recognize. The term refers to an idea or problem that cannot be fixed, where there is no single solution to the problem. A wicked problem is complex, its causes are complex, and its solution is complex (Alford and Head, 2017; Peters, 2017). Examples of wicked problems are climate change, biodiversity loss, persisting poverty, the advancing obesity epidemic, food insecurity, zoonotic diseases and many others. Climate change is an example of a super-wicked problem because those responsible for it are least interested in doing something about it and the longer we wait, the more wicked it becomes. Rittel and Webber (1973) have described factors associated with wicked problems, indicating that every wicked problem is unique, and solutions are not 'right or wrong', but better or worse. However, there is a strong body of evidence describing the solutions for addressing many of these problems. The risk of NOT taking action to solve a wicked problem is much higher than using a solution that is very wrong. Why not act now at an affordable cost to address wicked problems, rather than wait for a future catastrophe? Unfortunately, policy makers have great difficulty responding effectively to complex or 'wicked' problems. These challenges are a result of the defining features of wicked problems – their complex, numerous and sometimes undefined causes, which are often globalized, their contested understandings and framings among stakeholders with different and strongly held beliefs and values, and their need for collective action, sometimes on a global level, complicated by the lack of simple planning responses (Dentoni *et al.*, 2012; Head, 2014). With obesity, for example, no country to date has reversed its obesity epidemic (Roberto *et al.*, 2015), despite a considerable amount of attention devoted to the importance of this issue (Freudenberg *et al.*, 2011) and a growing evidence base of the effectiveness of various solutions (Raine *et al.*, 2013). To a significant extent, this is due to the ideological debates surrounding the issue, often driven by industry actors and their well-funded lobbies defending vested economic interests and deliberately exploiting the complex or wicked nature of the problem, and thereby creating further uncertainty about causes and consequences. These debates include those of personal vs collective responsibility for action, supply-type vs demand-type explanations for consumption of unhealthy food, the relative roles of physical inactivity and diet in weight gain, government regulation vs industry self-regulation and treatment vs prevention priorities (Roberto *et al.*, 2015). Similar debates and controversies surround discussions of the nature of and how best to respond to other wicked problems, and there is a documented industry strategy to influence country positions, create debate and confusion and delay government regulatory responses (Moodie *et al.*, 2013; Wall *et al.*, 2015). Wicked problems are systemic problems and require systems thinking to move towards systems-wide solutions. Unlike wicked problems, simple or 'tame' problems are those in which solutions are either evident or attainable, even if challenging.

There are two examples of wicked problems in the health sector that require a One-Health approach in their solution. These wicked problems are emerging pandemic threats (EPTs) and antimicrobial resistance (AMR).

Emerging pandemic threats

This chapter defines and describes the emerging pandemic threats, their hot spots, risk elements, reasons for the emergence and their strategic approaches for early detection, prevention and response. New and re-emerging diseases spread quickly across the globe, resulting in outbreaks that overwhelm health systems and affect lives and economies. Increased population growth and mobility and urbanization promote the spread of zoonotic diseases. Climate change continues to alter and increase the distribution of disease vectors. Political and social instability undermine health systems and abilities to prevent, detect and respond to public health threats. The misuse of antimicrobials and the emergence of pathogens with antimicrobial resistance (AMR) affect human, animal and environmental health.

Most of the emerging diseases are transmissible between animals and humans (zoonoses), which means that the disease has emerged from an animal and crossed the species barrier to infect humans (Wolfe *et al.*, 2007; Morse *et al.*, 2012). They include diseases or global health threats whose incidence in humans has increased in the past two decades or whose incidence threatens to increase soon. The largest proportion of these zoonoses comes from wildlife, while a small proportion comes from domesticated animals to be transmitted to humans through direct contact, droplets, food, water, vectors or fomites (Wallis and Rick Lee, 1999; Loh *et al.*, 2015).

Africa has been an epicentre for zoonotic outbreaks with Ebola virus disease (EVD) and other viral haemorrhagic fevers constituting nearly 70% of these outbreaks, and with dengue fever, anthrax, plague, monkeypox and a range of other diseases making up the remaining 30% (Pigott *et al.*, 2014).

Re-emerging diseases are diseases that reappear after they have been on a significant decline. They may re-occur due to a weakening or breakdown in public health measures or due to new strains of a known disease-causing organism (Feldmann *et al.*, 2002). In other words, it is any infection that had decreased in incidence in a local area or the global population and was brought under control through effective health interventions and began to resurge leading to changes in the health status of a susceptible population (Polgreen and Polgreen, 2017). These are diseases that once were major health problems globally or in a particular country, and then declined dramatically, but are again becoming health threats for a significant proportion of the population. During recent decades, infectious diseases that have shown regional or global re-emergence include tuberculosis, malaria, cholera, yellow fever, dengue, chikungunya, Crimean-Congo haemorrhagic fever, meningococcal meningitis, plague, Rift Valley fever, human African trypanosomiasis, rabies, Zika and monkeypox (Morens *et al.*, 2004; Loh *et al.*, 2015; Saxena *et al.*, 2023).

Antimicrobial resistance

Antimicrobial resistance (AMR) occurs when bacteria, viruses, fungi and parasites change over time and no longer respond to medicines, making infections harder to treat and increasing the risk of disease spread, severe illness or death. Recently, AMR has emerged as among the major global threats to public health systems and is recognized as a silent pandemic that threatens to kill up to 10 million people by 2050 (Founou *et al.*, 2021). Currently, up to 700,000 people die annually due to AMR, with 90% of these deaths being reported in low- and middle-income countries (Pokharel *et al.*, 2019). The prevalence of both community- and hospital-acquired AMR is increasing and is being associated with the over-use, misuse and abuse of antimicrobial drugs in humans, animals and agriculture (Mshana *et al.*, 2021). In clinical settings in Tanzania, the prevalence of multidrug-resistant bacteria ranges from 25 to 50% (Moremi *et al.*, 2012; Mshana *et al.*, 2013; Moyo *et al.*, 2014).

Tanzania suffers from high rates of AMR which may be contributing to high rates of misuse of antimicrobials in both the human and animal sectors The prevalence of multidrug-resistant bacteria in clinical settings in Tanzania ranges from 25 to 50% (Moremi *et al.*, 2012; Mshana *et al.*, 2013; Moyo *et al.*, 2014; Mshana *et al.*, 2021). The prevalence of resistance to antimicrobials such as tetracycline, trimethoprim-sulfamethoxazole, ciprofloxacin and gentamicin is at 97%, 69 and 44% respectively (Wellington *et al.*, 2013). A higher prevalence of acquired drug resistance (ADR) mutations among people living with HIV who had been on ART for ≥24 weeks have been reported in Dar es Salaam (Sangeda *et al.*, 2021). Antimalarial drug resistance has been observed for *Plasmodium falciparum*, *P. vivax*, and *P. malariae* globally (Antony and Parija, 2016). In Africa, the increase in antimicrobial use (AMU) and AMR are contributed largely by weak regulations in plant, human and animal health practices, weak enforcement of available laws and regulations on AMU, weak surveillance systems for AMR and AMU in humans, animals and crops, lack of policies and regulations regarding disposal of antimicrobials and lack of updated standard treatment guidelines for human and animal diseases (Mshana *et al.*, 2021).

In 2012, the World Health Assembly urged states to take the necessary steps to prepare and carry out appropriate national implementation plans to ensure the availability of the required strengthening, development and maintenance of the core public health capacities as provided for in IHR 2005. To provide a transparent process of gauging progress at the national level, in 2015, the WHO developed the joint external evaluation (JEE) tool. The tool aims to assess the country's capacity to detect, prevent and rapidly respond to public health threats independently of whether they are naturally occurring, deliberate or accidental. In countries where the JEE has been conducted, it provided the necessary information on what needs to be done to strengthen preparedness.

To address threats due to the negative impacts of these complex health problems, collective efforts by all sectors and at national levels as well as subnational levels are required. These efforts will ensure that the individual national systems are resilient, can prevent and facilitate early detection of disease outbreaks and ultimately prevent or limit their spread in communities and across international borders. Actions taken to strengthen health security in one country or nation are a starting point for enhancing global health security. In 2017, the World Bank's International Working Group on Financing Preparedness found that most countries are still not adequately prepared for pandemics (Oppenheim *et al.*, 2019). In line with this concern, it recommended that strengthening preparedness at the national level should be undertaken early since it reinforces the first line of defence against the threat of pandemics. Additionally, the group recommended that there is a need to strengthen capabilities and coordination at a global level, as well as to accelerate research and development to give more scientific weapons to fight diseases.

The One Health approach

Although the term 'One Health' is fairly new, the concept has long been recognized globally by many pioneers in public health and veterinary medicine. Since the 1800s, scientists have noted the similarity in disease processes among animals and humans, although human and animal medicine had been practised separately until the 20th century. In recent years, through the support of key individuals, meetings and conferences, the One Health concept has gained more momentum and recognition in the public health and animal health communities than ever before due to the emergence of zoonotic diseases of epidemic or pandemic potential. To support and complement the efforts against infectious diseases through both IHR 2005 and PVS 2007, the One Health approach was launched. One Health is loosely defined as the collaborative efforts of multiple disciplines, working locally, nationally and globally, to attain optimal health for people, animals and the environment. In Tanzania, the One Health approach was launched in 2013 by the then vice president, the Hon. Garib Bilal, and, late in 2018, the One Health Strategic Plan was launched by the prime minister, the Hon. Kassim Majaliwa.

Currently, it has become clear that collaboration between the different sectors can help countries to better face current and upcoming health threats. The benefits of the One Health approach go beyond emerging infectious diseases. It is also a much-needed approach for other major global health challenges, such as antimicrobial resistance food safety (Gudipati *et al.*, 2020; McEwen and Collignon, 2018), bioterrorism disaster recovery and response (Kumar, 2022), and climate change (Zinsstag *et al.*, 2018) among others. Addressing these challenges is critical to prevent and controlling emerging and re-emerging diseases.

The HIV/AIDS epidemic broke out in Tanzania in 1983, beginning in the Kagera region. In response to this epidemic, the Ministry of Health developed a short-term plan (STP) in 1985–1986 and established the National AIDS Control Programme in 1986. Later the first medium-term plan (MTP I, 1987–1991) was developed, followed by multisectoral participation in MTP II (1992–1996), which was enhanced in MTP III (1998–2002). The ministry coordinated the development of five-year health sector HIV and AIDS strategic plans to provide specific guidance for the health-sector response.

It was at this point that Tanzania realized the importance of multisectoral and collaborative efforts to curb the epidemic. Following this realization, the Tanzania Commission for AIDS was formed (TACAIDS).

Over the last decade, nations worldwide have been grappling with an increase in emerging and re-emerging diseases at the human, animal and environmental interface. The pathogens responsible for the emergence or re-emergence of these diseases can spread rapidly, not only nationally, but regionally and globally. Recently, the unprecedented Ebola outbreak in West Africa triggered a crisis that, for a period, seemed to evade effective national and international response, with catastrophic results for human health and well-being, food security and economic prosperity (Peterson and Samy, 2016). In 2005–2006, facing the threat

Bibliography

Alford, J. and Head, B.W. (2017) Wicked and less wicked problems: a typology and a contingency framework. *Policy and Society* 36(3), 397–413. DOI: 10.1080/14494035.2017.1361634.

Antony, H.A. and Parija, S.C. (2016) Antimalarial drug resistance: an overview. *Tropical Parasitology* 6(1), 30–41. DOI: 10.4103/2229-5070.175081.

Bech, M.M. (2013) Changing policies and their influence on government health workers in Tanzania, 1967–2009: perspectives from rural Mbulu district. *The International Journal of African Historical Studies* 46(1), 61–103.

Biddle, L., Wahedi, K. and Bozorgmehr, K. (2020) Health system resilience: a literature review of empirical research. *Health Policy and Planning* 35(8), 1084–1109. DOI: 10.1093/heapol/czaa032.

Biermann, W. and Wagao, J. (1986) The quest for adjustment: Tanzania and the IMF, 1980-1986. *African Studies Review* 29(4), 89. DOI: 10.2307/524008.

Brown, A. and WHO (2000) *Current Issues in Sector-Wide Approaches for Health Development: Tanzania Case Study* (No.WHO/GPE/00.6). World Health Organization, Geneva, Switzerland.

Brown, G.W., Bridge, G., Martini, J., Um, J., Williams, O.D. *et al.* (2022) The role of health systems for health security: a scoping review revealing the need for improved conceptual and practical linkages. *Globalization and Health* 18(1), 51. DOI: 10.1186/s12992-022-00840-6.

Dentoni, D., Hospes, O. and Ross, R.B. (2012) Managing wicked problems in Agribusiness: the role of multi-Stakeholder engagements in value creation: editor's introduction. *International Food and Agribusiness Management Review* 15(B), 1–12.

de Savigny, D., Kasale, H., Mbuya, C., Munna, G., Mgalula, L, *et al.* (2002) *Tanzania Essential Health Interventions Project: TEHIP 'interventions': An Overview*. Discussion Paper/Ministry of Health's Tanzania Essential Health Interventions Project (TEHIP); No.2, Ministry of Health, Dodoma. Available at: https://idl-bnc-idrc.dspacedirect.org/bitstream/handle/10625/40912/129019.pdf?sequence=1 (accessed 18 May 2023).

Feldmann, H., Czub, M., Jones, S., Dick, D., Garbutt, M. *et al.* (2002) Emerging and re-emerging infectious diseases. *Medical Microbiology and Immunology* 191(2), 63–74. DOI: 10.1007/s00430-002-0122-5.

Forsgren, L., Tediosi, F., Blanchet, K. and Saulnier, D.D. (2022) Health systems resilience in practice: a scoping review to identify strategies for building resilience. *BMC Health Services Research* 22(1), 1173. DOI: 10.1186/s12913-022-08544-8.

Founou, L.L., Founou, R.C. and Essack, S.Y. (2021) Antimicrobial resistance in the farm-to-plate continuum: more than a food safety issue. *Future Science OA* 7(5), FSO692. DOI: 10.2144/fsoa-2020-0189.

Freudenberg, N., Pastor, M. and Israel, B. (2011) Strengthening community capacity to participate in making decisions to reduce disproportionate environmental exposures. *American Journal of Public Health* 101(Suppl 1), S123–130. DOI: 10.2105/AJPH.2011.300265.

Fridell, M., Edwin, S., von Schreeb, J. and Saulnier, D.D. (2019) Health system resilience: what are we talking about? A scoping review mapping characteristics and keywords. *International Journal of Health Policy and Management* 9(1), 6–16. DOI: 10.15171/ijhpm.2019.71.

Ghebreyesus, T.A. (2020) Strengthening our resolve for primary health care. *Bulletin of the World Health Organization* 98(11), 726–726A. DOI: 10.2471/BLT.20.279489.

Ghebreyesus, T.A., Jakab, Z., Ryan, M.J., Mahjour, J., Dalil, S. *et al.* (2022) WHO recommendations for resilient health systems. *Bulletin of the World Health Organization* 100(4), 240–240A. DOI: 10.2471/BLT.22.287843.

Gottlich, H.C. (2018) Colonialism and the development of the Tanzanian health system. Thesis, Baylor University, Texas.

Gudipati, S., Zervos, M. and Herc, E. (2020) Can the one health approach save us from the emergence and reemergence of infectious pathogens in the era of climate change: implications for antimicrobial resistance? *Antibiotics* 9(9), 599. DOI: 10.3390/antibiotics9090599.

Hanefeld, J., Mayhew, S., Legido-Quigley, H., Martineau, F., Karanikolos, M. *et al.* (2018) Towards an understanding of resilience: responding to health systems shocks. *Health Policy and Planning* 33(3), 355–367. DOI: 10.1093/heapol/czx183.

Hartwig, G.W. (1979) Demographic considerations in East Africa during the nineteenth century. *The International Journal of African Historical Studies* 12(4), 653–672. DOI: 10.2307/218071.

Head, B.W. (2014) Evidence, uncertainty, and wicked problems in climate change decision making in Australia. Environment and Planning C: Government and Policy 32(4), 663–679. DOI: 10.1068/c1240.

Hermann, K., Van Damme, W., Pariyo, G.W., Schouten, E., Assefa, Y. *et al.* (2009) Community health workers for ART in sub-Saharan Africa: learning from experience--capitalizing on new opportunities. *Human Resources for Health* 7(1), 31. DOI: 10.1186/1478-4491-7-31.

Honest, P.N. (2009) Economic development and change in Tanzania since independence: the political leadership factor. *African Journal of Political Science and International Relations* 3(5), 259–267.

Iflaifel, M., Lim, R.H., Ryan, K. and Crowley, C. (2020) Resilient health care: a systematic review of conceptualisations, study methods and factors that develop resilience. *BMC Health Services Research* 20(1), 324. DOI: 10.1186/s12913-020-05208-3.

Ikingura, J.K., Mvungi, V.P., Nkwera, A.J., Senkoro, K.P., Malacela, M.N. *et al.* (2001) Twenty years of the National Institute for medical research (1980–2000): a Synopsis. *Tanzania Journal of Health Research* 2(2), 1–5.

Kalolo, A., Gautier, L., Radermacher, R., Stoermer, M., Jahn, A. *et al.* (2018) Implementation of the redesigned community health fund in the Dodoma region of Tanzania: a qualitative study of views from rural communities. *The International Journal of Health Planning and Management* 33(1), 121–135. DOI: 10.1002/hpm.2403.

Kapologwe, N.A., Kalolo, A., Kibusi, S.M., Chaula, Z., Nswilla, A. *et al.* (2019) Understanding the implementation of direct health facility financing and its effect on health system performance in Tanzania: a non-controlled before and after mixed method study protocol. *Health Research Policy and Systems* 17(1), 11. DOI: 10.1186/s12961-018-0400-3.

Kapologwe, N.A., Meara, J.G., Kengia, J.T., Sonda, Y., Gwajima, D. *et al.* (2020) Development and upgrading of public primary healthcare facilities with essential surgical services infrastructure: a strategy towards achieving universal health coverage in Tanzania. *BMC Health Services Research* 20(1), 218. DOI: 10.1186/s12913-020-5057-2.

Kengia, J.T., Igarashi, I. and Kawabuchi, K. (2013) Effectiveness of health sector reforms in reducing disparities in utilization of skilled birth attendants in Tanzania. *The Tohoku Journal of Experimental Medicine* 230(4), 241–253. DOI: 10.1620/tjem.230.241.

Killewo, J., Bazeyo, W. and Mdegela, R. (2017) One health central and Eastern Africa: historical and future perspectives. In: *International Encyclopedia of Public Health*. DOI: 10.1016/B978-0-12-803678-5.00512-9.

Kopoka, P.A. (2000) Provision of health services in Tanzania in the twenty first century: lessons from the past. In: *Economic Policy Environment in Tanzania in the Twenty-First Century: Lessons from the Nyerere Legacy*. Available at: http://www.tzonline.org/pdf/provisionofhealthservicesintanzania.pdf (accessed 18 May 2023).

Kruk, M.E., Ling, E.J., Bitton, A., Cammett, M., Cavanaugh, K. *et al.* (2017) Building resilient health systems: a proposal for a resilience index. *BMJ* 357, j2323. DOI: 10.1136/bmj.j2323.

Kumar, A. (2022) Disaster response under "One Health" approach: contribution of veterinary public health. In: Verma, S. and Prem, H.T. (eds) *Management of Animals in Disasters*. Springer Nature, Singapore, pp. 245-261.

Kwesigabo, G., Mwangu, M.A., Kakoko, D.C., Warriner, I., Mkony, C.A. *et al.* (2012) Tanzania's health system and workforce crisis. *Journal of Public Health Policy* 33(Suppl. 1), S35–44. DOI: 10.1057/jphp.2012.55.

Lamberti-Castronuovo, A., Valente, M., Barone-Adesi, F., Hubloue, I. and Ragazzoni, L. (2022) Primary health care disaster preparedness: a review of the literature and the proposal of A new framework. *International Journal of Disaster Risk Reduction* 81, 103278. DOI: 10.1016/j.ijdrr.2022.103278.

Lea, R.A. (1993) World Development Report 1993: 'Investing in Health.' World Bank, Washington, DC.

Loh, E.H., Zambrana-Torrelio, C., Olival, K.J., Bogich, T.L., Johnson, C.K. *et al.* (2015) Targeting Transmission Pathways for Emerging Zoonotic Disease Surveillance and Control. *Vector Borne and Zoonotic Diseases (Larchmont, N.Y.)* 15(7), 432–437. DOI: 10.1089/vbz.2013.1563.

Magesa, S.M., Mwape, B. and Mboera, L.E.G. (2011) Challenges and opportunities in building health research capacity in Tanzania: a case of the National institute for medical research. *Tanzania Journal of Health Research* 13(5), 427–443. DOI: 10.4314/thrb.v13i5.11.

Maluka, S.O., Hurtig, A.-K., Sebastián, M.S., Shayo, E., Byskov, J. *et al.* (2011) Decentralization and health care prioritization process in Tanzania: from national rhetoric to local reality. *The International Journal of Health Planning and Management* 26(2), e102–120. DOI: 10.1002/hpm.1048.

Manongi, R.N., Marchant, T.C. and Bygbjerg, I.C. (2006) Improving motivation among primary health care workers in Tanzania: a health worker perspective. *Human Resources for Health* 4, 6. DOI: 10.1186/1478-4491-4-6.
Martinez-Álvarez, M. (2014) *Development Assistance for Health in Tanzania: Has the Sector Wide Approach Achieved the Principles of Aid Effectiveness?* London School of Hygiene & Tropical Medicine, London.
McEwen, S.A. and Collignon, P.J. (2018) Antimicrobial resistance: a one health perspective. In: Schwarz, S., Cavaco, L.M., Shen, J. and Aarestrup, F.M. (eds) *Antimicrobial Resistance in Bacteria from Livestock and Companion Animals*. Wiley, Chichester, pp. 521–547. DOI: 10.1128/9781555819804.
McMahon, D.E., Peters, G.A., Ivers, L.C. and Freeman, E.E. (2020) Global resource shortages during COVID-19: bad news for low-income countries. *PLoS Neglected Tropical Diseases* 14(7), e0008412. DOI: 10.1371/journal.pntd.0008412.
Mghamba, J.M., Mboera, L.E.G., Krekamoo, W., Senkoro, K.P., Rumisha, S.F. *et al.* (2004) Challenges of implementing an integrated disease surveillance and response strategy using the current health management information system in Tanzania. *Tanzania Journal of Health Research* 6(2), 57–63. DOI: 10.4314/thrb.v6i2.14243.
Mkony, C.A. (2012) Emergence of a university of health sciences: health professions education in Tanzania. *Journal of Public Health Policy* 33(Suppl 1), S45–63. DOI: 10.1057/jphp.2012.51.
Moodie, R., Stuckler, D., Monteiro, C., Sheron, N., Neal, B. *et al.* (2013) Profits and pandemics: prevention of harmful effects of tobacco, alcohol, and ultra-processed food and drink industries. *Lancet* 381(9867), 670–679. DOI: 10.1016/S0140-6736(12)62089-3.
Moremi, N., Mshana, S.E., Kamugisha, E., Kataraihya, J., Tappe, D. *et al.* (2012) Predominance of methicillin resistant Staphylococcus aureus -ST88 and new ST1797 causing wound infection and abscesses. *Journal of Infection in Developing Countries* 6(8), 620–625. DOI: 10.3855/jidc.2093.
Morens, D.M., Folkers, G.K. and Fauci, A.S. (2004) The challenge of emerging and re-emerging infectious diseases. *Nature* 430(6996), 242–249. DOI: 10.1038/nature02759.
Mori, A.T, Christopher Bulula, N., Magodi, R. and Mwengee, W. (2022) Domestic funding opportunities for Tanzania as five new middle-income countries brace for reduced Gavi support for immunization. *Vaccine* 40(24), 3278–3285. DOI: 10.1016/j.vaccine.2022.04.058.
Morse, S.S., Mazet, J.A., Woolhouse, M., Parrish, C.R., Carroll, D. *et al.* (2012) Prediction and prevention of the next pandemic zoonosis. *The Lancet* 380(9857), 1956–1965. DOI: 10.1016/S0140-6736(12)61684-5.
Moyo, S.J., Aboud, S., Blomberg, B., Mkopi, N., Kasubi, M. *et al.* (2014) High nasal carriage of methicillin-resistant Staphylococcus aureus among healthy Tanzanian under-5 children. *Microbial Drug Resistance* 20(1), 82–88. DOI: 10.1089/mdr.2013.0016.
Mshana, S.E., Matee, M. and Rweyemamu, M. (2013) Antimicrobial resistance in human and animal pathogens in zambia, democratic republic of congo, mozambique and Tanzania: an urgent need of a sustainable surveillance system. *Annals of Clinical Microbiology and Antimicrobials* 12(1), 1–10. DOI: 10.1186/1476-0711-12-28.
Mshana, S.E., Sindato, C., Matee, M.I. and Mboera, L.E.G. (2021) Antimicrobial use and resistance in agriculture and food production systems in Africa: a systematic review. *Antibiotics (Basel, Switzerland)* 10(8), 976. DOI: 10.3390/antibiotics10080976.
Mtei, G. and Mulligan, J. (2007) *Community Health Funds in Tanzania: A Literature Review*. Ifakara Health Research and Development Centre, Ifakara, Dar es Salaam, Tanzania.
Ngadaya, F.D. (2022) Health system costs and feasibility of alternative mechanisms for expanding domestic resources mobilization to finance malaria, HIV/AIDS, and TB services in Tanzania. *Tanzania Journal of Health Research* 23(Suppl), 99–100.
O'Brien, G.L., Sinnott, S.-J., Walshe, V., Mulcahy, M. and Byrne, S. (2020) Health policy triangle framework: narrative review of the recent literature. *Health Policy Open* 1, 100016. DOI: 10.1016/j.hpopen.2020.100016.
Oppenheim, B., Gallivan, M., Madhav, N.K., Brown, N., Serhiyenko, V. *et al.* (2019) Assessing global preparedness for the next pandemic: development and application of an epidemic preparedness index. *BMJ Global Health* 4(1), e001157. DOI: 10.1136/bmjgh-2018-001157.
Peters, B.G. (2017) What is so wicked about wicked problems? A conceptual analysis and a research program. *Policy and Society* 36(3), 385–396. DOI: 10.1080/14494035.2017.1361633.
Peterson, A.T. and Samy, A.M. (2016) Geographic potential of disease caused by Ebola and marburg viruses in Africa. *Acta Tropica* 162, 114–124. DOI: 10.1016/j.actatropica.2016.06.012.

Piatti-Fünfkirchen, M. and Ally, M. (2020) *Tanzania Health Sector Public Expenditure Review 2020*. World Bank, Washington, DC. DOI: 10.1596/34620.

Pigott, D.M., Golding, N., Mylne, A., Huang, Z., Henry, A.J. *et al.* (2014) Mapping the zoonotic niche of Ebola virus disease in Africa. *ELife* 3, e04395. DOI: 10.7554/eLife.04395.

Pokharel, S., Raut, S. and Adhikari, B. (2019) Tackling antimicrobial resistance in low-income and middle-income countries. *BMJ Global Health* 4(6), e002104. DOI: 10.1136/bmjgh-2019-002104.

Polgreen, P.M. and Polgreen, E.L. (2017) Emerging and re-emerging pathogens and diseases, and health consequences of a changing climate. *Infectious Diseases* 40–48, e4.

Raine, L.B., Lee, H.K., Saliba, B.J., Chaddock-Heyman, L., Hillman, C.H. *et al.* (2013) The influence of childhood aerobic fitness on learning and memory. *PloS ONE* 8(9), e72666. DOI: 10.1371/journal.pone.0072666.

Rittel, H.W.J. and Webber, M.M. (1973) Dilemmas in a general theory of planning. *Policy Sciences* 4(2), 155–169. DOI: 10.1007/BF01405730.

Roberto, C.A., Swinburn, B., Hawkes, C., Huang, T.T.-K., Costa, S.A. *et al.* (2015) Patchy progress on obesity prevention: emerging examples, entrenched barriers, and new thinking. *Lancet (London, England)* 385(9985), 2400–2409. DOI: 10.1016/S0140-6736(14)61744-X.

Rogers, H.L., Barros, P.P., Maeseneer, J.D., Lehtonen, L., Lionis, C. *et al.* (2021) Resilience testing of health systems: how can it be done? *International Journal of Environmental Research and Public Health* 18(9), 4742. DOI: 10.3390/ijerph18094742.

Ruhago, G.M., Ngalesoni, F.N., Msasi, D., Kengia, J.T., Mganga, M. *et al.* (2022) The public health sector supply chain costs in Tanzania. *PLOS Global Public Health* 2(11), e0000960. DOI: 10.1371/journal.pgph.0000960.

Rumisha, S.F., Mboera, L.E., Senkoro, K.P., Gueye, D. and Mmbuji, P.K. (2007) Monitoring and evaluation of integrated disease surveillance and response in selected districts in Tanzania. *Tanzania Journal of Health Research* 9(1), 1–11. DOI: 10.4314/thrb.v9i1.14285.

Sangeda, R.Z., Gómes, P., Rhee, S.-Y., Mosha, F., Camacho, R.J. *et al.* (2021) Development of HIV drug resistance in a cohort of adults on first-line antiretroviral therapy in Tanzania during the Stavudine Era. *Microbiology Research* 12(4), 847–861. DOI: 10.3390/microbiolres12040062.

Saxena, S.K., Ansari, S., Maurya, V.K., Kumar, S., Jain, A. *et al.* (2023) Re-emerging human monkey-pox: a major public-health debacle. *Journal of Medical Virology* 95(1), e27902. DOI: 10.1002/jmv.27902.

Sue, K., Rosenberg, J. and Weintraub, R. (2016) *Addressing Tanzania's Health Workforce Crisis through a Public–Private Partnership: The Case of TTCIH*. Harvard Business Publishing, Cambridge, Massachusetts.

Thomas, S., Sagan, A., Larkin, J., Cylus, J., Figueras, J. *et al.* (2020) *Strengthening Health Systems Resilience: Key Concepts and Strategies*. European Observatory on Health Systems and Policies (European Observatory Policy Briefs), Copenhagen. Available at: http://www.ncbi.nlm.nih.gov/books/NBK559803/

Titmuss, R.M. (1964) *The Health Services of Tanganyika: A Report to the Government*. Pitman Medical Publishing Company, London.

URT (2014) *Human Resource for Health and Social Welfare Strategic Plan 2014–2019*. Ministry of Health and Social Welfare, Dar es Salaam, Tanzania.

van de Pas, R., Ashour, M., Kapilashrami, A. and Fustukian, S. (2017) Interrogating resilience in health systems development. *Health Policy and Planning* 32(suppl.3), iii88–iii90. DOI: 10.1093/heapol/czx110.

van Etten, G.M. and Raikes, A.M. (1975) Training for rural health in Tanzania. *Social Science & Medicine* 9(2), 87–92. DOI: 10.1016/0037-7856(75)90099-2.

Vaughan, J.P. and Walt, G. (1984) Implementing primary health care: some problems of creating national programmes. *Tropical Doctor* 14(3), 108–113. DOI: 10.1177/004947558401400304.

Wall, D.H., Nielsen, U.N. and Six, J. (2015) Soil biodiversity and human health. *Nature* 528(7580), 69–76. DOI: 10.1038/nature15744.

Wallis, J. and Rick Lee, D. (1999) Primate conservation: the prevention of disease transmission. *International Journal of Primatology* 20(6), 803–826. DOI: 10.1023/A:1020879700286.

Wellington, E.M.H., Boxall, A.B., Cross, P., Feil, E.J., Gaze, W.H. *et al.* (2013) The role of the natural environment in the emergence of antibiotic resistance in gram-negative bacteria. *The Lancet Infectious Diseases* 13(2), 155–165. DOI: 10.1016/S1473-3099(12)70317-1.

WHO (2021) *Building Health Systems Resilience for Universal Health Coverage and Health Security during the COVID-19 Pandemic and beyond: WHO Position Paper*. World Health Organization, Geneva, Switzerland.

WHO and UNICEF (2020) *Operational Framework for Primary Health Care: Transforming Vision into Action*. World Health Organization. Available at: https://apps.who.int/iris/handle/10665/337641 (accessed 18 May 2023).

Wiedenmayer, K., Mbwasi, R., Mfuko, W., Mpuya, E., Charles, J. *et al.* (2019) Jazia prime vendor system- a public-private partnership to improve medicine availability in Tanzania: from pilot to scale. *Journal of Pharmaceutical Policy and Practice* 12(1), 1–10. DOI: 10.1186/s40545-019-0163-4.

Wolfe, N.D., Dunavan, C.P. and Diamond, J. (2007) Origins of major human infectious diseases. *Nature* 447(7142), 279–283. DOI: 10.1038/nature05775.

Young, T.K. (1986) Socialist development and primary health care: the case of Tanzania. *Human Organization* 45(2), 128–134. DOI: 10.17730/humo.45.2.17p75666m4347g14.

Zinsstag, J., Crump, L., Schelling, E., Hattendorf, J., Maidane, Y.O. *et al.* (2018) Climate change and One Health. *FEMS Microbiology Letters* 365(11), fny085. DOI: 10.1093/femsle/fny085.

10 Beyond Health-System Building Blocks: Context and Determinants of Health

Rutasha Dadi[1]*, Albino Kalolo[2], Ntuli A. Kapologwe[3,4], Stephen M. Kibusi[4,5], Marcel Tanner[6,7] and Don de Savigny[6,7]

[1]Health Technical Specialist–FSSP, Tanzania; [2]Department of Public Health, St Francis University College of Health and Allied Sciences, Ifakara, Tanzania; [3]President's Office–Regional Administration and Local Government, Dodoma, Tanzania; [4]University of Dodoma, Tanzania; [5]School of Nursing and Public Health, University of Dodoma, Tanzania; [6]Swiss Tropical and Public Health Institute, Basel, Switzerland; [7]University of Basel, Switzerland

Abstract

The WHO health-system building block framework represents a construction that has been widely used to analyse health systems. While the framework has shown success and become a useful analytical tool, however, gaps exist in relation to critical elements and the dynamic interplay required to effectively implement some interventions. As countries move to universal health coverage, in particular through the primary health-care approach, more gains could be achieved if the framework addresses the context and determinants of health. This chapter, using the primary health-care context in Tanzania, suggests an expansion of the WHO health-system building blocks to recognize interventions targeting families and households, community resources and structures, social representations, societal partnerships, multisectoral actions and a wide spectrum of determinants of health.

10.0 Introduction

Since the introduction of the six health-system building blocks framework as the way of addressing the global health challenges systematically, there has been notable successes reported in different parts of the world hailing the invention (WHO, 2007; Shakarishvili *et al.*, 2011). There exist also other health system frameworks that have been put forward over time, which have not been widely adopted, but are often taken as an integral part of the operationalization of WHO health-system building blocks or reforming the health system (Shakarishvili *et al.*, 2011). While the six WHO building blocks have become a useful reference point and framework for national and global policy makers, however, gaps exist in relation to critical elements and the dynamic interplay required to implement some interventions effectively, for example, interventions targeting families and households, community resources and structures, social representations, societal partnerships and multisectoral actions to health (Mfutso-Bengo *et al.*,

*Corresponding author: drrutashadadi@gmail.com

 Primary Health Care in Tanzania through a Health Systems Lens (eds N.A. Kapologwe *et al.*)
DOI: 10.1079/9781800623330.0010

2017; Sacks *et al.*, 2019; Takian and Raoofi, 2021; Kalolo *et al.*, 2022). The fact that service delivery and the human workforce often rely on community resource persons (such as community health workers and community groups), strategies and availability of alternatives to health care (medical pluralism), emphasis and investment in community health systems and their complex structures are not clearly featured in the building blocks. Furthermore, community organizations, commercial bodies, societal partnerships and networks, efforts related to household production of health and information systems are often not seen as part of the health system (Sacks *et al.*, 2019). Therefore, a framework that goes 'beyond the building blocks' may be more meaningful as countries prioritize and invest resources in the stride forward to reaching universal health coverage. Embracing the systems-thinking approach (de Savigny and Adam, 2009; Adam and de Savigny, 2012) and taking health systems to a next level means investment beyond the WHO health-system building blocks framework so as to address the health-system challenges holistically in the direction of promoting health, maintaining health and sustaining the system to be resilient and responsive to shocks and adverse events, while putting people at all points in the system.

The fact that health services include specific activities undertaken by a health system to maintain or to improve health or to prevent the deterioration of health (Strasser, 2003; Kruk *et al.*, 2018) calls for rethinking how actions that are inherent to the communities and their structures affect service delivery and effectiveness of the activities. Health care is derived from the general process as part of the social and welfare system and not a narrow sense of illness care and disease interventions. It is therefore not possible to separate the nature of health care from the social, cultural and economic structures, or indeed the local community organization in which the system operates (Institute of Medicine (US) Committee on Health and Behavior: Research (2001); Wilson *et al.*, 2012; Alderwick *et al.*, 2021). Thus, the health-care system organization featured in Tanzania and elsewhere is beyond the modern biomedical system articulated by the WHO's framework consisting of the six building-block framework (WHO, 2007; de Savigny and Adam, 2009)

It is also important to note that the health system should look at the local community context by recognizing that health is both individually and collectively a local issue that requires local data and information to constantly create awareness in the community and its leaders on the unique challenges they face. Here we argue for the need to think beyond the six blocks by bringing in other left out but important aspects of the health system, including looking at aspects of the community and corresponding determinants of health, either as additional elements or two separate ideas for consideration.

Health systems always arise within a social, cultural, political and economic context as summarized in Fig. 10.1. As an integral component of social systems health systems are affected by various external forces such as global health initiatives and actions, commercial determinants, political determinants and socio-economic determinants and, when resourced well (problematic resourcing of PHC systems across settings), population health outcomes can be realized. As such there is worldwide diversity in size, scope and form of primary health-care (PHC) systems. Even if there are identifiable basic universal features of health systems that are similar and which are important for optimal PHC in a country, there will always be notable differences in the social-cultural and economic context and functioning of a health system. We use this framework for guiding discussion of this chapter.

10.1 The Tanzanian Primary Health-Care System in Perspective

Looking at the history of the struggle to strengthen the primary health-care system, this section uses a health system lens to shed light on the issues that are important (components) for the functioning of the health system but which are left behind or are less emphasized in the WHO health-system building blocks. These issues are categorized into: (i) contextual issues of the PHC system and (ii) determinants of health.

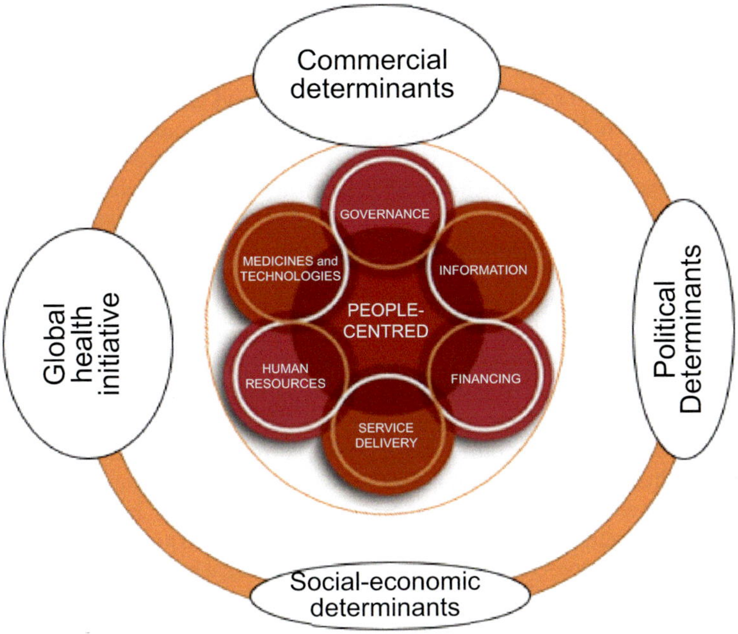

Fig. 10.1. Health systems beyond classical WHO health-system building blocks. (Adapted from de Savigny and Adam, 2009.)

10.1.1 Contextual issues of the PHC system

Overall, this section demonstrates why there is a need to think beyond the six building blocks, looking at how the Tanzania's PHC system has evolved over the years and demonstrating vividly how the current understanding fails to address local challenges as a result of a seemingly restricted definition of the concept of health system, which is confined to the only six building blocks. For example, failure to recognize the household and community as part of the building blocks has led to a lot of challenges in Tanzania's performance on prevention and health promotion to address non-communicable diseases (NCDs) and COVID-19 and to respond to and mount mitigation efforts for epidemics and other shocks. Omission of this component has seen resources for health-system strengthening and other related policy objectives only go to the listed building blocks at the expense of community health programming and household empowerment and health promotion. The key issues of focus here are: (i) health-care pluralism and (ii) community and societal partnerships.

Pluralistic health-care system in Tanzania

As in other countries, Tanzania's health-care system has been and is currently still characterized by the coexistence of different options when it comes to seeking care when one falls ill (Clyde, 1962; Görgen and Eckart, 2001). Care can be sought from conventional health-care facilities, alternative and traditional medical practices and religious healing. The existence of a variety of health-seeking behaviours and the use of a wide range of therapeutic sources, traditional and modern and static and evolving, is generally referred to as medical or health-care pluralism. Different authors have described the coexistence of health-care systems in different ways which might be applicable in Tanzanian context and beyond. For example, Helman has suggested three dimensions that describe the health-care system in any society as the popular, the folk or traditional and the modern professional health sector (Helman, 1994).

Each subsystem has its way of explaining and treating ill-health and of defining who a healer is and who a patient is, and as such the six building blocks described by WHO are more applicable to the modern biomedical health-system model and exclude an important aspect of health-care seeking behaviour in the local context. According to Helman, the popular system consists of the lay, non-professional and non-specialist domain of a society, where ill-health is first felt and recognized and health-care activities initiated. It includes all initiatives taken by family, self-medication or self-treatment, and friends' advice. With regard to alternative medicine, it includes traditional and alternative medicine practices other than indigenous or traditional health care, for example, yoga, Ayurveda, acupuncture, and Chinese traditional medicine practices, which are common nowadays. Its practitioners must undergo internationally recognized training and registration, relying exclusively on various established bodies of the respective alternative medicine or discipline.

Furthermore, unlike the modern health-system model, the folk or traditional healing subsystem is composed of heterogeneous groups of practitioners, with much variation in style and outlook. The voodoo practitioners, the healing ministries, the vendors of magical herbs, the spiritual healers who operate in the temples and in churches, they are all part of this category of health-care subsystem. Similarly, this category is associated with Christian miracle-based healing through the use of religious beliefs and magical practice (Webster, 2001). Different from modern health system workforce, who undergo a certain approved and accredited professional training process, traditional curers in folk/traditional health-care subsystems emerge through a culturally defined process of parental prodding, inheritance, visions, dream instructions and training.

The third category, according to Helman and Webster, is professional biomedicine, which comprises the organized and legally sanctioned healing of the professional, modern health-care system (Helman, 1994; Webster, 2001). Modern biomedicine health systems are characterized with formally linked health services, with a possibility of including formalized financing arrangements and health systems that are joined together to provide more coordinated and comprehensive health services.

In countries like China and India, strong indigenous systems of treatment enjoy almost the same legitimacy and popularity as modern systems, with the governments providing support for both of them to offer their citizens parallel systems of health care (Patwardhan *et al.*, 2005). In recognizing and promoting these parallel systems of health care of which traditional care is a major component, governments have also been supporting the training of medical practitioners from undergraduate to postgraduate levels to both indigenous and modern medicine. Table 10.1 shows major forms of traditional or indigenous health-care

Table 10.1. Summary of major global therapeutic systems.

Type	Characteristic
African traditional health system	Although each African community has its own medical system, disease aetiology and treatment, procedures tend to be similar.
Homeopathy	Homeopathy is a medical system based on the belief that the body can cure itself. It was developed in the 1700s in Germany and practised in Europe and elsewhere.
Yoga	Used in India and wherever Indian communities have settled.
Chinese	Used in mainland China and among the Chinese population elsewhere.
Ayurveda	Hindu medicine practised by the Indian population and immigrants elsewhere.
Unani	Arabic medicine – the practice of Eastern cultures, mostly now used in South India. The Unani system of medicine originated in Greece.

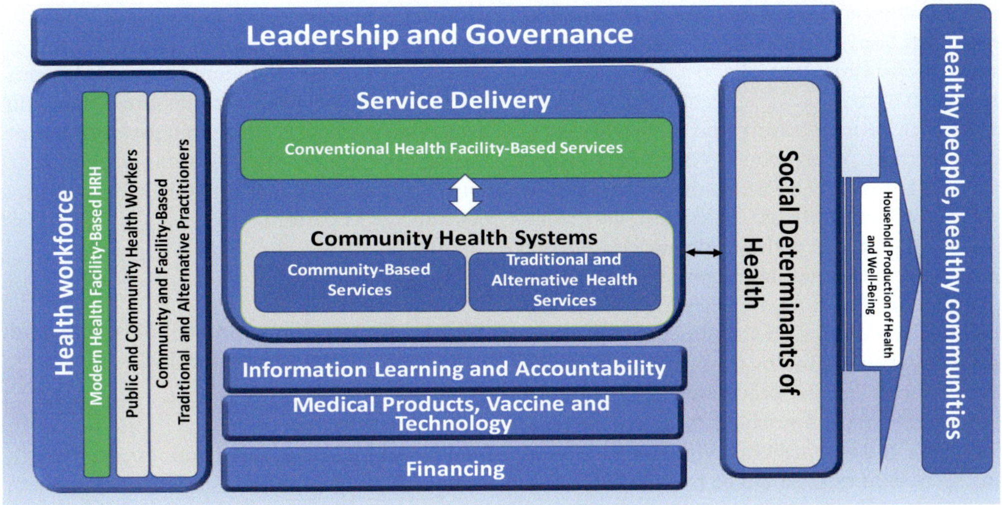

Fig. 10.2. Summary of pluralistic health system context in Tanzania.

systems globally, which most governments have been supporting.

Dadi (2012), in his work in Bagamoyo, Tanzania, found out that medical pluralism can be classified in four main forms: herbalists (*waganga wa miti shamba*); traditional diviners (*wapunga maruhani*); Koranic (*waganga wa kitabu*); Christian faith-healers (*wanamaombi*); and traditional birth attendants (*wakunga wa jadi*). The majority, seven (38%) used herbs, four (33%) used Islamic books, four (22%) cured by using exorcising spirits, and one used prayer. Of the seven who used herbs as their main method of curing, four, or over half, used only herbs; two used herbs and a Koran; and one used both herbs and divination. Of the six who used a Koran (*kitabu*) for treatment, three used a Koran alone, while two used the book along with herbs, and one used both a Koran and spirits. Of the four diviners, two used a combination of herbs and a Koran, and two performed divinations only. Similar categories were observed by a study in urban Dar es Salaam (Swantz, 1990; Gessler *et al.*, 1995; Obrist, 2006). Thus, this finding expresses in a nutshell that traditional health practitioners often combine more than one healing method. Table 10.1 summarizes the major global therapeutic systems.

Community and societal partnerships

Health-care pluralism in the context of Tanzania cannot be fully understood and operationalized with disregard of the community subsystems in which the health-care system operates. By definition, the community is a group of families, individuals and other types of networks and social circles that provide support and are often the units based on which health activities are organized and focused (MacQueen *et al.*, 2001). The importance of community in the provision of health care is centred on its nature as a platform where many services are provided at the community level, from familial provision of preventive or curative care in the household, to systematic clinical outreach from facilities. While most curative and specialized care should be provided in facility settings, many preventives, preliminary screening and basic treatments may be provided outside of formal facilities and, if this is not prioritized, poses the challenge to get data about the population that receives care in this model. Bringing these elements together, the PHC context framework is summarized in Fig. 10.2, with the grey areas representing areas of PHC which should be considered for mainstreaming.

At the community level, society organizations, partnerships and networks, household livelihood and neighbourhood production of health and protection are important parameters, but they have often been less reported as part of elements within the health system. The operation and implementation of most of the current building blocks, particularly service delivery and the health workforce approach, often rely on community-owned resource persons (CORPS), commonly known as community health workers, for community mobilization and strategies, without adequate investment in them or recognition at the policy level of their contribution. The human-centred approach and analysis should focus on the family and community level when examining the provision of health services, from familial provision of preventive or curative care in the household, to systematic clinical outreach from facilities. While most curative and specialized care should be provided in facility settings, many preventives, preliminary screening and basic treatments may be provided outside of formal facilities.

10.1.2 Social representation

There exist a multitude of definitions of social representation (Bauer and Gaskell, 1999; Stangor, 2004; Marková, 2012, 2017; Gautier, 2013). In this chapter, social representation is defined as 'a pattern of beliefs, values, norms, and practices that are shared by the member of a culture and that provide meaning for the culture' (Stangor, 2004). The context in Tanzania and other African settings is characterized by strong ties to social representation and some interventions could barely reach the communities if they are not designed in the way that social representations are taken onboard (Obrist, 2006; Winskell *et al.*, 2011; Kalolo *et al.*, 2022). Taking social representation as an important element when designing and implementing interventions is among the ways to optimize uptake of intervention by the beneficiary community.

10.2 Determinants of Health and PHC Systems

As detailed earlier on, health systems arise within social, cultural, political and economic contexts. Tanzania, like any other country, is undergoing triple transitions of an economic, demographic and epidemiological nature, presenting opportunities and challenges important for PHC evolution and struggle. Various determinants of health come into play and determine the health status and performance of the health system. Such determinants include social, commercial, political and environmental determinants of health.

10.2.1 Social determinants of health and PHC programming

Social determinants of health (SDH) influence health-seeking behaviours and the health outcomes of the population. Understanding them helps inform the design of sustainable interventions that take care of the interests of the population in question. SDH are non-medical factors that influence health outcomes. They are the conditions which we are born into, grow up in, live with and age with, and other forces and systems that shape the daily conditions of all people. SDH are driven by inequities and inequalities in the distribution of income and access to money and resources. Evidence shows that addressing SDH appropriately can be of more importance than a focus on health care or the lifestyle choices that influence one's health. For example, the WHO acknowledges that between 30 and 50% of gains in health outcomes of the population are attributable to SDH.

Programming approaches that include SDH, and in particular undertaking gender-equality measurements, are considered as appropriate efforts that bring a human-centred approach into programming, thus placing people at the centre of development in order to ensure the survival, thriving and flourishing of societies. The gender gap, gender-based analysis plus (GBA +), is often used when the aim is to programme PHC using a gender-based lens. GBA + is an analytical process used to assess how diverse groups of women and men may experience policies, programmes and initiatives (Hankivsky and Mussell, 2018). The 'plus' in GBA + acknowledges that GBA goes beyond biological (sex) and socio-cultural (gender) differences. All people have multiple identity factors that intersect to make them who they are; GBA + also considers many other identity factors such as race, ethnicity, religion, age, education, culture and income.

This analysis seeks to bring the human centred approach in PHC programming by putting population suffering and death at the centre of development planning to ensure the survival, thriving, and flourishing of women and girls.

In another work (Bishai *et al.*, 2016), evidence on declining maternal and child mortality revealed that, in aggregate, about 50% of the mortality reductions were attained from health-sector improvements and the other 50% gains were due to mortality reduction outside the health sector. These findings highlight the importance of promoting PHC in a more integrated manner across sectors and through a human-centred approach. SDH are driven by inequities and inequalities in the distribution of poor access to money and other resources. For example, early years experiences and exposure to education, poverty, work quality, housing and sanitation, and social classes and discriminations related to social position that affect peoples' lives are socially important determinants of health. SDH are one of the effective human-centred approaches with which to analyse, plan, and determine how PHC programming should be designed and how it responds to the needs of women's health and well-being beyond the traditional health systems blocks. Bringing these elements together, the SDH framework is summarized in Fig. 10.3, using information from the World Bank human development indexing.

Recent studies have linked social circumstances or socio-economic status to individual and population health (Rasanathan *et al.*, 2011; Braveman and Gottlieb, 2014; Wang and Geng, 2019; Kivimäki *et al.*, 2020). One's health status is proposed to be influenced by social circumstances through three pathways: behavioural, material and psychological (Matthews and Gallo, 2011; Braveman and Gottlieb, 2014). The social-economic status of an individual is presumed to influence behaviour. For instance, a behaviour often found in low-income individuals, such as smoking, directly influences one's health because it is a risk factor for lung cancer, asthma, emphysema and other respiratory diseases. Ongoing research is exploring the association of low economic status with other behaviours, such as drinking, risky sexual behaviour, drug use and violence.

Furthermore, material circumstances portrayed in Fig. 10.3 are the second pathway expressed by deprivation due to low income, represented by the inability to provide for basic needs such as food, shelter, and safety, result in malnutrition as well as exposure to community violence, lack of warm clothing, inadequate home heating or susceptibility to environmental exposures. These factors are considered to

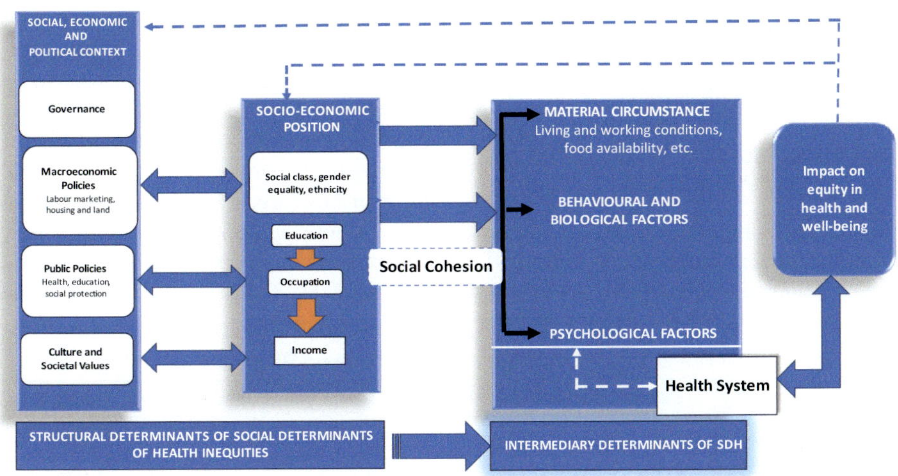

Fig. 10.3. Summarized SDH and health system in a wider social system. (Adapted from Solar and Irwin, 2010.)

influence the lower health status of the population and facilitate exposure to infectious diseases due to substandard housing and overcrowding, malnutrition, limited access to appropriate medical care and the risk of being a victim of violence.

The psychosocial pathway is considered more complex, and the psychobiological stress response is an essential link in this pathway of social structure to health. Extensive research established a connection between social structures, stress and biology. Stress can act as both a protective factor and a risk factor: when in survival mode, it is a protective factor, but, in contrast, prolonged exposure to stress can result in long-term health effects such as cardiovascular diseases, cancer, infection or cognitive decline. The psychological pathway is becoming common as we observe economic changes and rapid urbanization in developing countries.

The SDH approach embraces the key human development pillars of health, education, standard of living and good quality of work. The SDH approach has been used to look at the urban environment in a different context: the measurement of gender equality. Research shows that SDH can be more important in health programming than biomedical health-care interventions or lifestyle choices in influencing health. For example, various studies have shown that SDH account for between 30 and 55% of health outcomes (Rasanathan *et al.*, 2011; Braveman and Gottlieb, 2014). Furthermore, estimates show that the contribution of health to population health outcome exceeds the contribution from the health sector.

Human development and health outcomes, 1990–2019

The human development approach in programming has the explicit purpose of shifting the focus of development economics away from national income accounting towards people-centred policies. The basic tenet of the human development approach is the simple notion that people should be at the centre of development, and that development must enlarge people's choices and increase their well-being. Tackling health-related issues requires addressing other related challenges such as low educational attainment and poverty simultaneously, such as through human capital analysis. The World Bank measures human development through a simple comprehensive assessment of health-related elements of population longevity, education and income through a human development index (HDI) score (see Table 10.2). HDI is a summary measure that is used to assess long-term progress in life in three basic dimensions: a long and healthy life, access to knowledge and a decent standard of living (Roser, 2014). A long and healthy life is measured by life expectancy, while knowledge is measured by means of years of schooling among the adult population, which is the average number of years of schooling received in life by the age 25 and older and expected number of years of schooling for children of school entry age. The standard of living is measured by gross national income (GNI), as presented in Table 10.2.

A recent Tanzania Development Report from 2017, with data collected from the Tanzania Population and Housing Censuses (2012), showed that the average life expectancy of women is 63.7, higher than that of men at 59.7. Recently there has been a paradigm shift, with major improvements observable in healthy life expectancy in the rural population (62.6 in 2021, up from 49.4 in 2002), perhaps because of huge investment made in PHC which focused more on rural areas. Similarly, rural women and men live longer than their urban counterparts. However, when it comes to standard of living measured by GDP, females lag significantly

Table 10.2. Evolution of HDI in Tanzania 1990 to 2019. From: World Bank (2019).

Year	Life expectancy	Expected years of schooling	Mean years of schooling	GNI	HDI
1990	50.2	5.5	3.6	1343	0.368
2000	50.8	6.2	4.2	1396	0.390
2010	58.6	8.8	5.1	1972	0.481
2019	65.5	8.1	6.1	2600	0.529

behind their male counterparts, with regional variations. Data identifies regions such as Lindi, Njombe and Iringa as having the lowest gender disparities, whereas Singida, Tabora and Geita are the regions with the widest gender gaps in terms of education, health and standard of living.

Tanzania has been successful in increasing access to primary education, and more recently to secondary education, in a quest to achieve universal primary education. Education improves capabilities and is strongly associated with various socio-economic variables, such as lifestyle, income, health-seeking behaviour and fertility for both individuals and societies. However, the World Bank's Human Capital Index indicates that lack of access to education (especially for girls) is holding back Tanzania's development, with a human capital index of just 0.531, meaning Tanzanians are only reaching 53% of their potential (World Bank, 2019). Women who are less educated or not educated at all are the least likely to be consuming health services; see for example, the range of 0.75 in Kilimanjaro to a low of 0.44 in Kagera region. Specifically on education, Katavi region, with 30.4% of women with no education, has a teenage pregnancy rate of 45% and contraceptive prevalence rate of 18%, as compared to Kilimanjaro region, with only 2.3% of women with no education and 48% of women using modern contraceptives. This scenario calls for more investment in education for yielding better health outcomes.

When it comes to health outcomes and SDH and HDI, the same regions with the lowest levels of educational attainment and the highest basic poverty needs met have the highest total fertility rates (Simiyu 7.6, Geita 6.9, Tabora 6.9, Mara 6.4, Mwanza six in the Lake and West Zone), the highest basic needs poverty (Simiyu 39.2, Geita 37.5, Tabora 34.5, Mwanza 34.6), and the highest adolescent pregnancy rates (Katavi 45%, Tabora 43%, Dodoma 39%, Morogoro 39%, Shinyanga 34%) (as shown in Table 10.3). This analysis is in harmony with the gender-based analysis of multidimensional poverty in Tanzania which identifies Shinyanga, Tabora, Dodoma, Katavi, Mara, Kagera, Kigoma, Geita and Simiyu as regions with high-ranking inequality based on the 11 indicators, including poverty, gender-based violence, family planning use, female genital mutilation and HIV among women.

Gender equality and health outcomes

Gender equality is measured by the gender inequality index (GII). The GII is meant to measure across three dimensions of human development: reproductive health, empowerment and economic activities. Reproductive health is measured by maternal mortality and adolescent birth rates, while empowerment is measured by representation of women in Parliament and the relative percentages of men and women aged 25 years and above that have attained secondary education. Economic activities are measured by labour-market participation rate for women and men. Generally, Tanzania is doing well in closing gender gaps.

In Tanzania, women are more likely than men to experience lower opportunities of development because of existing inequalities, for example teenage pregnancy, in access to education, health services and economic opportunities. The recurrent theme emerging from the literature review and reinforced by the GBA + is that tackling issues such as high fertility and adolescent pregnancy require addressing other related challenges such as low educational attainment and poverty simultaneously.

Gender inequality and women's health outcomes

The GII mirrors how the health system is functioning and responding to women's health needs, aspirations and health outcomes. GII measures gender across the three aspects of reproductive health, empowerment and economic activity. While in GII reproductive health is measured by maternal mortality and adolescent birth rates/teenage pregnancy, empowerment is measured by the share of parliamentary seats held by women and the relative percentages of men and women aged 25 years and above that have reached secondary education. Economic activity is measured by the labour-market participation rate for women and men. The GII can be interpreted as the loss in human development due to inequalities in opportunities between women and men across the three GII dimensions. It entails women dying because of poorly organized health systems. A low

Table 10.3. Selected GII indicators as related to selected reproductive health (RH) Indicators.

Regions	GII 2017 World Bank	Maternal mortality rate 2012 census	Teenage pregnancy 2015 Demographic and Health Survey	Contraceptive prevalence rate 2015 Demographic and Health Survey
Kilimanjaro	0.75	283	6	48
Dar es Salaam	0.72	499	12	34
Arusha	0.70-	585	15	32
Iringa	0.70-	292	20	32
Njombe	0.67	788	20	45
Mbeya	0.66	776	33	45
Songwe	0.66	776	33	45
Ruvuma	0.66	365	32	51
Tanga	0.65	593	21	30
Mwanza	0.65	305	28	18
Manyara	0.63	376	33	28
Lindi	0.61	456	28	52
National	**0.61**	**432**	**27**	**33**
Mara	0.61	362	37	29
Morogoro	0.60	415	39	47
Mtwara	0.60	579	26	50
Simiyu	0.56	187	30	17
Geita	0.56	289	30	13
Pwani	0.53	687	30	39
Shinyanga	0.53	259	30	21
Katavi	0.52	670	45	18
Dodoma	0.48	512	39	41
Kigoma	0.47	248	32	18
Tabora	0.47	330	43	21
Singida	0.47	468	30	38
Kagera	0.44	391	15	39

GII value indicates low inequality between women and men, and vice-versa.

With respect to indicators on reproductive health, recent studies indicate the maternal mortality rate has declined due to improvements in PHC services, such as the expansion of PHC services, having delivery points closer to people with the capacity to offer comprehensive emergence and newborn care. However, the issue of safe surgery remains a challenge for these facilities. This could be the reason for the persistently high maternal mortality rate, which remains at 434 per 100,000 live births. While the number of women delivering at health facilities has increased from just over half of all women (50.2%) in the Tanzania Demographic Health Survey (TDHS) 2010 to two-thirds (63%) in the TDHS 2015/16, with an observable continued increasing trend from 65 to 72% during 2015–2017, followed by an acceleration in 2018 to 81% coverage. However, maternal mortality has remained high in Tanzania at 432 deaths per 100,000 live births in 2015. The maternal death rate is higher in urban areas (443 deaths per 100,000 live births) than in rural areas (336 deaths per 100,000 live births). It was also found that the maternal mortality rate for teenagers (15–19 years) was high (341 deaths per 100,000 live births). The millennium development goal by 2015 was to reach 133 maternal deaths per 100,000 live births. The observed level of maternal mortality from 2012 PHC none the less falls short of Tanzania's national target. The recent mid-term review of the Health Sector Strategic Plan IV and the review of the One Plan II show that maternal mortality and newborn deaths have stagnated, and that more mothers and new-borns die in health facilities where they go to seek care and expect to be saved (NBS (Tanzania) and ICF Macro, 2011; MOH, 2016). Tanzanian women and girls remain among the most marginalized and underutilized citizens in sub-Saharan Africa (Kabeer, 2005). In Tanzania there is a strong correlation between child marriage, pregnancy, HIV and school drop-out rates and poverty. Social and gender norms, such as early marriage and gender-based violence, are rooted in the community and in the socio-cultural beliefs and practices to which they adhere. They pose significant barriers to health and development, particularly for adolescent girls and young women. The synthesis of an ideology of male superiority and female inferiority continues to structure gender relationships and is still changing today as Tanzania is drawn into the global economy.

10.2.2 Commercial determinants of health

In 2013, Millar introduced the term 'corporate determinants of health' to refer to both the positive and negative influence that corporations have on population and global health, an idea further developed by other academics (Millar, 2013; Rochford *et al.*, 2019, 2021). The term became popular after 2016 when used by Kickbusch (2012) and defined commercial determinants of health (CDoH) as 'strategies and approaches used by the private sector to promote products and choices that are detrimental to health', entailing products and services provided by private entities to gain a financial profit, as well as market strategies, working conditions, production externalities and political activities, such as misinformation and lobbying donations to foster business to flourish. In other aspects, the private sector uses instrumental and conversational power to undermine public health policies that threaten profit gains (Allen, 2021; van Schalkwyk *et al.*, 2022). Concurrently, the corporate sector is an indispensable partner of most governments for development by, for example, building infrastructure and delivering health services or by ensuring food security through the fulfilment of corporate social responsibilities (Valente and Crane, 2010).

Through a human-centred lens, we take CDoH to be efforts and approaches employed by the private sector to promote choices to commodities that are harmful to health, including conditions, actions and omissions by corporate actors that affect health and well-being. Commercial determinants arise in the context of the provision of goods or services for payment and include commercial activities, as well as the environment in which commerce takes place. They can have beneficial or detrimental impacts on health. This concept embraces both macro- and micro-level influences on consumer behaviour and global and national political and business community.

Four major channels of corporate influence, as presented in Fig. 10.4, include: marketing strategies, which promote the desirability and acceptability of unhealthy products; lobbying, which entails influencing policy barriers, such as imposing a minimum age for drinking and smoking; corporate social responsibilities capable of deflecting attention and wiping out tarnished images and reputations; and an extensive supply chain, which intensifies company influence around the world. In Tanzania, the Global Adult Tobacco Survey (GAT) revealed that mass media play an important role for demand creation for tobacco products. However, tobacco advertising, promotion and sponsorship (TAPS) is prohibited in Tanzania by the Tobacco Act and its Regulation (2003). The health and economic impact on poor households increases their health risks and pushes them further into poverty. According to Tanzania's 2018 GAT, current cigarette smokers spend an average of TZS 28,840 per month.

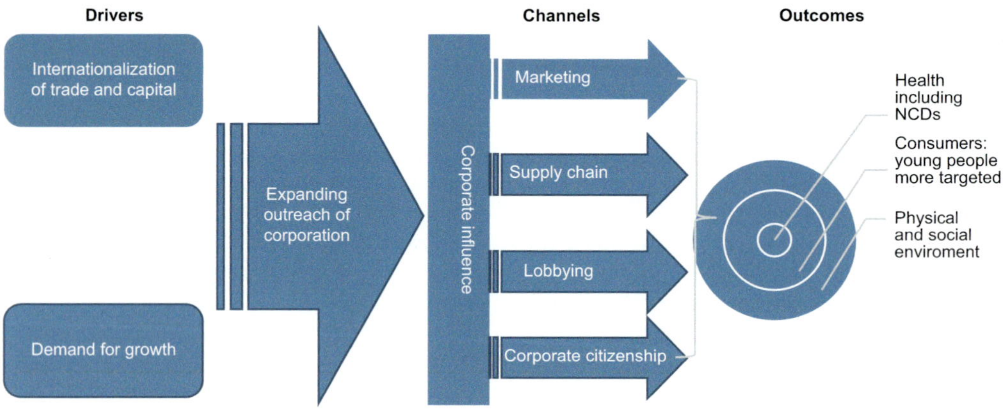

Fig. 10.4. Main drivers and channels which influence health outcome.

CDoH's economic and health outcomes

Commercial determinants of health are currently becoming a public health concern. Sales of processed and flavoured foods and drinks and the demand for tobacco and alcohol are booming, especially in developing low- and middle-income countries. Margaret Chan, former WHO director noted that the effort 'to prevent Non-Communicable Diseases (NCDs) has been against the corporate business profit'. Analysis of the impact of profit-driven harmful products and the power of the private sector, especially in the field of tobacco and alcohol and attention to other commodities, has been identified as a major driver and channel through which corporations propagate unhealthy practices and lifestyles. For example, it is estimated that one person dies from tobacco-related disease every 6 seconds, equivalent to 6 million people per year. Alarmingly, tobacco use is on the rise, having doubled in the last decades and having become more prevalent among young people and the poor. Overall, 14% of men and 3.2% of women currently use tobacco (smoking/or smokeless tobacco) (Bonnie *et al.*, 2015; West, 2017).

It is estimated that governments collect nearly US$270 billion in tobacco excise tax revenue each year. As such, tobacco has consistently been identified as an important source of new, sustainable funding for the health sector. In Tanzania, the Tanzania Cigarette Company (TCC), with over 95% of market share, contributed less than 1% of GDP 2015/16. Increasing tobacco taxation has proven to be one of the high-impact measures to reduce the consumption of tobacco products. It is a win–win policy for the government, where increasing taxes will both generate more revenue, cutting consumption by 2 to 8%. In low-income countries a doubling of cigarette excise tax increases cigarette tax by more than 30%.

Availability of data on corporate practices and influence on health and well-being is one of the worldwide major issues in quantifying these channels, which are important for public health analysis. For example, there is a paucity of information on how global commercial systems and the broader political economy shapes the inequalities. These corporate systems have a profound influence over population health and the social context. It is widely acknowledged that corporate social responsibility, for example, plays an important role in building customer loyalty, based on distinguished values, enhancing brand image and increasing sales (which eventually contributes to profits). Many of the promotion messages are targeted at the youth population. For example, seven students were supported with full sponsorship to pursue a diploma at Bagamoyo College of Arts, and 1520 assistive devices were given to people with disabilities.

Globally, alcohol misuse has been associated with over 3.3 million deaths annually and it contributes over 5.9% of the overall global burden of diseases and injuries. Some alcohol-attributable disability-adjusted life years (DALYs) lost result from injuries and

45% attributable deaths are due to violence. The 2018 World Health Organization alcohol-use status report revealed that, of all deaths attributable to alcohol consumption worldwide, 28.7% were due to injuries, 21.3% were due to digestive problems, 19% were due to cardiovascular diseases, 12.9% were due to infectious diseases and 12.6% were due to cancers (Lim *et al.*, 2012). About 49% of DALYs are due to NCDs. Liver cirrhosis, road traffic accidents and cancers are major health problems attributable to alcohol in Tanzania.

As more of the effects of commercial and corporate influences on population health are being identified and recognized in the developed world, information emerging from this field of public health has yet to be comprehensively integrated within CDoH framing in low-income developing countries. PHC literature lacks definition and is not well-articulated nor communicated, with analyses often narrowly formulated around specific interventions, especially for young people, and it is yet to be included systematically within public health policy frameworks and interventions. Together, these represent 'an elephant in the room': the increasingly obvious but often ignored problem of the profound influence of commercial and corporate influences on human and planetary health. In their paper, de Lacy-Vawdon *et al.* (2022) urge that there is also limited research on the activities of industries other than the food, alcohol and tobacco industries. The discussion on CDoH offers a unique opportunity to shift the dominant paradigm in public health, where individual behaviours are considered to be driven by inadequate environments. Ill health, damage to the environment and health and social inequalities could rather be understood as shaped by CDoH.

WHO response

The WHO addresses the wider economic factors impacting on health and health equity through the WHO workstreams on trade and health, as well as health and development. It also promotes the use of fiscal instruments, including taxation policies, to invest in and improve health outcomes. Private sector engagement is also addressed through different streams of work, including through the Advisory Group on the Governance of the Private Sector for Universal Health Coverage, as well as through programmatic and treaty approaches, such as WHO Framework Convention on Tobacco Control.

The WHO has initiated a new programme of action, the Economic and Commercial Determinants of Health, which has four goals: to strengthen the evidence base; to develop tools and capacity to address the commercial determinants; to convene partnerships and dialogue; and to raise awareness and advocacy.

Key facts

- Commercial determinants of health (CDoH) are the private-sector activities that affect people's health positively or negatively.
- The private sector influences social, physical and cultural environments through business actions and societal engagements; for example, supply chains, labour conditions, product design and packaging, research funding, lobbying, preference shaping and others.
- Commercial determinants of health impact a wide range of health outcomes, including obesity, diabetes, cardiovascular health, cancer, road traffic injuries, mental health and malaria.
- Commercial determinants of health affect everyone, but young people are especially at risk, and unhealthy commodities worsen pre-existing economic, social and racial inequities. Certain countries and regions, such as small island states and low- and middle-income countries, face greater pressure from multinational actors.
- There are effective public health actions to respond to these determinants, which are key to building back better after COVID-19.

10.2.3 Global health initiatives and the role of donors and global health actors

The sustainable development goals (SDGs) represent policy areas in the three dimensions of economy, environment and society, and together create an intersectoral vision for improvements in human and planetary health, peace, partnership and prosperity. It was acknowledged by the heads of states that health is a pre-requisite condition for positive outcomes and an indicator of the social, economic and environmental dimensions of sustainable development and of the implementation of the 2030 Agenda for Sustainable Development Goals. They recognized that PHC brings people into first contact with health systems and is a more inclusive, effective and efficient way of achieving universal health coverage and health-related SDGs, as declared in the Alma-Ata Declaration (1978) and reaffirmed in the Astana Declaration (2018).

As such, sustainable development goal 3, on the health of people, 'ensuring healthy lives and promoting well-being for all at all ages' can only be achieved if other actions are realized. The SDGs list many actions on determinants of health, highlighting reductions of within country inequalities in health determinants as a key priority, calling for an intersectoral vision of health. This includes supporting services as well as actions in the SDGs for universal health coverage as important for good population health and health equity. The first target of SDG (3.1) is on reducing maternal mortality ratio to less than 70 per 100,000 live births, providing universal access to sexual reproductive health and universal health coverage, including financial risk protection and access to quality health services, especially among poor and vulnerable communities. According to recent DHS 2015/16, Tanzania's maternal mortality rate is 456 per 100,000 live births. There are promising signs of a decline in the maternal death rate, although it is still unacceptably high. However, no woman should die before, during or after giving birth. Maternal health is one of the key indicators which can be used to measure the equity and gender equality of any given society.

In terms of SDG 5 (achieving gender equality and empowering all women and girls), including universal access to sexual and reproductive health and the elimination of all forms harmful practices and early forced marriage, over the period 2000–2010 Tanzania made some progress, including the creation of an enabling policy and a legal environment for the promotion of gender equality in the country. This has led to the ratification of key international and regional policy instruments such as CEDAW and the SADC Protocol on Gender Equality, the incorporation of progressive clauses for women's rights in the country's Constitution that has facilitated the improved representation of women's voices in Parliament and local government councils, the enhancement of progressive laws such as the Sexual Offences Special Provision Act (SOSPA) of 1998, and the development of the National Women and Gender Policy (2000) and the National Strategy for Gender Equality (2005).

Regarding the other aspect, the country's polices have underscored inclusive population development for sustainable development. Most official policy during the first decade of independence echoed Nyerere's perception of human development, which shows that Tanzania has long-defined national development in a manner consistent with the human development approach currently championed by UNDP. In 1967, Tanzania adopted the Arusha Declaration, which pronounced socialism and self-reliance as the guiding principles of the country's social and economic development. The declaration acknowledged the primacy of people-centred development, and the importance of enhancing human capabilities in promoting social and economic development.

10.2.4 Political effects on health in national public policies

Health is a political choice, and politics is a continuous struggle for power among competing interests. The political determinants of health involve the systematic process of structuring relationships, distributing resources and administrating the power over structuring relationships, operating simultaneously in a way such that they mutually reinforce or influence one another to shape opportunities that either advance health equity or exacerbate health inequities (Kickbusch, 2015; Dawes, 2020). Looking at health through the lens of political determinants means analysing how different power constellations, institutions, processes, interests and ideological positions affect health within different political systems and cultures and at different levels of governance, and it also involves looking into how the ruling party manifesto is implemented and how the balance between the technocrats or the executive branch and the politicians affects implementations of

Fig. 10.5. Political influence on health-systems policies, programmes and health outcomes.

health interventions (see Fig. 10.5). Bambra *et al.* (2010) provide three arguments why health is political: health is unevenly distributed, many health determinants are dependent on political action and health is a critical dimension of human rights and citizenship.

Helman (1994) asserts that different types of societies, depending on their dominant ideology, produce different types of medical systems, and different attitudes to health and illness. These dominant ideologies can be grouped into cultural ideology, political ideology and economic ideology.

The dominant political ideology concerns whether a country pursues a capitalist, socialist or mixed political economy, which subsequently produce different types of medical systems. On ideology that is driven by politics, generally there are three major types of dominant ideologies: capitalist, socialist or communist and mixed. The political dimension involving opinions framed in ideological and in programmatic terms impact on how different medical systems should exist in a certain place or country. As such, if the dominant political ideology is capitalistic, the prevailing kind of health-care system will be dominated by private sector, out-of-pocket and various kinds of pre-payment schemes, generally referred to as health insurances, and other social-security mechanisms. In the case of the socialist dominant political ideology, the government takes care of health-care costs. From a dominant political perspective and its relation with health-seeking behaviour, one society may see free health care or giving a waiver and exemption to the underprivileged and most vulnerable groups as a basic citizens' right. Mixed ideologies will create mixed health-care systems, in that two or more different types of therapeutic options may exist. These include both free forms of treatment and out-of-pocket modes. In countries with market-led political economies the health-care system is dominated by the private sector, unlike socialist public-led economies in which public sector is the main health-care provider.

In brief, just as in the spheres of economy and politics, an existing health-care system will be initiated or changed based on the fusion of political and social as well as economic conditions prevalent in a given country, according to one German philosopher and political theorist, human identity and idea activations are produced by the material economics and social conditions in which they exist. We further argue that the ultimate moving force of human history (and thus a health-care system) is economics or in a broader term, political economy.

In view of this, Tanzania, like many other countries, adopted different political and economic ideologies in different historical periods. Thus, the health-care system in Tanzania can be summarized in three historical epochs, during which the changing political and economic ideologies of the country have been experienced: the colonial – capitalistic; the post-independence – socialistic under Arusha Declaration; and the contemporary mixed political economy of today. Under this system, while free services are provided for maternal health, for people living with HIV/AIDS (PLWHs) and for other chronic illnesses, cost-sharing prevails for other health conditions. Waiver and exemptions policies are mechanisms that have been put in place for the execution of pro-poor free services policy. This scenario implies that although health-services provision in Tanzania is market-oriented, PLWHs access free biomedicine services under the exemption system, thus allowing them to make choices without restrictions. However, traditional medicine also remains a major feature provided under mixed charity and market-led practice.

Globally, as well as in Tanzania, there is an increasing interest in advocating for advancing universal health coverage (UHC), which calls for all nations to provide quality health-care services to all citizens without facing financial difficulties. Tanzania envisioned to ensure her citizens had access to quality services through introducing and implementing the Community Health Fund (CHF) Act of 2001 with all its amendments and an ongoing health-sector reform. Although the government has been implementing CHF for more than 20 years, the implementation and uptake of the scheme has been persistently low (Kamuzora and Gilson, 2007; Stoermer *et al.*, 2011; Kalolo *et al.*, 2017). In response to these challenges, a new, improved community health fund was established in 2018 with a marked improvement in enrolment rate. Further analysis indicates regional variations; enrolment has increased more steadily in regions that were supported by the first and second phases of the HPSS project (Kalolo *et al.*, 2021; SDC, 2022).

10.2.5 Environmental determinants of health and PHC

Despite its importance to sustainable development, very little information exists on environmental health-system context linkages. Being multisectoral, it escaped focused attention during project design. SDG target 3.9 underscores links to SDG 2, improved nutrition and sustainable agriculture. SDG 6, 'clean water and sanitation for all', and SDG11, 'make cities and human settlements inclusive, safe, resilient and sustainable', support monitoring of environment/health dimensions with a focus on linking urban health with urban equity dimensions and, if implemented appropriately with a system approach within an expanded health system, these building blocks could make a substantial impact on preventing deaths and illnesses from hazardous chemicals and air, water and soil pollution and contamination. These targets can only be achieved through joint action in other goals. Social determinants of health and environmental conditions predispose people to certain conditions, influence the effects of services and household efforts towards health, affect overall well-being and nutrition and directly determine ability to reach and optimally utilize health facilities. Environmental determinants include housing and community design, the built environment, the natural environment (green space and climate) and access to clean water. Individuals can be at higher risk for poor health outcomes due to 'compounded disadvantage' across multiple social determinants of health. This further limits access to health prevention, promotion and curative services.

Achieving ambitious global goals, such as the sustainable development goals, requires attention to social determinants of health. Health systems need to appropriately gauge these determinants' effects on community health at the local level, and to tailor health interventions to correct for social exclusion and prevalent negative social determinants. Beyond health interventions, multisectoral approaches (e.g. food security, access to clean water, improved sanitation) will be required to extend services to the hardest to reach, addressing the underlying causes of poor health, and implementing effective and sustainable health interventions. Three types of determinants: community, social and environment are critical, although not comprehensive, pathways for achieving health in communities. While not under the exclusive mandate of health-care services delivery systems, they are under the horizon of public health systems programmers, and policy makers need to intentionally develop the elements to address services, household production and social determinants as part of the community health equation asserted by the recent World Bank assessment on environment and health dimensions.

10.3 Summary and Policy Implications

The WHO building-blocks framework has become a useful reference point for national and global health policy making. This framework, however, has insufficiently addressed critical elements and the dynamic interplay required to implement and produce health outcomes effectively. Critical elements that have been insufficiently represented and are important in producing health outcomes include: the role of families and households in the production of health, community health systems (resources, structures, and initiatives), social representations and medical pluralism, determinants of health, societal partnerships and multisectoral actions to health. The critical components left behind have been analysed and their role in influencing health outcomes has been demonstrated in this chapter, and also by existing literature such as that by Sacks *et al.* (2019) and Mfutso-Bengo *et al.* (2017). Using evidence generated from this chapter, we support an expansion of the WHO building-block framework, showing dynamism between health-system components, and explicit community health needs and determinants of health, which central policy makers should proactively address and resource in order to institutionalize the wider health system.

A framework which goes 'beyond the building blocks' may be useful for national and subnational levels to recognize, prioritize and invest resources in aspects of the health system that promote equity and equality in efforts to improve access to health care, equity, quality of services and health outcomes, hence reaching universal health coverage.

Bibliography

Adam, T. and de Savigny, D. (2012) Systems thinking for strengthening health systems in LMICs: need for a paradigm shift. *Health Policy and Planning* 27(suppl 4), iv1–iv3. DOI: 10.1093/heapol/czs084.

Alderwick, H., Hutchings, A., Briggs, A. and Mays, N. (2021) The impacts of collaboration between local health care and non-health care organizations and factors shaping how they work: a systematic review of reviews. *BMC Public Health* 21(1), 753. DOI: 10.1186/s12889-021-10630-1.

Allen, L.N. (2021) Commercial determinants of global health. In: Haring, R., Kickbusch, I., Ganten, D. and Moeti, M. (eds) *Handbook of Global Health*. Springer, Cham, Switzerland, pp. 1275–1310. DOI: 10.1007/978-3-030-45009-0.

Bambra, C., Gibson, M., Sowden, A., Wright, K., Whitehead, M. *et al.* (2010) Tackling the wider social determinants of health and health inequalities: evidence from systematic reviews. *Journal of Epidemiology & Community Health* 64(4), 284–291. DOI: 10.1136/jech.2008.082743.

Bauer, M.W. and Gaskell, G. (1999) Towards a paradigm for research on social representations. *Journal for the Theory of Social Behaviour* 29(2), 163–186. DOI: 10.1111/1468-5914.00096.

Bishai, D.M., Cohen, R., Alfonso, Y.N., Adam, T., Kuruvilla, S. *et al.* (2016) Factors contributing to maternal and child mortality reductions in 146 low- and middle-income countries between 1990 and 2010. *PloS One* 11(1), e0144908. DOI: 10.1371/journal.pone.0144908.

Bonnie, R.J., Stratton, K. and Kwan, L.Y. (2015) *The Effects of Tobacco Use on Health, Public HealthImplications of Raising the Minimum Age of Legal Access to Tobacco Products*. National Academies Press (US), Washington, D.C. DOI: 10.17226/18997.

Braveman, P. and Gottlieb, L. (2014) The social determinants of health: it's time to consider the causes of the causes. *Public Health Reports* 129(Suppl 2), 19–31. DOI: 10.1177/00333549141291S206.

Clyde, D.F. (1962) *History of the Medical Services of Tanganyika*. Government Press, Dar es Salaam, Tanzania.
Dadi, R. (2012) *Seeking health under pluralistic medical system: determinants of resort patterns among people living HIV in Bagamoyo, Tanzania*. PhD thesis, Mzumbe University, Mzumbe, Tanzania.
Dawes, D.E. (2020) *The Political Determinants of Health*. Johns Hopkins University Press, Baltimore, Maryland. DOI: 10.56021/9781421437903.
de Lacy-Vawdon, C., Vandenberg, B. and Livingstone, C.H. (2022) Recognising the elephant in the room: the commercial determinants of health. *BMJ Global Health* 7(2), e007156. DOI: 10.1136/bmjgh-2021-007156.
de Savigny, D. and Adam, T. (2009) *Systems Thinking for Health Systems Strengthening*. World Health Organization, Geneva, Switzerland.
Gautier, L. (2013) Understanding the impact of social representations in health microinsurance schemes: a preliminary theoretical framework to guide empirical research. *International Journal of Behavioural and Healthcare Research* 4(3/4), 358–368. DOI: 10.1504/IJBHR.2013.058853.
Gessler, M.C., Msuya, D.E., Nkunya, M.H.H., Mwasumbi, L.B., Schär, A. *et al.* (1995) Traditional healers in Tanzania: the treatment of malaria with plant remedies. *Journal of Ethnopharmacology* 48(3), 131–144. DOI: 10.1016/0378-8741(95)01293-M.
Görgen, H. and Eckart, W.U. (2001) *The History of Health Care in Tanzania*. GTZ, Dar es Salaam, Tanzania.
Hankivsky, O. and Mussell, L. (2018) Gender-based analysis plus in Canada: problems and possibilities of integrating intersectionality. *Canadian Public Policy* 44(4), 303–316. DOI: 10.3138/cpp.2017-058.
Helman, C.G. (1994) *Culture, Health and Illness: An Introduction for Health Professionals*, 3rd edn. Butterworth Heinemann, Oxford, UK.
Institute of Medicine (US) Committee on Health and Behavior: Research (2001) *Organisations, Communities, and Society: Models and Interventions, Health and Behavior: The Interplay of Biological, Behavioral, and Societal Influences*. National Academies Press (US), Washington, DC.
Kabeer, N. (2005) Gender equality and women's empowerment: a critical analysis of the third millennium development goal 1. *Gender & Development* 13(1), 13–24. DOI: 10.1080/13552070512331332273.
Kalolo, A., Gautier, L. and De Allegri, M. (2022) Exploring the role of social representations in micro-health insurance scheme enrolment and retainment in sub-Saharan Africa: a scoping review. *Health Policy and Planning* 37(7), 915–927. DOI: 10.1093/heapol/czac036.
Kalolo, A., Gautier, L., Radermacher, R., Srivastava, S., Meshack, M. *et al.* (2021) Factors influencing variation in implementation outcomes of the redesigned community health fund in the Dodoma region of Tanzania: a mixed-methods study. *BMC Public Health* 21(1), 1. DOI: 10.1186/s12889-020-10013-y.
Kalolo, A., Gautier, L., Radermacher, R., Stoermer, M., Jahn, A. *et al.* (2017) Implementation of the redesigned community health fund in the Dodoma region of Tanzania: a qualitative study of views from rural communities. *The International Journal of Health Planning and Management* 33(1), 121–135. DOI: 10.1002/hpm.2403.
Kamuzora, P. and Gilson, L. (2007) Factors influencing implementation of the Community Health Fund in Tanzania. *Health Policy and Planning* 22(2), 95–102. DOI: 10.1093/heapol/czm001.
Kickbusch, I. (2012) 21st century determinants of health and wellbeing: a new challenge for health promotion. *Global Health Promotion* 19(3), 5–7. DOI: 10.1177/1757975912454783.
Kickbusch, I. (2015) The political determinants of health: 10 years on. *BMJ* 350, h81. DOI: 10.1136/bmj.h81.
Kivimäki, M., Batty, G.D., Pentti, J., Shipley, M.J., Sipilä, P.N. *et al.* (2020) Association between socioeconomic status and the development of mental and physical health conditions in adulthood: a multicohort study. *The Lancet Public Health* 5(3), e140–e149. DOI: 10.1016/S2468-2667(19)30248-8.
Kruk, M.E., Gage, A.D., Arsenault, C., Jordan, K., Leslie, H.H. *et al.* (2018) High-quality health systems in the sustainable development goals era: time for a revolution. *The Lancet Global Health* 6(11), e1196–e1252. DOI: 10.1016/S2214-109X(18)30386-3.
Lim, S.S., Vos, T., Flaxman, A.D., Danaei, G., Shibuya, K. *et al.* (2012) A comparative risk assessment of burden of disease and injury attributable to 67 risk factors and risk factor clusters in 21 regions, 1990–2010: a systematic analysis for the Global Burden of Disease Study 2010. *The Lancet* 380(9859), 2224–2260. DOI: 10.1016/S0140-6736(12)61766-8.
MacQueen, K.M., McLellan, E., Metzger, D.S., Kegeles, S., Strauss, R.P. *et al.* (2001) What is community? An evidence-based definition for participatory public health. *American Journal of Public Health* 91(12), 1929–1938. DOI: 10.2105/ajph.91.12.1929.

Marková, I. (2012) Social representations as anthropology of culture. In: Valsiner, J. (ed.) *Oxford Handbook of Culture and Psychology*. Oxford University Press, Oxford, UK, pp. 487–509.

Marková, I. (2017) The making of the theory of social representations. *Cadernos de pesquisa* 47, 358–375.

Matthews, K.A. and Gallo, L.C. (2011) Psychological perspectives on pathways linking socioeconomic status and physical health. *Annual Review of Psychology* 62, 501–530. DOI: 10.1146/annurev.psych.031809.130711.

Mfutso-Bengo, J., Kalanga, N. and Mfutso-Bengo, E.M. (2017) Proposing the LEGS framework to complement the WHO building blocks for strengthening health systems: one needs a LEG to run an ethical, resilient system for implementing health rights. *Malawi Medical Journal* 29(4), 317–321. DOI: 10.4314/mmj.v29i4.7.

Millar, J.S. (2013) The corporate determinants of health: how big business affects our health, and the need for government action! *Canadian Journal of Public Health* 104(4), e327–e329. DOI: 10.17269/cjph.104.3849.

MOH (2016) *Tanzania Demographic and Health Survey and Malaria Indicator Survey 2015–2016*. Ministry of Health, Dar es Salaam, Tanzania, and Rockville, Maryland.

NBS (Tanzania) and ICF Macro (2011) *Tanzania Demographic and Health Survey 2010*. NBS and ICF Macro, Dar es Salaam, Tanzania.

Obrist, B. (2006) *Struggling for Health in the City: An Anthropological Inquiry of Health Vulnerability and Resilience in Dar es Salaam, Tanzania*. Peter Lang, Bern.

Patwardhan, B., Warude, D., Pushpangadan, P. and Bhatt, N. (2005) Ayurveda and traditional Chinese medicine: a comparative overview. *Evidence-Based Complementary and Alternative Medicine* 2(4), 465–473. DOI: 10.1093/ecam/neh140.

Rasanathan, K., Montesinos, E.V., Matheson, D., Etienne, C. and Evans, T. (2011) Primary health care and the social determinants of health: essential and complementary approaches for reducing inequities in health. *Journal of Epidemiology and Community Health* 65(8), 656–660. DOI: 10.1136/jech.2009.093914.

Rochford, S., Dodd, P. and Austin, C. (2021) The public health approach to suicide prevention in Ireland. *Irish Journal of Psychological Medicine* 40(1), 97–102. DOI: 10.1017/ipm.2021.72.

Rochford, C., Tenneti, N. and Moodie, R. (2019) Reframing the impact of business on health: the interface of corporate, commercial, political and social determinants of health. *BMJ Global Health* 4(4), e001510. DOI: 10.1136/bmjgh-2019-001510.

Roser, M. (2014) Human development index (HDI). Our World Data.

Sacks, E., Morrow, M., Story, W.T., Shelley, K.D., Shanklin, D. *et al*. (2019) Beyond the building blocks: integrating community roles into health systems frameworks to achieve health for all. *BMJ Global Health* 3(Suppl 3), e001384. DOI: 10.1136/bmjgh-2018-001384.

SDC (2022) Country evaluation.

Shakarishvili, G., Lansang, M.A., Mitta, V., Bornemisza, O., Blakley, M. *et al*. (2011) Health systems strengthening: a common classification and framework for investment analysis. *Health Policy and Planning* 26(4), 316–326. DOI: 10.1093/heapol/czq053.

Solar, O. and Irwin, A. (2010) *A Conceptual Framework for Action on the Social Determinants of Health*. World Health Organization, Geneva, Switzerland.

Stangor, C. (2004) *Social Groups in Action and Interaction*. Psychology Press, New York.

Stoermer, M., Radermacher, R. and Vanderhyden, M. (2011) Transforming community health funds in Tanzania into viable social health insurance schemes: the challenges ahead. *Bulletin/Medicus Mundi Schweiz* 120, 22–28.

Strasser, R. (2003) Rural health around the world: challenges and solutions. *Family Practice* 20(4), 457–463. DOI: 10.1093/fampra/cmg422.

Swantz, L.W. (1990) *The Medicine Man among the Zaramo of Dar es Salaam*. Nordic Africa Institute, Dar es Salaam, Tanzania.

Takian, A. and Raoofi, A. (2021) We must redesign the WHO's building blocks to create more resilient health systems for the future. *The BMJ Opinion*. Available at: https://blogs.bmj.com/bmj/2021/04/14/we-must-redesign-the-whos-building-blocks-to-create-more-resilient-health-systems-for-the-futur (accessed 1 May 2023).

Valente, M. and Crane, A. (2010) Public responsibility and private enterprise in developing countries. *California Management Review* 52(3), 52–78. DOI: 10.1525/cmr.2010.52.3.52.

van Schalkwyk, M.C., Maani, N. and McKee, M. (2022) The commercial determinants of health. In: McKee, M. and Krentel, A. (eds) *Issues Public Health Challenge*. Open University Press/McGraw Hill, London, pp. 90–110.
Wang, J. and Geng, L. (2019) Effects of socioeconomic status on physical and psychological health: lifestyle as a mediator. *International Journal of Environmental Research and Public Health* 16(2), 281. DOI: 10.3390/ijerph16020281.
Webster, C. (2001) *Caring for Health: History and Diversity*. Open University Press, Milton Keynes, UK.
West, R. (2017) Tobacco smoking: health impact, prevalence, correlates and interventions. *Psychology & Health* 32(8), 1018–1036. DOI: 10.1080/08870446.2017.1325890.
WHO (2007) *Everybody's Business – Strengthening Health Systems to Improve Health Outcomes: WHO's Framework for Action*. World Health Organization, Geneva, Switzerland.
Wilson, M.G., Lavis, J.N. and Guta, A. (2012) Community-based organizations in the health sector: a scoping review. *Health Research Policy and Systems* 10, 36. DOI: 10.1186/1478-4505-10-36.
Winskell, K., Hill, E. and Obyerodhyambo, O. (2011) Comparing HIV-related symbolic stigma in six African countries: social representations in young people's narratives. *Social Science and Medicine* 73, 1257–1265.
World Bank (2019) *Tanzania Economic Update, July 2019: Human Capital –The Real Wealth of Nations*. World Bank, Washington, DC.

11 Looking to the Future of Primary Health Care in Tanzania

James Tumaini Kengia[1,2]*, Albino Kalolo[3], Eric van Praag[4], Don de Savigny[5,6], Marcel Tanner[5,6], Japhet Killewo[7] and Ntuli A. Kapologwe[1]
[1]President's Office - Regional Administration and Local Government, Dodoma, Tanzania; [2]University of Dodoma, Tanzania; [3]Department of Public Health, St Francis University College of Health and Allied Sciences, Ifakara, Tanzania; [4]Independent Consultant, Dar es Salaam, Tanzania; [5]Swiss Tropical and Public Health Institute, Allschwil, Switzerland; [6]University of Basel, Basel, Switzerland; [7]School of Public Health, Muhimbili University of Health and Allied Sciences, Dar es Salaam, Tanzania

Abstract
Primary health care (PHC) is key to achieving universal health coverage and sustainable development goals. Tanzania, as a pioneer of PHC among other countries, has made substantial progress in fulfilling its population health needs despite many obstacles encountered during its implementation. Addressing unfinished agenda and implementation of regional and global level agreements and treaties geared towards making PHC strong, enduring and responsive is critical for the future of PHC in Tanzania. A call for action for strengthening promotive, preventive services, quality of health care, real data use for decision making, prepayment health insurance schemes, integration of services, intersectoral collaboration, people-centred care, emphasis on individuals' well-being and the decentralization of screening services at the PHC level for early detection and treatment is inevitable while strengthening the evidence-informed policies that will make health systems resilient. Moreover, dedicated efforts are needed to address severe shortages of health-care workers at lower-level facilities, as well as geographical disparities between regions and pronounced urban–rural maldistributions.

11.0 Introduction

Primary health care (PHC) is key to achieving universal health coverage and sustainable development goals. Therefore, it is essential that PHC should always be seen as an investment and not as a cost. To make this happen in Tanzania, stakeholders recommend prioritizing primary health care as a three-for-one investment in universal health coverage, health security and better health and wellbeing for all (Allies for Improving PHC, 2022). Taking PHC to the next level means committing more resources to PHC while also prioritizing health promotion and disease prevention, in addition to curative services. Existing evidence attests to the fact that PHC can contribute to UHC if there is a deliberate effort to increase PHC expenditure (Arhin *et al.*, 2022). The current PHC system in Tanzania cannot achieve this, as per sustainable development goal 3 (SDG3) because it still primarily focuses on making curative services more available, while paying little attention

*Corresponding author: jtkengia@yahoo.com

DOI: 10.1079/9781800623330.0011

to health promotion and disease prevention. Health threats start with people in their homes, communities and workplaces and not in health facilities such as hospitals, clinics or outreach areas. Therefore, a people-focused investment plan is needed. The basic principles of generating sustainable and cost-effective facility- and community-based health services must aim for a continuum of care from promotion to preventive, curative, rehabilitative, and finally, palliative care.

The preceding chapters of this book have documented the evolution of PHC in Tanzania and highlighted the struggles suffered over time. We need to learn from them for future reforms and investments in PHC from a health-systems perspective as the country moves towards achieving health security, universal health coverage (UHC) and addressing the SDGs.

11.1 Reflections on the Progress of Addressing Key Principles of PHC in Tanzania

Since the Alma-Ata Declaration in 1978 with its motto of 'Health for All', primary health care has remained a benchmark in most countries as an approach to reorienting health-service provision of cost-effective interventions towards achieving universal health care. In principle, PHC is a whole-of-society approach to health and aims to attain the highest possible level and distribution of health and well-being. It does so by providing an accessible and wide range of cost-effective services in a spectrum which includes health promotion, disease prevention, illness treatment, rehabilitation and palliative care (Hone *et al.*, 2018; Behera and Prasad, 2022). PHC builds on the principles of equity in access to health services and the right of people to participate in decision making about their health care and well-being (Appiah-Agyekum, 2020; Behera and Prasad, 2022). These principles are based on justice and empowerment, and when services are organized by following these principles, existing evidence indicates improvement in health outcomes (Perveen *et al.*, 2022). The fundamental PHC principles include: (i) Universal access to health care (also dubbed universal health coverage), that is, all people receive the health services they need with sufficient quality and affordability; (ii) Community participation: active community involvement in defining health problems and needs, developing solutions and implementing and evaluating programmes; (iii) Intersectoral coordination: the linkage between health and development; and (iv) Appropriateness: services should be effective, culturally acceptable affordable and manageable.

Over time in Tanzania, fundamental health system reforms through a wide range of policies and strategies have been implemented to promote PHC principles, which in turn have underpinned the expansion of comprehensive PHC. Reforms focused on universal health care based on equity principles include decentralization reforms, villagization policy, distribution of resources, resource allocation formulae, comprehensive council health planning, human resources for health, capacity building and development of essential health packages (de Savigny *et al.*, 2008) .

Reforms that focused on community participation have also been implemented and include the formation of user committees (lay health services boards, facility governing committees and village committees) (Frumence *et al.*, 2013; Kamuzora *et al.*, 2013; Kesale *et al.*, 2022a), task shifting through the community health workforce (Knettel *et al.*, 2021; Munga *et al.*, 2012), planning of health services (Kamuzora *et al.*, 2013; Maluka and Bukagile, 2016), and health financing through community health funds (Kamuzora and Gilson, 2007; Mtei and Mulligan, 2007; Kalolo *et al.*, 2017). The presence of social services (education, health and water) committees at the council level (Maluka and Bukagile, 2016), the formation of multisectoral nutrition committees and the 'One Health' approach represent examples of intersectoral coordination (Kitua *et al.*, 2019; te Lintelo *et al.*, 2020). Reforms that insist on comprehensive health planning at the council and health-facility level attempt to ensure the appropriateness of services provided in different settings. Moreover, the country has continuously tried to use available technology to address the PHC elements. Accordingly, such efforts include the ongoing digitalization of primary health care (Watts, 2020). Table 11.1 provides details on the reforms in line with PHC principles.

Table 11.1. PHC reforms in Tanzania and PHC principles.

S/N	Reform	PHC principle by reform objective	PHC principle by reform implementation	PHC principle in outcomes
1	Decentralization	Universal health coverage Intersectoral collaboration Community participation	Universal health coverage Community participation Community participation	Universal health coverage Appropriateness
2	Health-sector reforms of 1990s	Universal health coverage	Universal health coverage	Universal health coverage
3	Expansion of health facilities	Universal health coverage	Universal health coverage Community participation	Universal health coverage
4	Comprehensive council health planning	Universal health coverage Appropriateness	Universal health coverage	Universal health coverage Appropriateness
5	Essential health interventions	Universal health coverage	Universal health coverage	Universal health coverage
6	Health financing reforms	Universal health coverage Community participation	Universal health coverage	Universal health coverage
7	Formation of governance structures for PHC	Community participation	Community participation	Appropriateness
8	Human resource development	Universal health coverage	Universal health coverage	Universal health coverage
9	Supply chain reforms	Universal health coverage	Universal health coverage	Universal health coverage
10	Strengthening community health systems	Universal health coverage Community participation	Community participation Intersectoral collaboration	Universal health coverage Appropriateness

Although there are gains in abiding by the PHC components with regard to service delivery, there are significant areas for improvement of the principles of PHC, which require efforts and commitment to address weaknesses in the following areas:

1. Underfunding of PHC and resource prioritization favouring curative services. This will limit funding for other equally essential services for health promotion, prevention and rehabilitation activities.
2. PHC services in the private sector, including self-care at drug outlets, have not been monitored adequately for quality, affordability and appropriateness.
3. Harmonization with the 'One Health' approach as complementary to the PHC system.
4. Fragmented care as a result of the existence of vertical and disease-specific programmes that embrace a narrow selective PHC concept, which was meant to be time-limited and thus not realizing the UHC principles.
5. Inadequate investment in solving the health workforce crisis for PHC addressing maldistributions and shortages.
6. Growing burden of health issues of an ageing population affecting PHC service-delivery effectiveness.
7. Limited recognition of civil society efforts in the provision of PHC services, in particular, community-based services.
8. Addressing medical pluralism in the context of PHC is required.
9. Inadequate attention to promotive, preventive and palliative care at PHC levels.

Future efforts should address the challenges discussed above while sustaining the gains over time with the aim of progressive universalism in every aspect of PHC. There is a growing experience (also endorsed by the 75th World Health Assembly) that, although complex, PHC can serve as an easy road to UHC (WHO, 2008; Walker and Peterson, 2021; Martin and Sturmberg, 2022). However, what works in one country may not work in another and, therefore, any policy transfer (lesson drawing) will require contextualization and thus modification. Context and social norms of a country are crucial. It is also important to examine where Tanzania stands in comparison to other LMICs in terms of adhering to PHC principles. The key principles considered here are equity in universal access, intersectoral actions for PHC, community participation and basic quality across the care continuum. The following LMIC countries have been taken as a comparison to Tanzania: Ghana (Appiah-Agyekum, 2020; Appiah-Agyekum *et al.*, 2022), Ethiopia (Kloos, 1998; Assefa *et al.*, 2020), Bangladesh (Rahman, 2001; Joarder *et al.*, 2019) and Bolivia (Bristow, 2010; Alvarez *et al.*, 2016). Table 11.2 provides a comparative analysis of PHC principles in selected LMICs.

11.2 Unfinished Agenda

To achieve UHC through the provision of quality primary health care, all three elements of quality PHC need to be in place: empowered people and communities; a multisectoral policy and action; and integrated health services prioritizing essential public health functions and primary care (WHO and UNICEF, 2018). Adaptation to Tanzania's social and health-system context is one of the critical sustainability traits of the PHC system that is constantly subject to changes because of evolving demands of communities and the introduction of innovations (Fig. 11.1).

As a pioneer of PHC among other countries, Tanzania has made significant progress in fulfilling its population health demands despite many obstacles encountered in the implementation of interventions (Maluka, 2017). The government has made progress in improving some key indicators for service delivery, as shown in Box 11.1. Nevertheless, the pace of reduction of maternal, neonatal and child mortality recorded is currently below the SDG targets (Ogbo *et al.*, 2019; MOHCDGEC, 2020a, b). Moreover, the country is experiencing a double burden of diseases with a notable increase in non-communicable diseases (NCDs), but at the same time still having infectious diseases as a significant health problem. The double burden of diseases coupled with novel public health threats such as the recent COVID-19 pandemic and antimicrobial resistance automatically affect the already over-burdened and over-stretched health systems, which carry a high risk of lowering the quality of care. This will require redefining the balance

Table 11.2. Comparative analysis on PHC principles in selected LMICs.

Country (references)	Human development index	Universal health coverage	Intersectoral collaborations	Community participation	Appropriateness
Tanzania	0.55	Decentralization Health-sector reforms of 1990s Expansion of health facilities Health financing reforms Human resource development	Limited intersectoral collaborations, especially at community level	Formation of governance structures for PHC Strengthening community health systems	Presence of essential health interventions for PHC services and comprehensive health plans at council and health facility levels Supply chain reforms
Ghana	0.63	Decentralization of services National community-based health planning and services (CHPS) policy	The CHPS approach lays down an avenue for intersectoral actions and bottom-up approach to PHC	The CHPS approach lays down an avenue for maximum community participation Presence of community commitees	Presence of essential health package for health services and community-based health planning and services (CHPS) plans Medical nemesis of PHC
Ethiopia	0.485	Decentralization on progress (keeping the momentum despite ongoing conflicts), uneven distribution of PHC services	Presence of health extension workers as one of the important approaches to intersectoral collaborations	Community participation is limited due to political unrest in some settings	Presence of essential health package for health services

Continued

Table 11.2. Continued

Country (references)	Human development index	Universal health coverage	Intersectoral collaborations	Community participation	Appropriateness
Bolivia	0.718	Decentralization of PHC, but UHC cant be achieved fast due to geography, multinational population, high poverty levels Limited health-system inputs jeopardizes the odyssey to UHC Progress to UHC is envisaged to be achieved by implementation of the following: (a) The unified family, community and intercultural health system (SAFCI law, 2008) (b) Law 475 of 2014 on provision of comprehensive PHC services (c) Other laws and legal frameworks that promote equity and UHC in general	Implementation of the unified family, community and intercultural health system (SAFCI law, 2008)	Implementation of the unified family, community and intercultural health system (SAFCI law, 2008)	Presence of essential health package for health services
Bangladesh	0.661	Decentralization–centralization dilemma persists Health financing arrangments as barrier to UHC	Intersectoral collaboration for PHC remains limited	Community participation is limited and there is poor collaboration between the government and the civil society and other actors	Presence of the essential package of health services and health benefit plans

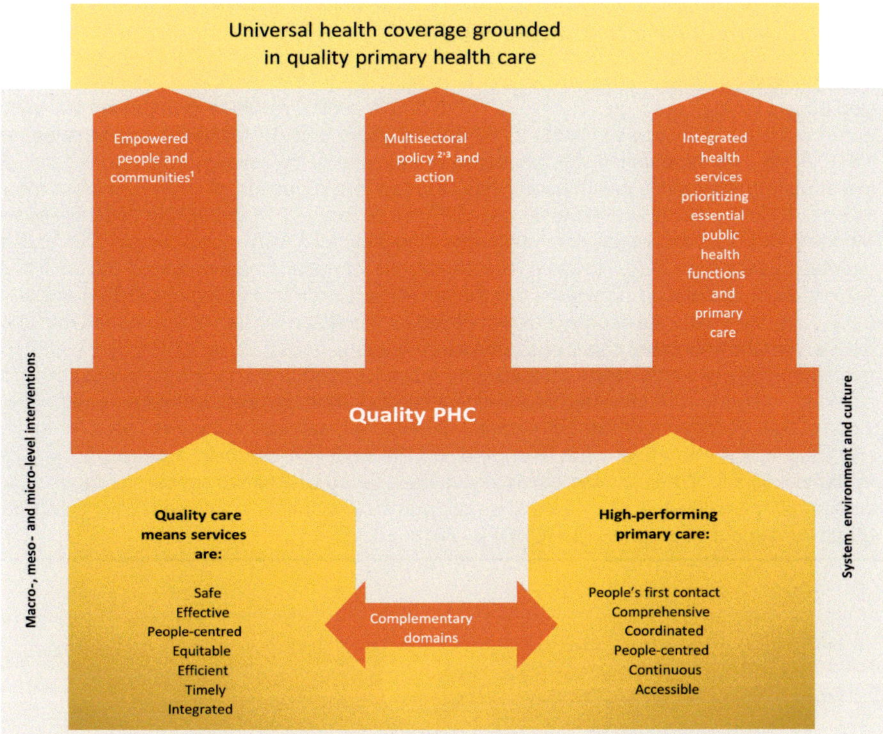

[1] Social accountability between village leadership, CHWs and village dispensary in 11 districts (Sikika, 2020)

[2] United Republic of Tanzania, National Action and Investment Agenda for Adolescents' Health and Wellbeing 2020/21–2023/24 (NAIA_AHW, 2020)

[3] United Republic of Tanzania, Office of the Prime Minister, National One Health Strategic Plan 2022–2027

Fig. 11.1. Universal health coverage grounded in quality PHC, with examples from Tanzania.

between surveillance, preventive and curative services, and a paradigm shift towards strengthening promotive and preventive services. This can only flourish through multisectoral collaboration based on mutual responsibilities and addressing the challenge of fragmentation whereby vertical and integrated approaches can move together harmoniously. Surveillance, including decentralization of screening and diagnostic services at health centres and dispensaries to enable timely detection and swift follow-up care, and systems research to learn what meets the needs of communities in a sustainable way (Donev *et al.*, 2013; Maluka, 2017; Kiologwe *et al.*, 2022) are both required. The current situation calls for action from the government and supportive donors to invest more in a newly defined PHC.

Leadership and governance are crucial to ensure success in implementing systemic strategies geared towards improving PHC (WHO, 2007; de Savigny and Adam, 2009; Markuns *et al.*, 2009) and services delivery at large. Through a series of reforms and implementation of decentralization-by-devolution policies, Tanzania has organized itself to establish and modify structures, systems, governance, and managerial tools to facilitate decision making, proper coordination, community participation, planning, resource mobilization and utilization to ensure efficiency and effectiveness in providing PHC services, as detailed in Chapter

Box 11.1. Achievements and calls to actions.

Over the last decades, Tanzania has made remarkable investments and progress to ensure organized efforts for improved quality of care in the health sector, resulting in improved life expectancy at birth from 50 and 51 years in 2000 to 60 and 63 years in 2012 for males and females respectively (URT, 2014). Life expectancy was projected to increase to 66 years in 2020. During this period, the investment in Tanzania's health sector has resulted in a reduction of under-five child mortality from 147 per 1000 live births in 2000 to 81 per 1000 live births in 2012 and 43 per 1000 live births in 2020. Mortality due to three major communicable diseases, HIV/AIDS, tuberculosis (TB) and malaria, is decreasing (see Fig. 11.2). However, the prevalence of malaria has increased from 7.5% in 2017 to 8.1% in 2022, despite an increase in low transmission rates from five regions in 2017 to nine regions in 2022. Over the years, the country has witnessed an increased burden of non-communicable diseases (NCDs) and the estimated share of deaths has increased from 27% in 2010 to 33% in 2016, which is overstretching the whole health-care system. A call for action for strengthening promotive, preventive services, integration of services, intersectoral collaboration, people-centred care, emphasis on individuals' well-being and the decentralization of screening services at the PHC level for early detection and treatment is inevitable, while strengthening the evidence-informed policies that will make health systems resilient. Moreover, dedicated efforts are needed to address severe shortages of health-care workers at lower-level facilities as well as geographical disparities between regions and pronounced urban–rural maldistributions (MOHCDGEC, 2019, 2021b).

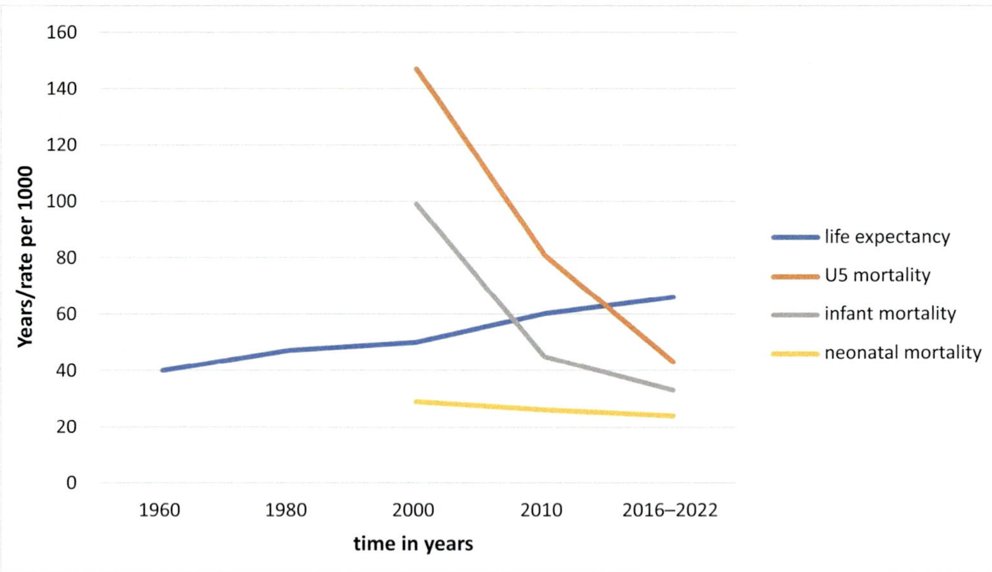

Fig. 11.2. Trends in major impact indicators for PHC over the decades since independence.

2. Nevertheless, more efforts are required to strengthen further the functionality of such structures and systems addressing quality and affordability, as described in Table 11.3.

Planning has evolved from paper-based and central planning towards decentralized planning at the facility level using web-based software for planning, budgeting and reporting, the PlanREP tool. Such tools simplify consolidation and tracking of budget implementation, now integrated with other financial and accounting management systems such as the Facility Financial Accounting and Reporting System (FFARS) and MUSE (*Mfumo wa Ulipaji Serikalini*) (Ruhago *et al.*, 2022). Since its introduction in 2017, direct health facility financing (DHFF)

Table 11.3. Unfinished agenda: key issues that require operational and strategic actions.

S/N	Thematic area	Unfinished agenda
1	Service delivery	Despite the improvement in access through the construction of PHC facilities, quality of care is still low, with fragmentation of services provision due to the existence of vertical programmes still a challenge. Moreover, expertise and capability for the provision of early diagnosis and treatment to NCD patients and palliative care is limited. Furthermore, PHC is mainly curative-oriented with limited promotive and preventive health services.
2	Governance and leadership	There is limited leadership and managerial capacity and resources (financial and tools such as updated guidelines) to support the functionality of decentralized governance and managerial structures. Morever there is limited decision making space and authority within the decentralization framework.
3	Human resources for health	There is a severe shortage of health-care workers of about 53% for the PHC with pronounced effects in radiology, eye care and dental services. Limited budget to absorb more staff, rural–urban maldistribution and regional disparities in human resource capacity are a persistent problem.
4	Health financing and resource mobilization	There is a high reliance on out-of-pocket payments to finance health care. This is associated with highly inequitable and high-level dependence on external financing. Also a significant proportion of donors' support goes off-budget by direct funding of fragmented vertical programmes or projects which create inefficiencies and low enrolment to pre-payment schemes. Overall, health insurance coverage remains very low at 14.7% of the total population, leaving about 85% of the population without health insurance.
5	Health commodities and technologies	There is an erratic supply of health commodities as a result of inadequate capacity for demand planning and quantification, problematic supply-chain issues, poor data quality and ineffective use of data for decision making.
6	Health information and evidence	There is limited infrastructure for electronic data collection and management, inadequate integration and interoperability of digital systems, limited use of data for decision making at different levels of the health system from practice to policy, and limited capacity for conducting research. Moreover, the digital health information system (DHIS2) does not yet capture real-time PHC individual level data for inputs to aggregate system.
7	Community health systems	There is fragmentation of initiatives with inadequate mechanisms for standardization of rewards and incentives for community volunteers. A costed strategic plan for community health initiatives is not available to date. There is an insufficiently integrated system for capturing routine community data and linkage to health-care facilities, inadequate mechanisms for the coordination of all actors within medical or health-care pluralism and limited participation of the community in planning, monitoring and evaluation.

Continued

Table 11.3. Continued

S/N	Thematic area	Unfinished agenda
8	Health-system resilience	There are inadequate health-system inputs (broadly defined, see Chapter 9), inadequate capacity for psychosocial care during emergencies, inadequate capacity for community-led responses during outbreaks and emergency situations and low capacity for analysis of routine data to inform decisions at the facilities, and no professionalized ambulance system.
9	Social determinants of health	There is inadequate intersectoral collaboration for addressing emerging challenges related to change in lifestyle and modernization influenced by external forces such as commercial determinants of health as detailed in Chapter 10.

has helped in the fiscal decentralization and empowerment of the lower health management system, enabling it to be more autonomous in planning, managing and using mobilized funds to provide health services to the catchment population (Wiedenmayer *et al.*, 2019). The reform also helps to ensure effectiveness, efficiency, transparency, accountability and workload reduction during the planning process (Tukay *et al.*, 2021; Kesale *et al.*, 2022c). However, more actions are needed to enhance quality in service delivery at primary care level, the capacity and participation of the community in the planning process, social accountability, demand creation for quality and comprehensive fiscal decentralization for all financial resources.

There has been documented progress and success in the struggle towards improving human resources for health capacity through the use of the 'Ajira portal', which has enhanced transparency and accountability in recruitment and deployment of health-care workers. However, Tanzania continues to experience a shortage and maldistribution of health-care workers with severe constraints for lower-level facilities (MOHSW, 2013; URT, 2020), geographical disparities between regions and persisting urban–rural and hard-to-reach maldistributions (MOHCDGEC, 2019, 2020a; URT, 2020). Moreover, the number of faculty required in health training institutions is insufficient to cope with the increasing demand for PHC training (MOHCDGEC, 2019).

Another unfinished agenda includes the regular availability of quality health commodities which play a pivotal role in providing PHC. Availability of health commodities is often equated to a high level of customer satisfaction irrespective of the quality of services (WHO, 2010a). Besides advocating for the availability and accessibility of medicines and medical devices, there is a significant gap between primary and tertiary health-care levels (Githendu *et al.*, 2020). The availability of essential basic medicines in rural and hard-to-reach PHC facilities in Tanzania has always been low, with frequent unavailability. In contrast, essential medical supplies and drugs are usually available in urban areas and in private drug outlets, pharmacies and clinics (Maluka, 2017).

Ensuring the availability of human resources and health commodities is almost impossible without sustainable financing mechanisms. Health-care financing is fundamental to the full functionality of any health system's performance (WHO, 2010b). The pooling of resources is critical to ensure effective utilization for the provision of PHC services (WHO, 2010b). Financing for PHC has always been part of a country's holistic health-financing strategy, although the balance during the last 20 years has favoured curative services above preventive and community services. In the last decade, there has been progress in fiscal decentralization in Tanzania. This has resulted in more public resources channelled to PHC. The introduction and operationalization of the DHFF initiative has enhanced the flow of funds to lower-level health-service providers and increased provider autonomy in planning and implementing health services (Tukay *et al.*, 2021). Despite such success, challenges still exist, including over-reliance on external funding, fragmentation and inadequate integration through additional resources being channelled through vertical programme and projects, low health-insurance coverage and a heavy reliance by the majority of Tanzanians on out-of-pocket payments which has made health care unaffordable and may push them towards catastrophic health expenditures, for self-care directly to drug outlets or delaying early health-care seeking until emergencies (Piatti-Fünfkirchen and Ally, 2020).

A sound PHC system relies on functional community health systems and moves beyond health-system building blocks, addressing interventions targeting families and households, harnessing community resources and structures, enhancing social representations and societal partnerships, multisectoral actions and a broad spectrum of determinants of health. Tanzania has made some progress in creating enabling environments and advocacy, mounting community linkages and partnerships. However, fragmentation and harmonization of actors in the community health system are still challenging. Like in other countries, addressing issues beyond the health-system building blocks has been a problem when resources must be prioritized. For example, community care has been entirely dependent on externally financed projects, and this presence of a fragmented and unharmonized pluralistic health system has resulted in unnecessary health-seeking behaviour. Furthermore, the capacity of PHC to address wider determinants of health, such as social, political and commercial determinants of health, has been constrained. Engaging the community meaningfully by recognizing its contribution and district-wide partnerships to address underlying needs has been suboptimal and will need extra efforts. The immediate challenge remains the lack of the costing of the strategic plan for CHWs which hampers government from having a coordinated approach to harnessing financial resources from different stakeholders and helping to address the fragmentation challenges.

PHC is the entry for communities into the health system and the basis for universal health coverage (WHO, 2007). An effective strategy for monitoring PHC implementation at the facility and community level is, therefore, crucial to understand progress and areas that require further improvements. To date, substantial advancement has been made to develop a monitoring and evaluation system for PHC in Tanzania, with recent reforms geared towards digitalization of health information systems to improve efficiency, effectiveness, planning, resource management, reporting, continuum of care and service delivery (MOHCDGEC, 2020b). Despite the progress made, more efforts need to be invested in the future to address monitoring and evaluation issues that are still challenging as detailed in Table 11.3.

As a part of monitoring, evaluation and learning, the strengthening of implementation research capacities at the PHC level is equally essential. The WHO recommends strengthening the research capability beyond academicians to include implementers and frontline workers in designing and conducting health research that will produce innovations and local solutions to curb the challenges that limit progress towards the realization of universal health coverage (WHO, 2013). In Tanzania, as in other countries in the low- and middle-income world, research capacity is still low. Hence, dedicated effort is needed to improve research capacity among health-care workers through tailor-made research training, coaching and mentorship, accessing the necessary research infrastructure and financial resources and strengthening local and international collaboration for conducting research. To move forward towards strengthening PHC in the stride for achieving universal health access, addressing the unfinished agenda is critical. Table 11.3 provides a detail account of key issues that require operational and strategic actions.

11.3 New and Re-Emerging Challenges

11.3.1 Poverty

According to the Tanzania Mainland Poverty Assessment report, in 2018, about 26 million (about 49% of the population) lived below the $1.90 per person per day international poverty line (Swinkels, 2019). Living in poverty-concentration areas is also associated with poor health outcomes and low service utilization rates (Khan *et al.*, 2005). The poor suffer more with limited access to health care and social protection, possibly dying at younger ages due to poor health outcomes and higher disease burdens (OECD and WHO, 2003). Globally, concern for the health of the poor is becoming a central issue in the development agenda. In improving PHC, addressing poverty is therefore very important. For poverty reduction, a multisectoral and systems-thinking approach, including addressing social (access to education, energy and health care), economic (improvements in infrastructure, mining, promoting industrialization and agriculture-sector structural transformation-diversification) and environmental issues are essential and will ultimately lead into better health status of the poor. On the other hand, poor health status of the community can result in productivity loss and minimal engagement in economic activities. Investment in health is therefore required as an important ingredient for reducing poverty (OECD and WHO, 2003).

11.3.2 Crises (climate change, food security, pandemics)

Global and regional health security is becoming an important priority due to the threats posed by emerging and re-emerging diseases at the global and continental levels. In response to that, the World Health Organization and its member states have signed several agreements that are geared towards making sure there is a collective response to international health threats. At the continental level, the African Union, through its technical arm the Africa CDC, has issued several guidelines including Africa's New Public Health order which, among other things, emphasizes investment in public health institutions that are responsive to all global health security threats. Therefore, health security threats such as air pollution and climate change, non-communicable diseases, emerging and re-emerging infectious diseases such as pandemics, influenza, Ebola, COVID-19, Dengue fever and other high-threat pathogens, HIV, monkeypox, weak primary health care, vaccine hesitancy, fragile and vulnerable settings and antimicrobial resistance (WHO, 2019b) are critical issues that need to be tracked and addressed as we look into the future of PHC in Tanzania.

Emerging and re-emerging diseases are also becoming essential issues that need dedicated and rigorous attention. Tanzania, like many other countries, is vulnerable to public health hazards and emergencies because of its geographical location. Both the Congo Basin and the Rift Valley ecosystems harbour pathogens and disease-transmitting vectors in an environment with high frequency of human and animal interactions. The threat is worsened by interactions and movement of people, animals and commercial goods across conventional national borders. In addition, globalization and booming international trade significantly increased the risk of disease transmission across international borders (Kapata *et al.*, 2020; Rugarabamu *et al.*, 2022). Addressing health security concerns at all levels requires robust health systems that are PHC-oriented. Some of the lessons learnt following the recent pandemics have shown that areas where community-based primary-care systems were weak, experienced a relatively substantial negative impact of the pandemic (Li *et al.*, 2021). This evidence necessitates the need for many countries to reorient and strengthen surveillance in their primary health-care systems, leading to a general strengthening of the PHC.

PHC is an essential foundation for the global response to disease epidemics. It plays a significant role in the health-care response: identifying and triaging potential cases, making an early diagnosis, helping vulnerable people cope with their anxiety about the outbreak and strengthening compliance with prevention and protection measures. In the context of emergency preparedness, response and resilience, specific consideration should be given to training and retaining the PHC workforce, strengthening health-information systems, strengthening community engagement and risk-communication interventions and provision of essential infrastructure and constant supply of health commodities.

Food security and consumption levels are linked to nutritional status and overall health status of the community. In Tanzania, food insecurity in some regions and districts poses a substantial threat to the attainment of satisfactory health outcomes particularly for the under-fives who may succumb into stunting and underweight. Food insecurity and undernutrition are prevalent, with 55% of Tanzanians experiencing moderate or severe food insecurity, 31% of the population undernourished and 35% of children stunted (Randell *et al.*, 2022). Dedicated efforts and innovative solutions are required to improve food production.

Regarding the climate crisis, documented evidence in the literature shows that health care is one of the most carbon-intensive sectors, accounting for 4.4% of global net greenhouse gas emissions and toxic air pollutants (Karliner *et al.*, 2020). The International Panel on Climate Change and the World Health Organization have made a call to action to reduce health care's ecological impacts (WHO, 2017; Hinrichs-Krapels *et al.*, 2022). The use of renewable energy in primary health-care facilities, such as solar energy, is one of the alternatives with the potential to reduce greenhouse gas emissions and mitigate climate change, which is critical to protecting humans, wildlife and ecosystems (Drennen *et al.*, 1996). Moreover, other initiatives are necessary to improve the eco-friendly environment in health facilities, including embarking on innovative approaches for health-care waste-management mechanisms to minimize environmental pollution (Zikhathile *et al.*, 2022). Investment in eco-friendly technology is, therefore, inevitable as we envision the future of PHC in Tanzania.

SDG gridlock

In accordance with the Voluntary National Review of the United Republic of Tanzania (VNR) 2019, the main sustainability challenges that have not yet been adequately addressed include SDG 1, SDG 13, SDG 14, SDG 15 and SDG 17. The consequences for Tanzania include persistent poverty and inequality, climate changes leading into global warming, endangered life and biodiversity loss, desertification, drought, hunger and resource deficit. This has an implication to PHC in terms of affecting community well-being and the ability to pay for health services, particularly for disadvantaged groups. Other consequences include increasing disease risk to the community, the reduction of budgets for the health sector and increasing attention to other competing priorities related to the SDG gridlock.

11.3.3 Demographic and epidemiologic transition

Another vital area is the epidemiological transition of diseases with a paradigm shift in the burden of diseases as Tanzania, among other developing countries, is experiencing a double burden of diseases with a notable increase in non-communicable diseases but at the same time having infectious diseases as a significant health problem (Mayige *et al.*, 2012). Other literature argues more on the triple burden of diseases, which includes malnutrition in addition to infectious diseases and NCDs (MOHCDGEC, MOH, NBS, OCGS and ICF, 2016). This shift has been largely attributed to social demographic changes, nutritional transition and urbanization that drives people into sedentary lifestyles and unhealthy diets (Mayige *et al.*, 2012). To respond to the rising burden on NCDs, including mental health, oral health diseases and injuries, there is a call to reorganize PHC services to meet the current needs, in particular, to improve the system to be able to deliver a comprehensive package of services from preventive to early diagnosis and treatment, as well as palliative care. More effort and emphasis should be placed on implementing the strategies for primary and secondary prevention and health promotion which are necessary to curb the rising disease burden. Moreover, PHC facilities need to be equipped and staffed to provide services for early diagnosis, treatment and rehabilitation.

11.3.4 Antimicrobial resistance

Recently, antimicrobial resistance (AMR) has emerged as one among the major global threats to public health. Emerging AMR is recognized as a silent pandemic that threatens to kill up to 10 million people by 2050. Currently, up to 700,000 people die annually due to AMR, with 90% of these deaths being reported in low- and middle-income countries. The prevalence of both community and hospital-acquired AMR is increasing and is being associated with over- and misuse of antimicrobial drugs in both human and animal health.

The misuse and abuse of antimicrobials in agriculture, veterinary and human medicine practices have been described as the major contributing factors. In clinical settings in Tanzania, the prevalence of multidrug-resistant bacteria ranges from 25 to 50% (Moremi *et al.*, 2012; Mshana *et al.*, 2013; Moyo *et al.*, 2014). As AMR is currently regarded as a complex health problem that cannot be solved by a single sector alone, the One Health approach, involving multidisciplinary efforts from national to subnational levels where PHC has the main foundation, will be the ultimate solution.

11.3.5 Urgent action on NCD prevention

The burden of non-communicable diseases (NCD), including diabetes, cardiovascular diseases, cancers, nutritional disorders, injuries, mental health disorders and substance abuse, is increasing while the health sector, particularly within PHC, is less prepared to meet the evolving demands. It is estimated that there was an increase of NCD deaths from 27% in 2010 to 33% in 2016, followed by a dramatic increase in the number of NCD cases in subsequent years (MOHCDGEC, 2016). To respond to the rising burden of NCDs, dedicated efforts are needed to strengthen promotive, preventive and rehabilitative services to ensure that basic services such as screening, early diagnosis and treatment and rehabilitation for NCDs are readily available in PHC facilities. NCDs are predominantly chronic diseases with high mortality. When NCD prevention and treatment have failed, patients are often sent home for end-of-life palliative care which PHC does not yet provide (e.g. pain medication for terminal cancer patients).

11.4 New Outlooks Needed

Looking to the future of PHC in Tanzania, we see a need for a strong paradigm shift that will guide a move towards strengthening health promotion, prevention and people-centred care (WHO, 2007) to counter-balance the current focus on the curative. This shift should be coupled with innovative revolutions for addressing challenges around the primary health system's responsiveness to the eight domains for increasing people's satisfaction and benefit, with services rendered at the PHC-level facilities (Kapologwe *et al.*, 2020). Moreover, with emerging recent challenges due to epidemiological transition of diseases and public health threats, strengthening multisectoral coordination through the motto of Health in All policies and the One Health approach is essential. These efforts will increase the capability of public health institutions and PHC facilities to implement community-based event-surveillance systems and should be a priority in the future in response to emerging and re-emerging health threats in order to yield success. Evidenced-based policies, guidelines and strategies are needed for the sound implementation of interventions that have a high likelihood to yield such benefits. Therefore, a paradigm shift must be made to investing more on evidence enquiry (primary research) through evidence synthesis (secondary research) to evidence products (tertiary research) plus knowledge translation, for the benefit of the general public. Tanzania also needs to learn from the well-being policies as recently enshrined in the broad national policies of several countries including New Zealand, Chile, Gibraltar and Wales. Transition towards a comprehensive emphasis on individuals' well-being, i.e. health, social, cultural, economic and environmental, is needed (Lindert *et al.*, 2015; WHO, 2022).

11.5 Specific Actions for the Future of Tanzanian PHC

Addressing the unfinished agenda and tackling the paradigm shifts is critical for the future of PHC in Tanzania. Dedicated efforts are needed to ensure that the PHC system is responsive, people-centred and resilient, backed by the availability of all necessary resources on the supply side, a supportive policy environment, effective community engagement and a system for monitoring in the spirit of surveillance, evaluation and learning.

In looking into the future of PHC in Tanzania, first and foremost it is crucial to ensure that established structures and systems are functional and operational to full capacity to facilitate the coordination and implementation of comprehensive PHC services. More efforts are needed to ensure that members of respective governance and managerial structures have the required skills, resources and tools. Appointed members should have the required competencies and leadership skills necessary to spearhead the development and implementation of innovative plans in line with local priorities, national and international strategies and policy directives (Mubyazi *et al.*, 2007; Kesale *et al.*, 2022b). The role of PO-RALG through the Department of Health, Social Welfare and Nutrition Services, regional health management teams (RHMTs) and council health management teams (CHMTs) need to be strengthened to spearhead the decentralization process, translation of policies and guidelines into actions and monitoring and evaluation of the provision of PHC.

Furthermore, lower-level management and governance of health-facility teams must also be capacitated to discharge their roles and responsibilities accordingly. This should go hand in hand with the routine implementation of health reforms geared towards making RHMTs and CHMTs respond to meet the current demands of the PHC. To better utilize the available decision making space and authority within the decentralization framework, central government must delegate more power to the district and subdistrict levels in priority setting and resource management (Maluka, 2017). With more roles, responsibilities and resources decentralized to lower health facilities like health centres and dispensaries, there is a need to invest in capacity building at that level. This will equip health managers and their teams to take up responsibilities to govern well, implement their budgets and translate available resources into quality service delivery while improving the outcomes and well-being of the population in question (Gilson *et al.*, 1994).

The second important aspect is to address gaps related to the availability of necessary resources. For the human resource for health shortage, it is worthwhile to continue investing in increasing production through face-to-face training and distance learning, recruitment and deployment to areas with critical shortages, implementing innovations for staff retention in particular in hard-to-reach regions, conducting workload assessment with innovative tools such as workload indicator of staffing needs (WISN) and the prioritization and optimization analysis (POA) and redistribution of staff to enhance accountability and efficiency in the use of available workforce (MOHCDGEC, 2021a), utilization of digital solution telemedicine, strengthening public–private partnerships, task sharing (WHO, 2010a) strategic task-shifting for proven workable solutions (Wiedenmayer *et al.*, 2015) and volunteerism (MOHCDGEC, 2020a). Apart from human resources for health, constant availability of health commodities is a key ingredient for the functionality of the PHC system. In order to have an effective supply chain to primary health-care facilities, it is necessary to obtain budget from the central government, strengthen pre-payment schemes such as NHIF and improved community health fund (iCHF) and invest in capacity building for health commodities demand-planning and quantifications through a bottom-up approach. This must be coupled with the implementation of a public–private partnership through a mechanism such as the Jazia Prime Vendor System (Wiedenmayer *et al.*, 2019) and drug revolving funds. Investment in preventive services to cater for primary and higher-level prevention care is needed to reduce the cost of procurement of health commodities. The backbone of an effective supply chain will rely on the availability of quality data and use for decision making. The implementation of the IMPACT (information mobilized for performance analysis and continuous transformation) team approach needs reinforcement to all stakeholders in the country to improve the culture of data use to inform demand planning and quantification. In looking into the future, it is also imperative to develop a universal financial protection strategy that seeks to maximize equitable access to quality health services for all and provides financial protection against ill health. Moreover, additional funding to complement the universal health insurance pool will be required from general budget support (from tax revenues and development assistance). In its effort to improve the health-financing system, the government is currently making a law that will ensure everyone has enrolled in health insurance. The Universal Health Insurance (UHI) Bill (URT, 2022) was presented for the first time in Parliament in September 2022. It is anticipated that, if well implemented, the UHI law will be a major step towards achieving universal health coverage by guaranteeing access to needed health care and financial protection to the whole population. However, the government will need to secure sustainable financing sources to enrol the poor into health-insurance schemes. Otherwise, it will be a challenge to guarantee access to health care for this population group. For efficiency, the utilization of fund integration of services needs to be encouraged based on available evidence from research (Tanahashi, 1978; Bulstra *et al.*, 2021). It is also essential to have a comprehensive financing mechanism, not only funding for clinical services but also spending for preventive and health-promotion interventions that address the underlying social determinants of health (Atashbahar *et al.*, 2022). Furthermore, harmonization of partners to avoid duplication of resources is critical. With the already matured SWAp (sector-wide approach) mechanism at the central level, it is high time for the decentralization of SWAp to the subnational level to improve the coordination of partners and efficiency in the utilization of resources.

The third important issue that requires action includes addressing the quality issue in the provision of services and efficiency through the integration of services to optimize the use of limited resources. The provision of services also needs to be redesigned and improved to accommodate emerging issues such as the need for early diagnosis and treatment for NCDs (this will require the improvement of point-of-care diagnostics and case-management capability at the PHC level), the need for palliative and geriatric care, psychosocial care and services to address gender-based violence.

The fourth area is the community health system that is also key to the success of PHC system in Tanzania and requires the following actions: (i) recognition of community-owned resource persons (CORPS) by government, communities and development partners as multitask cadres representing various sectors who can contribute to healthier living, integrated within the overall health system; (ii) remuneration of efforts made by CORPS in a standardized and regular way; (iii) ownership of the community health system in planning and executing services by the community themselves through social accountability as can be done through the community score cards; (iv) regular dialogue and agreements with vertically run projects to gradually integrate with and directly support community, council and national health systems; (v) alignment by all health-care partners to the competency-based and comprehensive modular training package for a multi-purpose community health worker; and (vi) recognition that basic health services are part and parcel of the preventive, promotive and rehabilitative service package of community health workers and often is in high demand by communities, boosting their acceptability.

Other important areas that require attention include strengthening promotive and preventive services, promoting healthy living and well-being, enhancing community engagement and social accountability, improving data use for decision making, integrating and enhancing digital system interoperability, building effective community surveillance and response systems within PHC and building capacity for the implementation of Health in All policies and the One Health approach to address social determinants of health and emerging and re-emerging diseases.

11.6 Conclusion

11.6.1 The Tanzanian path forward

Tanzania is signatory to a number of agreements and treaties at the regional and global level that are geared towards making its primary health systems strong, perseverant and responsive to regional and global health insecurities. In the East Africa region, Tanzania is the main contributor of inputs that are incorporated into the collaboration framework for improving health-services provision and population health in the region. Through the African Union 2023 Agenda 'Africa We Want', Tanzania, together with the other 54 member-states, have endorsed and ratified the strategy and started implementing its strategic objectives. The health technical arm of the African Union, the Africa Centers for Disease Control and Prevention (Africa CDC), has issued the New Public Health Order for the continent, which Tanzania has endorsed. The order has five pillars that focus mainly on: having strong public health institutions that represent African priorities in global health governance and that drive progress on key health indicators; expanded manufacturing of vaccines, diagnostics and therapeutics to democratize access to life-saving medicines and equipment; investment in the public health workforce and leadership programmes to ensure Africa has the workforce it needs to address health threats; increased domestic investment in health, including the domestic mobilization of financial resources, human capital, technical resources and networks; and respectful, action-oriented partnership to advance vaccine manufacturing, health workforce development and strong public health institutions.

In implementing the global agreements and declarations, Tanzania was one of the countries that endorsed the Alma-Ata Declaration in 1978 and the Astana Declaration in 2018 which, among other things, focused on achieving health for all with equity at the centre of the vision. In an attempt to achieve these declarations, there has been the introduction of initiatives and strategies, namely, millennium development goals (MDGs), universal health coverage (UHC) and sustainable development goals (SDGs) by 2030. Achieving these ambitious visions and strategies will require a vibrant primary health system that is resilient, capable of adaptation and able to sustain gains.

11.6.2 Framework for the future of PHC in Tanzania

PHC is a gateway towards achieving both universal health coverage and sustainable development goals. To strengthen PHC in Tanzania, five key components must be addressed as critical domains towards universal health access (Fig. 11.3). The first essential component covers the supply-side domain. For health services to be utilized and appreciated, adequate resources must be in place (Tanahashi, 1978).

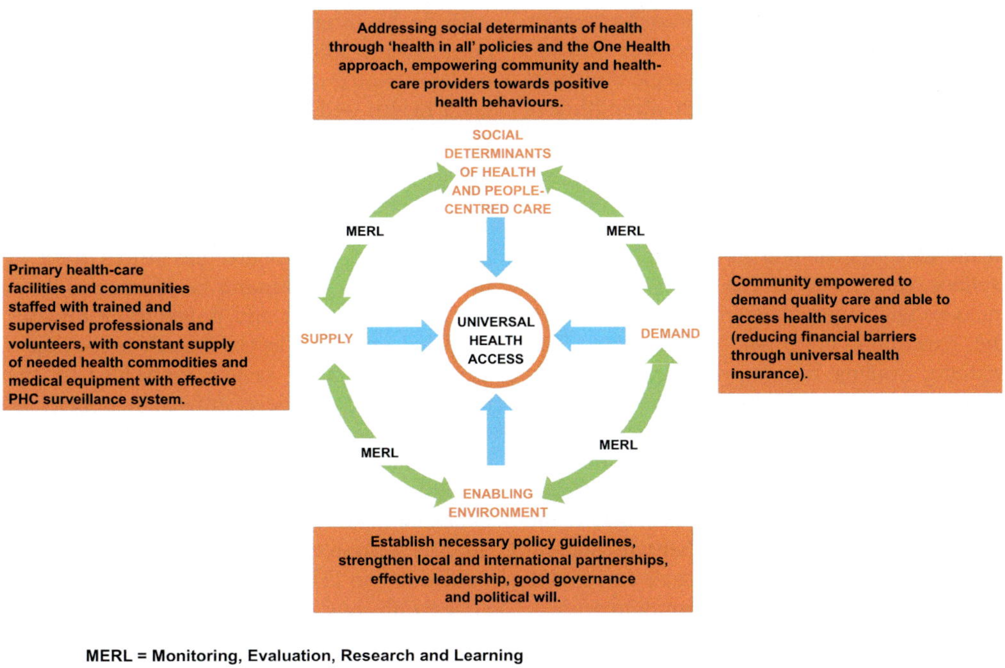

Fig. 11.3. Envisioning the future of primary health care in Tanzania. A framework for action.

Addressing human resource shortages and the constant availability of health commodities, medical equipment and financial resources is paramount. It needs dedicated efforts, strategies, attention and organized actions, from policy to implementation. Apart from the supply-side domain, the demand side is the second important domain that needs to be looked at. The community needs to be empowered to be able to demand quality health care and access services without barriers; in particular, the ability to pay for medical costs without vulnerability or succumbing to catastrophic health expenditure. The pending issue of the Universal Health Insurance Bill and addressing quality concerns in the primary health-care system requires urgent action (WHO, 2010a, 2019a). A comprehensive primary health-care system needs to be designed with the capability to address and adapt to social determinants of health so as to combat preventable diseases from occurring in the community with cost-effective interventions, hence minimizing the possibility of overburdening primary health-care facilities with conditions and diseases that could have been prevented (NASEM, 2016), and this is the third important strategic component. The people-centred care approach needs to be over-emphasized and strategically financed (Hanson *et al.*, 2022) among crucial strategic directions of the future of PHC in Tanzania. Strengthened intersectoral collaboration to address social determinants of health through Health in All policies and the One Health approach must be accentuated and operational within the primary health-care system and its structures (United Nations, (n.d.), 2023). The fourth component includes enabling the environment to support the execution of other components. This includes availing necessary policy guidelines, strengthened partnerships, effective leadership, governance and political will. Moreover, the fifth domain covers effective systems for monitoring in the spirit of surveillance, near-real-time evaluation of surveillance to enable swift action and in-depth research leading together with surveillance to learning. This component is essential to provide feedback in the implementation process, learn from the successes, and provide early hints or alarms for corrections to the areas that may require improvement or modifications (WHO, 2018, 2019c).

11.6.3 Call to action

To provide sustainable and high-quality primary health care, there is a need for a strong and robust service-delivery system that is people-centred and responsive to community demands. This can be achieved through building a strong system which is availed with adequate resources addressing socio-economic determinants of health, while empowering communities to engage in planning and discussions that foster an increase in access to quality health services without geographical or financial barriers. Moreover, there is a need to invest in evidence-informed policies coupled with an enabling environment, strong leadership and management and political good governance. The current primary health-care model will require ongoing reforms that will help to make it more sustainable and adaptable to the evolving demands of the quality services within and beyond Tanzania. Investing in the original model of primary health-care delivery that begins with health promotion and prevention, and is curative, rehabilitative and palliative cannot be underestimated for the populations to achieve good health and well-being. This will succeed by changing the current preferred model where the curative services have had dominance over health promotion and preventive medicine. The global health security agenda through initiatives like One Health and others needs to be at the centre of primary health care as there are many emerging and re-emerging diseases at global and local levels. Therefore, having a strong surveillance system embedded at the primary health-care level should be a priority for early detection and response to local, regional and global threats. Sustainable domestic health financing should be a top priority for PHC in Tanzania by exploring and leveraging domestic funding resources to meet the requirements needed to run PHC. The establishment of innovation hubs and new public health institutions will be used for nurturing primary health-care providers to be the future leaders and innovators.

Acknowledgements

The authors wish to thank George Kiwango for his advice on this chapter.

Bibliography

Allies for Improving PHC (2022) *Make This Time Different: Prioritize Primary Health Care as a 3-for-1 Investment towards Health for All*. Available at: https://www.phc3for1.org/ (accessed 16 May 2023).

Alvarez, F.N., Leys, M., Mérida, H.E.R. and Guzmán, G.E. (2016) Primary health care research in Bolivia: systematic review and analysis. *Health Policy and Planning* 31(1), 114–128. DOI: 10.1093/heapol/czv013.

Appiah-Agyekum, N.N. (2020) Primary healthcare implementation in practice: evidence from primary healthcare managers in Ghana. *African Journal of Primary Health Care & Family Medicine* 12(1), a2183. DOI: 10.4102/phcfm.v12i1.2183.

Appiah-Agyekum, N.N., Kayi, E.A., Appiah-Agyekum, J., Tetteh Nyanyofio, J.G. and Otoo, D.D. (2022) Capacity issues in primary health care implementation: examples from Ghana. *Health Education* 122(6), 633–648. DOI: 10.1108/HE-06-2021-0095.

Arhin, K., Frimpong, A.O. and Acheampong, K. (2022) Effect of primary health care expenditure on universal health coverage: evidence from sub-Saharan Africa. *ClinicoEconomics and Outcomes Research* 14, 643–652. DOI: 10.2147/CEOR.S380900.

Assefa, Y., Hill, P.S., Gilks, C.F., Admassu, M., Tesfaye, D. *et al*. (2020) Primary health care contributions to universal health coverage, Ethiopia. *Bulletin of the World Health Organization* 98(12), 894–905A. DOI: 10.2471/BLT.19.248328.

Atashbahar, O., Sari, A.A., Takian, A., Olyaeemanesh, A., Mohamadi, E. *et al*. (2022) The impact of social determinants of health on early childhood development: a qualitative context analysis in Iran. *BMC Public Health* 22(1), 1149. DOI: 10.1186/s12889-022-13571-5.

Behera, B.K. and Prasad, R. (2022) Primary health-care goal and principles. *Healthcare Strategies and Planning for Social Inclusion and Development* 2022, 221–239. DOI: 10.1016/B978-0-323-90446-9.00008-3.

Bristow, K. (2010) Exploring the challenges of implementing socio-culturally appropriate primary health-looking at community health worker training in Bolivia. *Medical Sociology Online* 5(1), 16–31. Available at: https://britsoc.co.uk/files/MSo-Volume-5-Issue-1.pdf (accessed 18 May 2023).

Bulstra, C.A., Hontelez, J.A.C., Otto, M., Stepanova, A., Lamontagne, E. *et al*. (2021) Integrating HIV services and other health services: a systematic review and meta-analysis. *PLoS Medicine* 18(11), e1003836. DOI: 10.1371/journal.pmed.1003836.

de Savigny, D. and Adam, T. (2009) Systems thinking for health systems strengthening: an introduction. In: de Savigny, D. and Adam, T. (eds) *Systems Thinking for Health Systems Strengthening*. World Health Organization, Geneva, Switzerland, pp. 27–36.

de Savigny, D., Kasale, H., Mbuya, C. and Reid, G. (2008) *Fixing Health Systems*, 2nd edn. IDRC, Ottawa. Available at: https://www.idrc.ca/sites/default/files/openebooks/411-6/index.html (accessed 4 May 2023).

Donev, D., Kovacic, L. and Laaser, U. (2013) The role and organization of health care systems prevention and control of non-communicable diseases view project. In: Burazeri, G. and Zaletel-Krageli, L. (eds) *Systems, Lifestyles, Policies*, 2nd ed., Vol. 1. Jacobs Verlag, Lage, Germany, pp. 3–14. Available at: https://www.researchgate.net/publication/257830385 (accessed 4 May 2023).

Drennen, T.E., Erickson, J.D. and Chapman, D. (1996) Solar power and climate change policy in developing countries. *Energy Policy* 24(1), 9–16. DOI: 10.1016/0301-4215(95)00117-4.

Frumence, G., Nyamhanga, T., Mwangu, M. and Hurtig, A.K. (2013) Challenges to the implementation of health sector decentralization in Tanzania: experiences from Kongwa district council. *Global Health Action* 6(1), 20983. DOI: 10.3402/gha.v6i0.20983.

Gilson, L., Kilima, P.M. and Tanner, M. (1994) Local government decentralization and the health sector in Tanzania. *Public Administration and Development* 14(5), 451–477. DOI: 10.1002/pad.4230140503.

Githendu, P., Morrison, L., Silaa, R., Pothapregada, S., Asiimwe, S. *et al.* (2020) Transformation of the Tanzania medical store department through global fund support: an impact assessment study. *BMJ Open* 10(11), e040276. DOI: 10.1136/bmjopen-2020-040276.

Hanson, K., Brikci, N., Erlangga, D., Alebachew, A., De Allegri, M. *et al.* (2022) The Lancet Global Health Commission on financing primary health care: putting people at the centre. *The Lancet Global Health* 10(5), e715–e772. DOI: 10.1016/S2214-109X(22)00005-5.

Hinrichs-Krapels, S., Diehl, J.-C., Hunfeld, N. and van Raaij, E. (2022) Towards sustainability for medical devices and consumables: the radical and incremental challenges in the technology ecosystem. *Journal of Health Services Research & Policy* 27(4), 253–254. DOI: 10.1177/13558196221110416.

Hone, T., Macinko, J. and Millett, C. (2018) Revisiting Alma-Ata: what is the role of primary health care in achieving the sustainable development goals? *Lancet* 392(10156), 1461–1472. DOI: 10.1016/S0140-6736(18)31829-4.

Joarder, T., Chaudhury, T.Z. and Mannan, I. (2019) Universal health coverage in Bangladesh: activities, challenges, and suggestions. *Advances in Public Health* article ID 4954095. DOI: 10.1155/2019/4954095.

Kalolo, A., Gautier, L., Radermacher, R., Stoermer, M., Jahn, A. *et al.* (2017) Implementation of the redesigned community health fund in the Dodoma region of Tanzania: a qualitative study of views from rural communities. *The International Journal of Health Planning and Management* 33(1), 121–135. DOI: 10.1002/hpm.2403.

Kamuzora, P. and Gilson, L. (2007) Factors influencing implementation of the community health fund in Tanzania. *Health Policy and Planning* 22(2), 95–102. DOI: 10.1093/heapol/czm001.

Kamuzora, P., Maluka, S., Ndawi, B., Byskov, J. and Hurtig, A.-K. (2013) Promoting community participation in priority setting in district health systems: experiences from Mbarali district, Tanzania. *Global Health Action* 6, 22669. DOI: 10.3402/gha.v6i0.22669.

Kapata, N., Ihekweazu, C., Ntoumi, F., Raji, T., Chanda-Kapata, P. *et al.* (2020) Is Africa prepared for tackling the COVID-19 (SARS-CoV-2) epidemic? Lessons from past outbreaks, ongoing Pan-African public health efforts, and implications for the future. *International Journal of Infectious Diseases* 93, 233–236. DOI: 10.1016/j.ijid.2020.02.049.

Kapologwe, N.A., Kibusi, S.M., Borghi, J., Gwajima, D.O. and Kalolo, A. (2020) Assessing health system responsiveness in primary health care facilities in Tanzania. *BMC Health Services Research* 20(1), 104. DOI: 10.1186/s12913-020-4961-9.

Karliner, J., Slotterback, S., Boyd, R., Ashby, B., Steele, K. *et al.* (2020) Health care's climate footprint: the health sector contribution and opportunities for action. *European Journal of Public Health* 30(Suppl. 5), ckaa165–843. DOI: 10.1093/eurpub/ckaa165.843.

Kesale, A.M., Mahonge, C.P. and Muhanga, M. (2022a) The functionality of health facility governing committees and their associated factors in selected primary health facilities implementing direct health facility financing in Tanzania: a mixed-method study. *Health Science Reports* 5(3), e611. DOI: 10.1002/hsr2.611.

Kesale, A.M., Mahonge, C. and Muhanga, M. (2022b) The functionality variation among health facility governing committees under direct health facility financing in Tanzania. *PLOS Global Public Health* 2(5), e0000366. DOI: 10.1371/journal.pgph.0000366.

Kesale, A.M., Mahonge, C. and Muhanga, M. (2022c) The quest for accountability of health facility governing committees implementing direct health facility financing in Tanzania: a supply-side experience. *PloS One* 17(4), e0267708. DOI: 10.1371/journal.pone.0267708.

Khan, M.M., Hotchkiss, D.R., Berruti, A.A. and Hutchinson, P.L. (2005) Geographic aspects of poverty and health in Tanzania: does living in a poor area matter? *Health Policy and Planning* 21(2), 110–122. DOI: 10.1093/heapol/czj008.

Kiologwe, J.C., Kusirye, U., Hoffman, A. and Kalolo, A. (2022) Operational challenges of engaging development partners in district health planning in Tanzania. *BMC Public Health* 22(1), 200. (accessed 4 May 2023). DOI: 10.1186/s12889-022-12520-6.

Kitua, A.Y., Scribner, S., Rasmuson, M., Kambarage, D., Mghamba, J. *et al.* (2019) Building a functional national One Health platform: the case of Tanzania. *One Health Outlook* 1(3), 3. DOI: 10.1186/s42522-019-0003-0.

Kloos, H. (1998) Primary health care in Ethiopia under three political systems: community participation in a war-torn society. *Social Science & Medicine* 46(4–5), 505–522. DOI: 10.1016/s0277-9536(97)00194-9.

Knettel, B.A., Muhirwa, A., Wanda, L., Amiri, I., Muiruri, C. *et al.* (2021) Patient perspectives on the helpfulness of a community health worker program for HIV care engagement in Tanzania. *AIDS Care* 35(7), 1014–1021. DOI: 10.1080/09540121.2021.1995840.

Li, D., Howe, A.C. and Astier-Peña, M.P. (2021) Primary health care response in the management of pandemics: learnings from the COVID-19 pandemic. *Atencion Primaria* 53(Suppl 1), 102226. DOI: 10.1016/j.aprim.2021.102226.

Lindert, J., Bain, P.A., Kubzansky, L.D. and Stein, C. (2015) Wellbeing measurement and the WHO health policy Health 2010: systematic review of measurement scales. *European Journal of Public Health* 25(4), 731–740. DOI: 10.1093/eurpub/cku193.

Maluka, S. (2017) *Primary Health Care Systems (PRIMASYS): Comprehensive Case Study from United Republic of Tanzania*. Available at: https://apps.who.int/iris/handle/10665/341165 (accessed 16 May 2023).

Maluka, S.O. and Bukagile, G. (2016) Community participation in the decentralised district health systems in Tanzania: why do some health committees perform better than others? *The International Journal of Health Planning and Management* 31(2), E86–E104. DOI: 10.1002/hpm.2299.

Markuns, J.F., Culpepper, L. and Halpin, W.J. (2009) Commentary: a need for leadership in primary health care for the underserved: a call to action. *Academic Medicine* 84(10), 1325–1327. DOI: 10.1097/ACM.0b013e3181b6c8e7.

Martin, C. and Sturmberg, J. (2022) Universal health (UHC) and primary health care (PHC): a complex dynamic endeavor. *Journal of Evaluation in Clinical Practice* 28(2), 332–334. DOI: 10.1111/jep.13654.

Mayige, M., Kagaruki, G., Ramaiya, K. and Swai, A. (2012) Non communicable diseases in Tanzania: a call for urgent action. *Tanzania Journal of Health Research* 14(2). DOI: 10.4314/thrb.v13i5.7.

MOHCDGEC (2016) *Strategic and Action Plan for the Prevention and Control of Non-Communicable Diseases in Tanzania 2016–2020*. Government of the United Republic of Tanzania, Dodoma. Available at: https://www.worlddiabetesfoundation.org/sites/default/files/NCD%20Stategic%20Plan%202016%20-%202020.pdf (accessed 19 May 2023).

MOHCDGEC (2019) *Staffing Levels for Ministry of Health and Social Welfare Departments, Health Service Facilities, Health Training Institutions and Agencies 2014–2019*. Ministry of Health and Social Welfare, Dar es Salaam, Tanzania.

MOHCDGEC (2020a) *National Health Workforce Volunteering Guideline*. Ministry of Health and Social Welfare, Dar es Salaam, Tanzania.

MOHCDGEC (2020b) *Monitoring and Evaluation Strategic Framework (MESF) 2020–2025*. Ministry of Health and Social Welfare, Dar es Salaam, Tanzania.

MOHCDGEC (2021a) *Health Sector Strategic Plan July 2021 – June 2026 (HSSP V)*. Ministry of Health, Dodoma.

MOHCDGEC (2021b) *National Human Resources for Health Strategy 2021–2026 Strengthening Health Systems, Improving Services*. Ministry of Health, Dodoma.

MOHCDGEC, MOH, NBS, OCGS and ICF (2016) *Tanzania Demographic and Health Survey and Malaria Indicator Survey (TDHS-MIS) 2015–16*. MOHCDGEC, MOH, NBS, OCGS, and ICF, Dar es Salaam, Tanzania, and Rockville, Maryland.

MOHSW (2013) *Mid Term Review of the Health Sector Strategic Plan III 2009–2015, Main Report*. World Health Group 59, Ministry of Health, Dodoma.

Moremi, N., Mshana, S.E., Kamugisha, E., Kataraihya, J., Tappe, D. *et al*. (2012) Predominance of methicillin resistant Staphylococcus aureus -ST88 and new ST1797 causing wound infection and abscesses. *Journal of Infection in Developing Countries* 6(8), 620–625. DOI: 10.3855/jidc.2093.

Moyo, S.J., Aboud, S., Blomberg, B., Mkopi, N., Kasubi, M. *et al*. (2014) High nasal carriage of methicillin-resistant Staphylococcus aureus among healthy Tanzanian under-5 children. *Microbial Drug Resistance* 20(1), 82–88. DOI: 10.1089/mdr.2013.0016.

Mshana, S.E., Matee, M. and Rweyemamu, M. (2013) Antimicrobial resistance in human and animal pathogens in Zambia, Democratic Republic of Congo, Mozambique and Tanzania: an urgent need of a sustainable surveillance system. *Annals of Clinical Microbiology and Antimicrobials* 12, 28. DOI: 10.1186/1476-0711-12-28.

Mtei, G. and Mulligan, J.A. (2007) *Community Health Funds in Tanzania: A Literature Review*. Consortium for Research on Equitable Health Systems (CREHS), London School of Hygiene and Tropical Medicine, London.

Mubyazi, G.M., Mushi, A., Kamugisha, M., Massaga, J., Mdira, K.Y, *et al*. (2007) Community views on health sector reform and their participation in health priority setting: case of Lushoto and Muheza districts, Tanzania. *Journal of Public Health* 29(2), 147–156. DOI: 10.1093/pubmed/fdm016.

Munga, M.A., Kilima, S.P., Mutalemwa, P.P., Kisoka, W.J. and Malecela, M.N. (2012) Experiences, opportunities and challenges of implementing task shifting in underserved remote settings: the case of Kongwa district, central Tanzania. *BMC International Health and Human Rights* 12, 27. DOI: 10.1186/1472-698X-12-27.

NASEM (2016) *A Framework for Educating Health Professionals to Address the Social Determinants of Health*. National Academies of Sciences, Engineering, and Medicine, The National Academies Press, Washington, DC. DOI: 10.17226/21923.

OECD and WHO (2003) *Poverty and Health*, DAC guidelines and reference series. OECD Publishing, Paris. DOI: 10.1787/9789264100206-en.

Ogbo, F.A., Ezeh, O.K., Awosemo, A.O., Ifegwu, I.K., Tan, L. *et al.* (2019) Determinants of trends in neonatal, post-neonatal, infant, child and under-five mortalities in Tanzania from 2004 to 2016. *BMC Public Health* 19(1), 1243. DOI: 10.1186/s12889-019-7547-x.

Perveen, S., Lassi, Z.S., Mahmood, M.A., Perry, H.B. and Laurence, C. (2022) Application of primary healthcare principles in national community health worker programmes in low-income and middle-income countries: a scoping review. *BMJ Open* 12(2), e051940. DOI: 10.1136/bmjopen-2021-051940.

Piatti-Fünfkirchen, M. and Ally, M. (2020) *Tanzania Health Sector Public Expenditure Review 2020*. World Bank, Washington, DC. DOI: 10.1596/34620.

Rahman, S.A. (2001) Utilisation of primary health care services in rural Bangladesh: the population and provider perspectives. PhD thesis, London School of Hygiene & Tropical Medicine, London . DOI: 10.17037/PUBS.00682288.

Randell, H., Gray, C. and Shayo, E.H. (2022) Climatic conditions and household food security: evidence from Tanzania. *Food Policy* 112, 102362. DOI: 10.1016/j.foodpol.2022.102362.

Rugarabamu, S., George, J., Mbanzulu, K.M., Mwanyika, G.O., Misinzo, G, *et al.* (2022) Estimating risk of introduction of Ebola virus disease from the Democratic Republic of Congo to Tanzania: a qualitative assessment. *Epidemiologia* 3(1), 68–80. DOI: 10.3390/epidemiologia3010007.

Ruhago, G.M., Kapologwe, N.A., Ngalesoni, F.N., Kengia, J.T., Kibusi, S.M, *et al.* (2022) Cost-efficiency analysis of the improved web-based planning, budgeting, and reporting system (PlanRep) in Tanzania. *Frontiers in Health Services* 1, 787894. DOI: 10.3389/frhs.2021.787894.

Sikika (2020) *Community Score Cards: A Comprehensive Report of Interventions from 11 Districts in Tanzania*. Sikika, Dar es Salaam, Tanzania.

Swinkels, R.A. (2019) *Tanzania – Mainland Poverty Assessment 2019: Executive Summary (English)*. World Bank, Washington, DC. Available at: http://documents.worldbank.org/curated/en/431111575939381087/Executive-Summary (accessed 2 May 2023).

Tanahashi, T. (1978) Health service coverage and its evaluation. *Bulletin of the World Health Organization* 56(2), 295–303.

te Lintelo, D.J.H., Page, P., Kaganda, J. and Esau, D. (2020) Tanzania's story of change in nutrition: political commitment, innovation and shrinking political space. *Global Food Security* 24, 100350. DOI: 10.1016/j.gfs.2020.100350.

Tukay, S.M., Pasape, L., Tani, K. and Manzi, F. (2021) Evaluation of the direct health facility financing program in improving maternal health services in Pangani District, Tanzania. *International Journal of Women's Health* 13, 1227–1242. DOI: 10.2147/IJWH.S333900.

United Nations (n.d.) Goal 17 of SDG: strengthen the means of implementation and revitalize the Global Partnership for Sustainable Development. Multi-stakeholder partnerships and voluntary commitments. Available at: https://sdgs.un.org/topics/multi-stakeholder-partnerships-and-voluntary-commitments (accessed 16 May 2023).

URT (2014) *The 2012 Population and Housing Census: Basic Demographic and Socio-Economic Profile, Key Findings*. NBS and OCGS, Dar es Salaam, Tanzania.

URT (2020) *United Republic of Tanzania National Human Resources for Health Strategy for 2020–2025. November 2020*.

URT (2022) *The Universal Health Coverage Bill of 2022*.

Walker, C. and Peterson, C.L. (2021) Universal health coverage and primary health care: their place in people's health. *Journal of Evaluation in Clinical Practice* 27(5), 1027–1032. DOI: 10.1111/jep.13445.

Watts, G. (2020) The Tanzanian digital health agenda. Available at: https://www.readcube.com/articles/10.1016%2Fs2589-7500%2820%2930005-4 (accessed 18 May 2023).

WHO (2007) *People-Centred Health Care: A Policy Framework*. World Health Organization, Western Pacific Region, Geneva, Switzerland. Available at: https://www.who.int/publications/i/item/9789290613176 (accessed 4 May 2023).

WHO (2008) *World Health Report (2008): Primary Health Care – Now More Than Ever*. World Health Organization, Geneva, Switzerland. Available at: https://apps.who.int/iris/handle/10665/43949WHO

WHO (2010a) *Monitoring the Building Blocks of Health Systems: A Handbook of Indicators and Their Measurement Strategies*. World Health Organization, Geneva, Switzerland. Available at: https://apps.who.int/iris/bitstream/handle/10665/258734/9789241564052-eng.pdf (accessed 4 May 2023).
WHO (2010b) *The World Health Report: Health Systems Financing: The Path to Universal Coverage*. World Health Organization, Geneva, Switzerland. Available at: https://apps.who.int/iris/handle/10665/44371 (accessed 4 May 2023).
WHO (2013) *The World Health Report 2013: Research for Universal Health Coverage*. World Health Organization, Geneva, Switzerland. Available at: https://apps.who.int/iris/handle/10665/85761 (accessed 18 May 2023).
WHO (2017) *Environmentally Sustainable Health Systems: A Strategic Document*. World Health Organization, Regional Office for Europe, Copenhagen. Available at: https://apps.who.int/iris/bitstream/handle/10665/340375/WHO-EURO-2017-2241-41996-57723-eng.pdf?sequence=3&isAllowed=y (accessed 19 May 2023).
WHO (2018) *World Health Statistics 2018: Monitoring Health for the SDGs, Sustainable Development Goals*. World Health Organization, Geneva, Switzerland. Available at: https://apps.who.int/iris/handle/10665/272596
WHO (2019a) *Review of 40 Years of Primary Health Care Implementation at Country Level*. World Health Organization, Geneva, Switzerland. Available at: https://www.who.int/publications/m/item/review-of-40-years-of-primary-health-careimplementation-at-country-level (accessed 2 May 2023).
WHO (2019b) *Ten Threats to Global Health in 2019*. World Health Organization, Geneva, Switzerland. Available at: https://www.who.int/news-room/spotlight/ten-threats-to-global-health-in-2019 (accessed 4 May 2023).
WHO (2019c) *World Health Statistics Overview 2019: Monitoring Health for the SDGs, Sustainable Development Goals*. World Health Organization, Geneva, Switzerland.
WHO (2022) *Bending the Trends to Promote Health and Well-Being: A Strategic Foresight on the Future of Health Promotion*. World Health Organization, Geneva, Switzerland. Available at: https://www.who.int/publications/i/item/9789240053793 (accessed 4 May 2023).
WHO and UNICEF (2018) *A Vision for Primary Health Care in the 21st Century: Towards Universal Health Coverage and the Sustainable Development Goals*. World Health Organization and the United Nations Children's Fund (UNICEF), Geneva (WHO/HIS/SDS/2018.15), Switzerland. Available at: https://apps.who.int/iris/handle/10665/328065 (accessed 4 May 2023).
Wiedenmayer, K.A., Kapologwe, N., Charles, J., Chilunda, F. and Mapunjo, S. (2015) The reality of task shifting in medicines management: a case study from Tanzania. *Journal of Pharmaceutical Policy and Practice* 8(1), 13. DOI: 10.1186/s40545-015-0032-8.
Wiedenmayer, K., Mbwasi, R., Mfuko, W., Mpuya, E., Charles, J. *et al.* (2019) Jazia Prime Vendor System, a public–private partnership to improve medicine availability in Tanzania: from pilot to scale. *Journal of Pharmaceutical Policy and Practice* 12, 4. DOI: 10.1186/s40545-019-0163-4.
Zikhathile, T., Atagana, H., Bwapwa, J. and Sawtell, D. (2022) A review of the impact that healthcare risk waste treatment technologies have on the environment. *International Journal of Environmental Research and Public Health* 19(19), 11967. DOI: 10.3390/ijerph191911967.

Index

Note: **bold** page numbers refer to tables and *italic* page numbers refer to figures.